Towns and Topography

David Henry Hill in 1985
(Photograph: Keith Maude)

Towns and Topography

Essays in Memory of David H. Hill

Edited by

Gale R. Owen-Crocker
and
Susan D. Thompson

Oxbow Books

Oxford & Philadelphia

Published in the United Kingdom in 2014 by
OXBOW BOOKS
10 Hythe Bridge Street, Oxford OX1 2EW

and in the United States by
OXBOW BOOKS
908 Darby Road, Havertown, PA 19083

© Oxbow Books and the individual authors 2014

Hardcover Edition: ISBN 978-1-78297-702-5
Digital Edition: ISBN 978-1-78297-703-2

A CIP record for this book is available from the British Library

Library of Congress Cataloging-in-Publication Data

Towns and topography : essays in memory of David H. Hill / edited by Gale R. Owen-Crocker and Susan
D. Thompson. -- First English edition.
       pages cm
  Contains bibliography of the publications of David H. Hill.
  Includes bibliographical references and index.
  ISBN 978-1-78297-702-5 (hardcover) -- ISBN 978-1-78297-703-2 (e-book) 1. Great Britain--History--
Anglo-Saxon period, 449-1066. 2. Cities and towns, Medieval--England--History. 3. Anglo-Saxons--Social
life and customs. 4. Anglo-Saxons--Social conditions. 5. Civilization, Anglo-Saxon. I. Hill, David, 1937
July 15- II. Owen-Crocker, Gale R. III. Thompson, Susan D.
  DA152.T68 2014
  941.01'4--dc23
                                    2014033984

Printed in the United Kingdom by Short Run Press, Exeter

For a complete list of Oxbow titles, please contact:

UNITED KINGDOM
Oxbow Books
Telephone (01865) 241249, Fax (01865) 794449
Email: oxbow@oxbowbooks.com
www.oxbowbooks.com

UNITED STATES OF AMERICA
Oxbow Books
Telephone (800) 791-9354, Fax (610) 853-9146
Email: queries@casemateacademic.com
www.casemateacademic.com/oxbow

Oxbow Books is part of the Casemate Group

Front cover: *Anglo-Saxon Canterbury (c. AD 600), a reconstruction based on archaeological evidence.
Drawing by J. A. Bowen. © Canterbury Archaeological Trust Ltd.*
Back cover: *David Hill with students.*

CONTENTS

PART THREE: TOPOGRAPHY

ILLUSTRATIONS

PREFACE

David Hill joined the then Victoria University of Manchester the same year as I did (1971), and I well remember our first meeting for the exuberance of his personality. More easily tracked down in the refectory than his office, and always crackling with creative energy, he would wave aside practicalities, assigning them to an army of supporters to whom he referred with old fashioned formality: 'My wife, Ann, will drive me to your house with the scripts'; 'My secretary, Mrs Burns, will put the lecture in my diary'; 'My colleague, Mrs Worthington, will know the answer to that question'.

I occasionally gave lectures for the Extra-Mural Department, for which he was warmly appreciative (even bringing flowers on one occasion when I stood in at short notice – though I WAS being paid for it!) and in later years he double-marked the final year scripts for my course 'Anglo-Saxon Art and Archaeology'. It was a popular course and there were a lot of scripts (and he WASN'T paid for it!); but he very much enjoyed the fluency with which English students wrote, and I enjoyed our collaboration. When he transferred to the English Department it was natural to invite him to share the teaching of this course, and he took over the lectures on Towns and Church Architecture, to the benefit of the students. He also ran a course called 'From Alfred to Edgar' in the English Department until he was forced to retire. Despite that official retirement he never stopped working and was often to be found in the University, rarely alone, the Christie Bistro being his favourite place for meetings and cameraderie. As a founder member of the Manchester Centre for Anglo-Saxon Studies, David contributed enormously to its development and success, particularly by organising conferences and excursions.

In spite of his frequent travels his family was of primary importance to David, and he was always proud of the achievements of his children and grandchildren. He nearly always included a reference to them in his lectures and his daughters, Rachel and Virginia, often accompanied him on digs when they were young. Later it always gave him great pleasure and pride to speak of Rachel's husband as 'my son-in-law the doctor' and he conquered his dislike of flying to attend, with delight, Virginia's wedding in America.

David died on 19 July 2011, just four days after celebrating his 74th birthday, when, with typical generosity, he had hosted a party at Tatton Park. On that occasion, despite chronic ill-health, he was in fine spirits, delighting in his recent marriage to Margaret Worthington, and hugely pleased that my colleague Maren Clegg Hyer and I had used his drawings on the cover of our recent book.[1]

As the current Director of MANCASS I arranged a memorial symposium in his honour which was held at The University of Manchester on 7–8 June 2012, named 'Towns, Topography, [Bayeux] Tapestry' to reflect his main interests. The conference papers on towns and topography are published here, with the personal tributes of each author.[2] I invited Susan Thompson to join me in editing these papers. A graduate of the part time MA in Medieval Studies course, in which David played a major role, she also completed her PhD at Manchester and is currently an Honorary Research Fellow of the University. Long-time neighbours and friends of the Hill family, she and her husband Brian were particularly supportive of David when he bravely returned to work and to his house in Sale after his first wife, Ann, died in 2003, shortly after they had moved to the north-east to be close to their elder daughter and her family; and Susan and Brian provided string music for David's wedding to Margaret in August 2010. Susan was therefore a natural choice to contribute to the preparation of this volume in his honour.

GALE R. OWEN-CROCKER
Professor of Anglo-Saxon Culture, The University of Manchester
Director, Manchester Centre for Anglo-Saxon Studies

Notes

1 *The Material Culture of Daily Living in Anglo-Saxon England*, ed. Maren Clegg Hyer and Gale R. Owen-Crocker, Exeter, University Press, 2011; paperback edition Liverpool, University Press, 2013.
2 Some of the Bayeux Tapestry papers are to be published in *Text* 42 (2014–15).

CONTRIBUTORS

MARTIN ALLEN is a Senior Assistant Keeper in the Department of Coins and Medals at the Fitzwilliam Museum, Cambridge, and an Affiliated Lecturer in Cambridge University's Faculty of History. He administers the Corpus of Early Medieval Coin Finds (EMC) and edits the *British Numismatic Journal*, which includes annual surveys of coin hoards and single coin finds and articles on Anglo-Saxon coinage. His recent publications include *Mints and Money in Medieval England* (Cambridge: University Press, 2012).

MARK ATHERTON teaches Old and Middle English and History of the Language at Regent's Park College and at Mansfield College, Oxford University. He previously taught at universities in Cologne and Brussels and worked for two years on the *Fontes Anglo-Saxonici* project at Manchester University. He has published on Hildegard of Bingen, Henry Sweet and Victorian philology, and on Old English literature. Recent publications include *There and Back Again: J. R. R. Tolkien and the Origins of The Hobbit* (London: I.B. Tauris, 2012) and *Teach Yourself Complete Old English* (London: Hodder and Stoughton, 2010).

DAVID BEARD is a freelance archaeologist specializing in the medieval period. He has worked as a field archaeologist for the Department of Environment (Northern Ireland) and the Museum of London. He has been involved in continuing education for many years and has taught for the University of Oxford Department for Continuing Education (OUDCE) and the Universities of London, Essex, Ulster, and the London College of the University of Notre Dame; he was also the Archaeological Consultant for Southwark Cathedral. He is the author of and tutor for an OUDCE online course on the Vikings, and the Programme Director and Academic Director for the Oxford Experience Summer School. info@archeurope.com

GILLIAN FELLOWS-JENSEN was formerly Reader in Name Studies at the Institute of Name Research in the Department of Scandinavian Research at the University of Copenhagen, retiring in 2003. Her major field of interest has been place-names and personal names in Scandinavia, the British Isles and Normandy. Although resident in Denmark, it was always a pleasure for her to return to her home town, Manchester, and talk to David Hill and his colleagues there.

ERIK GRIGG is at present nearing completion of his PhD on early medieval dykes (400 to 850 AD) at The University of Manchester. He works as the Education Officer at the Collection Museum in Lincoln. He has taught at The University of Manchester and the University of Lincoln. He completed his MA in Medieval History at Manchester University in 2007 and

his BA in History and Geography at Christ Church College, Canterbury, in 1990. He has written on a variety of subjects including Cornish literature, the Welsh Annals and the 1217 Charter of the Forest.

CHRISTOPHER GROCOCK read Latin and French at Royal Holloway College, University of London, and studied medieval Latin epic for his PhD at Bedford College, University of London. He has been Project Director of the Bede's World Museum, Jarrow, a museums consultant and freelance lecturer, and currently combines teaching Classics at Bedales School with research writing. He is editor of *Ruodlieb* (Aris and Philips, 1985), Gilo of Paris' *Historia Vie Hierosolimitane* (Oxford: OMT, 1997; with Elisabeth Siberry); *Apicius* (Prospect Books, 2006; with Sally Grainger), and *Abbots of Wearmouth and Jarrow* (Oxford: OMT, 2013, with Ian Wood). He has been a regular contributor to MANCASS conferences since 2006.

MICHAEL HARE is an honorary research fellow in the Department of Archaeology and Anthropology of the University of Bristol. His research interests focus on the history, archaeology, architecture and art of the early medieval period. Recent publications include a study of the historical evidence for Anglo-Saxon Berkeley (Gloucestershire) designed to accompany Bristol University's excavations there and several papers concerned with the church of St Mary at Deerhurst (Gloucestershire), an outstanding survival from the early ninth century; he is in the early stages of writing a book about Deerhurst. In addition to Anglo-Saxon England, he has also published papers concerned with Ottonian and Salian Germany, and he has a developing interest in early medieval Italy, especially Rome. His paper in this volume is a spin-off from his contributions to the recently published Western Midlands volume of the *Corpus of Anglo-Saxon Stone Sculpture*.

JEREMY HASLAM is a Senior Research Fellow at the Institute of Historical Research, University of London. He has worked for many years as an archaeologist, excavating on, supervising and directing early medieval sites in English towns such as Oxford, Southampton, London, Cricklade and elsewhere, and has also excavated a number of early industrial sites in England, Europe and Africa. In addition, he has been involved professionally as a photographer of architectural and landscape subjects. His main research focus has for some time been situated on the boundaries of archaeology, geography and history, analysing the evidence for the physical morphology and early development of Anglo-Saxon and early Norman towns within a wider landscape in England. This has led to the examination of the place of towns and fortifications within territories as evidence of the political and strategic aspects of the development of the late Anglo-

Saxon state. He recently published *Urban-Rural Connections in Domesday Book and Late Anglo-Saxon Royal Administration*, BAR British Series 571 (Oxford: Archaeopress).

NICK HIGHAM is Professor Emeritus at The University of Manchester, since his retirement in 2011. He is best known for his work on early Anglo-Saxon England and King Arthur, including *King Arthur: Myth-Making and History* (2002), *(Re-) Reading Bede: The Ecclesiastical History in Context* (2006), and the Jarrow Lecture in 2011, *Bede as an Oral Historian*. He has recently edited *Wilfrid: Abbot, Bishop and Saint* (2012), and with Martin Ryan published *The Anglo-Saxon World* with Yale U. P. in 2013.

SIMON KEYNES is Elrington and Bosworth Professor of Anglo-Saxon in the University of Cambridge, and a Fellow of Trinity College, Cambridge. He is a co-editor of and contributor to the *Wiley Blackwell Encyclopedia of Anglo-Saxon England* (2nd ed., 2014), and a contributor to *Kingship, Legislation and Power in Anglo-Saxon England*, ed. G. R. Owen-Crocker and B. W. Schneider (2013).

GALE R. OWEN-CROCKER (editor) is Professor of Anglo-Saxon Culture at The University of Manchester and Director of the Manchester Centre for Anglo-Saxon Studies. She co-founded and co-edits the interdisciplinary journal *Medieval Clothing and Textiles*, and is a general editor of the series Medieval and Renaissance Dress and Textiles. Her books include *The Bayeux Tapestry: Collected Papers*, Variorum Collected Studies Series (2012), *An Encyclopaedia of Dress and Textiles of the British Isles, c. 450–1450* (with Elizabeth Coatsworth and Maria Hayward, 2012); *The Material Culture of Daily Living in Anglo-Saxon England* (with Maren Clegg Hyer, 2011); *Working with Anglo-Saxon Manuscripts* (2009); *An Annotated Bibliography of Medieval Textiles of the British Isles, c. 450–1100* (with Elizabeth Coatsworth, 2007); *King Harold II and the Bayeux Tapestry* (2005); *Dress in Anglo-Saxon England: revised and enlarged edition* (2004); *The Four Funerals in Beowulf and the Structure of the Poem* (2000).

JONATHAN PARKHOUSE is a graduate of Manchester University, where he first met David Hill when taken on as a digger on the Offa's Dyke Project. He then became David's first research student, and also worked with him at Quentovic. He has subsequently directed a wide range of excavations and field projects in South Wales and Buckinghamshire, and spent thirteen years as Warwickshire's County Archaeologist before establishing himself as a consultant. He is archaeological advisor to the Diocese of Coventry, and a former vice-chair of the Institute for Archaeologists. The nature of his career means that he has had perforce to be something of a generalist, although he has retained an interest in both Anglo-Saxons and quernstones, themes to which he returns in this paper. (jp@jparchaeology.co.uk)

DOMINIC POWLESLAND was taught by and worked with David Hill in the mid 1970s before going on to start the Heslerton Parish Project and then the Landscape Research Centre, a charitable research trust, established in 1980 and based in the Vale of Pickering in Yorkshire. He is best known for his research on the archaeological landscapes of the Vale of Pickering as well as his contributions to Anglo-Saxon settlement and cemetery studies, excavation techniques, archaeological computing and remote sensing. He holds an honorary doctorate from the University of York and Honorary or Visiting chairs in Leeds, York, Huddersfield and Vienna and is currently the Field Archaeologist in Residence at the McDonald Institute of Archaeological Research, University of Cambridge.

ALEXANDER R. RUMBLE recently retired as Reader in Palaeography at the University of Manchester and is a former Hon. Director of MANCASS. He has published extensively on Anglo-Saxon Studies, Domesday Book, onomastics and palaeography. He co-edited with David Hill *The Defence of Wessex: The Burghal Hidage and Anglo-Saxon Fortifications* (Manchester, 1996). He is currently editing the charters of the Old Minster, Winchester.

DONALD SCRAGG is Emeritus Professor of Anglo-Saxon Studies at the University of Manchester, and has published widely on English up to 1100. His major works include editions of *The Battle of Maldon* and the *Vercelli Homilies*, and in 2012 he published the reference book *A Conspectus of Scribal Hands Writing English, 960–1100*. In 1984 he initiated discussions relating to the foundation of the Manchester Centre for Anglo-Saxon Studies which came into being in the following year, and he was its first Director until his retirement in 2005.

SUSAN D. THOMPSON (editor) is a graduate of the Manchester MA in Anglo-Saxon Studies followed by a PhD on the Palaeography of the Royal Anglo-Saxon Diplomas, both completed while still working as a peripatetic 'cello and class music teacher. She joined the MANCASS 11th century Project on Script and Spelling as a research assistant in 2000 and later published *Royal Anglo-Saxon Diplomas: A Palaeography* (2006) and *Anglo-Saxon vernacular Charters: A Palaeography* (2010).

DAMIAN TYLER studied history at the University of Manchester in the 1990s. After taking his BA he remained at Manchester, taking an MA in Medieval History before commencing doctoral research. His PhD, on the impact of Christian conversion on early Mercian kingship, was awarded in 2002. His research interests focus on early Anglo-Saxon England and include kingship, religion and conversion, warfare and violence, and ethnicity and identity. He has taught at the University of Manchester and currently teaches at Manchester Metropolitan University.

MARGARET WORTHINGTON HILL (portharch@btinternet.com) is an independent teacher and archaeologist. Her research interests focus on the Early Medieval period having taught both Anglo-Saxon and Celtic Studies in the University of Manchester Extra-Mural Department. Excavations and survey co-directed with David Hill included research on Offa's Dyke, Quentovic, France and Monemvasia, Greece. Publications include: 'Quentovic – local and imported wares' (1993), *La Ceramique du Ve au Xe siecle dans L'Europe du Nord-Ouest*. Conference proceedings of the Groupe de Recherches et d'Etudes sur la Ceramique dans le Nord/Pas-de-Calais; 'Wat's Dyke: An archaeological and historical enigma' (1997) in *Anglo-Saxon Texts and Contexts*, ed. Gale R. Owen-Crocker, *Bulletin of the John Rylands University Library of Manchester*, 79, No. 3.

ABBREVIATIONS

ASE	*Anglo-Saxon England*. Cambridge: Cambridge University Press
BL	London, British Library
CW	number in Rumble 1980
DB	Domesday Book
DMV	deserted medieval village
EEE	*Epistola ad Ecgbertum Episcopum*, Bede's 'Letter to Bishop Egbert'; the fourth text included in Grocock and Wood, *Abbots of Wearmouth and Jarrow*
EHR	*English Historical Review*. London: Longman
GDB	Great Domesday Book
HA	Bede's *History of the Abbots of Wearmouth and Jarrow*
ODNB	*Oxford Dictionary of National Biography*. 2004. Oxford: Oxford University Press
OMW	number in Rumble forthcoming
RCHM[E]	Royal Commission for Historical Monuments [of England]
S	number in P.H. Sawyer, *Anglo-Saxon Charters: An annotated List and Bibliography*. Royal Historical Society Guides and Handbooks 8 (London, 1968), with additions and revisions by Susan Kelly and Rebecca Rushforth http://www.esawyer.org.uk
VC	*Vita Ceolfridi*

Part One

David Hill

1

David Henry Hill PhD FSA

Nicholas J. Higham

The unexpected death in July 2011 of Dr David Hill robbed Anglo-Saxon academe, and the Manchester Centre for Anglo-Saxon Studies in particular, of one of its most exciting and innovative thinkers. It was very fitting that we remembered David through a memorial symposium in Manchester (in July 2012), as, though I don't think his heart ever really shifted far north of Somerset, it was here in Manchester that he did so much to develop and promote studies of the Anglo-Saxon.

Aged 34, he came to Manchester University as the first Extra-Mural tutor ever to be appointed in archaeology, taking up his post in the summer of 1971. Over the next few years he built up archaeology as one of the most dynamic subject areas in a then flourishing Department of Extra-Mural Studies. This was a time when archaeology was becoming established as a subject across Britain and was commanding wide popular interest and media exposure. David's achievements were many. He saw the opportunity to offer a wide variety of short courses – day trips, one-day schools, short study trips at home and abroad – which brought many of the leading academics of the day into the orbit of Manchester's archaeological enthusiasts, or took coach loads of his students to visit henges, hill forts, Roman forts, ancient churches and medieval towns, all under expert guidance. But in many respects more important, David developed a suite of longer courses, 3-year long certificate programmes, which enabled adult learners to engage with organised study and achieve high levels of understanding and engagement with the discipline. For many of these students David unlocked the door through which they could pass to gain a real working knowledge of archaeology in the field. At the core of this initiative lay the Methods in Archaeology certificate course, which at its height was running in all three years consecutively, with anything up to 60 students in total spread across them. Alongside there were in addition smaller certificate classes in both Egyptology and Roman Britain. A particular need was for field work: Extra-Mural groups visited collections of Egyptian and Roman antiquities at home and abroad, and David took his Methods classes all over Britain and Western Europe; but most of all he needed a theatre in which to train and develop their skills in survey and excavation.

David was first and foremost an Anglo-Saxon archaeologist. It was at Winchester with Martin Biddle that he had first cut his archaeological teeth, as it were, and then at Southampton he studied for his PhD the towns of later Anglo-Saxon England. Until 1973, all David's publications were in some sense or other about these urban sites, that enigmatic early tenth-century document the Burghal Hidage, or Frankish parallels – he was very interested in the siege of Paris for example. But Anglo-Saxon towns are concentrated very much in southern and eastern England – as you get closer to Manchester they become as rare as hen's teeth; the few that might be considered were small, temporary and difficult to locate: the only large and permanent example close by is Chester, where archaeology was already pretty well sewn up by Romanists working with or from the Grosvenor Museum. If you were going to select a modern English city from which to conduct research on King Alfred's urban legacy, Manchester would be pretty much the bottom of the list of candidates.

So David chose instead to focus his attention, and that of his students, on the great dykes of the Welsh Marches, Offa's and Wat's, which had been largely neglected since the great survey of Cyril Fox published in 1955. Professor Owen Ashmore, the Director of Extra-Mural Studies, approved the purchase of a small collection of equipment, wheel barrows, spades, and so on, but students in the early days had largely to provide their own gardening equipment, all of it transported on a royal blue, open-back lorry which one of them happened to own – the inspired purchase of a horse-box to store and transport equipment came later. So began decades of weekends, weeks and even fortnights spent under canvas along the Marches, surveying and sectioning the dykes, with groups of students working scattered along the line each under the command of one of the final year students, often working up their projects, with David carried backwards and forwards by car (he did not drive of course), rather like some first world war general in *Black Adder* visiting the trenches. Vast numbers of profiles were surveyed and the hundredth trench was reported in 1984 – to place this in context, previous excavations by Fox were barely a handful. Numerous short reports resulted, leading up to the publication of a final overview, with Margaret Worthington, in 2003, which has made a major contribution to the way that today we read the great earthworks of the period. The work on Offa's Dyke won the BBC Chronicle Award in 1977. I have no doubt that it was by far the most successful archaeological project run out of any Extra-Mural Department of a British University since the last war and it brought both David himself and, more particularly, all those participating, considerable acclaim.

At the same time, of course, David was pursuing other academic interests, and in particular working on a cartographic representation of mid- to late Anglo-Saxon England. His great *Atlas* was published in 1981, providing Anglo-Saxonists with by far the best researched and most accomplished body of maps ever produced, all painstakingly hand-drawn and letrasetted. The *Atlas* contained some non-British images, such as his map of early settlements in Iceland as recorded in *Landnámabók* (map 75 on p. 52) but David's intention to continue and provide a comparable atlas of early medieval Europe was eventually frustrated by his worsening eye-sight, as diabetes took its toll. At the same time he was deeply interested in Anglo-Saxon coinage and trade, publishing papers on *sceattas* in 1977 and joining with D. M. Metcalf to publish a major multi-authored volume in 1984. In 1984 and 1985, in collaboration with a team from Sheffield University, David took a small group of Extra-Mural students and others to the Canche valley, where for the first time Quentovic, the main port of northern Francia, was located near Montreuil-sur-Mer, and this led to articles in *Antiquity* in 1990 and 1992, and a contribution to a multi-authored work published in Rotterdam. Excavations continued each year from 1985 up until 1992.

When David was researching the Atlas of Early Medieval Europe he travelled extraordinarily widely. These journeys took him at one point to Monemvasia, a now almost deserted medieval and later town on the eastern edge of the Peloponnese which was founded by Greek refugees from Slav invaders in the late sixth century. Going back some time later with the aid of the British School at Athens, he and a group of Extra-Murals met Harris Kalligas, an architect who was researching the history of the town and re-building some of its houses, and agreed to survey the upper town and defences – something which Harris needed doing but could not do herself. The result was 3-week seasons each summer from 1991 to 1996, with the results lodged both with Harris and at the British School. There was no publication, nor any intention to publish: David was waxing lyrical one day in the University's senior common room to two colleagues, one of whom asked him to what research project the Monemvasia surveys were attached. Without pause for thought, David replied 'the F.U.N. project' – they nodded wisely, and Margaret nearly choked.

But David could also take a joke. My own doctoral research in Cumbria centred on Kirkby Stephen, where I came across a run-down old antique shop – a junk shop really – with the name David Hill above the window in large, peeling letters.

At a Saturday Day School at which we were both speaking I slipped a slide of it into the carousel for the start of his talk: he stopped in mid flow and looked at it slightly quizzically then moved on to the intended image with a smile, never as far I know even asking afterwards who had tampered with his lecture – though he probably guessed.

The 1990s saw David establish a new interest in Anglo-Saxon agriculture and the equipment used. Again, this was largely driven by textual research as much as artefacts, starting in many instances with the illustrative material provided by the calendars; papers on the hayrake, beekeeping, a winepress, the oxcart, vine-dressers' knives and the heavy plough all followed. There was, however, a great deal more going on: David was interested in mills, leather and metal working and a wide range of further craft areas. It is a sad fact that he has left a substantial body of unpublished research, mostly in the form of short papers, some at least of which it is to be hoped will appear in due course. Alongside his agricultural interests, David also shifted his research towards the Bayeux Tapestry, once again in highly innovative ways, studying the back as much as the front of this massive embroidery to assess the degree of damage and alteration it had undergone over the last millennium.

David was highly collaborative throughout his working life, as his publications and more particularly his numerous projects show. The *Atlas* aside, he was not the producer of major single-authored monographs, rather his research was generally carried out through teamwork, often with his students but also joining with other Anglo-Saxonists near and far, for example to edit conference proceedings. He had an extraordinarily wide circle of academic friends, both at home and abroad, and was for ever making fresh contacts. Sharing a room with him in the late 1970s was always an interesting experience. Quite unexpectedly you might find his footprints all over the papers on your desk, though it was rarely apparent just why he had needed to clamber up there; or he would empty his entire case over your work then scoop up your papers along with his, leaving you to go out to take a class that evening without the lecture you had prepared. But his telephone conversations were always entertaining. To those who had not yet met him but were about to he would tell them that he would be the tall handsome one with the curly hair so they could not miss him. His research journeys were many and various, though few were as extraordinary as his walk from Canterbury to Rome in 1985, following in the footsteps of archbishops on their way to receive the pallium and using the same schedule, with a support team led by Margaret. There followed a walk across Ireland, again with Margaret, in the footsteps of both saints and traders; but ill-health finally put an end to such endeavours.

The running-down and eventual closure of the Extra-Mural Department was a tragedy for David, as much as for his students, cutting him off from the adult education which had been such a central feature of his working life. David moved into English, where he joined a distinguished and welcoming group of fellow Anglo-Saxonists, but his teaching was not well adapted to the needs and interests of English undergraduates and he missed the whole arena of adult education, as did others of us. He continued to be very active within MANCASS, but worsening health reduced his ability to travel and to write, with periods of near blindness, then damage to his circulation leading to surgery. His continuing productivity throughout was very much against the odds.

David will be remembered widely as a brilliant lecturer, a hugely entertaining raconteur with a whole fund of stories stemming from his own youth as well as his many travels, and a brilliant ideas man, capable of casting whole new insight onto a subject which you might otherwise have thought was sorted. He cared deeply about his students, providing them with guidance, advice and aid. He was jointly instrumental in the 1980s in instigating an MA programme in the History Department to provide those who wanted it with a further level of attainment – 16 students began that part-time programme, the vast majority coming from David's Certificate courses. One, who had no first degree, went on from the MA to attain a PhD, an achievement which would have been unthinkable without the help and grounding that David and the Certificate provided. Without such Extra-Mural students, MANCASS itself would never have emerged as the force that it has been in Anglo-Saxon studies. It is fair to say that David has been instrumental in placing Anglo-Saxon archaeology and history on the map at Manchester, stimulating and enthusing many who might otherwise have had little interest to follow his lead. Alongside, he was a man of great integrity and deep personal loyalty, who touched the lives of very many. The two-day symposium from which these papers derive served as a fitting commemoration of his service at Manchester and to the wider community, and their publication can only cement his memory. He would have been delighted at the breadth and depth of the contributions on offer and at the coming together of so many of his old friends. David hardly ever missed a MANCASS meeting: even at his own memorial symposium, I am sure many will have expected him to shuffle in to listen and then to comment, his taxi having turned up a bit on the late side that morning; he was certainly present in spirit.

2

Published works by David H. Hill

Compiled by Margaret Worthington Hill
edited and augmented by Gale R. Owen-Crocker with the Assistance of Celeste Andrews

1967a The Burghal Hidage – Lyng. *Proceedings of the Somerset Archaeological and Natural History Society* 111, 65–6.

1967b The Burghal Hidage – Southampton. *Proceedings of the Hampshire Field Club* 24, 59–61.

1968 with P. V. Addyman. Saxon Southampton: a review of the evidence, Part 1. *Proceedings of the Hampshire Field Club* 25, 61–93.

1969 with P. V. Addyman. Saxon Southampton: a Review of the evidence, Part 2. *Proceedings of the Hampshire Field Club* 26, 61–96.

1970a Late Saxon Bedford. *Bedford Archaeological Journal* 68, 96–100.

1970b The Burghal Hidage: the establishment of a text. *Medieval Archaeology* 13, 84–92.

1970 with D. Austin. The bounds of Crondall and Itchell. *Proceedings of the Hampshire Field Club* 27, 63–5.

1970 with J. Hassall. Pont de l'Arche: Frankish Influence on the West Saxon Burh? *Archaeological Journal* 127, 188–95.

1971 ed. with M. Jesson. *The Iron Age and its Hillforts: Papers Presented to Sir Mortimer Wheeler*. Southampton, Millbrook Press.

1971a with J. Hassall. The Siege of Paris. *Ago* 9, 16–22.

1971b with J. Hassall. The Siege of Paris. *Ago* 10, 16–23.

1971c with J. Hassall. The Siege of Paris. *Ago* 11, 1–10.

1971 with M. Biddle. Late Saxon Planned Towns. *Antiquaries Journal* 51, 70–85.

1971 with F. Aldsworth. The Burghal Hidage – Eashing. *Proceedings of the Surrey Archaeological Society* 68, 198–201.

1972 Maps and diagrams. In C. M. Heighway (ed.), *The Erosion of History*. London, Council for British Archaeology, Urban Research Committee.

1974a Offa's and Wat's Dykes – some exploratory work on the frontier between Celt and Saxon. In T. Rowley (ed.), *Anglo-Saxon Settlement and Landscape: papers presented to a symposium, Oxford 1973*. British Archaeological Reports 6, 102–7. Oxford, British Archaeological Reports.

1974b The inter-relation of Offa's and Wat's Dykes. *Antiquity* 48, 309–12.

1974 with David Wilson. Frontier Dykes in the Wrexham Area, Recent Work, 1972. *Journal of Chester Archaeological Society* 58, 93–6.

1974 with John Sharples. The Lutje-Saaksum Hoard: a correction. *Jaarboek voor Munt- en Penningkunde*, 60/62, 156–8.

1975–6 The Cambridgeshire Dykes: II The Bran Ditch. *Proceedings of the Cambridgeshire Archaeological Society* 66, 126–9.

1976a London Bridge: a reasonable doubt? *Transactions of the London & Middlesex Archaeological Society* 27, 303–4.

1976b Problems associated with the Borough of Thelwall on the Mersey. In Shelagh Grealey (ed.), *The Archaeology of Warrington's Past*. Warrington, Warrington Development Corporation.

1976c The Case of the Disappearing Dyke. *Rescue News* 12, 1.

1976d The Death of the Ailsworth Witch. *Durobrivae* 4, 13.

1977a Continuity from Roman to Medieval: Britain. In M. W. Barley (ed.), *European Towns: their Archaeology & History*, 293–302. London, Academic Press for the Council for British Archaeology.

1977b Die-Adjustment in the Woden-Monster series of Sceattas. *Numismatic Chronicle* 7th series 17, 171–2.

1977c Notes on Offa's and Wat's Dykes. *Medieval Archaeology* 21, 210–222.

1977d Offa's and Wat's Dykes: some aspects of recent work 1972–76. *Transactions of the Lancashire and Cheshire Antiquarian Society* 79, 21–33.

1977e The 'Hanover' Hoard of Porcupine Sceattas. *Numismatic Chronicle* 7th series 17, 173–4.

1978a ed. *Ethelred the Unready, Papers from the Millenary Conference*. British Archaeological Reports, British Series 59. Oxford, British Archaeological Reports.

1978b The origins of the Saxon Towns. In P. Brandon (ed.), *The South Saxons*, 178–89. London, Phillimore.

1978c Trends in the development of Towns in the reign of Ethelred II. In D. Hill (ed.), *Ethelred the Unready, Papers from the Millenary Conference*. British Archaeological Reports, British Series 59, 213–26. Oxford, British Archaeological Reports.

1978 with C. Heighway. St Oswald's Priory: the history and context of its foundation. In C. Heighway, Excavations at Gloucester, 4th Interim Report: St Oswald's Priory 1975–1976. *Antiquaries Journal* 58.1, 118–23.

1979 Siege-craft from the Sixth to the Ninth Century. In M. W. C. Hassall (ed.), *De Rebus Bellicis*, British Archaeological Reports, International Series 63, 111–17. Oxford, British Archaeological Reports.

1980 After Chronicle – What Next. *Popular Archaeology* 2.3, 35–6.

1981a *An Atlas of Anglo-Saxon England*. Oxford, Blackwell.

1981b Notes on Offa's and Wat's Dykes. *Medieval Archaeology* 25, 184–5.

1981c The 'How to' Series 2: Learn to Dig. *Popular Archaeology* 2.8, 38–9.

1982 The Anglo-Saxons 700–1066 AD. In M. Aston and I. Burrow (ed.), *The Archaeology of Somerset*, 109–18. Taunton, Somerset County Council.

1983 The Excavations, Sites XI and X2, Pound Lane. In K. S. Jarvis (ed.), Excavations in Christchurch, 1969–80. *Dorset Natural History and Archaeological Society*. Monograph series 5, 22–7. [Dorchester,] Dorset Natural History and Archaeological Society.

1984a Offa's Dyke – 100th Trench. *Popular Archaeology* 5.9, 32–5.

1984b The Dyke Systems in the North – Recent Work and Reconsiderations. *Archaeology in Clwyd* 6, 11–14.

1984 With D. M. Metcalf (eds). *Sceattas in England and on the Continent: The Seventh Oxford Symposium on Coinage and Monetary History*, British Archaeological Reports, British Series 128. Oxford, British Archaeological Reports.

1985a The Construction of Offa's Dyke. *Antiquaries Journal* 65.1, 140–2.

1985b The road to Rome. *Popular Archaeology* 6.7, 7–11.

1986a Notes on Offa's and Wat's Dykes. *Medieval Archaeology* 30, 150–2.

1986b To another Far Horizon – the Road to Rome. *Popular Archaeology* 6.14, 9–13.

1987a Period Surveys – The Saxon Period. In J. Schofield and R. Leech (eds), *Urban Archaeology in Britain*. Council for British Archaeology Research Report No. 61, 46–53. London, Council for British Archaeology.

1987b June (Unsigned) The search of Saddleworth Moor. *Police* 19.10, 20–1.

1987 with D. Barrett, K. Maude, M. Worthington and A. Mayer. The Canche Valley Survey 1984–1985. *Manchester Archaeological Bulletin* 1, 10–17.

1988a Towns as structures and functioning communities through time: the development of central places from AD 600 to 1066. In D. Hooke (ed.), *Anglo-Saxon Settlements*, 197–212. Oxford, Blackwell.

1988b Unity and diversity – a framework of European towns. In R. Hodges and B. Hobley (eds), *The Rebirth of Towns in the West, AD 700–1050*, Council for British Archaeology Research Papers No. 68, 8–15. London, Council for British Archaeology.

1988 with B. Dearden. Charles the Bald's bridgeworks at Pitres: Recent excavations at Pont de l'Arche and Igoville. *Haute-Normandie Archaeologique* 1, 63–70.

1988 with D. Barrett, K. Maude and M. Worthington. The Canche Valley Survey: A search for the Carolingian Port of Quentovic, the 1986 Season. *Manchester Archaeological Bulletin* 3, 35–52.

1989 with R. Greig. Early medieval Pilgrimage. *Manchester Archaeological Bulletin* 4, 9–14.

1990 with M. Worthington. From Sea to Sea: across Ireland following the footsteps of the pilgrims and traders. *Irish Heritage* 6, 6–7.

1990 with D. Barrett, K. Maude, J. Warburton and M. Worthington. Quentovic defined, *Antiquity* 64.242, 51–8.

1991a Offa's and Wat's Dykes. In J. Manley, S. Grenter and F. Gale (eds), *The Archaeology of Clwyd*, 142–56. Mold, Clwyd County Council.

1991b The Eadred Reliquary: The riddle in the Park. *Manchester Archaeological Bulletin* 6, 5–11.

1992a Sept. A hayrake: insights into Offa's agricultural landscape. *Offa's Dyke Newsletter* 69, 14–15.

1992b At last People. *Offa's Dyke Association Newsletter* 58, 16.

1992c Illustrations. In S. Lewis, *Buried around Buckingham*. [Buckingham,] The Author.

1992d The siting of the early medieval port of Quentovic. In A. Carmiggelt (ed.), *Rotterdam Papers VII, A contribution to medieval archaeology*, 17–23. Rotterdam [n.p.].

1992 with M. Worthington, J. Warburton and D. Barrett. The Definition of the Early Medieval Site of Quentovic. *Antiquity*, 66.253, 965–9.

1993 La Calotterie, Monthuis. *Bilan Scientifique* 1992, 55. Direction Regional des Affaires Culturelles, Nord-Pas de Calais.

1994a Summer. A handful of grit, Anglo-Saxon bee-keeping. *Beekeepers Quarterly* 38, 28.

1994b An urban policy for Cnut? In A. Rumble (ed.), *The Reign of Cnut, King of England, Denmark and Norway*, 101–5. Leicester, University Press.

1994c Autumn. Some drawings of R. H. Watt. *Cheshire History* 34, 37–8.

1994d August. The earliest representation of an Anglo-Saxon ship. *The Mariner's Mirror* 80.3, 326–7.

1995a Asser not a forgery. *British Archaeology* 9, letters.

1995b The crane and the gyrfalcon in Anglo-Saxon England. *Medieval Life* 3, 32, 24 [eccentric numbering].

1996a April. Chepstow. *Offa's Dyke Association Newsletter* 71. [Page numbers not available.]

1996b Gazetteer of Burghal Hidage sites. In D. Hill and A. Rumble (eds), *The Defence of Wessex. The Burghal Hidage and Anglo-Saxon Fortifications*, Appendix IV, 189–231. Manchester: Manchester University Press.

1996c The nature of the figures. In D. Hill and A. Rumble (eds), *The defence of Wessex. The Burghal Hidage and Anglo-Saxon Fortifications*, 74–87. Manchester: Manchester University Press.

1996d September. To Chepstow – again. *Offa's Dyke Association Newsletter* 72, 15–16.

1996 ed. with A. R. Rumble. *The Defence of Wessex: The Burghal Hidage and Anglo-Saxon Fortifications*. Manchester, University Press.

1997 Spring. Anglo-Saxon Mechanics: a winepress. *Medieval Life* 6, 7–10.

1997 with S. Sharp. An Anglo-Saxon Beacon System. In A. R. Rumble and A. D. Mills (eds), *Names, Places and People, an onomastic miscellany for John McNeal Dodgson*, 157–65. Stamford, Paul Watkins.

1998a Autumn. Anglo-Saxon Technology 1: The Oxcart. *Medieval Life* 10, 13–18.

1998b Autumn. Anglo-Saxon Technology 2: Wingeard Seax: the Anglo-Saxon vine dresser's knife. *Medieval Life* 10, 18–20.

1998c The Bayeux Tapestry – the case of the Phantom Fleet. *Bulletin of the John Rylands Library* 80, 23–31.

1998 with D. Seddon. An unrecorded Anglo-Saxon Cross Shaft, now at Blackden, Holmes Chapel, Cheshire SJ 789 707. *Transactions of the Lancashire and Cheshire Antiquarian Society* 94, 145–9.

1999a Eleventh century Labours of the Months in Prose and Pictures. *Landscape History* 20, 29–39.

1999b Summer. Riddle 8: a problem of identification or a problem of translation. *Medieval Life* 11, 22–3.

1999c Winter. The Bayeux Tapestry and its commentators: the case of Scene 15. *Medieval Life* 11, 24–6.

1999d The labours of the month. *Landscape History* 20, 29–40.

2000a A frontier in flames, the eighth century in south-west Shropshire. In J. Leonard, *et al.* (eds), *The Gale of Life, two thousand years in south-west Shropshire*, 65–73. Woonton: South-West Shropshire Historical and Archaeological Society in association with Logaston Press.

2000b Anglo-Saxon Mechanics: 1: *Blaestbel(i)g* – the Bellows. *Medieval Life* 13, 9–11.

2000c Athelstan's Urban Reforms. *Anglo-Saxon Studies in Archaeology & History* 11, 173–85.

2000d Offa's Dyke: pattern and purpose. *Antiquaries Journal* 80, 195–206.

2000e December. Offa versus the Welsh. *British Archaeology* 56, 18–23.

2001a A byway of history: Harold Harefoot. *Medieval Life*, 11 [error for 14?] 25.

2001b Spring. *Cyrn*: The Anglo-Saxon Butter Churn. *Medieval Life* 11 [error for 14?] 19–20.

2001c End Piece: Definitions and Superficial Analysis. In D. H. Hill and R. Cowie (eds), *Wics: The Early Medieval Trading Centres of Northern Europe*, 75–84. Sheffield, Academic Press.

2001d Mercians: the dwellers on the boundary. In M. P. Brown and C. A. Farr (eds), *Mercia, an Anglo-Saxon Kingdom in Europe*, 173–82. Leicester, University Press.

2001e '*Sulh*'– The Anglo-Saxon Plough *c.* 1000 AD. *Landscape History* 20, 1–15.

2001f The Shiring of Mercia – again. In N. J. Higham and D. Hill (eds), *Edward the Elder: 899–924*, 144–59. London, Routledge.

2001 ed. with R. Cowie. *Wics: the early mediaeval trading centres of Northern Europe*. Sheffield, Sheffield Academic Press.

2001 ed. with N. J. Higham. *Edward the Elder: 899–924*. London, Routledge.

2001 Winter, with R. Greig. The Bayeux Tapestry: a dramatic colour change. *Medieval Life* 11 [error for 14?], 15 and rear cover.

2002 The Origin of Alfred's Urban Policies. In T. Reuter (ed.), *Alfred the Great: Studies in Early-Medieval Britain* 3, 219–233. Aldershot, Ashgate.

2002a with M. Worthington. Le Site de Quentovic. In S. Curveiller and C. Seillier (eds), *Archéologie du littoral Manche – mer du Nord, II Le haut Moyen Age*, Bulletin Historique et Artistique du Calais 65–76, Calais, Association historique des Amis du Vieux Calais.

2002b with M. Worthington. Offa's Dyke. *Reallexikon der Germanischen Altertumskunde* 22, 24–8. Berlin, Sonderdruck.

2002–3 A Note on the Shad. *Cheshire History* 4, 4–15.

2003 with M. Worthington. *Offa's Dyke: History and Guide*. Stroud, Tempus.

2004 The Bayeux Tapestry: the establishment of a text. In P. Bouet, B. Levy and F. Neveux (eds), *The Bayeux Tapestry: embroidering the facts of history*, 383–401. Caen, Presses universitaires de Caen.

2004 transcribed and ed. with S. Matthews. *Cyril Fox on tour 1927–1932, Two of Sir Cyril Fox's notebooks*. British Archaeological Reports, British Series 364. Oxford, Archaeopress.

2005 ed. with M. Worthington. *Æthelbald and Offa: Two Eighth-Century Kings of Mercia*. British Archaeological Reports, British Series 383. Oxford, Archaeopress.

2010a The Anglo-Saxon Plough: A Detail of the Wheels. In N. J. Higham and M. J. Ryan (eds), *Landscape Archaeology of Anglo-Saxon England*, 169–74. Woodbridge, Boydell.

2010b The Quality of Life. Deerhurst Lecture 2005. Deerhurst, The Friends of Deerhurst Church.

2010 with M. Worthington. La Contribution des fouilles britanniques à la connaissance de Quentovic. In S. Lebecq, B. Bethouart and L. Verslype (eds), *Quentovic: Environnement, archéologie, histoire*, 253–64. Villeneuve d'Ascq: Université Charles-de-Gaulle-Lille 3.

2011a Prelude: agriculture through the year. In M. Clegg Hyer and G. R. Owen-Crocker (eds), *The Material Culture of Daily Living in the Anglo-Saxon World*, 9–22. Exeter, The University of Exeter Press.

2011b with J. McSween. The storage chest and the repairs and changes to the Bayeux Tapestry. In M. J. Lewis, G. R. Owen-Crocker and D. Terkla (eds), *The Bayeux Tapestry: New Approaches*, 44–5. Oxford, Oxbow Books.

Part Two

Towns

3

Quentovic

Margaret Worthington Hill

David was my mentor, colleague and friend for more than thirty years and, towards the end of his life, my husband. I became one of his Manchester University Extra-Mural students and a tutor and I count some of the adult students I met and worked alongside among my best friends. Generosity with his ideas enabled several students, including myself, to complete research degrees. Offa's Dyke, Wat's Dyke and the Welsh border began to feel like home as we recorded and excavated the earthworks, and I eventually moved there and for me it has been home for the last fifteen years. With people who had completed the Methods in Archaeology course, his 'Trained Brains', we went to France to excavate Quentovic and Pont-de-L'Arche and to Greece to record the ruins of the early medieval town of Monemvasia. The study tours and day visits he organised took us to many early medieval sites in England, Ireland, Denmark, Iceland, France and Italy, including his 'Walk to Rome'. My life was certainly the richer in so many ways for knowing David.

Locating Quentovic

The excavations in the valley of the River Canche to locate the early medieval trading site of Quentovic were carried out by a team from Manchester and Sheffield Universities under the overall direction of David Hill and with the permission and oversight of M. Pierre Leman, Head of Archaeology for the region. The investigations were carried out between 1984 and 1992, each season lasting for between three and six weeks with occasional long weekends for survey.

The group of early medieval settlements known as *wic* sites were known from coin and documentary evidence and many of these undefended, international trading sites had been identified by excavation so that the archaeological world had become familiar with continental sites such as Dorestad, Ribe, Hedeby and in England Hamwic and Eoforwic. The site known as Quentovic from both coins and documents had proved more elusive.

The name Quentovic means '*vicus* on the Canche' and in some sources is mentioned in connection with St Josse.

David Hill had explored the documentary sources and the valley some years before and thought initially that Quentovic could be located at a point where a side valley on the south side of the Canche led to the church and village of St Josse. Our initial excavations therefore were in the valley bottom adjacent to where this side valley entered the main Canche valley at a property called Le Tertre. Twelve minor excavations and nine boreholes were opened but on this site no evidence for occupation was found. In one area a deep clay layer with large quantities of naturally crushed marine shells was of potential importance as shell-tempered pottery is found on many *wic* sites.

Further research and discussion with M. Leman showed that the River Canche had been canalised in modern times and now runs close to the northern side of the wide flat-bottomed valley. The river today is tidal up to Montreuil-sur-Mer and the low-lying area of the hamlet of Visemarest in the commune of La Calotterie has numerous drainage ditches with sluice gates that prevent the incoming tide from flooding the area. The valley sides are of limestone with flints and rise to wide, fertile plateaux to north and south.

A Roman road ran from the northern plateau crossing the Canche near Beutin, passing through the commune of La Calotterie and on to the southern valley side and plateau beyond. In 1973 M. Jean Couppé of Etaples had excavated a Roman pottery kiln of the second and third centuries AD adjacent to the southern valley road. In 1981 human bones were exposed when a nearby field in Visemarest was cut by drainage ditches to enable the farmer to convert it from pasture to arable. Investigation by M. Couppé of the numerous cuts showed that there were two areas of burials and that early medieval artefacts were to be found across the whole area. It was declared to be 'La Nécropole de Quentovic'. No research excavations were carried out at this time.

Early in our research M. Leman had pointed us to this field and the two mounds (M1 and M2). M. Leman had also shown us the results of a geophysical survey that had been carried out in an adjacent field by himself and M. Jeanson

and this had shown a number of features in the northeast corner. As the necropolis field was under a crop we turned our attention in our first seasons in 1985 and 1986 to the area of the geophysical survey that had appeared to show the remains of buildings.

The Area of the Geophysical Survey

Four trenches (G1–4) were laid out adjacent to each other and evidence for the flint and rubble foundation walls of a fourteenth-century farmhouse were found in each of the trenches excavated. The farmhouse foundations were close to the surface and clearly explained the geophysical evidence. Once the farmhouse layer had been removed, a grey, sterile context was revealed and below this a humic layer containing animal bones, pottery, worked amber, hone stones, worked antler and high quality glass fragments of the type in use during the seventh to ninth centuries. The area proved to be where a number of rubbish pits had been cut into clean sand and had overflowed to produce the dark humic layer. It seemed likely that this was an area close to early medieval habitation although no trace of associated buildings was found within our excavations.

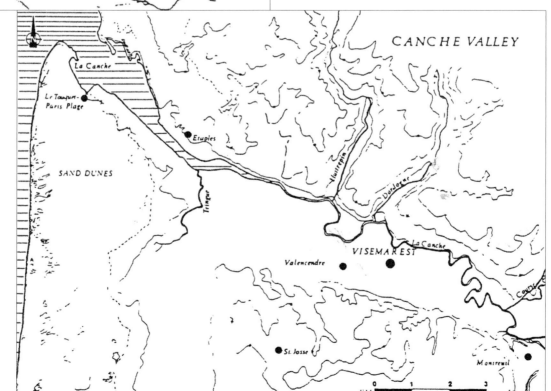

Fig. 3.1. Quentovic: top: Location Map of northern France bottom: The Canche Valley (Drawn by David Hill).

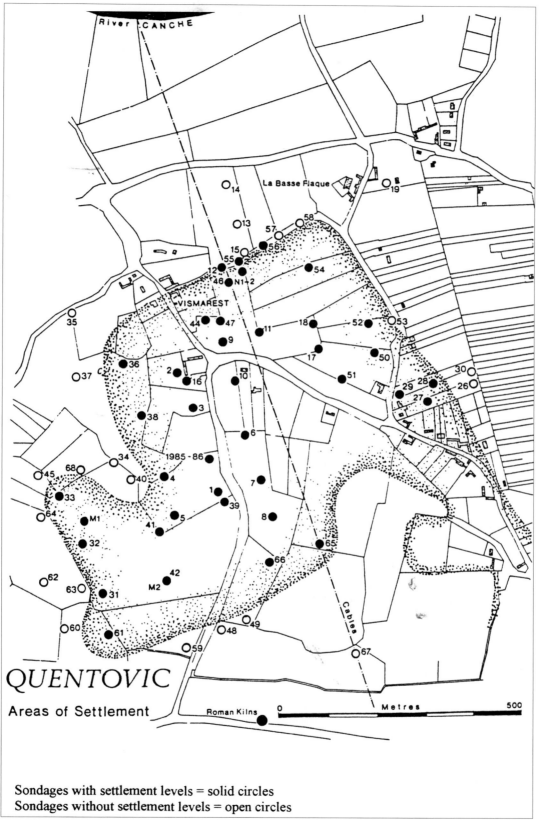

Fig. 3.2. The settlement area of Quentovic (Drawn by David Hill).

The Sondages

After the first full season of excavation and the discovery of early medieval activity on the site we were hopeful that we were within the *wic*. However, encouraging as this was, it did not necessarily identify the site as that of Quentovic. To be certain that this was the *wic* site, we needed not only the evidence of long-distance contact demonstrated by the wide range of non-local materials found in the rubbish pits but we also needed evidence to show that the occupied area was extensive and not simply one or two dwellings. We therefore developed a two-fold approach; firstly, to find further evidence for the type of settlement and its material culture during the early medieval period in area excavations, and secondly, to determine the size of the area occupied. To define the extent of the site a series of 1 × 3m sondages (S1–S68) were planned at 100m intervals on a grid pattern as far as landowners and the terrain allowed. We felt that archaeologically it was not acceptable to excavate into the early medieval context in so many small excavations that they would damage the site for future research; the decision was therefore taken to excavate to a point where the early medieval contexts were clearly visible, to record the excavation and then backfill the sondage.

Figure 3.2 shows the location of the sixty-eight sondages. The solid circles on the map show where early medieval occupation evidence was found; the open circles are where no evidence was found. When a sterile sondage was found, an intermediate sondage closer to the last productive one was excavated until the boundary of the site became clear. To the south and west of the occupied area the evidence was for a gently sloping sandy beach with no structures to define it (S31, 32, 33, 61). The sand gave way to a peaty deposit outside the settled area in S59, 60. We understand from local, verbal sources that there was once a southern branch of the River Canche between the settlement site and the valley side and that in times of flood it occasionally runs again. The excavations to define the northern boundary are described below under The Waterfront.

The Necropolis

In 1987, with a second season in 1990, we were able to turn our attention to the burial mounds at the southern side of the site as the farmer gave us access after the harvest and before ploughing. Excavations were carried out at both the northern mound (M1) and the southern mound (M2). The early medieval material was close to the surface in both mounds, and the stratigraphy could be observed in the drainage ditches that cut each of the mounds. In M1 pottery, glass, flint cobbles and fragments of human bone were all found within the plough soil adjacent to the ditch. This would seem to be material that had been thrown up from the cutting of the drainage ditches and then regularly ploughed. Our excavated area on the undisturbed mound contained six separate burials, all of which were articulated and most of which had flint cobbles

associated with them, placed round or over the head. There were no clear grave cuts to be seen, but the undisturbed nature of these burials and the associated flint cobbles suggest that they were carefully buried and in an ordered manner; all were laid east/west. There were no grave-goods. It was clear that there were a considerable number of additional burials within the area of M1 but these were left undisturbed. The recalibrated radiocarbon date for one of the burials gave a date centred on AD 820 (GrN-16140, 1235±30BP). Below the burials there was evidence for early medieval occupation with artefacts that included animal bone, antler tines, glass fragments, early medieval pottery sherds and a Series G sceat, usually dated to about AD 720.

The excavation in M2 showed a similar sequence of plough soil disturbance to that found in M1. The surface of the mound seemed to have had a chalk and flint layer that had been disturbed and contained fragments of human bone. Articulated skeletons were discovered immediately below this level. As in M1, there were no grave-goods and the bodies had been carefully laid east/west. In some cases a grave cut could be seen. Although the burials were close together both horizontally and vertically, and had a date span of over a hundred years, there seemed to have been little disturbance of the earlier burials or intercutting of graves. Some burials at the lower level showed slight evidence for wooden boards or coffins and associated metalwork including corner brackets and, rather surprisingly, what seemed to be a lock. The lowest burials had cut shallowly into the sterile grey silt layer below the mound material. Two radiocarbon dates for the bones in M2 gave recalibrated dates centred on AD 690 and 820 for the lower and upper burials (GrN-18956, 1235±25BP and GrN-18957, 1310±25BP). These two dates show that the mounds had been used for burials over a considerable length of time and they were not the result of one devastating event.

Cut into the structure of the mound was a rectangular pit, 1m × 0.5m, of which the south side was vertical but the north side sloped to the flat bottom of the pit. The south-east corner of the pit contained the carbonised remains of a large squared post, 0.25m across, which had been set against the southern, vertical side of the pit and its base packed with chalk. The fill of the pit contained charcoal but no human bone despite the fact that the cut was below the burials in the mound into the sandy silt layer below. Although the original extent of the mound was difficult to identify because of the years of ploughing and the cutting of the drainage ditches, the post seemed to have been set into the centre of the mound. A recalibrated radiocarbon date for the remains of the post gave a date centred on AD 890 (GrN-18959, 1145±35BP), suggesting that the mound may have continued to have a significance after burials ceased. A number of cut chalk blocks were also found within the mound and may once have been part of a structure, although this could not be determined; similar blocks, one with a cross cut into it, were found by M. Couppé in his original examination when the field was first brought into arable cultivation.

In both mounds, the lowest level of burials had been cut into the top of grey, silty sand that contained no evidence of occupation and formed a sterile layer as appears to have been the case across the whole area of the site. It had not been possible to excavate below the burials at M1 but at the M2 site, below the sterile layer and sealed by it, there was significant evidence of occupation. A large quantity of worked antler was found together with separate piles of off-cuts that had been discarded at various stages during the production of combs: the bosses of antlers in one pile, lengths of antler in another and a third with the tips of the tines. That this was evidence for comb making came from the number of sub-rectangular billets that had been cut from the tops of the combs after the billets had been fixed between their back plates. No complete combs were found but parts of the back plates of two combs were recovered, one of which had a small bronze nail in place.

In addition to sherds of early medieval pottery, many fragments of amber were found, including two complete annular amber beads. There were also a glass bead and many fragments of glass from vessels that could be identified as palm cups and cone beakers. Glass working was shown by a droplet, a part of a crucible glass attached and a reticella glass rod for decorating glass vessels. An incomplete silver back-plate for a composite brooch was also found. A number of iron artefacts corroded together were recovered and x-rays, courtesy of Manchester Museum laboratory, seemed to indicate evidence for annular brooches. It would seem that an area of workshops had existed and been abandoned, possibly after a flood that deposited the sterile layer, and the burials with their mounds of soil imported from the valley side. As these workshops were sealed below the burials they must have been in use prior to the late seventh century, the date for the earliest burials.

The earth that formed both M1 and M2 was not the same as that found elsewhere within the settlement and on investigation it proved to be the same as that from the southern valley side. Within this context, and without doubt brought to the site with the soils, were found small, abraded sherds of pottery of the same distinctive type of fabric as that made at the Gallo-Roman kiln excavated by M. Couppé. No other pottery from the kiln, or any pottery of Roman date, was found in any other excavation that we carried out. It is also clear from the radiocarbon dates from the burials within the mound material that burials were of a considerably later date than the Roman pottery from the kiln.

The Football Field

In 1988 and 1989 a 15m × 5m area was excavated in the northeast corner of the Football Field (N1 & N2) adjacent to an overgrown disused road or farm track that we called the Old Road. There was a 0.35m depth of topsoil under which a series of settings and alignments in flint and chalk cobbles were revealed, a rectilinear layout that may have formed the foundations of a timber framed building similar to the

foundations found in G1–4. There was much evidence for later medieval occupation within the topsoil and between the cobbles, including a substantial quantity of glazed and unglazed fourteenth- to fifteenth-century pottery. No early medieval artefacts were found in the layer below this. There were darker areas within the layer below but these seemed to be the result of mole activity. We felt that this was proved to be the case when a mole fell into the excavation as the side of the trench had cut through its run! This excavation was extended into the Old Road (N2) with similar results initially, but see below.

The Waterfront

Sondage 12 within the Old Road had provided evidence for early medieval activity. Sondages 13, 14 and 15 to the north of the Old Road, towards the river, proved to be an area of thick clays that had been heavily water-logged indicating that it had been frequently inundated by the river in the past. No evidence of occupation was found in this area. An extension of N2 across the Old Road was therefore started by hand, as all our excavations were, and extended and excavated by machine to a depth of 2m across the full width of the road (courtesy of M. Leman). This revealed significant archaeology for a post and wattle revetted bank five metres wide. The bank itself appeared to be of horizontally interleafed clay and sand. The vertical posts were c.15cm in diameter and some appeared to have been split from a tree trunk giving them a triangular section; these posts were visible in the west side of the trench. At the bottom of the trench a line of posts running east/west had been cut through by the machine; these gave a clear indication that there was a revetment along the bank as well as the north/south line towards the river.

Further sondages within the Old Road and to the east (S55 & 56) confirmed that posts with interwoven wattles revetted the front face of a linear east/west aligned bank and the recalibrated radiocarbon date from the thin interwoven branches in Sondage 56 confirmed that it dated from the mid-eighth century, centred on AD 830 (GrN-18958, 1190±30BP). No evidence for a north/south line of posts was found here, but these excavations were much less extensive than the one previously described.

In Sondage 55 the layering of clay and sand was again observed within the bank. It was felt that layers of turfs might have been laid within the bank to help to stabilise it. To the front (north) side of the revetment in each sondage a series of interleaved water-laid deposits, varves, had built up naturally, suggesting periods of clear water silts and humic silts being deposited, and in one area the upright remains of reeds that had grown at the water edge could be identified. Below the varves early medieval pottery, the waterlogged remains of leather off-cuts from shoe making and animal bone were found.

When Sondages 57 and 58 were excavated further east of the Old Road no evidence for the bank was found; it seemed that either the bank had terminated between S56 and S57 or the alignment of the early medieval bank was not identical to that of the Old Road. The orientation of the revetment seemed to point to the south-east; unfortunately these fields were not available for excavation and the line of the waterfront in that direction could not be determined. However boreholes taken by Manchester geography students to the west did identify similar varves and again they seemed to mark the boundary between the sandy area where settlement had taken place and the area of the tidal waters of the Canche to the north. That the river once reached this revetment as the tide came in was well-demonstrated one afternoon when the local person responsible for closing the sluice gates to the drainage ditches forgot to do so. A gurgling was heard and water flowed along the Old Road and filled our excavations. The tidal waters of the Canche did not flow onto the occupied areas and it all disappeared when the tide went out.

We interpreted the bank and revetment as the main waterfront area with at least one line of posts that stretched out into the uninhabitable tidal area, the one radiocarbon date suggesting that this was built or repaired in the mid-eighth century. Comparisons can be made from the riverside structures at Dorestad.

Since our excavations the French Archaeological Service has carried our excavations to the south-east of the Old Road and further evidence of timber and wattle linear structures was found. Here also it was close to the probable limit of occupation and the tidal reach.

The Artefacts

Taken together, the artefacts recovered from our excavations gave evidence of manufacturing processes including part of a crucible and a reticella rod from glass working; hone stones of various grades and sources including Scandinavia indicating metalworking; antler comb-making waste; jewellery making in amber, glass and silver; and probably pottery as indicated by an antler-tine pot-stamp.

The artefacts also showed evidence for long-distance trade: the single sceat of series G, the high quality soda glass that would have been imported either as vessels or cullet, the amber and schist hone stones from Scandinavia, jet from north-east England and Neidemendig lava from the Mayen area (see Parkhouse, this volume, pp. 19–25). The pottery included white wares from the Rouen area, red painted wares from the Beauvais area and a decorated blackware vessel that is identical to one from Arras (Worthington, 1993). The shell-tempered ware could have been of local manufacture, but analysis proved it to be identical to that found in Hamwic, and it could have been made at either or both sites. Some of the blackwares from Ipswich, York and Quentovic were analysed by York Archaeological Trust using both thin-section analysis and neutron activation analysis (Mainman, 1993). They showed that some sherds found at Quentovic matched some sherds from Ipswich and some from York, although no kiln site is known for this particular pottery at any of these sites.

Fig. 3.3. Trench 1 David with the team (Photograph: Margaret Worthington).

Fig. 3.4. Trench 2 Looking into drainage ditch with M. Bakowski, DHH & M. Leman (Photograph: Margaret Worthington).

Fig. 3.5. David Hill with students (Photograph: Margaret Worthington).

Thus the excavations have given good evidence for early medieval occupation, the manufacture of goods, and for long distance contacts, all requisites for identifying a *wic* site. The sixty-eight sondages revealed the limits of the site, giving it an overall size of 800m east/west and 700m north/south, making it one of the largest *wic* sites identified to date, as can be seen from Figure 3.2, which places Quentovic within the top rank of similar sites in the early medieval period.

Our interpretation is that the open trading settlement was on a low-lying sandy island in the braided stream of the River Canche, with a timber and earth retaining wall to the north where the river would have been most active. However this was not a defensive structure, and the settlement seems to have been open and undefended with areas of shelving sand on the southern side where boats could be beached, if indeed there was a southern channel at this time. The inhabitants were involved in the manufacture of artefacts and materials were available to them from a wide area, including Scandinavia, Britain and France. The material assemblage closely parallels that found across The Channel in the *wic* sites at Southampton, London, Ipswich and York. However, to date, no Rhenish pottery has been found at Quentovic.

The evidence from coins with the mint mark Quentovic from other sites indicate that there was an active mint using the name of Quentovic in the early seventh century, as shown by one of the coins found at Sutton Hoo (Bruce-Mitford 1975, 579). However coins continued to be struck in the name of Quentovic after the abandonment of the Visemarest site. A series of Viking destructions of Quentovic were recorded as taking place in the middle of the ninth century in the Annals of St-Bertin (Nelson 1991 *sa* 842) and the date of the Viking raids fits well with the end dates given by the radiocarbon analysis and the pottery evidence from our excavations.

The whole area identified by our work is now protected in French law. Minimal development is allowed and excavation is required prior to any building work.

We received considerable assistance from the commune of Attin and its Mayor, M. Bakowski, throughout our time in France, and each year we put on an improvised display of our finds in the school; and they provided us with a *frite* supper each year.

The original team was led by David Hill with David Barrett, Keith Maude, Margaret Worthington and Julia Warburton plus the 'trained-brains', the occasional undergraduate and a number of professional archaeologists who gave freely of their expertise during the excavations and in the post-excavation analyses.

Calendar

1984	Survey and Sampling
1985	Le Tetre (winter); G1, G2 and G3 (summer)
1986	G1, G4; Sondages 1–16
1987	M1, M2; Sondages 17–43
1988	N1, N2; Sondage 44–49
1989	N1, N2; Sondages 50–55
1990	M1, M2; Sondages 56–59
1991	Season Cancelled
1992	Sondages 60–68

Note

1 Note on re-calibrated radiocarbon dates: The original dates were recalibrated in 2008 as recommended by the laboratory that supplied them. They are therefore different from those given in Hill, David *et al.* 1992. Revised dates were given in Hill 2010.

4

Putting Lava on the Map

Jonathan Parkhouse

Quernstones made from the lava of the Eifel mountains have long been recognised as an indicator of trade links within early medieval northwest Europe (*e.g.* Dunning 1956). In 1975 David Hill suggested that the author examine this material as the basis of an MA. The map which accompanied the resulting thesis (Parkhouse 1977) has been reproduced in a number of publications (*e.g.* Parkhouse 1976; Hodges 1982, 125) including David's own *An Atlas of Anglo-Saxon England* (Hill 1981, 120). An updated map taking account of more recent excavated and published material was presented in 1997 (Parkhouse 1997), although the earlier version still continued to be reproduced (*e.g.* Hill 2001, 82). This paper will summarise recent work which adds to the general picture of the distribution of lava and the trade which it represents.

Introduction

Many of the items for which we have archaeological evidence for long-distance trade or exchange are luxury items; some will have been primarily packaging rather than commodities *per se*, and some will have been for the personal use of traders and other travellers rather than commodities. Quernstones and millstones, on the other hand, are utilitarian objects which will represent actual trade, rather than, say, gift exchange.

Mayen Lava (also known as Niedermendig or Rhineland lava) was distributed beyond the immediate vicinity of the quarries in the Eifel from prehistory onwards (Hörter *et al.* 1951, 1955; Steuer 1987; Mangartz 2008). Long-distance export was well established by the Roman period and continued well into the post-medieval period. The quarries were still being worked in the mid-twentieth century.

Mayen lava has been found at a large number of sites in early medieval Europe from the later seventh century onwards. Querns have been found in significant quantities at a number of continental and English emporia, notably Dorestad (Parkhouse 1976; Kars 1980); Haithabu (Jankuhn 1963; Schön 1995), London (Parkhouse 1991; Freshwater 1996; Goffin 2003), York (Rogers 1993), Hamwic (Andrews 1997), Ipswich

(unpublished), Groß Strömkendorf/Reric (Tummuscheit 2003) and Ribe (Feveile 2010) as well as single fragments at Birka (a single fragment, the most northerly findspot, and the most isolated) and Quentovic (Hill *et al.* 1990). Away from the sites which clearly had importance for long-distance trade, lava tends to be found in much smaller quantities, although there are some sites, such as Flixborough, Lincolnshire (Loveluck 2009), and Dorney, Buckinghamshire (Roe 2002) with larger quantities. Nevertheless, the total quantity of early medieval lava recovered by archaeologists is only a tiny fraction of the entire output of the quarries. Fritz Mangartz (2008) has estimated that between *c.* AD 450 and 800 the total production in the Eifel was of the order of 2,250,000 quern pairs; the main activity in the quarries was during the late fifth century (although none appears to have been reaching England at that date) and the eighth century, with only limited production during the sixth and much of the seventh centuries. The annual production may thus have been in the order of 15,000 whole querns, or between six hundred and seven hundred and fifty tons. Even allowing for the fact that during the life of a quern some 50–70% literally vanishes to dust, the sample which has been archaeologically recovered is minute.

Whilst Mayen lava is very distinctive and readily identifiable, studying early medieval material presents problems and limitations. Unsurprisingly almost all quern finds are fragmentary; the majority of finds are not particularly diagnostic, even in terms of basic characteristics such as size and recognition of a grinding surface. Often burial conditions are such that the material may be very fragile and brittle, particularly on sites on river gravels where slightly acidic groundwater may circulate freely, whilst its vesicular nature also enables groundwater to penetrate more readily (Roe 2002). Furthermore, whilst there are typological differences between Roman and later material, it is often impossible to determine this from minute fragments, and residuality may also be a problem on sites where there is continuity of occupation.

One further difficulty is that whilst lava is distinctive, the Eifel was not the only source of basalt lava from geological activity in the Cenozoic Era used for quernstones and millstones (Kars 1980, 400–3). The occurrence of Cenozoic lava outcrops in southern Europe need not concern us here, but it is worth noting that lava from Volvic in the Massif Central in France was exploited during the Roman and possibly also the early medieval period (Peacock 1980). Although mineralogical differences between the Volvic and Eifel may be distinguished by thin-section analysis, macroscopically the two lavas are identical (Gluhak and Hofmeister 2011, cited in Picavet 2011, 178). The available evidence suggests very strongly that the early medieval material in the part of northwest Europe covered by this paper is from the Eifel; nevertheless, there may be some uncertainty as to provenance along the southern edge of the distribution, particularly as the Massif Central, rather than the Eifel, appears to have been the major source of lava querns in Roman Gaul (Gluhak and Hofmeister 2008, 2009).

Typology

There is not a great deal of typological variation amongst the early medieval material. The most variable assemblage remains that from Dorestad. A variant type, which as far as the author is aware is peculiar to Dorestad, has an integral rynd, rather than relying upon one made of metal or wood (Parkhouse 1976, 185). These would probably have been much harder to manufacture and it is difficult to see what the benefits from the additional effort and risk of breakage would have been.

These basic categories may be subdivided further according to the means by which motive power is applied, usually by means of a handle socket drilled vertically near the edge of the runner or (less frequently) obliquely from the upper surface to the side. Diagnostic features (handle holes, hopper flanges, rynd sockets) are more prevalent on upper stones and upper stones are thus more readily identifiable.

Early medieval stones differ from Roman examples in that the grinding surfaces tend to be relatively flat and level; the Roman examples generally have a more prominently angled grinding surface (King 1986, 96). Further, whilst the grinding surfaces of Roman stones often show evidence for dressing, usually with radial grooves, such evidence is generally absent from the early medieval material; where dressing is visible it is usually crudely pecked in 'harps' with short grooves in parallel groups at right angles to each other (*e.g.* the assemblages from the Royal Opera House, London; Goffin 2003).

Lava was also used for mechanical mills, with evidence in the form of larger diameter stones from the ninth-century mill at Tamworth (Rahtz and Meeson 1992), and also from London, Springfield, Essex (David Buckley, excavator, *pers. comm.*), and from Mildenhall, Suffolk (Fiona Roe, *pers. comm.*). It is possible, however, that some mechanical mills made use of stones which were no larger than hand-querns. At the water mill site at Omgård, Denmark, what is presumed to be a millstone (of gneiss, although there were a number of lava stones from the site) had a diameter no larger than a handquern, but was

substantially thicker (14.5cm; Nielsen 1986: it is not clear from the published report how many stones were hand querns and how many were millstones). A near-complete stone from Dorestad appears to have had no handle, but does have a rynd-socket on the underside and may also have been mechanically driven (Parkhouse 1975, 185 and fig. 4a).

The other significant category of material to be considered is part-worked rough-outs or 'blanks', which come mainly from the emporia, although as we shall see there are other instances where they occur. Where rough-outs occur in quantity it is reasonable to suggest that the part-worked material may have been being processed into finished objects for onward trade.

The archaeological context

The extensive work which has taken place at Dorestad has yielded lava fragments in quantity, and its situation on the Rhine makes it a key site for understanding the distribution of lava querns. Study of the thicknesses of the major assemblage of lava fragments from Dorestad by Kars (1980) shows a bi-modal pattern of two distinct groups, one of *c.* 3cm and the other of *c.* 7cm, which contrasts strongly with the arithmetic mean thickness of 5.12cm. The 'thick' group, about a third of the whole population, represents the fragments of 'new' stones in Dorestad, including rough-outs and items broken during manufacture. In contrast the 'thin' group is the stones which were used and broken on site. Plotting of the two groups in relation to the excavated area shows that the rough-outs tend to come from the harbour area, with those of smaller diameter coming from close to the former river. On the basis of this, it is suggested that manufacture took place close to the harbour where the raw material was being unloaded. Another concentration of thicker fragments, however, within the main area of the settlement, seems to indicate the presence of a workshop further from the harbour.

The even larger assemblage from Haithabu, reported upon in detail by Volkmar Schön, shows similarity with the Dorestad material. There is again a distinct differentiation between used thinner stones and thicker half-finished examples (Schön 1989, 1995). In addition Haithabu includes material interpreted by Schön as evidence of the manufacturing process. Truncated cones and biconical fragments are interpreted as the 'core' of the hopper aperture, evidently removed with some care, either by inscribing a single groove around the hopper aperture from one side or by working from both sides. There are also small chips of stone which are interpreted as waste from dressing.

A workshop may also be deduced from the London material. In 1989 an assemblage of 235 fragments was recovered from behind a late tenth-century waterfront at Thames Exchange (Parkhouse 1991; Freshwater 1996), which could be clearly seen to consist predominantly of half-finished material, broken prior to deposition. Many were broken at or near the central hole; some fragments were partly drilled through, whilst there was also evidence for breakage near the edge of many stones, suggesting a degree of damage whilst being stacked on edge or during transport (Fig. 4.1).

The great majority of upper stones had traces of flanges around the hopper. None, however, showed any trace of handle holes or rynd sockets, features which would have been added at a late stage of manufacture. The Thames exchange assemblage differs from those from Dorestad and Haithabu in one further respect, in that there are no blanks with thickened but un-perforated areas in the centre corresponding to the hopper area. What we are seeing at London therefore seems to represent a different and later stage of the manufacturing process. The Thames Exchange assemblage of course comes from a single context, whilst those from Dorestad and Haithabu are derived from a large range of contexts across large excavation areas.

Given the nature of the Thames Exchange material it is difficult to be sure how many complete rough-outs are represented by the assemblage, but the minimum figure is around sixty-six. From a small sample of the more complete examples it was possible to calculate a mean weight of 39.55kg pre-breakage. Whilst there were no small chips which might be expected from a workshop, let alone the 'hopper cores' seen at Haithabu, the evidence for breakage of stones during drilling of the central hole seems to be clear indication that there was a workshop in the vicinity of where the material was discarded.

A large quantity of material has been recovered from various mid-Saxon sites in Ipswich (unpublished, but examined by the author in 1990). Whilst the greater part of the assemblage consists of small, heavily abraded, undiagnostic fragments, there are at least two pieces which are evidently parts of unworked 'blanks'; frustratingly, these are from post-medieval contexts although there is a likelihood that they are derived from middle Saxon contexts (Keith Wade, former Suffolk County Archaeologist, *pers. comm.*).

York may also have been the site of a workshop, with assemblages of moderate size from Anglian levels at Fishergate and Coppergate. There are no 'blanks', but a truncated cone *c.* 5cm in diameter was initially described as a possible 'core' removed to form the hopper of an upper stone, but apparently less carefully worked than the similar pieces from Haithabu (Rogers 1988). However, this interpretation was not sustained in the final report (Rogers 1993); the question of whether querns were worked up at York is thus not strictly proven.

Another site where the evidence for a workshop is weak is Ribe. Whilst the site was a significant trading centre, the evidence for manufacture amongst the published material consists of a single hopper 'core' and fragments of two unused querns (Feveile 2010, 139); it is impossible to state whether these items were for use by a Ribe resident or represent items being finished for onward distribution.

There are other sites which have produced rough-outs/'blanks', or material which has been interpreted as residue from quern manufacture. There are undressed rough-outs from Medemblik in the Netherlands (Besteman 1990), from Alt-Archsum (Sylt) and Elisenhof on the west coast

Fig. 4.1 Thames Exchange, London. Part of the assemblage of partly-finished lava querns from the rear of a late tenth-century waterfront.

of Schleswig Holstein (Schön 1995, 101 and fig. 37), and a single half-finished lava quern fragment from Winchester from later eleventh-century levels (Biddle 1990, 264–5). What this material appears to show is that the production of finished quernstones was not restricted to the emporia. Elsewhere material has been interpreted as possible waste from quern finishing, such as that from a pit at Hamwic (Andrews 1997, 240), and from the Eton Rowing Lake sites at Dorney, Buckinghamshire, where the suggestion that querns were being finished on site seems to be made largely on the basis of the small size of the lava fragments, although no roughouts were recovered and despite the condition of the assemblage many fragments were clearly from well-worn, well-used querns (Roe 2002), similar in many respects to the Flixborough assemblage (examined by the author in 1994; summary note in Loveluck 2009, 248).

There is, however, direct evidence for the transport of half-finished material in the form of boat finds in the Rhineland at Lüttingen (Nordrhein-Westphalia) and at Salmorth (Ellmers 1972, 1974). Comparable evidence from England comes from the early tenth-century Graveney boat, which contained two large unfinished fragments of quernstone. Within the main hold area, pairs of stones stacked on end and perpendicular to the keel would have fitted comfortably between each frame, packed in with the rest of the cargo, which consisted principally of hops, together with Kentish ragstone and some Roman tile, presumably salvaged building material. It is suggested that the boat would have been capable of carrying a cargo of approximately 280 querns, with twenty-eight querns in each of the ten frame spaces, weighing around seven tons (Fenwick 1978).

We may compare this calculation with the data extrapolated from the roughly contemporary Thames Exchange assemblage. Using the mean weights calculated above for the Thames Exchange querns, a cargo of 280 querns would perhaps have weighed around 10.9 tons, comfortably within the cargo capacity suggested for boats of the period, which may have been as high as twenty tons (Feveile 1995, cited by Pohl 2011). Taking the annual output/production figures for the Eifel quarries deduced by Mangartz and referred to above, one may suggest that the volume of river traffic was in the order of perhaps thirty to one hundred vessel loads per year.

The superior characteristics of Mayen lava, and the relative absence in many areas of other stone of comparable quality, were evidently major factors in the 'market penetration' which the lava achieved. Nevertheless, other stones were used for querns, and on many sites lava querns occur alongside those made of more local stone. Nor was Mayen lava the only stone traded over long distances. In the Baltic and Scandinavia the most important material was garnet muscovite schist (Glimmerchiefer), quarried at Hyllestad (Norway) from the tenth century (Rønneseth 1968). The distribution of this material has been studied by Peter Carelli and Peter Kresten (1997) and most recently by Meinrad Pohl (2010, 2011), who has looked in some detail at the boundary, or more strictly the overlap, between the distributions of lava and schist. Both are good quality commodities and moreover a type of commodity produced and used over wide areas.

Following Carelli and Kresten, Pohl describes a line between two 'trade spheres' running northwest – southeast across the Cimbrian peninsula from the Limfjord estuary in northwestern Denmark, to the Vejle Fjord, then south to the bay of Lübeck and then along the Elbe. This does not correspond with any political boundary, and Pohl looks to transport expenditure as a determinant factor. Long distance transport by sea from Hyllestad to eastern Jutland and beyond would have been cheaper than the relatively shorter journey from Mayen down the Rhine, along the North Sea coast, and possibly involving trans-shipments and even short stages over land. Pohl explains this in terms of the ratio of price to transport cost, and provides comparative estimates of the costs of transporting Mayen and Hyllestad stones to a range of destinations. Querns, though utilitarian, are a relatively high value commodity and the transport element of the cost was thus comparatively low, even if the costs of taking them short distances overland is factored in; with building stone, such as the Rhenish Tuff which was also exported to the Cimbrian peninsula, although the distribution is more limited, the transport cost is a much higher proportion of the total commodity value.

Nevertheless the boundary between the 'trade spheres' (if that is the right term) is not impermeable. A single find of lava from Birka, from a used and worn quern, is the most northerly find of this material, well beyond Pohl's trade sphere boundary; unfortunately it is from the backfill of the nineteenth-century excavations, and is effectively without a context (I am grateful to Dr Björn Ambrosiani for this information). There are also finds of lava in the Baltic within the area where Hyllestad schist querns predominate. At Haithabu, on Pohl's trade sphere boundary, lava querns predominate at 92% by weight of the assemblage with schist accounting for only 4%, whilst at its successor, Schleswig, the percentages (by weight) are lava 76% and schist 13% (Schön 1995). One also has to take account of the fact that merchants would have carried mixed cargoes; the supply-side economics would be different for each individual commodity. The picture may thus not be quite as clear cut as that suggested by Pohl, whose calculations assume cargoes consisting solely of stone.

Excavated finds only tell part of the tale. A recent paper by staff of Norfolk County Council's Historic Environment Service (Ashley *et al.* 2009) discusses the high percentage of medieval churches in Norfolk – 62% – which incorporate lava fragments in their fabric. Lava was noted in 425 of the 684 churches visited. Many of the fragments are clearly from querns; some thicker fragments may be from millstones or roughouts. There does not seem to be any demonstrable preference for use of lava in particular parts of churches, and the fabric in which lava was recorded ranges in date from the eleventh to fifteenth centuries.

The number of fragments per church ranges from single pieces to over eighty. There is a marked concentration of churches with over twenty fragments in south-east Norfolk, particularly in the Bure and Yare valleys. High concentrations are absent from west Norfolk, despite the presence of several mid-Saxon 'productive' sites, and a slightly greater abundance than elsewhere in Norfolk of mid-Saxon finds (Rogerson 2003). The concentration of churches with high counts of lava fragments in the Broadlands may indicate a workshop in the Norwich/Great Yarmouth area; indeed it is interesting to note the recovery of *sceattas* and metalwork from Burgh Castle, indicative of a 'productive' site (Pestell 2003). Most of the fragments are simply incorporated into the walls as pieces of rubble, but at St Andrew, Colney, just outside Norwich, large lumps of lava have been deliberately selected as the quoins of the north-western corner of the eleventh-century nave.

The distribution does not, of course, stop at the Norfolk border (Fig. 4.2). In Suffolk, this author has noted modest quantities (fewer than ten fragments) in churches in the Deben valley. Volkmar Schön (1995, 48) notes quern fragments in three churches in East Friesland.

What is one to make of this material? The high incidence is in part down to the frequent use of mass rubble walling or mortared flint as opposed to ashlar. Lava is not the only 'foreign' material incorporated into such walls; at Reedham, for example, there are several lava fragments along with much re-used Roman brick and *opus signinum*; the likelihood is that much of this material, including possibly the lava quern fragments, was stripped from the Roman fort at Burgh Castle.

Whilst some of the larger fragments may be from roughouts or even ballast, the greatest proportion of the lava in churches appears to be from broken quernstones. In most cases these have been built into the wall horizontally, so that it is difficult to see diagnostic characteristics to be able to suggest a date. Whilst some material will be Roman, the likelihood is that a significant proportion of it is later. Lava continues to be imported after the Norman conquest; however the suppression of querns in the twelfth century, in order to ensure revenues at manorial mills, means that querns tail off in the archaeological record. Nevertheless quern fragments are still being incorporated into church fabric after the twelfth century. What is not apparent is how long a period might elapse between discard of a quernstone and subsequent incorporation into church fabric. We need a better understanding of what happens to quernstones after they have been discarded and how they enter the archaeological record. Much of the material from churches shows relatively clean sharp edges, in contrast to much of the material recovered from excavations, which is often worn and in a fairly friable state. Presumably the church builders would have used whatever material was to hand, including, perhaps, material from field clearance, yet many of the stones from church walls do not look as though they had been exposed to abrasion or chemical deterioration in the ploughsoil for any great length of time.

The East Anglian church material shows that lava is being imported in larger quantities than is apparent solely from excavated material. The full extent of the church distribution beyond Norfolk is yet to be determined, including the

Fig. 4.2 A concentration of lava quern fragments (arrowed) incorporated into the exterior north nave wall of Holy Trinity church, Bungay, Suffolk.

correlation with the use of mass-rubble masonry. One would expect there to be fewer instances of quern fragments being re-used where there is good building stone suitable for ashlar masonry. Would there be a similar volume of material arriving in, say, the Yorkshire Ouse/Humber area, given that there are a number of sites where lava querns have been recovered from excavation as well as evidence for a reasonable level of economic activity at the various 'productive' sites in this region (Naylor 2004; appendix in Blackburn 2003b for list of potential 'productive' sites)?

Lava distribution and trade

Most or even all of the material was exported from the Eifel in partly-finished form. Breakage in transit was always a possibility and there was less commercial risk in trading lower value bulk material and adding the value with the completion of the finished artefact closer to the end user.

Frisian involvement in the trade, perhaps a large proportion of it, would have been significant, given the importance of Dorestad in the distribution network, and the documentary evidence for Frisian merchants in London in the seventh century, York in the eighth, and the Baltic in the ninth (Jellema 1955), although this does beg the question of who these Frisians actually were, and whether the term 'Frisian' may sometimes have simply denoted an international trader (Lebecq 1990). There were English traders in France in the eighth century, whilst in Charlemagne's correspondence with Offa he complains about Saxon traders circumventing customs by claiming to be pilgrims (Whitelock 1955, 779).

Lava was not the only commodity to come from the Rhineland, but its distribution is wider than that of Rhenish pottery, and the competition between Frisian and Frankish areas of commercial influence proposed by Richard Hodges on the basis of pottery (Hodges 1982, fig. 22) is not really reflected by the distribution of lava. Lava did not go directly from the quarry to the end user; it went via the emporia and doubtless then via more local markets, although the supply chain from emporium to user is difficult to reconstruct. We do not know whether the workshops in the emporia were working the material up into finished querns, or whether some were being traded on for final dressing at the point of use. We should not expect to find quantities of finished items at the workshops since they would have been traded on; the largest single context assemblage is that from Thames Exchange, London, which consists almost entirely of reject material and there is nothing that is a brand new 'factory fresh' quern. At Dorestad it is suggested (Kars 1980) that only stones destined for use within the settlement were actually finished there. The evidence that can be gleaned from the excavated material in the settlements is that dressing of early medieval querns was on the whole fairly basic, not necessarily reliant on a (possibly itinerant?) specialist.

Emporia were not the only places where international trade or specialist production took place, and the systematic correlation of numismatics, metal detecting data and excavated evidence has resulted in the identification of a growing number of 'productive' sites – essentially places that yield large quantities of coins and metalwork and which appear to be functioning as secondary redistributive centres (Ulmschneider 2000; Ulmschneider and Pestell 2003). Not all of these sites were necessarily permanently settled; for example Dorney (Lake End Road) in Buckinghamshire produced copious finds including exotic imports but no evidence for structures or permanent residence (Foreman *et al.* 2002, especially Chapter 5). Some of these sites may have been intermittent or temporary fairs, even where assemblages show superficial similarities to more settled sites; excavation of these sites will shed further light on the considerable variety of sites which have been categorised as 'productive'. As we have seen, some of these sites (*e.g.* Dorney, Flixborough) have produced large quantities of lava and whilst much of it is very fragmentary and/or abraded, and some of it is clearly from used querns, it raises the possibility that querns were being finished at some of these sites.

Who is organising and controlling this activity lies beyond the scope of this paper. Religious institutions certainly seem to have had a role in trade, with some 'productive' sites having ecclesiastical connexions, but other sites appear to be purely secular.

The utility of this data extends only as far as it illustrates behaviour and process. When David Hill set this author to looking at this material in 1975 it was accepted that lava indicated trade, but the extent of the network had not been defined nor likely workshops identified beyond a general assumption that emporia were involved. The frameworks in which we think about trade have also shifted considerably since David Hill was inspiring undergraduates and Extra-Mural students with his 'Anglo-Saxon Towns and Trade' courses at Manchester University in the 1970s. The 'Hodges model' has been developed and critiqued (see useful overview in the introductory chapter of Naylor 2004), and a vast amount of new data has come to light, if not yet entirely assimilated, both from controlled excavation and metal detecting, with new categories of site recognised.

Distribution maps show where one has looked, and this author's scanning of the literature (let alone any attempt to unlock data held in Historic Environment Records, which will vary in the level of detail in the data they hold) has been so inconsistent that he has not attempted to produce a comprehensive distribution map, or to compile a new corpus of material. Furthermore, maps need to be used with caution; the juxtaposition in David Hill's *Atlas* of the initial map of lava with one showing the *sceatta* coinage shows that there are similarities in the overall distributions, although one should avoid reading too much into this; the lava distribution represents a far longer slice of time than that within which *sceattas* were used. Nor may we assume that trade patterns remained static within this period; the role of the *wics* is eclipsed by the development of towns, whilst Vikings disrupt trade. Cargoes were mixed; lava is just one indicator of commercial activity amongst many, although one with a more widespread range than many of the other categories of artefact which make up the evidence for long-distance trade.

Nevertheless, the title of this paper probably commits one to providing something in the nature of a distribution map. The map produced here (Fig. 4.3) is an attempt to produce a definition of the extent of the area within which the material is known to occur, the principal sites for understanding mechanisms of production and distribution, and some of the 'hot spots' of distribution. There are deficiencies; in particular the southern limit of distribution is not well-defined, in part because of the problems of identification of provenance referred to above, and is an area requiring further work. We also need to think about the extent to which a map of this type is distorted by the biases and vagaries of the archaeological record; the lava now shown to be extensively incorporated in the fabric of Norfolk medieval churches serves to indicate the extent to which the material is likely to be under-represented in the archaeological record across much of its distribution.

But this is not intended to be a definitive map – it is a hypothesis in spatial format, demanding further testing and refinement.

Acknowledgements

Colleagues across Europe have provided ideas, advice, information and access to collections over many years; they are far too numerous to name individually but I hope they know who they are and will forgive the shortcomings of this contribution, which in any case is largely reliant upon the work of others. I must, however, thank Claus Feveile, Fritz Mangartz, Kenneth Penn, Paul Picavet, Meinrad Pohl and Fiona Roe, who have each provided information about recent work. Two people above all provided encouragement as well as friendship over many years; it is to my regret that I have not been able to discuss the content of this paper with either the late Gertrud Röder of Koblenz, whose knowledge of the Eifel quarries and hospitality were invaluable, or our much missed colleague David Hill, who set me to the task of looking at lava in the first place.

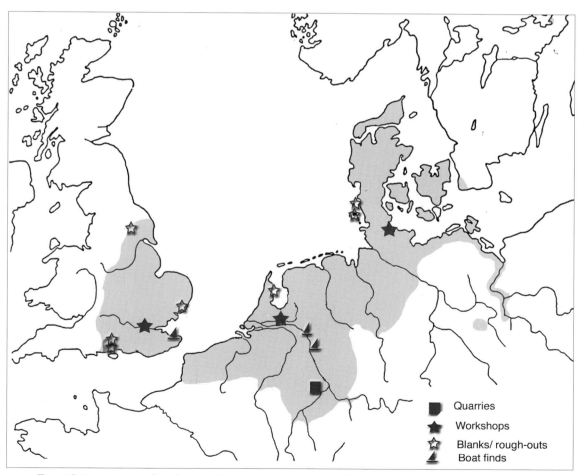

Fig. 4.3 Approximate distribution of lava querns from the Eifel in the seventh to eleventh centuries.

5

Hemming's Crosses

Michael Hare

I first met David at the Æthelred the Unready millenary conference in Oxford in 1978. Over the following 33 years I derived enormous benefit from his wide-ranging scholarship, as well as a great deal of pleasure and sheer fun from his friendship. This tribute is partly concerned with the topography of a town (Worcester), but principally with sculpture. Sculpture was not in the forefront of David's interests, but (together with Derek Seddon) he did publish a previously unknown Anglo-Saxon cross-shaft, and he also mapped much sculpture in his *Atlas* (Hill and Seddon 1998; Hill 1981, maps 250–8).

Introduction

My starting point is a narrative passage included in a charter entered in the late eleventh-century cartulary from Worcester Cathedral known as 'Hemming's Cartulary'. The passage describes the destruction of two standing crosses, one of which stood in the cathedral cemetery, the other outside the city. Although some scholars have made brief reference to this account, there is no detailed discussion of its implications for the study of early medieval sculpture; the passage also provides interesting information, which has not been fully evaluated, about Worcester in the late Anglo-Saxon and early Norman periods.

The charter in the name of Wiferd and Alta

Hemming named the saintly Bishop Wulfstan II (1062–95) as the source of inspiration behind the compilation of the cartulary which was written by Hemming and fellow-scribes among the monastic community at Worcester. It is unclear whether work actually began before Wulfstan's death on 20 January 1095, but most of the work would seem to have taken place in the years immediately following his death (Tinti 2002, 236). By this time there was a clear division of the estates of the church of Worcester between the bishop on the one hand and the monastic community on the other hand. We are concerned with a charter which purports to have been issued by one Wiferd and his wife Alta and which is found in part of the cartulary known to modern scholarship as 'Section K'. This section consists of thirteen spurious or interpolated charters relating to lands, all of which belonged to the monks in the late eleventh century (Hearne 1723, II, 319–46; Ker 1948, 59–60; Tinti 2002, 248–57). In the words of Francesca Tinti (2010, 145) 'in Section K the compilers focused on the production of documents which could prove the monks' right to the estates which they did effectively control when the cartulary was compiled'.

The charter in the name of Wiferd and his wife (S 1185) grants fifteen hides of land at Knighton-on-Teme, Newnham (in Knighton) and Eardiston (all Worcestershire) to the church of St Peter at Worcester, where the bodies of their ancestors (*parentes*) are said to lie.[1] The bounds show that the estate comprised a single block of lands on the north bank of the River Teme (Hooke 1990, 82–7).[2] The charter contains no dating clause or witness list, but a twelfth-century list of benefactions to Worcester (Dugdale 1817–30, I, 608) notes that the grant was made during the reign of King Offa (757–96) while Heathored (781–99) was bishop of Worcester; this would give dates of 781 × 96.[3]

However, it is easy to show that S 1185 is an eleventh-century forgery, compiled using elements taken from charters contained in *Liber Wigornensis*, the early-eleventh-century Worcester cartulary. The invocation and proem are borrowed from a charter of King Beorhtwulf of Mercia for Abbot Eanmund of Breedon dated 25 December 841 [for 840].[4] The dispositive section draws in part on Beorhtwulf's charter and in part on a charter dated 757 issued by Eanberht, *regulus* of the Hwicce, and his brothers, granting land at Tredington (Warwickshire); Eanberht's charter includes an identical phrase recording the burial of the donors' *parentes* in the church of St Peter.[5] The anathema is largely borrowed from one or other of two charters concerning Water Eaton (Oxfordshire) with almost identical anathemas; the first is in the name of King Burgred of Mercia dated 864, the second in the name of King Æthelstan dated 929.[6]

It is interesting to note that S 1185 is the only charter in Section K to record a grant as having been made to the church of St Peter; there are also no charters referring to St Peter in Section L, which is likewise concerned with lands held by the monks.[7] When a dedication is invoked in Sections K and L, it is normally St Mary, the patron of the monks' own church (Barrow 2005, 107, 112–13). It is unlikely that the forger of S 1185 was constrained to use Eanberht's charter as a model for the dispositive section, as he could easily have found many charters in the Worcester archive referring to gifts to St Mary's church. It is likely that S 1185 was produced at the same time as the narrative passage incorporated in it, and that the contents of this narrative passage influenced the choice of the patron invoked. I will return to this point later in this paper.

This narrative section, which follows the anathema, relates to events which occurred after the deaths of Wiferd and Alta. The text of the passage reads as follows:

Post finem autem uite illorum, lapidum structura, more antiquorum, super sepulchrum eorum, opere artificioso, cum cruce dominica, ob monumentum largitatis et monimentum animarum ipsorum, composita est. Juxta quem lapidem beatus pater Oswaldus, propter loci planiciem, sermonem facere ad populum sepius solebat, eo quod ecclesia sedis episcopalis in honore Sancti Petri, apostolorum principis, dedicata, admodum stricta multitudinem concurrentis populi capere nequibat, nec dum scilicet constructo honorabili monasterio beate Dei genetricis Marie, quod ipse beatus pater ad sedem episcopalem laudabiliter incepit, laudabiliusque consummavit. Perduravit igitur hec lapidum structura usque ad tempora Eadwardi regis quo regnante Alricus frater Berhteachi episcopi presbiterium supradicte beati Petri ecclesie ampliare studuit, ipsamque lapidum congeriem destructam operi immiscuit. Ab hoc quoque lapide miliarium mensurabatur ad lapidem, qui vocabatur candidus lapis, opere consimili extra civitatem ad aquilonem positi [sic], qui etiam tempore regis Willelmi majoris destructus, officio lavatorii monachorum necessarius operique admixtus est.

'After the end of their lives, as memorial of their munificence and monument to their souls, a structure of stone with a cross, in the manner of the ancients, was skilfully built above their grave. Beside this stone, the blessed father Oswald used to preach frequently to the people on account of the location's tract of level ground, since the church of the episcopal see dedicated in honour of St Peter, the prince of the apostles, being too small, could not contain the multitude of people assembling, that is to say while the monastic church of the blessed mother of God Mary was being honourably built, the church which that blessed father praiseworthily began and even more praiseworthily completed. This structure of stone [i.e. the grave-marker] lasted then until the time of King Edward, in whose reign Æthelric, Bishop Brihtheah's brother, applied himself to

enlarge the presbytery of the above-mentioned church of St Peter, and included in the work the destroyed pile of stones. One mile from this stone was also a stone, which was called "The White Stone", of very similar work, placed outside the city to the north, which, having likewise been destroyed in the time of King William the elder [i.e. William I], was deemed necessary for the provision of the monks' lavatorium and was thus incorporated in the work'.[8]

This narrative account is followed by a passage (perhaps deriving from a liturgical source) in the form of a prayer with several biblical quotations, praising the act of benefaction and seeking God's blessing on the community's benefactors; the document then concludes with a normal set of charter bounds.

It is uncertain whether the names of Wiferd and Alta given in the charter found in Hemming's cartulary were taken from a written source or whether they were in fact derived from names on an inscription on the cross which stood next to St Peter's. Wiferd and Alta are acceptable late-eleventh-century forms of Old English names. Wiferd represents an Old English name such as Wigfrith or Wilfrith or perhaps Wulfrith or Wulfheard,[9] while Alta probably represents the uncompounded Old English name Ealde (Redin 1919, 114). Just possibly Wiferd is to be identified with the Wulfferd who (according to a lost charter from the Worcester archive) received two hides at Seckley belonging to Wolverley (Worcestershire) from King Burgred in 866 in return for a lease of five hides for one life.[10] Wolverley (including Seckley) is in northern Worcestershire, some 13 miles (21km) to the north-east of Knighton-on-Teme, and it was one of the estates belonging to the monks of Worcester at the time of the Domesday survey in 1086 (Erskine 1986, fo. 174; Thorn and Thorn 1982, no. 2.83); it was presumably given to the Worcester community by Wulfferd or by one of his heirs. Hemming's cartulary includes a forged charter also dated 866 by which King Burgred gave Seckley directly 'to the brethren in the monastery of Worcester'.[11] At the time that Hemming's cartulary was being put together, the monks are thus likely to have had in front of them some documentation concerning Wulfferd of Seckley. However, while Wiferd and Wulfferd could be one and the same person, it should be stressed that this is no more than a possibility.

The narrative passage inserted in S 1185 is discursive and the last sentence concerning the 'white stone' is wholly irrelevant to Wiferd and Alta's donation. At first sight it might seem possible that (like much else in the charter) the narrative material was copied, in this case from an otherwise unknown source. However, such digressions are characteristic of the material preserved in Hemming's cartulary,[12] and it is likely that the narrative passage was composed as an integral part of S 1185. In any event the reference to King William the elder shows that the narrative passage cannot have been compiled in its present form before the Conqueror's death and the succession of William Rufus in 1087.

The Anglo-Saxon church of St Peter

In the late Anglo-Saxon period there were two major churches in the cathedral complex at Worcester. The ancient cathedral church, founded *c.* 680, was dedicated to St Peter. After the introduction of monks to the cathedral community in the 960s or 970s, a separate church of St Mary was established by Bishop Oswald for the monastic community; this church was completed by 983, but was probably in use by 977 (Tinti 2010, 25–33). A Worcester lease, probably to be dated to 991, indicates that the episcopal throne was still in St Peter's at that time,[13] though it must have been moved to St Mary's at some subsequent date.[14] The church of St Mary still stood until it was demolished during the construction of the new Norman cathedral by Bishop Wulfstan II, probably begun in 1084 (for the site of the new cathedral see Fig. 5.1); St Peter's was probably demolished at around the same time.[15] The exact location of both churches is unknown (Barker 1994, 9–17; Barker 2005, 167). In the narrative passage cited above, the church of St Peter is described as inadequate in size to hold the congregations attracted by St Oswald; although the church was the ancient cathedral, we can perhaps give some credence to the implication that it was not a large building for it probably survived until the 1080s and would thus have been known to the forger of S 1185.[16]

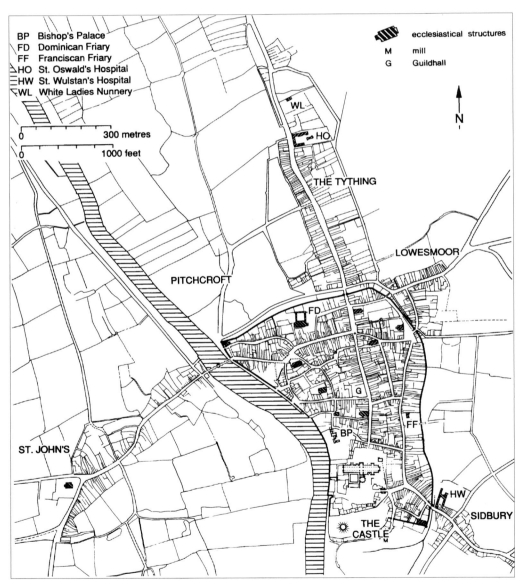

Fig. 5.1 Plan of Worcester, showing the principal features of the medieval city. The Cathedral is just north of the Castle, and Whiston Priory is indicated by the letters WL, referring to its alternative name of White Ladies. Reproduced (with permission) from Baker and Holt 2004, fig. 6.5.

The new presbytery referred to in the narrative passage under discussion has often been assigned to the 1030s, no doubt due to the reference to Bishop Brihtheah (1033–8; Dyer 1968–9; Baker and Holt 2004, 135). However, as Francesca Tinti (2010, 32 n. 94) has recently stressed, the passage in question assigns the construction to the reign of Edward the Confessor (1042–66). It is possible that Æthelric, who was probably a younger half-brother of Brihtheah, was undertaking a project begun or at least planned by Brihtheah.[17] The period between the death of Brihtheah on 20 December 1038 and the accession of Edward the Confessor in June 1042 was turbulent at Worcester. Bishop Lyfing was appointed in succession to Brihtheah by King Harold Harefoot, but on his accession in 1040, King Harthacnut suspected Lyfing of involvement in the murder of his half-brother, Alfred the Ætheling; Lyfing was deposed and the see was governed by Archbishop Ælfric Puttoc of York. Lyfing regained the see in the following year after he was reconciled with the king (Tinti 2010, 48–9). In 1041 there was a major upheaval, when two of the king's housecarls were slain 'within the town in the minster' on account of the severe geld which they were levying on behalf of the king; all Worcestershire was subsequently harried.[18] It seems unlikely that much progress could have been made with any project initiated or planned by Brihtheah in the period immediately following his death.

Brihtheah leased to Æthelric several estates forming part of the monks' manor of Hallow, and Æthelric was still alive in the period immediately after the Conquest, for it is known that Earl William fitzOsbern (who was appointed in 1067 and died in 1071) seized these lands from him during Æthelric's lifetime.[19] Æthelric and his family seem to have remained prominent under Bishops Lyfing (1038/9–1040, 1041–6) and Ealdred (1046–62). However, care must be exercised, for Æthelric is a common name and it is not certain that every reference in Worcester sources of this period is to the brother of Bishop Brihtheah, though no contemporary Worcester document lists more than one person of this name among the witnesses. Lyfing leased four estates to an Æthelric, in all of which he is described as Lyfing's faithful man (S 1392 (KCD 760); S 1394 (Robertson 1939, no. XCIV); S 1395 (KCD 765); S 1396 (KCD 764)); Ann Williams has shown that this Æthelric is one and the same as the Æthelric Kiu mentioned by Hemming, who in turn was probably Brihtheah's brother (Hearne 1723, I, 267–8; Williams 1996, 394–5). In addition an Æthelric witnessed four documents issued by Ealdred; in two of these he is described as 'the bishop's brother', and it is a moot point whether the reference is to Brihtheah's brother or to an otherwise unknown brother of Ealdred.[20] Æthelric's tenure of lands pertaining both to the bishop and the monks in 1066 (and in some cases into the reign of William I) is confirmed by Domesday Book (Erskine 1986, fos. 172v, 173, 173v, 180v; Thorn and Thorn 1982, nos. 2.4, 5, 7, 36, 58, 69, 70; Thorn and Thorn 1983, no. 1.45).

Æthelric's rebuilding of the presbytery of St Peter might thus have taken place at any time during the reign of Edward the Confessor. He may have been acting in an administrative capacity on behalf of Lyfing and/or Ealdred in the rebuilding, for both were pluralists with interests elsewhere, and both were active in the political affairs of the day; both of them are likely to have been absent from Worcester for long periods. However, the credit assigned to Æthelric for the rebuilding in the passage cited above suggests that he is also likely to have been a patron of the work, perhaps using resources generated from the substantial number of lands leased to him.

The estates which Æthelric held from the bishop and community might have provided building stone for the new presbytery. For instance in 1066 Æthelric held an episcopal estate at Holt (Worcestershire), which could have provided the red sandstone (the Bromsgrove Sandstone Formation of the Sherwood Sandstone Group) which was so extensively used in the later medieval cathedral.[21] This stone has not been identified in any standing building of Anglo-Saxon date in the region, but was used in Anglo-Saxon sculpture, for instance in northern Worcestershire at Belbroughton and Stoke Prior; there are also examples in Shropshire and Warwickshire (Bryant 2012, 36–8, 353, 364–5). In addition Æthelric held Elmley Castle (Worcestershire), a member of the monks' manor of Cropthorne.[22] This estate could have provided oolitic limestone from Bredon Hill. Bredon Hill does not seem to have been quarried extensively for use as building stone at Worcester, though in the late fourteenth-century gargoyles and crockets were supplied from Comberton (Worcestershire), immediately adjacent to Elmley Castle (Engel 2007, 28). Limited exploitation of limestone from Bredon Hill is possible at this early date.

Sadly there is no information which might indicate whether Æthelric's new presbytery was built in a traditional Anglo-Saxon style or whether it was a structure in the new Romanesque style; Edward the Confessor's contemporary rebuilding of Westminster Abbey, dedicated in December 1065, was a structure built in the Romanesque style showing a wide range of continental influences (Gem 1980). A possible hint that there was work of Romanesque character at Worcester in the reign of Edward the Confessor is provided by the fact that many of the columns and cushion capitals in the crypt of the Norman cathedral show signs of reuse from an earlier structure.[23] The cushion capital was first used in the German Empire in the early eleventh century. Its introduction to Worcester might, as I have suggested elsewhere (Hare 1997, 59), be due to the influence of Bishop Ealdred (1046–62), who spent nearly a year in Cologne in 1054–5 on a diplomatic mission. The cushion capitals in the crypt could thus derive from Æthelric's rebuilding of the presbytery of St Peter's, which might itself have had a crypt.

The purpose of Æthelric's rebuilding is also hard to gauge. The difficulty is compounded by the fact that we do not know whether there were still secular clergy at Worcester to perform the liturgical observances in St Peter's in the middle of the eleventh century; Julia Barrow (1996, 98) has remarked that the final disappearance of secular clerks from the cathedral community could have taken place as early as the beginning of the eleventh century, but might have been as late as the episcopate of Wulfstan II (1062–95). One possibility might be that the rebuilding of the presbytery was necessary to provide increased space as the monastic community had at some prior date taken over responsibility for the liturgy in St Peter's. However, other explanations are also possible. The previous presbytery is likely to have been of some antiquity and may have been dilapidated by this date. Very little is known about the burial-places of the bishops of Worcester, though the saintly Oswald (d. 992) was buried in St Mary's, as were two of his successors, Bishops Ealdwulf (995–1002) and Leofsige (1016–23; Darlington and McGurk 1995, 440, 452, 518). However, bishops before Oswald had presumably been buried in St Peter's, and a desire for an enlarged space for episcopal burial (and perhaps also for episcopal relatives) could have been one factor in Æthelric's rebuilding; Brihtheah is the only eleventh-century bishop of Worcester whose burial-place is unrecorded.[24] Another possibility is that Æthelric's rebuilding reflected the liturgical interests of Bishop Ealdred. A twelfth-century account of Ealdred written at York, where he became archbishop (1061–9), relates that during his year in Germany Ealdred learned 'many things which pertain to the character of religious observance, and many things which pertain to the authority of ecclesiastical discipline, he heard, saw and committed to memory, things which afterwards he caused to be adopted in the English churches' (Raine 1879–94, II, 345; Lapidge 1983; Hare 1997). It is interesting to note that Ealdred's works at Beverley Minster in the 1060s included a new presbytery (Raine 1879–94, II, 353–4).

Finally it should be noted while the principal altar of the new Norman cathedral built by Wulfstan II was dedicated to St Mary, the central altar in the crypt was probably dedicated to St Peter (Crook 2005, 198). The crypt may thus have taken over some of the functions of the previously separate church of St Peter; unfortunately little is known of the role played by the crypt in the liturgical life of the new cathedral church (Engel 2007, 190).

The monks' lavatorium

The reference to the monks' *lavatorium* in the passage quoted above has received little attention, but shows that work was in progress during the reign of William I (1066–87) on the claustral buildings, presumably associated with Bishop Wulfstan II's rebuilding in Norman style. The *lavatorium*, used for the washing of hands before meals, was usually sited close to the entrance to the refectory. The reference to a new *lavatorium* does not necessarily imply that work was being undertaken at the same time on a new refectory, but the possibility that the construction of a new refectory was undertaken at an early stage of the Norman rebuilding deserves consideration. College Hall, the successor of the medieval refectory, has a complex structural history. The refectory

itself was rebuilt in the fourteenth century, but work of early Norman date survives in the refectory undercroft; it is usually considered to have originated *c*. 1100 (Barker 1994, 45–6; Guy 2011). The eleventh-century *lavatorium* is likely to have been a freestanding structure in the cloister garth, whereas the present fifteenth-century *lavatorium* is located at the south end of the west walk of the cloister (for a photograph, see Barker 1994, fig. 39); it is constructed of red- and green-coloured sandstones, and there is no indication that it contains any early material from the 'white stone' mentioned in Hemming's cartulary.

Wulfstan's rebuilding of the cathedral is usually considered to have begun in 1084, based on an entry in the early fourteenth-century *Annales prioratus de Wigornia*.[25] It is thus possible that the work on the monks' *lavatorium* took place between 1084 and 1087 (the year of William I's death). However the construction of a new *lavatorium* seems unlikely to have been a high priority when the cathedral itself was being rebuilt, and another possibility also deserves consideration. It has long been considered a puzzle that the refectory and south walk of the cloister are on a different alignment from the Norman cathedral.[26] One may therefore wonder whether the refectory and monks' *lavatorium* were in fact begun before the construction of the cathedral itself. If so, then the rebuilding of the cathedral complex may have started rather earlier in Wulfstan's pontificate (1062–95) than is usually considered, perhaps in the 1070s. Just possibly the large increase in the size of the community during Wulfstan's lifetime (from twelve to fifty according to his Alveston charter of 1089)[27] meant that the most immediate requirement was the provision of a new refectory. The orientation of the cathedral itself is close to true east; by the time it was begun in 1084, the preference for correct orientation, which is a marked feature of many of the greater churches rebuilt in the Norman period, may have become the dominant factor (Rodwell 2001, I, 129).

The Anglo-Saxon crosses

The Anglo-Saxon cross-shaft demolished to make way for the enlargement of the presbytery of St Peter's church is stated to have been erected as a grave-marker, and there seems no reason to doubt the accuracy of this remark. The cross was not demolished until the reign of Edward the Confessor (1042–66), and it seems likely that there were members of the monastic community who might have remembered this cross long after its demolition. First and foremost among these would have been St Wulfstan himself, who had been professed as a monk of the community by Bishop Brihtheah (1033–8) and who became bishop of Worcester in 1062; Wulfstan died in January 1095 (Brooks 2005, 1–4). Whether Bishop Oswald actually preached beside the cross during the construction of the new church of St Mary is perhaps less certain. St Mary's was completed by 983, but Oswald's preaching beside the cross is not otherwise recorded until Hemming's cartulary was composed in the 1090s. It is possible that this was a legend that had grown up in the interim period; we can, however, safely say that the composer of this passage did not think it incongruous to describe St Oswald preaching in this manner.

It is more difficult to judge what purpose the cross known as the 'white stone' erected a mile to the north of the cathedral might have served. This cross is likely to have been on or close to the site of Whiston priory (also known as Whiteladies), a nunnery founded in the middle of the thirteenth century; the land on which the priory was established was a manor of the bishop of Worcester (Willis-Bund and Page 1906, 154–6; Goodrich 1994; Goodrich 2008). Whiston priory, which stood a little to the north of St Oswald's Hospital, is almost exactly one mile to the north of the cathedral (Fig. 5.1), and its name derives from the 'white stone'.[28]

The northern suburb of medieval Worcester is in the form of a long linear settlement, the southern half of which is called Foregate Street, while the northern part is called The Tything. Foregate Street lay within the city boundaries and formed part of the parish of St Nicholas. The Tything by contrast was outside the city boundary; it was part of the rural manor of Claines and took its name from the fact that it lay in the tithing of Whistones in the parish of Claines.[29] Baker and Holt (2004, 188–91, 338–9, 363) argue that the northern suburb of Worcester originated as a single design under the auspices of the bishops of Worcester and they suggest that this probably took place at a date between the tenth century and the early twelfth century. They know the reference to the 'White Stane' cross only from the eighteenth-century antiquary Valentine Green rather than from Hemming, but tentatively suggest that it may once have marked the northern limit of the bishops' suburb (Baker and Holt 2004, 191; Green 1796, I, 241–2). If the cross did mark the limit of the suburb, the date at which the suburb was laid out would need to be pushed back well before the Conquest, as the cross is unlikely to have been new at the time of its destruction between 1066 and 1087.

Alternatively the presence of a cross might indicate that there was an earlier focus of some sort in the vicinity of Whiston priory predating the establishment of the suburb. There was a church of uncertain function at Whiston by the middle of the twelfth century, when it was confirmed as a possession of the cathedral priory.[30] It is possible that this church stood close to the site formerly occupied by the cross. Unfortunately it is not clear whether this church was the precursor of one of the two later places of worship in the tithing of Whistones, the nunnery church on the one hand and the chapel of St Oswald's Hospital on the other hand; the latter was the customary place of worship of the inhabitants of the tithing until the sixteenth century (Baker and Holt 2004, 338). There are hints that in the middle of the eleventh century, the cathedral community at Worcester provided accommodation for religious women. Most notably the mother of St Wulfstan is said to have taken the nun's veil at Worcester; another of the religious women associated with Worcester was Eadgyth *monialis*, perhaps a daughter of Æthelric, brother of Bishop Brihtheah (Halpin

1994, 104; Foot 2000, II, 257–9; Williams 1996, 397 n. 94). There is no evidence as to where such women lived in the eleventh century, but it is possible that religious women had been housed at Whiston long before the formal establishment of a priory there in the thirteenth century.[31]

The name of the 'white stone' erected to the north of the town seems to provide a clear indication that this cross is likely to have been made of oolitic limestone; no other stone found locally would meet this description (Oliver 2007; Bristow and Freshney 2012). The use of oolitic limestone is no great surprise, for the known Anglo-Saxon sculpture from southern and central Worcestershire is almost entirely of oolitic limestone, including the limited amount of carved Anglo-Saxon stonework known from Worcester Cathedral; two small carved fragments found in excavation are both oolite, as are 23 of the 24 reused columns and bases in the eastern slype.[32] Much Anglo-Saxon sculpture is known to have been painted, but the name 'white stone' suggests either that this cross was never painted or that it had long lost any painted decoration which it might once have had (in which case it must have been of considerable antiquity). It is likely that the cross erected to commemorate Wiferd and Alta was also made of oolitic limestone, but in this case there is no evidence.

The reuse of the crosses

The account in S 1185 of the employment of the two crosses as building stone is (by some margin) the earliest written source to attest to the reuse of Anglo-Saxon sculpture in this way. However, a substantial percentage of the known body of Anglo-Saxon sculpture has been discovered reused as building material in churches and other buildings, as reference to any of the published volumes of the *Corpus of Anglo-Saxon Stone Sculpture* will demonstrate.[33] Much of this sculpture came to light during nineteenth-century restorations, and the context is rarely documented as fully as one would wish. In some cases Anglo-Saxon sculpture can still be seen reused in structures of later Anglo-Saxon date, for instance the cross-heads of pre-Viking date built into the towers of Hovingham and Middleton (both Yorkshire) or the late eighth-century cross-shaft built into a doorway in the eleventh-century building of St Peter's, Bedford (Bedfordshire) (Lang 1991, 146, 187, ills. 484, 694; Tweddle *et al.* 1995, 206–7, ills. 265–7; Taylor and Taylor 1965, I, 58–60, 326–8, 418–24). Within the medieval diocese of Worcester, a considerable quantity of sculpture has been recovered from the fabric of the church of St Oswald's, Gloucester, under modern standards of observation by Carolyn Heighway and Richard Bryant. The material discovered included two ninth-century cross-shafts from two different crosses built into the Period I structure, to be identified with the church erected c. 900 by Ealdorman Æthelred and his wife Æthelflæd; other carved stone from the site included early tenth-century grave-covers of very high quality built into the foundations of walls of later Anglo-Saxon date (Bryant 1999, nos. 32, 34, 37, 38, 40).

In an important study, David Stocker and Paul Everson (1990) have drawn attention to the different ways in which carved stone might be reused; they argue 'that almost all cases of re-use can be discussed under one of three general headings: casual, functional and iconic'. The first category, casual reuse, is certainly the commonest and is used to describe those cases where no account is taken of the original use of stone when used in a new context, for instance if a carved stone is used as walling material. Functional reuse consists of the reuse of a feature for the purpose for which it was originally cut, for instance a carved doorway reused as such in a later structure, while iconic reuse occurs when a stone is treated with especial respect and used in a context designed to impart some meaning, for instance to draw attention to the ancient inheritance of the site.

Examples of all these types of reuse may be found in the diocese of Worcester, for which coverage is provided by the recently published Western Midlands volume of the *Corpus of Anglo-Saxon Stone Sculpture* (Bryant 2012). Much of the material of known provenance falls within the category of casual reuse. Functional reuse is exemplified by the Anglo-Saxon capitals and bases reused in the eastern slype of Worcester cathedral during the Norman rebuilding (Bryant 2012, 369–71, ills. 677–701). Striking examples of iconic reuse are provided by a large tenth-century panel of Christ set in the south wall of the Norman tower at Beverston (Gloucestershire) (Fig. 5.2) and by an eleventh-century panel depicting Christ in Majesty over a Harrowing of Hell scene reused above the twelfth-century south doorway at South Cerney (Gloucestershire) (Bryant 2012, 133–4, 247–9, ills. 25–6, 437–40).

A further important study has recently been published by Deirdre O'Sullivan (2011) in which she examines the destruction of Anglo-Saxon sculpture in the north-east in the post-Conquest period, looking, for example, at the incorporation of four Anglo-Saxon cross-heads together with a fine grave-cover in the foundations of the Norman Chapter House at Durham Cathedral. She examines the case for a deliberate strategy of Normanisation in which monuments erected by Anglo-Saxon patrons were demolished and their visible tombstones defaced. She concludes that 'A global assertion that all destruction was inspired by overt political moves is not sustainable across the region, but some political context in Durham and York is hard to ignore' (O'Sullivan 2011, 187). She also offers alternative and less dramatic interpretations and comments that 'The argument that much destruction was purely functional, dull though it sounds, does carry force in the context of the monastic and episcopal sites that had to be rebuilt according to a predetermined, claustral ground plan' and she adds that at a more local level destruction probably resulted from the systematic rebuilding of local churches in the eleventh and twelfth centuries (O'Sullivan 2011, 186). Finally she touches on the possibility that the incorporation of crosses and other sculpture into new buildings may be what prehistorians have

termed 'structured deposition'; she suggests that the burial of carved stone in the foundations of new buildings may have been 'a tangible and material appropriation of both symbol and substance' (O'Sullivan 2011, 186).

If we look again at our text in the light of these ideas, we can very clearly set aside any concept of Normanisation in the case of Worcester. One of our crosses was pulled down before the Norman Conquest, while the other was destroyed after the Conquest, but at a time when Worcester was still ruled by an English bishop who governed a community still largely English-speaking and English-writing into the 1090s. At Worcester the reuse of crosses at this period should in my view be seen purely as part of a continuous tradition of reuse that was probably almost as old as the creation of Anglo-Saxon sculpture and indeed drew in turn on Roman traditions. We do not at present know whether the destruction of Anglo-Saxon stone sculpture at Worcester in the early post-Conquest period was on the same scale as at Durham and York, but given the scale of rebuilding, it may well have been.

The reuse of the 'white stone' in the monks' *lavatorium* is probably a case of casual reuse; this does not exclude the possibility that some of the carved faces of the cross could have been used decoratively in the new *lavatorium*.[34] It is impossible to know what was in the minds of those who planned and executed the removal of the 'white stone', but the text describing its reuse emphasises the purely practical aspect and gives no hint of structured deposition.

The case of the cross in the cathedral cemetery is more difficult. It may have been reused casually as mere building stone. However, the very fact that this cross was remembered some 40 or 50 years after its destruction perhaps suggests that part of it may have been meaningfully displayed in the new presbytery built by Æthelric in a fashion similar to the Christ in the south wall of the Norman tower at Beverston. Such iconic reuse would not be surprising for a cross believed to commemorate one of the community's early patrons and also thought to be associated with Bishop Oswald, the most important saint culted at Worcester in the late Anglo-Saxon period (Thacker 1996, 262–4; Crook 2005, 196–201). Display of this sort might have included the cross's inscription; if this inscription still survived when S 1185 was produced (or had at least survived until the demolition of St Peter's, perhaps in the 1080s shortly before the production of Hemming's cartulary), that might explain why the forger was constrained to invoke a gift to St Peter's rather than to St Mary's.

It is also worthy of note that the 'white stone' was moved a mile to the cathedral before its reuse.[35] Students of sculpture have long recognised that some stone sculptures may have been moved to central church locations in modern times (Blair 2005, 227 n. 195), and the text under consideration serves as a reminder that sculpture found at a particular site may not initially have been used there.

Fig. 5.2 Photograph of the south wall of the Norman tower at Beverston (Gloucestershire), showing the position of the reused figure of Christ between two small windows (Photograph: Michael Hare). Inset: detail of the figure of Christ (Photograph: Richard Bryant).

The decline of the custom of erecting standing crosses

The statement in S 1185 that the cross erected to commemorate Wiferd and Alta was built *more antiquorum*, 'in the manner of the ancients', is of considerable interest. It implies that the cartularist considered standing crosses to be old-fashioned in the 1090s, at least as regards crosses erected to commemorate graves and probably crosses erected for other reasons as well. There is no detailed study of the decline of the tradition of erecting carved standing crosses in England in the central Middle Ages,[36] and a full study would be outside the scope of this paper. It is certainly fair to say that elaborately carved stone crosses were still being produced in some numbers in the first quarter of the eleventh century, and that far fewer were being made by the last quarter of the century; by the end of the century sculptural decoration was being concentrated largely on architectural forms such as capitals and tympana (Zarnecki *et al.* 1984, 146–8).

A detailed study of the decline of the carved standing cross would probably throw up regional variations. In Lincolnshire large standing crosses in traditional Anglo-Saxon style were still being produced well into the eleventh century, as at Harmston and Stoke Rochford (Everson and Stocker 1999, 176–7, 253–4; ills. 195–200; 346–9, 355). Paul Everson and David Stocker have also noted as many as eight decorated cross-shafts from the Romanesque period in Lincolnshire, which 'continue the Anglo-Scandinavian tradition well into the twelfth century'; they note that 'the monuments reveal not only continuity but also some attempt at revival following a gap in time' (Everson and Stocker 1999, 89–91, 319–29; ills. 434–71). There are also groups of carved crosses of twelfth-century date in the east Midlands (Everson and Stocker 1991, 89–90) and in the Rotherham area of south Yorkshire (Baldwin Brown 1937, 142–7; Ryder 1982, 103, 116–17, 120–1, 125). Further afield there is, at least on present knowledge, less evidence for the production of carved crosses in any number. For instance Jim Lang (1991, 43) commented that in York and Ryedale, there are 'firm indications that the custom of creating stone monuments almost disappeared in the decades leading to the Norman Conquest'. The magnificent cross with elaborately carved decoration of mid-twelfth-century date from Kelloe (Co. Durham) stands in isolation in the area, and would seem to represent a revival in Romanesque form of the tradition of the carved standing cross (Lang 1977; Zarnecki *et al.* 1984, 66, 208–9).

The evidence from the recently published Western Midlands volume of the *Corpus of Anglo-Saxon Stone Sculpture* bears out this pattern. The volume lists thirty-nine fragments of crosses in the five counties of Gloucestershire, Herefordshire, Shropshire, Warwickshire and Worcestershire, of which twenty-four are considered to be of pre-900 date, with only fifteen assigned to the tenth and eleventh centuries.[37] Moreover the late crosses seem on the whole to have been much less ambitious pieces than those pre-900 date; two tenth-century cross-shafts, one from Diddlebury (Shropshire), the other from Billesley (Warwickshire), are the only pieces of which the workmanship bears comparison with the quality displayed in the crosses of eighth- and ninth-century date (Bryant 2012, 307, 335–6, ills. 543–4, 582–4). The tradition of standing crosses did not die out entirely in the area, but the only example of Romanesque date known to me from the western Midlands is a fine cross-head (Fig. 5.3) of the middle of the twelfth century from Mitton (Gloucestershire, formerly Worcestershire), now in Tewkesbury Town Museum (Bryant 2012, 270). In the Anglo-Saxon period, Mitton was part of the episcopal manor of Bredon; it was recovered by Bishop Ealdred (1046–62) and assigned by him to the support of the monks of Worcester (Tinti 2010, 176–83). It is, however, unlikely that Hemming's successors in the Worcester community were the patrons of the Mitton cross; it seems more probable that this cross was erected by one of their lay tenants (Page and Willis-Bund 1913, 286–7). The erection of a cross at Mitton is perhaps to be linked to the fact that there was a chapel there dedicated to the Holy Cross.[38] The cross at Kelloe (Co. Durham) mentioned above was linked by its iconography to St Helena (the patron saint of the church) and to the Invention of the True Cross by her (Lang 1977, 108–14). Such isolated examples of elaborate standing crosses in the twelfth century may therefore in some cases reflect a special focus on the cult of the cross.

Fig. 5.3 Photograph of the 12th-century cross-head from Mitton (Photograph: Richard Bryant).

Conclusion

A close reading of S 1185 suggests that the forger knew that he was on shaky ground and felt it necessary to throw dust in the reader's eyes. He would seem to have been constrained (perhaps by a surviving inscription) to use a model in which the donation was made to the church of St Peter rather than the church of St Mary, but for the proem he selected as a model the charter with the most elaborate Latin in the entire Worcester archive. The intention may have been to discourage the reader from paying close attention to the detail; the long prayer which follows the narrative passage may have served the same function.

The narrative passage incorporated in S 1185 has much to offer the historian, and it is perhaps surprising that it has not attracted more attention in the past.[39] Sources that provide information about contemporary attitudes to stone sculpture are few and far between, and the information about the treatment of standing crosses in the eleventh century is especially valuable, complementing the evidence provided by archaeology and by art history.

Worcester in the time of Bishop Wulfstan II (1062–95) has often been perceived as a surviving stronghold of Anglo-Saxon culture, though as Francesca Tinti (2010, 318) has observed, Worcester's championing of its own past at this time was a means of adaptation to new and insecure times. At Worcester, as elsewhere, Anglo-Saxon crosses were demolished and used as building stone in new structures in the late Anglo-Saxon and early Norman periods. In his aside to the effect that standing crosses were old-fashioned, the forger of S 1185 was expressing a view that is likely to have been current throughout much of England in the late eleventh century.[40]

Notes

1 S 1185 (BCS 1007). Anglo-Saxon charters are cited by their number in Sawyer 1968, abbreviated as S. Whenever possible, charter texts are cited from Birch 1885–99, abbreviated as BCS, or from Kemble 1839–48, abbreviated as KCD. A revised edition of Sawyer's catalogue is accessible on the website http://www.esawyer.org.uk

2 A separate set of bounds of the same estate (named as Pensax and not attached to a charter text) was added in the twelfth century to *Liber Wigorniensis* (Worcester's early eleventh-century cartulary): S 1595 (Hearne 1723, I, 246), discussed by Hooke 1990, 392–7.

3 In Page and Willis-Bund 1913, 444, Frank Stenton is quoted as considering it likely that Wiferd and Alta lived in the tenth century, but no reason is given for this date.

4 S 193 (BCS 434). This charter is especially notable for its literary qualities and has recently been printed and discussed by Kelly 2009, 365–8; Kelly argues that, although S 193 comes from the Worcester archive, it is likely that the original text concerned Breedon-on-the-Hill (Leicestershire) rather than Bredon (Worcestershire).

Julia Barrow (2005, 108–11) considers that the elaborate Latin in S 193 is an interpolation, probably to be dated shortly after 1002.

5 S 55 (BCS 183). S 55 is itself in all likelihood a later forgery: see Scharer 1982, 213–14.

6 S 210 (BCS 509) and S 402 (BCS 666). The charter in the name of Æthelstan is forged: Barrow 2005, 108, 112; Tinti 2010, 105–6.

7 For discussion of the purposes of the three different sections of Hemming's cartulary with charter materials, see Tinti 2002, 248–57; Tinti 2010, 144–7. In Section J, which seems to have been produced with the intention of preserving documents which might prove the monks' rights to lands which had been lost, several documents retain references to donations to St Peter.

8 Translation partly from Tinti 2010, 32 notes 92, 94 and 314 n. 360, partly by the present author. I am grateful to Francesca Tinti for explaining to me exactly how the last sentence should be construed.

9 For all these names, see the Prosopography of Anglo-Saxon England (PASE) database at http://www.pase.ac.uk, accessed 12 August 2011.

10 S 212 (BCS 513). This charter is known only from an eighteenth-century edition of a (now lost) original from the Worcester archive; it is usually considered authentic (see for instance Finberg 1972b, no. 261). In all likelihood the name of Wolverley (recorded as *Wulfferdinleh* in S 212) takes its names from Wulfferd (as suggested by Hooke 1990, 124).

11 S 211 (BCS 514). For comment on this forged charter, see Finberg 1972b, no. 262; Barrow 2005, 115 n. 45.

12 I am grateful to Francesca Tinti for advice on this point.

13 S 1308 (BCS 1166). This document is preserved in *Liber Wigorniensis*; it bears the date 965, but this is clearly in error, and the date must be *c*. 991: see Finberg 1972b, no. 138; Tinti 2010, 32–3.

14 Barrow 2005, 113, suggests that the throne is likely to have been moved to St Mary's in the early eleventh century.

15 The demolition of the church built by Oswald (*i.e.* St Mary's) is mentioned by William of Malmesbury in his *Vita Wulfstani*: Winterbottom and Thomson 2002, 122.

16 There is no evidence for alterations to the building other than the rebuilding of the presbytery, though it is certainly possible that other work took place on St Peter's between the 970s and the 1080s.

17 For discussion of Brihteah's kinship, see Williams 1996, 394–8, with a genealogical table at 403.

18 *Anglo-Saxon Chronicle* 1041 D: Cubbin 1996, 66 (text); Whitelock *et al.* 1961, 106 (translation). John of Worcester adds further information, stating that the two housecarls had taken refuge in the upper room of a tower and that both the city and the countryside were subsequently laid waste, the city expressly noted as having been burnt: Darlington and McGurk 1995, 532.

19 This information comes from the *Codicellus possessionum* which forms part of Hemming's cartulary: Hearne 1723, I, 266; Williams 1996, 394–7; Tinti 2010, 218–20.

20 The references to Æthelric as 'the bishop's brother' occur in S 1406 (KCD 923) and S 1409 (KCD 804); he also witnesses S 1405 (Earle 1888, 247–8) and S 1407, which has not yet been edited, but may be consulted in facsimile in Bond 1873–8, IV, 32.

21 For Holt, see Erskine 1986, fo. 172v; Thorn and Thorn 1982, no. 2.7. On the building stones used at Worcester, see Engel 2007, 27–8.

22 S 1396 (KCD 764); Hearne 1723, I, 267–8; for discussion, see Williams 1996, 394–5.

23 As argued by Barker 1994, 32 and by Guy 1994, 24–6. An alternative possibility is that these columns and capitals were carved at the quarry and damaged while in transit; I am grateful to Dr Richard Gem for this suggestion.

24 Among eleventh-century bishops, Wulfstan I, Lyfing, Ælfric Puttoc and Ealdred were not buried at Worcester.

25 Luard 1864–9, IV, 373. Paul Hayward has recently shown that the Worcester material in these annals derives largely or wholly from a lost breviate chronicle composed by John of Worcester in the 1120s; the similar entry in the C-text of the *Annales Cambriae* under 1083 confirms that the origin of the 1084 annal is to be sought in Hayward's 'common root': see Hayward 2010, I, 63–98, 169–76; II, 706, 711.

26 Barker 1994, 46. Excavation south of the Chapter House in 1999 revealed a wall on the same line as the north wall of the refectory. This wall is interpreted as a terrace or retaining wall, which perhaps divided the lay and monastic cemeteries in the pre-Conquest period; this wall is likely to be relevant to the alignment of the refectory: see Guy 2011, 4. The alignment of the refectory might also have been affected by the ditch of the new Norman castle built to the south in 1069 (I owe this point to Chris Guy).

27 Darlington 1968, no. 3. It is possible that the Alveston charter is a very early forgery, prepared soon after Wulfstan's death, but the information in respect of the size of the community is likely to be trustworthy: see Cheney *et al.* 2007, no. 8; Tinti 2010, 48.

28 Mawer and Stenton 1927, 115. The form of the name given by Leland in the sixteenth century is still *Whitestan*: Toulmin Smith 1906–10, II, 91.

29 For a map showing the boundaries of Claines parish (including its tithing in the northern suburbs of Worcester), see Baker and Holt 2004, fig. 7.2 (p. 212). On Claines, see also Bassett 1989, 232, 238, fig. 2. Claines appears in Domesday Book (under the name of Northwick) as a manor of the bishop of Worcester: Erskine 1986, fo. 173v; Thorn and Thorn 1982, no. 2.48.

30 Darlington 1968, nos. 73, 77. The earlier document is a charter dated 1149 issued by Bishop Simon of Worcester, while the latter is a confirmation of privileges by Pope Alexander III dated 1159 × 63. Bishop Simon's charter is probably a forgery of the late 1150s: see Cheney *et al.* 2007, no. 108.

31 Goodrich 1994, 131, also suggests possible continuity between the religious women of the eleventh and thirteenth centuries, though she does not touch on the possibility that they were resident at Whiston from the outset.

32 Bryant 2012, 367–71. The one base of sandstone (no. 3s) is probably Roman in origin.

33 Ten volumes have been published to date (November 2012).

34 For casual reuse to decorative effect, see Stocker with Everson 1990, 90.

35 I have assumed that the 'white stone' was used in the *lavatorium* itself, but Hemming's account does not exclude the possibility that it was used in a channel leading to the *lavatorium* or in some other structure concerned with the provision of water for it.

36 An initial attempt to discuss this and related issues was made by Baldwin Brown (1937, 138–49); however, there is much scope for a reassessment of this topic.

37 Bryant 2012. I am grateful to Richard Bryant for the figures (which take into account the inclusion in the volume at a very late stage of a cross from Lawrence Weston (Gloucestershire)).

38 The chapel is first mentioned in 1287 and its dedication is recorded in 1427: Page and Willis-Bund 1913, 291.

39 The fact that this passage has not received attention from historians of sculpture is largely accounted for by the fact that it is not included in the compendium of sources compiled by Lehmann-Brockhaus 1955–60. The fullest discussion of the written sources for early medieval sculpture in England is by Dodwell 1982, 109–28, who also does not discuss this passage.

40 I am extremely grateful to Richard Bryant and Francesca Tinti, who both read and made a number of useful comments on an early version of this paper. Various scholars discussed specific questions with me: Derek Craig shared his knowledge of twelfth-century crosses, Chris Guy provided information about the refectory undercroft at Worcester, Ann Williams sent me a long email about the prosopographical problems surrounding Æthelric, while Alex Rumble drew my attention to Mats Redin's discussion of the personal name Alta.

6

Control of London in the Seventh Century

Damian Tyler

I first met David Hill in the summer of 1998 in his room in the then Arts Building of the University of Manchester (currently the Samuel Alexander Building). I was about to start my PhD and David had very kindly agreed to act as a member of my supervisory panel. Over the course of the next three years we had numerous conversations which were, for me, always interesting and informative and, David being the man he was, generally also highly amusing and entertaining. My research was on pre-Viking Mercian kingship and so, of course, we mainly discussed Offa's and Wat's Dykes. We also, however, talked about mid-Saxon London, particularly the city's political status in the seventh century.

Introduction

Until the 1980s mid-Saxon London presented scholars with something of a paradox. Literary evidence portrayed the city as an important trade centre in the seventh and eighth centuries, but this picture was not supported by the archaeological record, which revealed no signs of any dense occupation or significant trading activity within the walled area before the early tenth century (Vince 1983, 33–7; Dyson and Schofield 1984, 292–3). The breakthrough in understanding came in 1984, when Alan Vince and Martin Biddle independently came to the same conclusion: that we had been looking for 'London' in the wrong place. Up to that time it had been assumed that the trading activities referred to in the documents took place within the Roman walls, *i.e.* the area known today as the City of London. Vince and Biddle suggested that in fact the emporium of London was located to the west of the walled city, on the north bank of the Thames, in the Strand area, between the valley of the Fleet river and what now comprises Trafalgar Square (Biddle 1984; Vince 1984). They argued that far more mid-Saxon material had been found in the Strand area than in the City (Biddle 1984, 25; Vince 1984, 310), that some of the churches there may have mid-Saxon origins (Vince 1984, 310–11) and that a number of place-names also support the hypothesis that the emporium was located west of the city

(Biddle 1984, 25–6, citing Birch 1885, no. 1048, Sawyer 1968, no. 670). What was in 1984 an inspired hypothesis has since been confirmed by extensive archaeological excavation which has demonstrated the existence of a thriving extramural riverine trading settlement in the area of the Strand. Since 1984 a model has emerged that sees mid-Saxon London as a binary system. The walled city, which is generally referred to as *Lundonburh*, was a sparsely-populated, high-status ecclesiastical and administrative centre, consisting of the cathedral complex of St Paul's and a royal hall or halls. Most of the area inside the walls was unoccupied and, though it occupied the site of Roman Londinium, *Lundonburh* was not, in our terms, an urban site. To the west of the walled area was the busy, populous trading centre which we term *Lundonwic*, and it was here that the economic activity of mid-Saxon London took place (Vince 1988; Cowie 1987; Tatton-Brown 1986, 21–8; Cowie and Whytehead 1989; Cowie 2001; Tyler 2002, 146–55).

Our understanding of the economic functioning of mid-Saxon London has thus been transformed over the last three decades. The city's political affiliation has received rather less attention from scholars, and is less well understood. The changing political status of London during the seventh century is, from the point of view of the modern scholar, extremely confusing, and may have seemed hardly less so to contemporaries. The general trend is easy enough to perceive – London moved from East Saxon to Mercian control (Cowie 2001, 195) – but this ignores much complicated detail. Mid-Saxon England was a politically fragmented land made up of a number of kingdoms, and during the latter part of the seventh century kings of several different peoples appear to have had interests and influence in London. This can partly be explained geographically. The city was located near the intersections of the kingdoms of the East Saxons, the West Saxons, the Mercians and Kent, and might be expected to have been the object of a certain amount of rivalry. It seems probable, however, that the chief attraction of London was the profits accruing to whoever controlled the emporium of

Lundonwic. This essay will trace, in so far as the sources allow, the influence wielded over London by different Anglo-Saxon kingdoms during the seventh century.

London in the early seventh century

The Northumbrian monk and scholar Bede, in his *Historia Ecclesiastica*, informs us that at the beginning of the seventh century London was in the control of Sæberht, the king of the East Saxons and nephew and tributary of the Kentish king Æthelberht, who was himself the patron of St Augustine and the first Christian Anglo-Saxon king. Bede states that in the year 604 Augustine consecrated Mellitus, one of his monks, as bishop of the East Saxons and that Æthelberht caused a church, dedicated to St Paul, to be built at London. Bede describes London as 'an emporium for many nations who come to it by land and sea', though this description probably owes more to conditions in Bede's own time than to those a century earlier (HE II, 3, Colgrave and Mynors 1969, 142–5).

The infant East Saxon Church, based on London, was dependent on the more well-established mission at Canterbury, and was ultimately under the protection of King Æthelberht of Kent. As such it was a symbol of Kentish hegemony, and this might explain the events subsequent to the deaths of Æthelberht and Sæberht. Æthelberht died in 616 and Bede implies that Sæberht died shortly after his uncle. Both kings left non-Christian heirs, and this led to the abandonment of the London and Rochester missions, and almost that at Canterbury also (HE II, 5, Colgrave and Mynors 1969, 148–55). The new king of Kent, Æthelberht's son Eadbald, soon accepted Christianity, and Bishop Justus was reinstalled at Rochester. The position at London, however, was more problematic. Bede says that the inhabitants of London refused to take Mellitus back, preferring, as he puts it, 'to serve idolatrous high priests', and that Eadbald, being less powerful than his father had been, was unable to reinstate the bishop against the will of the East Saxons (HE II, 6, Colgrave and Mynors 1969, 154–7). It seems likely that part at least of the aversion the East Saxons felt for Mellitus and his religion stemmed from a desire to be free of Kentish dominance. Both traditional religion and control of London thus appear intimately bound up with East Saxon independence, and in fact it would not be until the 650s that another East Saxon king would accept Christianity (HE III, 22, Colgrave and Mynors 1969, 280–7).

The gold coinage of King Eadbald of Kent provides a possible modifier to the testimony of Bede. Eadbald is the earliest English king known to have minted coins bearing his own name. A number of early seventh-century gold *tremissas* are inscribed with the legend *AVDVARLD REGES*, which is generally taken to indicate Eadbald, and were minted in London (Grierson and Blackburn 1986, 158, 162–3; Blackburn 2006b, 129; Williams 2008b, 18). The existence of these *tremissas* may indicate that despite Bede's testimony Eadbald had a certain amount of influence, or at least connections, in pagan London, and indeed that there was someone there with sufficient literacy to produce the admittedly garbled legend on these coins.

It is not until the second half of the seventh century that we encounter any further evidence of kings of other peoples exerting influence over London, and, significantly, the first such alien ruler is a Mercian king. Bede tells us that, after being expelled from Wessex by King Cenwalh, Bishop Wine bought the see of London from King Wulfhere of the Mercians (HE III, 7, Colgrave and Mynors 1969, 232–7). We cannot date these events precisely, but Wulfhere became king in 658 (HE III, 24, Colgrave and Mynors 1969, 288–95) and Cenwalh probably died in 672 and was certainly dead by 674 (ASC, *sub anno* 672, Swanton 1996, 34–5; Bede, *Historia Abbatum* IV, Plummer 1895, 367–8). If, as Bede elsewhere seems to imply, Agilbert, Wine's predecessor as bishop of the West Saxons, still held that see at the time of the Synod of Whitby in 664, Wine's simoniacal succession to London probably occurred in the period 664 to 672 (HE III, 25, Colgrave and Mynors 1969, 295–309).

London in the late seventh and early eighth centuries

Over the next three decades the picture becomes extremely confused. Wulfhere's ability to dispose of the see implies considerable Mercian influence over London, yet it was still the seat of the bishop of the East Saxons, and in addition to the Mercian and East Saxon rulers, the laws of Hlothere and Eadric suggest that Kentish kings had continuing interests in London. The relevant section of the code states 'If a man of Kent buys property in London, he shall have two or three trustworthy men, or the reeve of the king's estate, as witness', and goes on to say that, if there is any subsequent dispute about the transaction, this is to be resolved at the king's residence in London, before the king's reeve (Attenborough 1922, 22–3). Hlothere and/or Eadric thus had a hall and at least one official in London and an interest in and control over the market there, at least regarding the transactions of Kentish traders. Hlothere ruled Kent from 673 to 685, and his nephew and slayer Eadric died in either 686 or 687 (HE IV, 5, 26 [24], Colgrave and Mynors 1969, 348–55, 426–31). Their law code cannot be dated more precisely. So, in the second half of the seventh century East Saxon, Mercian and Kentish kings all appear to have had a degree of power at London.

The position is confused still further by the intrusion of the West Saxons. Bede states that Hædde was consecrated as bishop of the West Saxons by Archbishop Theodore at London at some point in the decade following Cenwalh's death *c.* 672 (HE IV, 12, Colgrave and Mynors 1969, 368–71). The next section of this chapter of Bede's *History* describes the ravaging of Kent by King Æthelred of the Mercians in 676, and we may be intended to suppose that Hædde's appointment occurred in or about that year.

The consecration of a West Saxon bishop in London is interesting, but does not necessarily indicate a significant West Saxon influence there, and indeed this seems unlikely in view of the temporary fragmentation of the West Saxon polity that followed the death of Cenwalh (*HE* IV, 12, Colgrave and Mynors 1969, 368–71). Such influence is more strongly suggested by the preface to the law code of King Ine. In this Ine describes Bishop Eorconwald of London as 'my bishop', and names him as one of those who advised him during the drafting of his code (Attenborough 1922, 36–7). These statements suggest that Ine had, or at least claimed, some degree of influence over London. Ine became king in 688, and Eorcenwold died in 693, so it seems probable that Ine's laws were issued in the early part of his reign (*HE* IV, 15, Colgrave and Mynors 1969, 380–1, V, 24, 360–71, *ibid.*, 367n. 1).

Despite the intrusion of Mercian, Kentish and West Saxon rulers, London still retained its connections with the East Saxon kingdom. In the mid-690s, after a reign of thirty years, the East Saxon king Sæbbi, in ill health and close to death, became a monk at London and, having died, was buried there in St Paul's (*HE* IV, 11, Colgrave and Mynors 1969, 364–9). It would be both overly cynical and anachronistic to maintain that Sæbbi's decision to enter a monastery was not motivated principally by piety. Nevertheless, it is not difficult to imagine a political aspect to his decision to spend his last days, and be buried, in this particular community.

The Mercian/East Saxon nexus at London at the turn of the seventh and eighth centuries can perhaps best be illuminated by a charter granting land at Twickenham to Bishop Waldhere of London (Birch 1885, no. 111, Sawyer 1968, no. 65). In seventh- and eighth-century England one of the ways in which powerful kings imposed their authority on weaker rulers was by insisting on the right to confirm, and by implication to deny, their land grants. The grant in question was made jointly by King Swafræd of the East Saxons and a man named Pæogthath, who is described as a *comes*, so presumably an ealdorman, of King Æthelred of the Mercians. The document is very precisely dated to 13 June 704. At the head of the witness list is a 'confirmation' by King Cenred, who succeeded his uncle Æthelred as king of the Mercians in this year. The 'confirmation' is, however, expressed in terms more suggestive of a grant, stating that Cenred had ordered the land to be given to Waldhere. Finally, there is a later confirmation by Cenred's successor Ceolred, which again seems to suggest that Cenred was the grantor, stating that Ceolred confirms the donation made by his predecessor Cenred.

Though doubts have been expressed as to the authenticity of this charter (see Sawyer 1968, no. 65, 'comments'), it survives in an eighth-century manuscript (BL Cotton Augustus ii, 82), and it is possible that it is a reliable record. If so, then it helps to illuminate the status of London at the beginning of the eighth century. Pæogthath is generally supposed to have been a Mercian official, an agent of Æthelred, resident in London and supervising his lord's business in the city (Yorke 1990, 49). We

have seen that the kings of Kent earlier had a similar official there, though there is no evidence to suggest that the Kentish reeve was in a position to make grants of land in association with the East Saxon king. It seems that the Mercian king possessed an agent in London whose remit extended considerably beyond the supervision of the business transactions of Mercian traders. The city at this time then appears effectively to have been a condominium, a territory over which two (or more) sovereign powers agree to share jurisdiction.

Another interesting feature of this diploma is the fact that the grant which it records seems to have coincided with the abdication of Æthelred. As noted above, he is cited as the Mercian king in the text, yet it is Cenred who confirms the grant. The domineering style adopted in the confirmation may be ascribable to the desire of a new king to demonstrate his power and influence over a dependent polity.

By the close of the seventh century London appears to have been, if not yet a Mercian city, a city firmly within the compass of the Mercian kings. This trend continued in the eighth century. Æthelbald, king of the Mercians 716–757, issued a number of charters which granted exemption from royal tolls at London (Kelly 1992; Tyler 2002, 156–85). These imply that, by the 730s at the latest, the *wic* and its tolls, and by implication the city as a whole, could be treated by the Mercian ruler as part of his own kingdom. Thereafter, except for a brief period when it was lost to the West Saxons (*ASC sub anno* 827 [829], Swanton 1996, 60–1), London remained a Mercian city until the collapse of the kingdom during the Viking wars of the ninth century.

Conclusions

In the long term, control of London was transferred from one kingdom to another – it was East Saxon, it became Mercian. This much is clear. What, however, are we to make of the confused situation in the final quarter of the seventh century, when East Saxon, West Saxon, Kentish and Mercian kings were competing for, and exerting influence over, London? It may be that the city repeatedly changed hands. This is essentially the line taken by Barbara Yorke (1990, 45–57). This is a possibility, and though one might expect Bede to have mentioned it, his silence need not be taken as refutation. Alan Vince, however, argued that we should perhaps see London as housing several kings' halls concurrently, and that several kingdoms profited from commercial activities there (Vince 1990, 54). Again, this is possible, but even if correct we should not assume that relations between the various royal households were relaxed and amicable. In view of the confused, volatile and violent state of politics in south-east England in the period *c.* 670–*c.* 690, which involved repeated clashes between Mercian, Kentish, East Saxon, West Saxon and South Saxon kings and their warbands, any joint control of London must have been fraught with tensions. That the Mercian rulers had been able to oust their rivals by the end of the seventh century may find some confirmation from developments at another *wic*. The West Saxon emporium at *Hamwic* seems to have originated, or at least expanded greatly, at just this time (Hodges 1989, 85–91; Scull 1997, 269–309; Russo 1998, 137–42). It has been suggested that *Hamwic* was a royally sponsored venture, planned by Ine (Hodges 1989, 85). It is possible that Ine took this step in order to replace lost revenues from London.

East Saxon influence at London probably declined rapidly during the early decades of the eighth century. By the central part of the reign of Æthelbald London was effectively a Mercian centre. Nevertheless, in the ecclesiastical sphere the association between London and the East Saxons lingered, and the county of Essex remained a part of the Diocese of London until the middle of the nineteenth century.

London: Archaeological Evidence
for the Events of 886 and its Aftermath

David Beard

This article is an update of a short paper on that I gave at a seminar on Alfredian London organized by David Hill in Manchester in 1986. Subsequent to that, David, Margaret Worthington and myself carried out a series of small investigations on Offa's Dyke with volunteers from MEMAS (the University of Manchester Extra-Mural Archaeological Society) and EMAS (the University of London Extra-Mural Archaeological Society). These were wonderful times – the day's work being driven by David's enthusiasm, and the evenings being enlivened by his wonderful sense of humour. (Margaret will remember the Zulu finger Puppets!)

Introduction

The work by Biddle (Biddle 1984) and Vince (Vince 1984) that led to the discovery of middle Saxon London helped clarify the problem of what was meant by the entry for 886 in the Anglo-Saxon Chronicles that stated that:

> *Ðy ilcan geare gesette Ælfred cyning Lunden burg, 7 him all Angel cyn to cirde, þæt buton Deniscra monna hæftniede was, 7 hie þa befæste þa burg Æþerede aldormen to haldonne.* (E 886, Plummer and Earle, 1972).

'The same year King Alfred occupied London fort (*Lunden burh*) and all the English race turned to him, except what was in captivity to the Danish men; and he then entrusted the fort to Ealdorman Æthelred to hold.' (anno 886, Swanton, 1996).

It is clear that *Lunden burh* refers to the area within the old Roman fort. Our knowledge of this area of Anglo-Saxon London prior to 886 is far from complete, but its relationship to the Strand settlement seems to have been similar to the relationship that Winchester had to Hamwih (Biddle 1976, 114).

It is presumed that the old walled area of Roman London had a minster from 604 – the parallels from Winchester and Canterbury would seem to make this likely, and most people accept that the location of the first minster church was on or near the present site of St Paul's. The distribution of the very few finds that can be closely dated to the later mid-Saxon period within the walled area are in the vicinity of St Paul's, which would appear to support this theory. This minster presumably had the necessary domestic buildings and perhaps stood within its own precinct. There was also possibly a royal palace, which may have been situated within the area of the old Roman fort at Cripplegate. The late seventh-century lawcode of Hlothere of Kent (*d.* 685) refers to a hall in London where Kentish merchants were to register their transactions (Whitelock 1955, 360–1), and medieval tradition held that the king's palace lay just within the city walls on the site of Cripplegate fort (Milne and Dyson 2002, 128). Such a location just within the city walls is perhaps supported by John of Worcester's annal for 1017 referring to when Cnut was in London: 'And at the Lord's Nativity when he [Cnut] was in London, he gave orders for the perfidious ealdorman Eadric to be killed in the palace ...' and the entry continues ' ... he ordered his body to be thrown over the wall of the city and left unburied' (Darlington and McGurk 1995, II, 504, 505).

The church of St Alban Wood Street is sited on the main north-south road of the fort, and a tradition recorded in the mid-sixteenth century held that it was the royal chapel of the Anglo-Saxon palace. Unfortunately the post-second world war excavations that revealed a small stone church under the medieval church were inconclusive and there is no evidence to suggest that the church can be dated to before the eleventh century.

A late eleventh-century source quoted by Matthew Paris in the thirteenth century (Riley 1867–9, I, 55) states that liberties of the old royal palace then lay with a small house which has been identified as Aldermanbury by Tony Dyson and John Schofield (Dyson and Schofield 1980, 308), the suggestion being that the east gatehouse of the fort survived as a prestigious accommodation. The fact that the line of Addle Street avoids the gatehouse is cited as evidence for the survival of the gatehouse into the Anglo-Saxon period. Once again, however, we lack firm archaeological evidence to show if the south and east walls of the fort even survived above ground after the northern and western walls were incorporated into the Roman city wall.

The discovery of the Roman amphitheatre in 1988 revealed another possible location for a royal centre. Re-use of amphitheatres in the early medieval period is well attested on the Continent, but the evidence from the Guildhall Yard excavation suggests that the area of the amphitheatre remained empty until the eleventh century. This has been questioned by Daniel Russo who writes 'Anglo-Saxon street topography suggests that this former public structure remained standing and had some significant function, if not as the site of a royal hall, then perhaps as the traditional gathering place of the London folkmoot' (Russo 1998, 118).

Alfredian London

Despite the lack of hard and fast archaeological evidence, the prevailing view is that London before 886 was (to use Martin Biddle's classic description of pre-Alfredian Winchester) 'royal, ecclesiastical, ceremonial' in its nature (Biddle 1976, 114). As with Winchester, in London after 886 there is a complete change in the nature of the settlement: new streets are laid out which (in some areas at least) bear little relation to the Roman street pattern, although the gates (or at least, their locations) are used. The major east-west thoroughfare of Cheapside uses the sites of the Roman gates, but follows a different line from its Roman predecessor.

There is disagreement, however, on how long the process of street construction took; most see 886 as the key date, but Jeremy Haslam has put forward arguments suggesting that the process of turning London into a *burh* began around 879, directly after the Peace of Wedmore (Haslam, 2011b). Clarity on this point is made difficult by the wide date range of most of the excavated finds. Both archaeological and documentary evidence indicate that the focus of this new settlement of London was within a block defined by Cheapside to the north and the Thames to the south.

In 1990 Gustav Milne suggested that Alfred's plan for the rebuilding of London could be shown to be within an area that includes 'Bread Street, Garlick Hill/Bow Lane and College Hill in the west, with Fish Street Hill and Botolph Lane in the east' (Milne 1990, 206). He points out that streets north of the line of Cheapside 'such as Milk Street, Ironmonger Lane, Gracechurch Street/Bishopsgate or Leadenhall Street do not seem to be intensely occupied until one or two generations later' than 886 (*ibid.* 206). The area indicated by Milne is 'ringed by markets and other major features, most of which functioned in the pre-Conquest period. They include the precinct of St Paul's; the possible site of the "King's Hall" at Cripplegate; the great markets at Cheapside, Poultry and (later) Leadenhall on the north side; the site of the old fishmarket on the eastern side, with the two documented harbours at Queenhithe and Billingsgate

sitting on the south-western and south-eastern corners' (*ibid.* 207). The position of markets on the periphery rather than in the centre of the settlement is a feature of many early town plans.

Milne's suggested plan has a lot to recommend it; certainly excavations on the waterfronts west and east of this area have so far failed to provide evidence of pre-Conquest activity, not showing waterfront development until the eleventh or twelfth centuries. However, although the excavations at Number 1 Poultry which fell within the north western area of the suggested grid show evidence of late ninth-/early tenth-century occupation, this occupation is not aligned on the Cheapside based grid (Treveil and Rowsome 1998, 284). It would seem that a considerable degree of flexibility had intruded into the original plans. As John Clark has pointed out: 'in the year before he died Alfred was still apparently involved in discussions about "the restoration of London" – and was meeting his advisors at the royal estate of Chelsea rather than London itself – it seems very likely that his plans for London were slow to get under way' (Clark 1999, 38).

Naturally, the waterfront would be an area of major importance in the new town. There is evidence to show that the Roman riverside wall still stood in most places, which may have initially restricted the areas of the waterfront that were available for use. In 1978 Tony Dyson examined two charters dating to 889 and 898–9 in which Alfred granted land to Wærferth, bishop of Worcester, in the earlier charter and to Plegmund, archbishop of Canterbury, and Bishop Wærferth in the later charter (Dyson 1978). The northern boundary of the estate was a road and the southern boundary the city wall. The earlier grant allowed the bishop's men to trade within the estate, but regulated trade on the public street and the riverside market (*ripa emptoralis*). The later charter granted both bishops the right to moor their ships on the foreshore along the width of their properties. Dyson gave convincing arguments to show that the area referred to in the charters was the parcel of land bounded by Bread Street Hill to the west and Little Trinity Lane to the east, and that the *ripa emptoralis* was Queenhithe; and concluded that the streets mentioned in the charter were being laid out around this time and that here was one of the earliest areas of Alfredian London (Dyson 1990). Excavations at Bull Wharf, adjacent to Queenhithe, have certainly confirmed that this was part of the early development of late Saxon London. The second-century Roman timber quay had been robbed to its base-plates and was covered with roughly one metre of alluvial silts (Wroe-Brown 1990, 12).

The highest inter-tidal foreshore produced two female burials: burial one was an east-west orientated supine burial that had been placed in a simple cut, the other burial was less than 5m away. The woman had died from a blow to the head which had broken out a piece of her skull. She had been laid on a bed of reeds between two layers of bark as a simple coffin, moss had been placed over her face, pelvis and knees, and the burial had been marked by posts, one above her head and one between her knees. A C14 date on the bark gave a

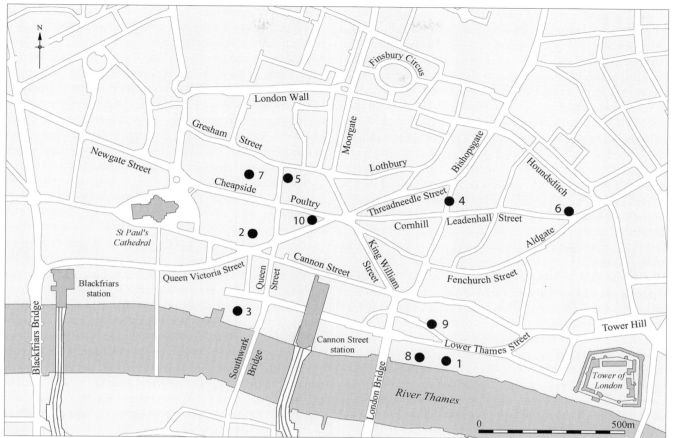

Fig. 7.1 Location of sites mentioned in the text (Map courtesy of Pre-Construct Archaeology Ltd). Key: 1. Billingsgate; 2. Bow Lane; 3. Bull Wharf; 4. Gracechurch Street/Bishopsgate; 5. Ironmonger Lane; 6. Leadenhall Street; 7. Milk Street; 8. New Fresh Wharf; 9. Peninsular House; 10. 1, Poultry.

result of AD 670–880 at a probability of 95% (*ibid.*, 13). Two Northumbrian *styccas*, similar in type to a hoard found at the Royal Opera House site, suggest that some sort of trading was being carried out here in the mid-ninth century, perhaps related to the minster site of St Paul's (*ibid.*, 13).

The earliest Anglo-Saxon structural phases at Bull Wharf consisted of several fairly insubstantial but well-preserved timber features: two lines of trestles which originally supported gang-planks with space between them to moor boats, to the east a low timber structure packed with foreshore gravel – tentatively identified as a barge bed – and a turf and wattle hut. Most of the timbers were not suitable for dendrochronological dating, but a timber from the barge bed gave a date of 890, while a possible bark edge and a timber from the trestles gave a terminus *post quem* of 880. There were also three coins of Alfred on the contemporary foreshore. Tenth-century finds indicated good trade with the Continent, as objects of Frankish, Carolingian and Scandinavian origin were found. Among the Scandinavian objects was an early to mid-tenth-century copper alloy comb connecting plate which has parallels from Hedeby, where both combs and moulds for their manufacture have been found (Hilberg 2009, 81).

In the late tenth century rapid development of the foreshore took place, possibly prompted by the shore line receding, or by shortage of space on the shore. A succession of two low timber revetments was constructed, which seem to have functioned as landing places for boats. In each case the method of construction was similar – a line of posts supporting horizontal planks with the area behind levelled with dumps of earth, stone and timber. These revetments extended the area of the built-up foreshore two metres to the west, and the second of these revetments represented an advance into the river of 1.5 metres. Much of the timber was reused, including fragments of a late tenth-century sailing vessel, identified as a Frisian Hulc, and timbers from a substantial late tenth-century aisled building (Wroe-Brown 1999, 14).

In the early eleventh century the method of construction changed to large embankments of dumped timber supported by rows of posts and stakes. Good dendrochronological dates were possible for these structures, giving an initial construction date of 1021 (perhaps as a result of the severe flooding in 1014, although it seems rather a late response). This structure was repaired and extended in 1045 (*ibid.*, 14).

Behind the area of the Queenhithe Dock the earliest buildings probably date to the eleventh century, although it is possible that their construction had removed evidence of earlier buildings. This part of the Roman riverside wall had been demolished to allow access to the reclaimed land. The excavated building remains were extremely fragmentary, and repeated repair and reuse made it impossible to be sure of the exact number of buildings present, but there seems to have been a total of twelve buildings here. All of these were timber-built, with earth or plank floors covered in rushes or sedges. A number of burnt posts suggest that fire had been an occasional hazard. One large post-built structure may have been an aisled building, as its posts were of the same diameter as the reused aisle posts found in the revetments. The most completely excavated building was *c.* 4m × 8m, but was later expanded to 6m ×11m. One building contained an oven almost one metre in diameter containing quantities of carbonised grain (*ibid.*, 15).

When we look to the waterfronts west of the Walbrook Valley we see somewhat later development. At New Fresh Wharf a mid-tenth-century rubble bank extended four metres south of the decayed Roman quay; this bank overlay river silts and extended 18 metres east to west. To the west of the bank was a grid of oak stakes, which may have been the posts of a jetty which led to the riverside wall. After mid-tenth- to eleventh-century silting, further embankments of clay and timber were built which were dated by dendrochronology to between 991 and 1000; these embankments were divided into plots by rough fences. After further eleventh-century silting a late eleventh-century revetment was built which was the first to be constructed with a vertical face. After further silting a front-braced revetment was built, which could be dated to 1188 ± 9 years (LAARC NFW74).

At Billingsgate Market Lorry Park the first sign of late Saxon activity was the removal of part of the old Roman quay at the east of the site to provide an inlet to the north. This inlet was formed by two stave-built revetments, at least two metres high, running off the site to both the east and the west. The area behind these revetments was filled with packed clay with timber lacing and they were further strengthened by braces in the body of the clay. These revetments continued in use throughout the tenth and the eleventh centuries, with occasional partial collapse necessitating repairs (LAARC BIG82).

Excavations at the Peninsular House site provided good evidence of streets and houses being laid out in the early tenth century. Floors were of brickearth and at least one building was of beam slot construction. It was not possible to excavate the associated street surfaces, as they lie under modern Botolph Lane, but it was possible to examine them in section (LAARC PEN79). At Bow Lane it could be seen that the late Saxon buildings directly overlay the latest Roman street, while the Saxon street overlay the latest Roman buildings (LAARC WAT78).

The excavations at Number 1 Poultry have provided an opportunity to examine the development of London immediately south of Cheapside. There was a large open space, probably a market area, at the eastern end of Cheapside from the late ninth or early tenth century, and it is likely that Poultry was originally a route way skirting this open area. The excavations at Number 1 Poultry revealed gravel and cobbled surfaces to the south of the later street frontage. At Poultry at least part of the layout seems to have been influenced by the Roman topography as the open market area was sited directly above the Roman street junction and the fenced hollow way that led to the area from the north-west followed the alignment of the Roman street (Treveil and Rowsome 1998, 284).

The earliest post-Roman structures were a number of late Saxon sunken-floored buildings, one of which was constructed against the wall of a late Roman masonry building. The construction methods for these buildings included horizontal planking, earth-fast posts and wattle hurdles, while the floors were of brickearth, planking or brushwood. In the first half of the eleventh century the sunken-floored buildings were replaced with rows of narrow timber buildings which fronted on to the south side of Poultry. Presumably by this time the Cheapside frontage had been developed in a similar fashion and the development of Poultry may reflect the need to create trading space in the vicinity of the Cheapside market. The earliest buildings were free-standing structures, *c.* 3m wide and extending back from the street frontage by *c.* 5.5m. Both earth-fast posts and beam slots set into the ground were used, and most floors were of brickearth, although examples of earth and mortar floors were also found. There were also a number of buildings with timber-lined hearths.

The eleventh-century parish church of St Benet Sherehog was constructed on the western side of the area. This was a single-celled rectangular structure set on the same alignment as the underlying Roman road, so that the church was on a different alignment from the surrounding buildings. The excavations showed that the Roman road was buried beneath a sequence of dumps and pits and so would not have been visible, unless as a low ridge. The church was built using reused Roman ragstone and tile, except for side-alternate quoins in limestone. Dating evidence for the construction of the building is extremely limited, and only a general date of the eleventh century can be given.

London Bridge

A certain amount of mystery surrounds the origins of the first Anglo-Saxon London Bridge. Archaeological and documentary evidence confirm the existence of a bridge by *c.* 1000, the archaeological evidence consisting of *ex situ* bridge timbers dating to *c.* 987–1032. This first bridge may have been built as a consequence of the Viking attack on London in 994 and was presumably the bridge around which Cnut's men dragged their ships in 1016. Comparison between Charles the Bald's defences at Pont de l'Arche, with its fortified town and a fortified site either side of the confluence of the Seine and the Eure, and the burghal town of London and the burghal fort of Southwark, have led people to suppose that a bridge must have been part of the original intention. Jeremy Haslam sees that 'two essential components ... of this new *burh* (*i.e.* London) would have been the formation of a garrison and the association of this *burh* with a new or reconstructed bridge over the Thames'. By linking with the *burh* already existing at Southwark this would have acted as a defence of the river against the passage of Viking ships (Haslam 2011b, 136), but as John Clark has pointed out, 'a Danish fleet sailed upriver past London unimpeded in 893' (Clark 1999, 38).

It is interesting to note that the *Anglo-Saxon Chronicles* record cases where the English built fortifications either side of a river to control Viking activity: 896 on the River Lea; 918 at Buckingham; 919 at Bedford; 922 at Stamford and 924 at Nottingham (Plummer and Earle 1972, 89, 100, 100,103,104). In each case the fortifications are mentioned (either *geweorc* or *burh*), but only in the case of Nottingham is there any mention of a bridge. Of course, this may be due to the width of the rivers at the point where the double *burhs* were constructed, but it could imply that the presence of a bridge was not seen to be of primary importance for defensive purposes. These examples may perhaps suggest that Alfred's original plan for London never included a bridge, or that if a bridge were part of the original plan, it was not of sufficient importance to have been built during the first stages of construction.

The late Saxon *burhs* of Somerset – a review

Jeremy Haslam

I have known David Hill – usually meeting in conferences – on and off for more than 30 years. I have over this period found his writings and lectures on *burhs* and the Burghal Hidage a constant source of challenge The principal reason is that in his earlier papers – in particular that on the Burghal Hidage in 1969 in *Medieval Archaeology*, and his joint paper with Martin Biddle on late Saxon town planning in 1974 in the *Antiquaries Journal* – he has set an agenda which has been instrumental in shaping further research and analysis over the last 40-odd years. This was perhaps begun with his pioneering study of the topography of Lyng in Somerset (1967), which with Athelney is discussed further in my own paper here. Through this work he has been largely instrumental in creating and sustaining two separate but inter-related paradigms – one concerning the development of late Anglo-Saxon towns, and the other concerning the origin and context of the Burghal Hidage and the appended Calculation. Both of these paradigms have underpinned this particular branch of historical and archaeological studies to this day. The fact that I fundamentally disagree with some (but not all) aspects of the former, and almost every aspect of his interpretation of the latter, has meant that I have had my own work cut out both to clarify my own ideas, and to argue in detail, going back to primary evidence and the first principles of historical, topographical and archaeological analysis, for alternative views to those which he has usually upheld down the years with persistence and clarity. So I have to thank David for his insights which have got to the heart of the matter in these as well as other topics (and for his cartographic skills in presenting evidence and data), as well as those ideas which (at least to my way of thinking) do not quite stand the test of detailed examination. In all these aspects, his work has stimulated me (and others) to think critically on these matters in ways which I probably would not have done if he had not gone before me and provided me with a mounting block.

Introduction

The four *burhs* at Axbridge, Langport, Lyng and Watchet in Somerset provide a particularly illuminating case study for examining general military strategies in Wessex in the ninth century, as well as the development of settlement patterns in Somerset in the period. For reasons given elsewhere (Haslam 2013a), and briefly below, Ilchester is also considered as belonging to the original Alfredian system. (Bath, also in Somerset, is omitted here, partly for lack of space – but see on this Cunliffe 1984; Aston 1986b; Manco 1998). These *burhs* (apart from Ilchester, but also including Bath) were included in the Burghal Hidage document, which gives a list of defended sites of the reign of King Alfred in the late ninth century (Hill and Rumble 1996) (Fig. 8.1). For a long time this has been considered as having been drawn up in the second decade of the tenth century, a paradigm which has become deeply engrained in historical studies in large measure through the writings of David Hill. I have however sought to demonstrate that the document itself was drawn up within the context of the setting up of the system of *burhs* which it records, and that this process belongs to the period 878–9, between the victory of King Alfred over the Viking forces of Guthrum at Edington in early 878 and Guthrum's subsequent withdrawal to East Anglia in the autumn of 879 (Haslam 2005; Haslam 2010; Haslam 2011b). The recent arguments of John Baker and Stuart Brookes (2011), which present an alternative course of development of the Wessex *burhs* of the Burghal Hidage, do nothing, in my view, to demonstrate that this is not the case, for various reasons which it is hoped to set out in detail on a future occasion. Some of these reasons are, however, discussed elsewhere (Haslam, 2012 chapters 8, 9 and 12; Haslam 2013b). The dating of the Burghal Hidage to this time, therefore, has some significant implications for the interpretation of the development of the burghal system, of which the four *burhs* discussed here were components. The usage of the contemporary term *burh* to refer to these fortified places, while

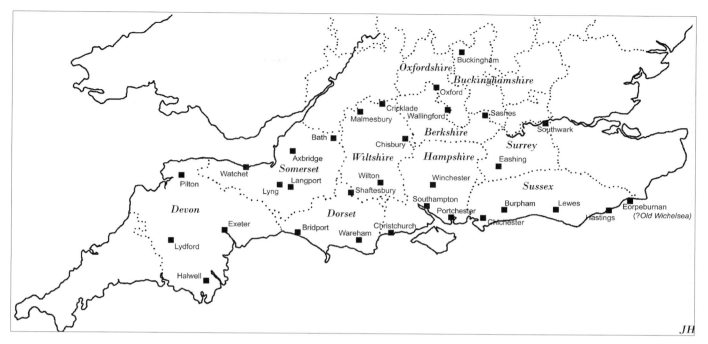

Fig. 8.1 The burhs of the Burghal Hidage in Wessex.

in some ways problematical (Draper 2008), has nevertheless seemed preferable to other terms. Axbridge and Langport are amongst a small group in the Burghal Hidage the names of which refer to post-Roman topographical or constructional elements generated by human activity. Others are those containing the *-bury* or *-geweorc* suffix, referring to a fortification, as at Burpham, Shaftesbury, Chisbury and Southwark, and the two fords at Wallingford and Oxford at crossing places of the river Thames (Dodgson 1996). The *-brycg* and *-port* elements in Axbridge and Langport are therefore unique in the place-names of the Burghal Hidage. The dating of the name-forms implied in the reassessment of the date of the Burghal Hidage to the period 878–9 allows conclusions to be drawn about the existence and significance of these topographical elements in these two places at this particular time. This in turn makes it possible to take a view not only about ways in which the creation of these and other sites in the system listed in the Burghal Hidage reflected the strategic thinking both of this period and earlier, but also about the development of sites with marketing or redistributive functions under royal control within the late Saxon landscape. These themes have been examined briefly by David Hill, who has also included small-scale (and in consequence somewhat unsatisfactory) topographical analyses (Hill 1967; Hill 1982; Hill 1996). In particular, however, this study extends a more general model for settlement development of the period put forward by Mick Aston (Aston 1984), which was subsequently refined by him in greater detail (Aston 1986a), as well as the general discussion on these matters by Michael Costen (Costen 2011, 44–7, 145–76) Fig. 8.2.

Langport

The basic premise that the Burghal Hidage was drawn up as part of the process of the creation of Alfred's new system of *burhs* in Wessex carries the implication that the occurrence of the name-form of *Langport* in the Burghal Hidage must mean that the 'long port' – the 'urban' development along the street leading to the bridge over the River Parrett (Dodgson 1996, 114–15) – was already a feature of the site by the time the place was incorporated into the burghal system. There is evidence of Roman occupation within the town and on the west side of the crossing over the River Parrett, as well as of extensive Roman settlement in the area, from which the use of the crossing and therefore of the causeway before the late ninth century can be reasonably inferred (Bush 1974, 16; Richardson 2003b, 4–6). The development and use of this causeway in the mid- and later Saxon period would therefore be expected. At this point a particularly narrow gap between high ground on either side of the tidal river (shown by the contours in Fig. 8.3) would have been crossed by a bridge at the western end of this street, since the street or causeway could not have had any meaningful existence without it.

This series of inferences implies that the relationship of this place as the marketing site or redistribution point to the royal centre of Somerton, 7km to its east (Fig. 8.2), pointed out for instance by Mick Aston (Aston 1984, 192), is likely to have already developed by this time. It was also somewhat closer to another royal estate centre at Curry Rivel 3.5km to its south-west, for which it may also have been the market outlet, though its thirty-four burgesses in Domesday are included in

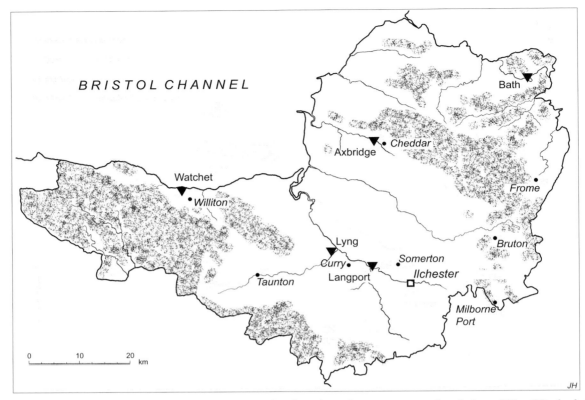

Fig. 8.2 Burhs in Somerset (including Ilchester), with selected royal estate centres. Land above 120m OD shaded.

the entry for Somerton (Darby and Finn 1967, 202). Its burghal territory – the area assigned for its upkeep – must have included much or all of the royal estate centred on Somerton (Aston 1984, 187 fig. 69; Dunning 1974), though the presence of five contributory burgesses at Langport held by the estate at North Curry in Domesday Book (Darby and Finn 1967, 202) arguably indicates that the extent of this burghal territory would also have included the royal estate of Curry Rivel on the other side of the river. The holding of a garden at Langport by Staple Fitzpaine, even further to the west, might well indicate that its territory extended this far. These evidences of heterogeneous tenure are largely a defining characteristic of *burhs*. I have argued elsewhere that these urban-rural connections in Domesday were the vestiges of a more complete system, whereby landholders within each of the burghal territories were given tenements within the *burh* in that territory, as one way in which the king could maintain the social, economic and strategic or military functions of the *burh* as sustainable settlements, as well as enhancing his overall political control of the kingdom (Haslam 2012, chapters 8 and 9; Haslam 2013b).

It has always been assumed that the defended site or *burh* constructed by King Alfred would have been situated on the hilltop immediately overlooking this settlement on its eastern side (Aston and Leach 1977; Aston 1984, 182; Hill 1996, 207; Richardson 2003b, 7) Fig. 8.4, and that this would have been 'founded to control this crossing and [to] take advantage of

transhipment facilities for land and water transport' (Aston 1984, 182). An alternative possibility, however, could be that the defended enclosure of the *burh* was situated along the causeway immediately to the east of the bridge, with a market-place outside the defences to the east (Fig. 8.5). Extensive excavations on the hilltop in 1976 have yielded no evidence of any defences or structures of any date (Aston 1984, 182), and another excavation on the south-west flank has produced no evidence of either occupation or defences on the postulated line (Leech 1986). The church on the hilltop could possibly have been contemporary with the foundation of the burh, its parish carved out of that of Huish Episcopi to its north, but an origin later in the Saxon period, possibly as part of a programme of refortification in the later tenth or early eleventh century under Æthelred, seems more likely. Further parallels to this situation are at Old Sarum, to which moneyers were moved from the *burh* at Wilton in 1003 (Shortt 1950; Dolley 1954; Crittal 1962, 53–60; RCHM 1980, xxix–xxxi; Haslam 1984b, 124–5; Blunt and Lyon 1990; Alcock 1995, 166), and at Daws Castle, Watchet (discussed below, and in Haslam 2011a), Dover (Tatton Brown 1988, 227–8) and South Cadbury (Alcock 1995).

The hilltop *burh* at Langport could therefore be considered as a strong point without a permanent garrison, and would have acted variously as a refuge, a rallying point for the local *fyrd* or mobile army, a lookout point or signalling station. Examples of such *burhs* in the Burghal Hidage system include Halwell,

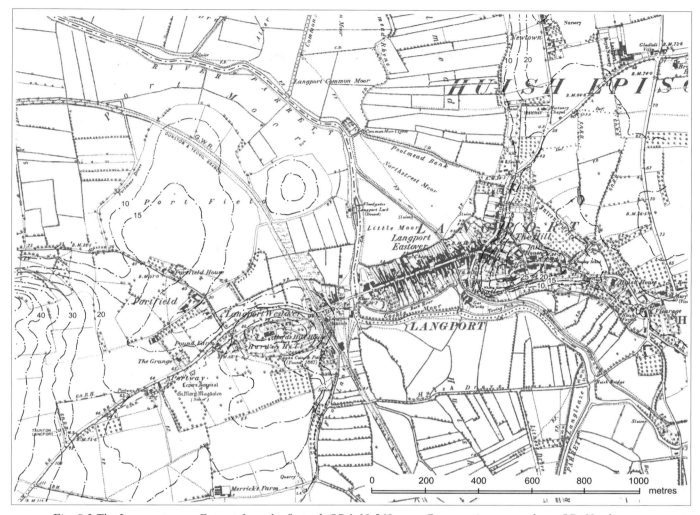

Fig. 8.3 The Langport area. Extract from the first ed. OS 1:10,560 map. Contours in metres above OD. North to top.

Pilton, Sashes, Eashing, Chisbury and Burpham (Biddle 1976; Hill 1996a). A further example could have been the first phase at Daws Castle, possibly a precursor to the urban *burh* at Watchet, a hypothesis discussed in detail elsewhere (Haslam 2011a), and summarised below. None of these shows evidence of organised habitation such as burgage plots or a street system, which would be indicative of the presence of a permanent garrison. One of the functions of the *burh* on the hilltop at Langport would therefore have been to act with the bridge as a strong point in preventing access up the tidal River Parrett to Viking ships, and guarding a vital routeway and access point to the royal sites and estates at Somerton and Curry Rivel.

Current opinion depicts the burghal defences as taking an extended course around and near the base of the western side of the hill (Fig. 8.4), based in part on the observation of a bank and ditch along this line (Bush 1974, 16; Aston and Leech 1977, map 32; Aston 1984, 184; Hill 1996a, 206–7; Richardson 2003b, map B). This topographical hypothesis is based on the

premise that the length of the defences on this line would equal the length postulated from the figures given in the Calculation of the Burghal Hidage (Aston and Leech 1977).

There are however several seemingly insurmountable objections to this line. Firstly, the creation of defences of a hillfort at the base of its slopes rather than along its crest would be contrary to common practice at any period. Secondly, excavations along this projected line on the western side have failed to find any evidence of these defences (Leech 1986). Thirdly, recent thinking on the relationship of the lengths of the defended perimeters of *burhs* of the Burghal Hidage to the 'theoretical' lengths given in the Calculation attached to the document suggests that there is no *necessary* correspondence between the hidage figures and the lengths of defences of *burhs* in the Burghal Hidage system, as has previously been assumed (Brooks 1996, 130–132; Haslam 2009, 111–4; Haslam 2011a). I have argued elsewhere that the Calculation was drawn up and appended to the List of the Burghal Hidage at a later date, and that it therefore does not bear any relationship to the sizes or lengths of the defences of the *burhs* as they were initially set out (Haslam 2011a, 211–7). The comparatively frequent occurrence of instances where the lengths of defences were not determined by the numbers of hides given to a *burh* (such as in the cases of the *burhs* of Devon: Brooks 1996, 138–141) means that this formula cannot be used in predictive ways. It is quite clear that the hidages recorded in the Burghal Hidage give the areas of the burghal territories which were set out to provide the *burhs* with general logistical support, rather than giving an accurate record of the lengths of their defended perimeters. This argument applies to the elucidation of the topography of all the *burhs* in this study – Langport included.

The 'entrenchments' marked on early Ordnance Survey maps (Fig. 8.4), and identified by previous commentators as early medieval defences, are therefore more likely to have originated in the Civil War of the seventeenth century.

The defences of the suggested hillfort can, however, be more naturally reconstructed as enclosing a relatively flat area on the top of the hill, with the line of the defences defined by the clear breaks of slope on all of its sides, and by the medieval gateway on the eastern side (Fig. 8.4). This would have enclosed the greatest area of flat land on top of the hill with the shortest length of defences, and would thus have been the most economical in terms of the maximum gain of useable area defended for effort expended. The line shown in Fig. 8.4 is very nearly the

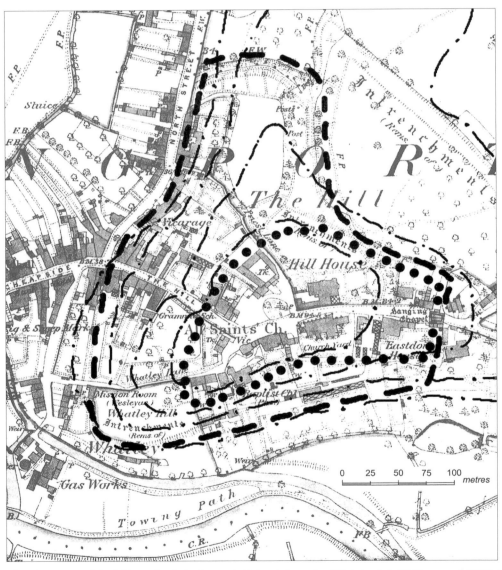

Fig. 8.4 Langport, showing area of the hill-top burh to the east. Extract from the OS 1st ed. 1:2500 map of 1886. Contours in metres above OD. Dotted line – suggested area of hill-top burh defences; dashed line – area of defences defined in Aston and Leach 1977, map 32, Aston 1984, 182, Hill 1996, 207, and Richardson 2003b map B. North to top.

same as that postulated in 1863, using similar reasoning (Warre 1863, 145). The conclusion is drawn in the same volume that this hillfort is 'evidently a Belgic British work' (Anon.1863, 7).

If this were the case, the hilltop site is very likely to have been utilised as a strategically-attractive fortifiable position in a number of different contexts in the few centuries before the Burghal Hidage system was put in place (Fowler 1971; Rahtz and Fowler 1972, 197; Burrow 1981; Burrow 1982), although the defences of this putative hillfort have been inferred only from the topography of the site rather than demonstrated from archaeological or other physical evidence. The lack of any material evidence of late Saxon development in extensive excavations on the hilltop is consistent with the suggested use of this area as a non-urban lookout post or signalling station within an earlier enclosure, either in the Alfredian phase of development or earlier.

The 'long port'

There are several factors in the layout of the 'long port' which are consistent with the thesis that this was the location of a settlement which would have been engaged in marketing and redistributive functions brought into being by its proximity to the waterfront and roadway. Its more recent layout shows burgage plots on both the northern and southern sides extending from the central spinal street to a common line defined at present by ditches with low-lying fields or the river beyond (Fig. 8.5). This has the characteristics of a single plan-unit, which is emphasised by the artificial water-filled cut or rhine (Portlake Rhine) which ran across it and which separated it from the area of the market place immediately to its east, and which was crossed by a bridge (Little Bow Bridge; Bush 1974, 19).The rhine is still visible to the north of Bow Street/ Cheapside. This rhine, and its extension to the east along the bank of the Parret, seems to have originated as the leet for the mill adjacent to the market area, which in the late nineteenth century was a flour mill. The course of the leet can be traced in the landscape for more than 6km upstream from Langport, following the line of the river.

This arrangement, including the cutting of the rhine, is unlikely to have arisen without some degree of planning of the layout as a whole, which has been interpreted as being the result of an episode of urban formation of the eleventh or twelfth century (Aston 1984, 182). This may well be so, but

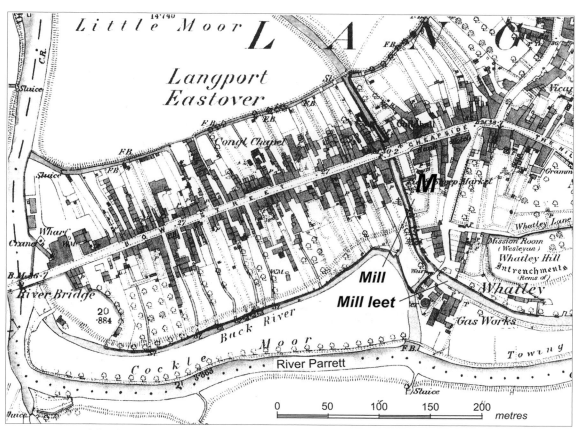

Fig. 8.5 Langport – area of the 'long port'. Extract from the 1st ed. OS 1:2500 map of 1886. North to top. For contours see Fig. 8.4 M is the area of the triangular market place, defined on its west by the mill leet (Portlake Rhine), on its east by Whatley Street and on its north by Cheapside. It is possible that the plan unit of Bow Street and its burgages, between the mill leet and the bridge, could represent the area of the fortified burh of the Burghal Hidage.

the evidence of the place-name, and the use of the causeway and river crossing in the Roman and perhaps earlier periods, would suggest strongly that this is likely to have been preceded by earlier settlement along the causeway and around the market area adjacent to the hillfort. The existence of burgages in the twelfth century is shown in the evidence from one excavation on Bow Street (Grant 1985), but the fact that the lower levels of made ground on this site were not investigated means that the absence of occupation in earlier periods is not demonstrated.

It could be reasonably suggested, therefore, that the spatial association of the ensemble of features comprising the market area which was adjacent or at least accessible to the waterfront, the mill with its leet, the bridge, and the causeway and its burgages, could reflect a functional association which could be reasonably taken back to an episode of quasi-urban planning associated with the formation of the *burh* in the late ninth century. As already suggested, it is not impossible that this was the site of the fortified enclosure or *burh* mentioned in the Burghal Hidage, which would certainly fit the meaning of the place-name. Also associated with this new settlement would have been the town fields, called Portfield on early Ordnance Survey maps, which lie to the west of the bridge on a relatively flat area of land lying above the 10m contour, together with the Port Moor on lower ground to the north next to the river (Fig. 8.3). The association of fields (often called 'Portfield') with new *burhs* is shown for instance at Axbridge (below), Christchurch, Dorset, as well as numerous other places (Haslam 2009, 110 and 99 fig. 2).

Lyng

A similar but contrasting pattern is shown at Lyng, a small *burh* assessed at 100 hides in the Burghal Hidage, which was sited immediately to the west of Athelney, a fort occupying an island site surrounded by marshes (Fig. 8.6). It is this fort to which King Alfred retreated after his rout at Chippenham in early 878. These two sites were connected by a causeway and a bridge over the former line of the River Yeo (the Baltmoor wall) which is referred to by both Asser and the *Anglo-Saxon Chronicle* (Hill 1967; Leach 1976, 29–30; Aston and Leech 1977, 87–90; Aston 1984, 183–5, Keynes 1992; Richardson 2003c, 5–8). Asser's description implies that the causeway and the fort built by Alfred were new constructions at the time (*cap.* 92; Keynes and Lapidge 1983, 102–3), but the archaeological and other evidence suggests that both the fort and the causeway were preceded by already-existing structures. Simon Keynes has suggested that the place-name *Ethelingaeigge*, which means 'the island of the princes', shows that the island 'was recognised for an association of some kind with the princes of the West Saxon royal dynasty', and that this may well have been so named from its occupation by Aethelwine, brother of King Cenwealh (642–72), as a hermit (Keynes 1992, 149). Its high status is, however, taken further back in time by the presence of late sixth-century imported Phocaean slipware

from the eastern Mediterranean, and general occupation in the early to mid-Saxon period is shown by other handmade pottery of the period. Athelney can thus be included in a select group of other high-status sites in Somerset such as South Cadbury, Cadbury-Congresbury and Glastonbury Tor which also show evidence of this imported pottery. This indication of early post-Roman occupation is further strengthened by the presence of extensive iron-smithing and possibly smelting, in the form of slag, hammer scale, parts of furnace structures and tuyeres, as well as evidence of the manufacture of tools, which can be broadly dated to this period. A Roman presence on the site is shown by the find of a mask of bronze (Somerset HER 10554) and by the presence of Roman pottery.[1] This activity invites comparison with other 'productive sites' of the period which can be identified for instance in East Anglia (Hutcheson 2006).

The 2002 excavations also demonstrated the presence of a ring-ditch of the Iron Age on the western part of the island, which continued into use in the early to middle Saxon periods. The existence of this defended area would have facilitated its occupation as a royal hermitage in the seventh century, and would by inference have formed the basis for its reconstruction as a fort in the late Saxon period during Alfred's occupation of the island. The importance of the site in the Iron Age is emphasised by the possible Iron-Age origin of the cross-promontory defences on the western side of Lyng, argued below, which would have formed a double defence of the island as a whole. The connecting causeway (the present Baltmoor Wall; Somerset HER 44863) appears to have had beginnings as a Bronze Age trackway (Somerset HER 12787, 12789, 15623; Richardson 2003c, 4). The find of two late Bronze Age palstaves on Athelney itself (Somerset HER 10555) takes the use of this island site even further back in time, though its functions within the historic landscape at this period are not directly evidenced. The special and long-standing significance of Athelney as a secure place which had royal and probably also religious associations must go a long way to explaining why King Alfred chose this site amongst so many other possible island sites in the area.

The *burh* at Lyng was situated on the western end of this causeway on the end of a low ridge projecting eastwards into the Levels, its topographical situation reflected in the place-name (Dodgson 1996, 114). The *burh* and its connection with Athelney by a bridge and/or causeway are referred to in the account of Asser, as well as in the *Anglo-Saxon Chronicle* (above). David Hill has located cross-promontory defences on the west of the *burh* near the church, arguing on the basis of the length implied by the Burghal Hidage figure of one hundred hides that this line would have been the main 'town bank', and that the other sides of the settlement would have been unprotected except for 'a light line of defence on the marsh shore line' (Hill 1967, 66; cf. Hill 1996a, 209–11). This view, however, needs to be reassessed in the light of more recent fieldwork and excavation. As I have argued in detail elsewhere, and above, the hidage figures cannot be used to predict the size, position or length of the defences of the burh. The cross-promontory defences here would anyway have been considerably longer (approximately 700 feet) than the 402.5 feet which the hidage assessment would in theory have allowed. Furthermore, to suppose that a *burh* created by Alfred would have been left open to attack along most of its length, in particular from the river, is contrary to the tactical thinking of the times. This same point has been argued in relation to the defences of another small Burghal Hidage *burh* at Christchurch, Dorset (Haslam 2009).

The course of the defences of the *burh* at Lyng can therefore be more reasonably inferred as enclosing the whole area of the end of the spur on which it lies, following a line which is marked approximately by the 7m contour (Leach 1976, 32 fig.) which is followed by the ends of property boundaries on either side of the main street, and located somewhat above the level of the presumed former marshland outside it (Fig. 8.7). What could be interpreted as the remains of just such

a defensive bank has been located on the south side of this defended *enceinte* (Croft and Adkins 1988). The course of the former bank and either one or two external ditches suggested in this arrangement is indicated by distinct breaks of slope which can be observed in several places on both the northern and southern sides, though these are untested by excavation. The area of the *burh* thus defined is considerably smaller than that defined by previous commentators, who have in general followed Hill's suggestion that it extended to the flood-plain levels on all sides (Aston and Leech 1977; Aston 1984, 183–5 and fig. 67; Richardson 2003c, map 3). The eastern end of this defended enclosure would appear to merge into the bank of the Baltmoor causeway (above).

It must be inferred from this arrangement that the Baltmoor causeway between Lyng and Athelney is, in its late Saxon form, contemporary with the formation of the *burh* at Lyng, with its antecedents and origin – as indicated by the rather scrappy archaeological evidence discussed above – lying in the Iron Age or earlier. Miranda Richardson has suggested

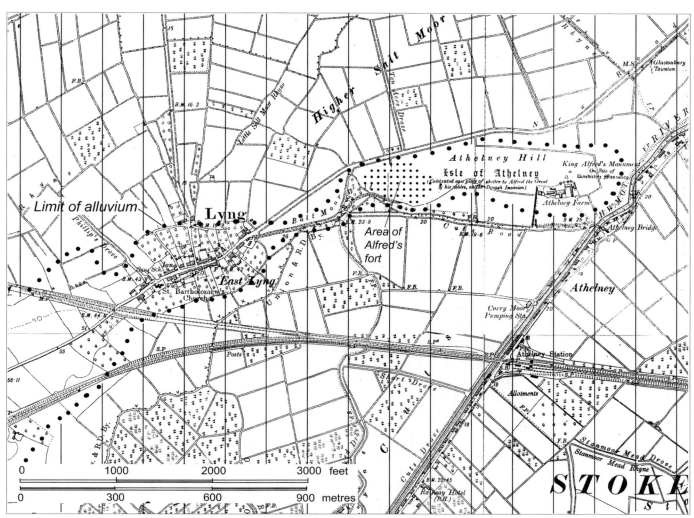

Fig. 8.6 Lyng and Athelney. North to top. Area of quaternary alluvium shown by vertical shading.

that the paucity of archaeological evidence from the Baltmoor Wall implies the existence of an alternative causeway between Lyng and Athelney to its north (Richardson 2003c, 6). However, not only has the Baltmoor wall not been investigated archaeologically to an extent which would demonstrate that it did not exist in the late Saxon period, but there is also no evidence of this alternative causeway. The topographical indications of its close association with the *burh* at both Lyng and the fortification at Athelney, suggested above, provides strong arguments for accepting that it was in existence when the new *burh* at Lyng was constructed, and that the causeway and the associated bridge over the former line of the Yeo river would have been constructed at this time, though on the line of a causeway which would already have been in existence. This original arrangement, though not entirely clear in detail, is reconstructed in Fig. 8.7.

Further support for this model of the layout of the *burh* at Lyng and its defences is given by the existence of several hollow ways leading towards the marshes on both sides of the main street (Fig. 8.7). One of these was found in an excavation by Peter Leach to have produced 'early medieval' pottery (of unspecified date) in silt layers at its base (Leach 1976, 33). It could be reasonably argued that if the silting and presumed disuse of this hollow way had occurred by the early medieval period, then this must have been preceded by an appreciable period of use to have created the hollow way in the first place. This evidence, combined with the fact that, as Leach has pointed out (Leach 1976, 32 and fig. 3; cf. Richardson 2003c, 7), these

hollow ways form symmetrically-placed elements in the layout of the settlement as a whole, they formed the main means of access to a line of defences on both sides of the *burh* from the central street. These defences would by inference have been serviced by an intra-mural track which would have enabled defenders to have reached all of its length. The origin of these may therefore be reasonably taken back to the formation of the late ninth-century *burh*, in which they would have formed planned components. The erosion of these tracks to form the medieval hollow ways would have happened after the defences were abandoned. This whole set-up suggests that the layout of the *burh* at Lyng was rather more sophisticated than previous commentators have allowed.

There is, furthermore, a reasonable doubt as to whether the cross-promontory defences on the western end belong to the period of the construction of the original Alfredian *burh*. The bank and ditch to the south of the church, noted by David Hill (Hill 1967, 65 and fig.), survive as much-spread features in a paddock and appear to extend some 250–300m from the northern to the southern edge of the spur. The bank is around 25m in width, with a ditch of the same order of magnitude immediately to its west. In both their size and arrangement these features are not typical of Anglo-Saxon *burh* defences. The defences at Cricklade, for instance, comprised a bank some 6–8m in width, separated from three relatively slight ditches by berms of the same width as the bank (Haslam 2003, period 1). At Lyng, the arrangement would appear to be more typical of an Iron Age cross-promontory defence than of a late Saxon

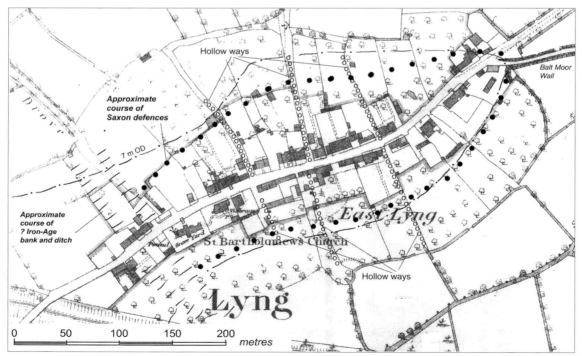

Fig. 8.7 Lyng. Extract from the OS 1:2500 map of 1886, with suggested course of Saxon defences and probable Iron-Age cross-promontory bank and ditch defences to the west. Position of hollow ways after Leach 1976.

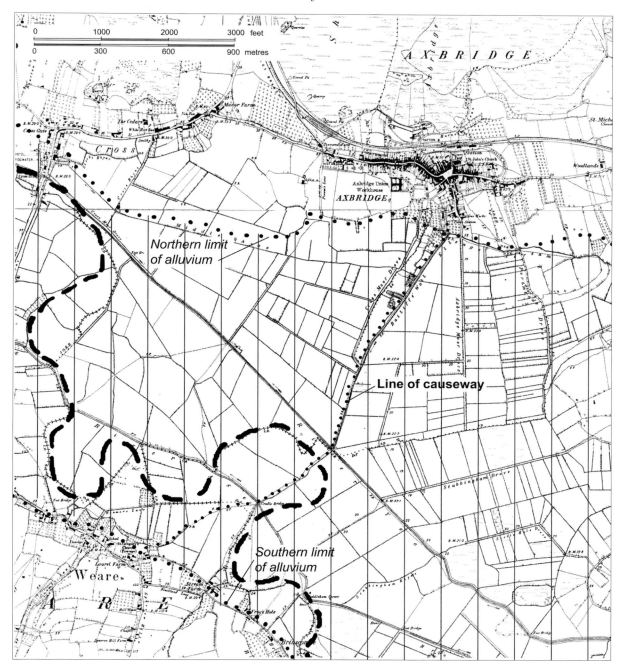

Fig. 8.8 Axbridge area, showing suggested line of the causeway (dotted line) running south-westwards from Axbridge to cross the Axe river and adjoining Levels to the high ground at Weare. The palaeochannel of the Axe (based partly on Batt 1975) is reconstructed with a broken line. Extract from the 1:10560 OS map of 1884. Area of quaternary alluvium is shown by vertical shading. North to top.

burh. This bank and ditch can be recognised in the disposition of features to the north of the church and main street, where a farm track appears to follow the line of the former ditch with a sharp rise in levels of at least 2m to its east. If this is the case, the relatively slighter burghal defences suggested above would have augmented this primary defence by creating a new defended space with a bank and one or more ditches which

would have butted up against the inside of the earlier bank. A parallel exists at Burpham in Sussex, where the temporary *burh* of the Burghal Hidage utilised similarly massive cross-promontory bank and ditch defences of the Iron Age.

On this interpretation, King Alfred would have taken occupation of a site in early 878 which was already defended by a ditched enclosure on Athelney itself, which would have had highly-charged royal associations and which may (as argued below) already have been functioning as a local and perhaps regional market and redistributive centre under royal control. This site would already have been connected to the mainland by a causeway and bridge, and its defences would, furthermore, have been augmented by the massive outworks crossing the promontory of land to the west. The complex as a whole would have taken little work to bring to defensive readiness. In effect, Alfred found at Athelney and Lyng an arrangement which was in essence a double *burh* connected with a bridge, a strategic device which had been used in Francia by Charlemagne in the 860s and which he and his successors in Mercia were to use to great effect later on (Abels 1988, 73–5). It is hardly surprising that the pre-existing defensive system at Lyng/Athelney (on the interpretation put forward here) was then strengthened through public obligations for labour, after Alfred's success in battle against the Viking forces, to form a *burh* in Alfred's new system.

Axbridge

The model developed here is of the existence of markets – or settlements with redistributive functions – at Langport and Lyng which were placed in a significant functional and spatial relationship to the royal estate centres and to royal citadels, and which were sited at important nodal points in the historic and strategic landscape which were already well developed by Alfred's time. The same model can also be applied to Axbridge, which was placed in an analogous position to the royal site at Cheddar to its east (Aston 1984, 173–4). The difference between Axbridge and the other two places discussed is that there is no identifiable citadel adjacent to it. As its name implies, this was named from a causeway (*brycg*; Dodgson 1996, 112–13; Parsons and Styles 2000, 51–7) which crossed the levels of the River Axe, with a presumed bridge over the river itself, and was sited at a point which in some way controlled access along this causeway and bridge as well as along the River Axe itself. The existence of the name in the Burghal Hidage has the same implications as that of Langport: the causeway and crossing over the Levels at Axbridge are likely to have already been in existence by the time the Burghal Hidage was drawn up and the *burh* at Axbridge created and named. This suggests the presence of a significant routeway which must have branched off southwards from the east-west road running from the royal site at Cheddar along the foot of the Mendips (Fig. 8.8). It may be the case, by analogy with those at Langport and Lyng, that the market at Axbridge, doubtless sited at its present position around and to the south of the church, could have been in existence as a settlement by the 870s. However, the new defended enclosure or *burh* of the burghal system of King Alfred of 878–9 was, as argued below, clearly a newly-laid-out defended settlement at the time, with the market and church sited outside its eastern gateway. This would imply that this pattern would have been a new creation at the time.

The existence by the 870s of the causeway at Axbridge crossing the Levels to the south and the inferred bridge over the Axe, the causeway and bridge at Langport associated with a market, and the existence at an early date of the causeway and bridge associated with the market centre at Lyng and the royal citadel at Athelney, all have considerable strategic implications for the period. As already argued, these features must have been a significant part of the strategic geography of the time before the creation of the respective *burhs* at these sites. An essential component of the model of *burh*-formation, discussed elsewhere by the writer and others, is that defended *burhs* were associated with bridges (Haslam 1984a, 262–7; Abels 1988, 69–78). These bridges would usually have formed the lowest crossing-places of the rivers on which these places were sited, and would themselves have had a defensive and military function. Nicholas Brooks has remarked some time ago that '… in [Saxon] England bridges were linked with fortresses … Bridge and fortress were a single military unit; together they secured the river crossing for the armies of the kingdom and together they prevented the movement of enemy troops either by land or by river' (Brooks 1971, 72). Richard Abels has pointed out that the *burhs* were also designed to operate with the reformed *fyrd*, the king's mobile field army, in such a way that the associated bridges and causeways not only blocked access to rivers by the Vikings but also gave the *fyrd* the mobility they required to carry out their function (Abels 1988, 63, 72). The association of *burh* and bridge is also shown, particularly at a number of places which I have discussed elsewhere (Haslam 2009, 108–9, and in relation to London/Southwark in Haslam 2010; this general association is examined in Gillmor 1988; Smyth 1995, 138–45; and Cooper 2006). That the public obligations of fortress-work, army service and work on bridges were incumbent on all landholders from the mid-ninth century in Wessex (and earlier in Mercia; Brooks 1971; Abels 1988, 43–57) shows how important these functions were in the strategic organisation of the landscape from this period. The existence of the name-forms of Langport and Axbridge by the 870s shows that these settlements, each with its associated bridge and causeway(s) across the Levels, as well as the causeway and bridge between Athelney and Lyng, would have played an important role in the maintenance of these strategic functions, very probably by the early or mid-ninth century. It is of interest that this *burh* and its causeway/bridge were not built at the royal site at Cheddar itself, with a crossing of the Levels between Cheddar and Clewer to its southwest, which would probably have formed a shorter routeway over the Axe and the marshy Levels. The position of the crossing at Axbridge would however have represented the lowest such crossing before the Levels widened out to the west.

The most likely route of the causeway at Axbridge can be traced for nearly 3 kilometres between the marketplace at Axbridge in a south-westerly direction to the church at Weare on the Isle of Wedmore on the other side of the valley of the present river Axe (Fig. 8.8). This causeway and bridge are not, however, shown in the analyses of the topography by any previous commentator (*e.g.* Batt 1975; Aston 1984, 172–4; Hill 1996, 189–90; Richardson 2003a). It leaves the southern side of the market at Axbridge probably along the line of Moorland Road (though there is an alternative route slightly to the west), forming a raised causeway (significantly named 'Bailiff's wall') running in a south-westerly alignment to cross the present course of the Axe at the site marked now by a footbridge. It continues along a clear alignment, shown by a crop mark in aerial photographs, to end at a position on higher ground near Weare church. This southern part of the route fits with the course of the palaeochannel of the earlier river Axe, reconstructed in Fig. 8.8 from aerial photographs (based partly on Batt 1975, 23 fig. B). The primacy of this route in the landscape (though not its absolute age) is demonstrated by the fact that the field systems on either side of its entire length are laid out on different alignments.

In gaining a clear view of the strategic significance of the *burh* at Axbridge and its associated causeway it is important to note that this causeway and river crossing would have been considerably more important in the early medieval period than today. Before about AD 1000 the River Brue flowed past Glastonbury to join with the Axe to the east of Axbridge, before the upper reaches of the Brue were diverted to a new channel to the south of the Isle of Wedmore at around this time (Williams 1970, 64; Rippon 2004, 96 fig. 2, 97 fig. 3, 98). This would have made the Rivers Brue/Axe and the Parrett the major drainage channels of the Somerset Levels to the sea in the tenth century and earlier. The River Brue/Axe would therefore have been particularly important from a strategic point of view in the ninth century, in that it would have represented a significant potential point of access to Viking ships deep into Somerset. The appearance of estuarine alluvium 10km to the east of Axbridge (Rippon 2004, 97 fig. 3) shows that the palaeochannel of the Axe would have been tidal, and therefore navigable, upstream of the Axbridge causeway and bridge. These considerations provide the essential context for the siting of a *burh* at a significant crossing of this major river, in that it would not only have offered protection to the adjacent royal site of Cheddar to its east, as well as the monastery of Glastonbury and its estates further upriver, but would also have provided a strategically-important river crossing enabling and facilitating movement of the local militias or *fyrd*. The occurrence of the name-form containing the *-brycg* element in the Burghal Hidage, arguably of 878–9, suggests that this causeway and bridging point over the river had been a feature of the landscape for some time before this date.

The siting of Langport has similar strategic implications. As already stated, the fact of the existence of the causeway forming the 'long port' by the 870s implies that the bridge was in existence at this time as well: the tidal river could not have been crossed by this route at this point by means of a ford. That the association of *burhs* and bridges is documented

from the middle of the ninth century in Wessex, noted above, carries the implication that Langport could well represent an instance of the application of this strategic device to the defence of Wessex which pre-dates the implementation of the more systematic provision of defensive points represented by the system described in the Burghal Hidage. The crossing at Langport would also, as with the causeway at Axbridge, have facilitated the movement of the *fyrd* across the Levels of Somerset. It is not beyond the bounds of possibility to suggest that King Alfred and his entourage would have used this crossing on journeys to and from Athelney and Somerton. In a similar way the causeway between Athelney and Lyng, and the bridge across the former line of the River Yeo between them, would have performed the same strategic function at this early date. The provision for the defence of the Levels shown by Axbridge, Langport and Lyng before the more systematic provisions by King Alfred mirrors the provision of defensive measures against the Vikings in south Devon in the mid-ninth century, discussed by Terry Slater and Paul Luscombe (Slater 1991; Luscombe 2005).

The *burh* at Axbridge

A location for the *burh* at Axbridge has been proposed by Michael Batt to the south of the market place, where it is seen as comprising a sub-rectangular area with a central street along Moorland Street (Batt 1975). The location of the *burh* in this position, though regarded as problematical, is nevertheless accepted by later commentators (Aston 1984, 172–4; Hill 1996, 189–90; Richardson 2003a, 7–8). Batt's hypothesis is based on slight indications in the physical and built topography, combined with two other premises: (a) that the 400 hides given to Axbridge in the Burghal Hidage would indicate a length of the defended perimeter as being 1650 feet (550yds) or 503 metres; and (b) that the plan of a typical *burh* of the Burghal Hidage would have been rectangular or nearly so.

There are, however, a number of reasons for regarding these factors as having little evidential value, and for proposing an alternative site for the *burh* immediately to the west of the market area. As has been argued in relation to Langport (above), the formula in the appendix to version A of the document cannot be used predictively to determine the lengths of the defences of a burh. The four hundred hides given to Axbridge in the Burghal Hidage cannot therefore be taken as an indicator of either the length or the position of the defended circuit. The rectilinear character of the layout of the *burhs* included in the Alfredian system is furthermore only shown by the larger *burhs* on new sites (Cricklade, Wallingford, Wareham). Even in these, the main emphasis of the new layout associated with their construction appears to have been a single main spinal street with side streets – a pattern also shown by most of the new *burhs* within earlier Roman defences (Biddle and Hill 1971; Biddle 1976). The preferred plan of these *burhs* appears to have been of a defended enclosure within which was laid out, or which incorporated, a single central market street, with or without side streets, whose dimensions and proportions reflected the local natural or built topographical conditions (see the example of Christchurch, which I have examined recently in detail: Haslam 2009), rather than assuming a plan determined by some abstract model imposed from without. It is not therefore appropriate to use these arguments in determining either the position or the size of the defended *enceinte* at Axbridge. Furthermore, the defences of the suggested *burh* are nowhere visible as earthworks on the line given or in any other position on the south side of the market area, in particular in undeveloped open ground on the eastern side. This is in contrast to the defences of other late Saxon *burhs* at, for instance, Cricklade, Wallingford, Wareham, Portchester and Christchurch, where defensive banks are (or were until recently) still visible in open ground. There is, furthermore, little relationship between the suggested line of defences and demonstrably early property boundaries within the area of the proposed burh.

Secondly, the position of the suggested *burh* does not directly control the main routeway along the foot of the Mendips, which runs east-west through the market area. As Miranda Richardson has argued, any such routeway is unlikely to have taken a course across the low-lying ground of the Levels, as Batt has suggested, but would rather have followed a more direct and dry route along the line of the foothills of the Mendips (Richardson 2003a, 7–8). It must be inferred therefore that it was the course of the early road, which approached the market area of Axbridge from the east and which continued westwards in the same way along the Mendip foothills (and perpetuated in the modern A371), which was the primary routeway in the Saxon period. It would be expected therefore that the *burh* would have been positioned on this east-west route along the foot of the Mendips within easy access to the causeway. Just such a solution is put forward below. In short, there is little positive evidence for Batt's hypothesis of the existence of the *burh* to the south of the market area.

There is however an alternative site for the *burh* which meets many of the criteria for a quasi-urban burh, and which obviates many of the difficulties inherent in Batt's proposal. It is suggested that the *burh* was placed astride the main east-west route along the foot of the Mendips on the western edge of the market area (Figs 8.9, 8.10). This area comprises closely-packed burgages fronting onto the north and south sides of the present High Street. Those on the south side have clearly been laid out between the street and a continuous property boundary, which today is marked by a considerable break in slope contained by a substantial wall. This feature may be reasonably inferred, in this reconstruction, to mark the line of the outer edge of the bank of the original burghal defences. At its eastern end the regular shapes of the tenement boundaries are distorted to conform to a curved alignment, which may be taken as reflecting an earlier boundary which curved round to the north to meet the putative gate of these defences on the line

of the main street of the *burh* at its junction with the market area to its east. (The details of this arrangement are fudged on the 25 inch first edition of the Ordnance Survey of 1886, and are left blank on the otherwise detailed Tithe Award map of 1839. The layout is best seen on aerial photographs, for which see Google Earth). It can be inferred from this arrangement that the layout of the tenements on the south side of the High Street are secondary to, or contemporary with, the formation of this envelope. A similar pattern is shown by the tenement boundaries on the north side of the street.

The western end of this suggested enclosure is marked by the furthest western end of the wall line on the south side of the street mentioned above, at the line now marked by a modern street. Further west, the regular burgage plots along the main street (West Street) take a different shape, and clearly belong to a different plan-unit. This hiatus in the regular layout of the properties to both the north and south sides of the High Street suggests the position of the western gateway on the street, at a position where the road begins to turn and to slope down to the west. This topographical hypothesis is strengthened by the fact that this suggested western alignment of the putative defended circuit marked the western limit of the borough of Axbridge, until the borough and the parish of Axbridge were extended westwards in the early seventeenth century (Richardson 2003a, 4, 10). This alignment, significantly, marks the position of a re-entrant of the parish of Compton Bishop in the Tithe Award map of 1839 (Fig. 8.9).

The northern defences of this enclosure, though not so clearly defined by the ends of property boundaries as the line on the south, can be suggested as being approximately equidistant from the southern defences, along a line marked by the ends of straight burgage plots facing onto the north of the High Street. The northern part of this line, though not obviously determined by any break in slope, nevertheless fits well into the space formed by the lines of the long properties to the east and to the course of a back lane. (It is possible, however, that the details of the micro-topography at this point have been obscured or altered by the building of the railway embankment immediately to its north.) This 'envelope' of burgages, which can be considered as a single 'plan unit' laid out at one moment in time (Lilley 2000; Baker and Holt 2004, 11–13), is defined on its north-eastern side by a contrasting block of burgages on a completely different alignment which front onto the northern side of the market place, and which have long plots which reach to a back lane to their north (Fig. 8.9).

The recognition that these topographical features are a survival of the former existence of the defended *burh* of Axbridge fits in with the wider topography of the place as a whole. Apart from the market-place, it is clearly the primary morphological element in the layout of the settlement as a whole. The road leading to the causeway southwards across the Levels, described above, leads to the southern side of the market, forming a natural layout with these plan-elements.

Secondary development along the High Street to the west of the burh, indicated by the extension of burgages on either side of the street of a contrasting size and shape, would have been the expected outcome of the prosperity of Axbridge as a marketing centre in the later Saxon and early medieval periods (Aston 1984, 172–4). The only difficulty with this suggested layout of the defences is that the northern line of the *burh* lies on an uphill slope, leaving it somewhat more vulnerable to attack from this side. Here, however, the *burh*-builders would have been left with little choice as to its exact location. The advantage of a defended *burh* in this position, however, would have been that it would have directly controlled all movement along the east-west route to and from the royal site at Cheddar; it would have dominated and therefore controlled activity in the market

immediately outside its gate, facilitating the collection of tolls by the agents of the king; and it would also have controlled access along the causeway to the south.

The relationship of Axbridge to the royal and minster site at Cheddar, only 3km to the east, is of some significance in terms of the general model proposed in this paper. John Blair has argued that the foundation of the *burh* at Axbridge would have been associated with a 'local restructuring of royal assets' at Cheddar in the late ninth or early tenth century, and has wondered ' ... why the borough was built 3 kilometres away rather than at Cheddar itself' (Blair 1997, 119–20). The answer to this, which derives from the analysis given above, lies in the key relationship of the new *burh* at Axbridge to the defensive causeway and bridge over the Axe river, which was arguably

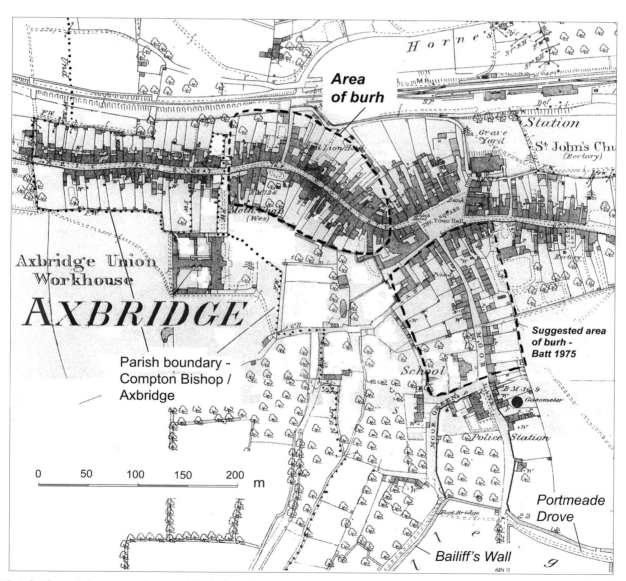

Fig. 8.9 Axbridge, with suggested area of burh from Batt 1975, and area of burh proposed here. Also showing parish boundary – Axbridge to the east, Compton Bishop to the west. Extract from the 1st ed. 1:2500 OS map of 1886. North to top.

of particular strategic importance from at least the mid-ninth century. Furthermore, it is commonly said that the *burh* was built to protect the royal site at Cheddar. But Blair's reappraisal of the dating and context of the royal palace at Cheddar has suggested that the palace was moved to Cheddar from an earlier site at Wedmore in the period 900–920, or possibly slightly earlier in the reign of Alfred (Blair 1997, 119). Given that the construction of the *burh* at Axbridge can be dated to 878–9, it would appear on this interpretation that the move of the royal palace to Cheddar could be seen as the consequence rather than the cause of the construction of the burh.

However, it would be consistent with the rather loose archaeological dating evidence from Cheddar which is the subject of Blair's reappraisal to suggest an alternative solution – that both the construction of the *burh* at a site which was already of some strategic significance and the relocation of the royal palace to an already existing minster site, were conceived as a single concurrent episode of restructuring of the administrative and strategic landscape of the area. As Blair has pointed out, it is very probable that a market would have developed at Cheddar at this time, in relation to both the royal palace and the minster sites, if Axbridge had not performed this role. This process can thus be seen as a way of facilitating and leveraging royal control of both the strategic and the marketing aspects of settlement development. These aspects are discussed further below. A not unimportant aspect of this (although one which is not so far directly evidenced) could well have been the protection and consolidation of the royal interest in the mining of lead and silver from the Mendips, as has been suggested in the case of the *burh* at Bath in north Somerset and the role of Lydford on Dartmoor in Devon in relation to the mining of tin (Maddicot 1989, 34–38, 46; Haslam 1984a, 256–9, 277).

As part of this process, it is envisaged that the *burh* was laid out at the most suitable position astride the routeway along the foot of the Mendips (above) to enable it to act as a defence of the causeway across the marshes to the south. It may even have been the case that a temporary fortification could have been provided at the southern end of this causeway at Weare. The layout of this enclosure at Axbridge suggests that the establishment of the closely-packed burgages, which can be seen on modern maps (Fig. 8.9), would have formed part of its original layout. At this time (or perhaps subsequently) the church would have been placed adjacent to a market area outside the eastern gateway of the enclosure, its small parish carved out of the larger minster parish to its east. At the same time, the town inhabitants would have had the use of an area of arable and/or pasture land, indicated by the existence of the name Portmeade Drove in the sixteenth century (Richardson 2003a, 4). This situation is paralleled at Langport (above). All these features form an ensemble of inter-functional elements which together indicate that the new *burh* is likely to have been planned as a newly-founded quasi-urban settlement from its inception.

Watchet

The relationship of the non-urban hilltop fortress at Langport and the *port* at its foot, both developing in close functional relationship to the neighbouring royal sites at Somerton and Curry Rivel, invites comparison of the Burghal Hidage *burh* at Watchet with the nearby fortress at Daws Castle (Aston 1984, 192–3; McAvoy 1986; Gathercole 2003, 6–7, Haslam 2011a). Both appear to have developed their respective defensive and commercial functions in relationship to the royal sites at Old Cleeve (3.5km to the south-west), Williton (2.5km to the south-east), Carhampton (6.5km to its west) and Cannington to its east (Aston 1984, 193; Dunning 1985, 151). This seems to have been the context for the payment in Domesday of the third penny of the 'borough right' of the royal estates of Carhampton, Williton, Cannngton and North Petherton, which was payable at the royal estate centre of Old Cleeve (Thorn and Thorn 1980, 1.13), just as the thirty-two burgesses of Axbridge are mentioned under, and presumably paid their dues to, the royal hall at Cheddar, and the thirty-four burgesses at Langport who are mentioned under and paid dues to the royal hall at Somerton. Similarly, the burgesses at Ilchester were appurtenant to the royal site at Milborne Port, and paid their dues there (see below). It seems likely that this 'borough right' would have represented the payment of the earl's third penny from dues from the borough of Watchet, which is otherwise not mentioned in the Domesday account (Tait 1936, 61 n. 3). The parish of St Decuman, its church probably a Celtic foundation (Calder 2004, 16–24) lying to the west of Watchet (Fig. 8.11), included Watchet and the royal site at Williton, 2.5km to its south (Dunning 1985, 142–3).

The discussion of the context of the development of the *burh* at Watchet within the landscape has been significantly widened by the results of the excavations conducted at Daws Castle, a hillfort on the coast immediately to the west of the town, in 1982 (McAvoy 1986). I have made a detailed case that the hillfort was constructed as a fort in the late eighth or early ninth century as part of a series of such forts, at least in south-west England, and that it would have been replaced by the *burh* at Watchet itself as one element in King Alfred's new defensive measures of 878–9 (Haslam 2011a). It is also argued that the second-phase defences observed in excavations at Daws Castle represent a secure fortress commissioned by King Æthelred in the late tenth or very early eleventh century, which would have been analogous in scale and function to the archaeologically better-documented example at South Cadbury (Alcock 1995, 154–7). The reorganisation of the defences on this part of the west Somerset coast, in the form of a *burh* which would have afforded some protection to the royal estates and their centres, can be placed in the same context as the construction of other *burhs* at South Cadbury and Old Sarum, at a time in the late tenth or the first decade of the eleventh century, and as a response to Viking raiding on coastal areas from the 980s, Fig. 8.11.

This leaves open the relationship of Watchet itself with the fortress at Daws Castle, which must have been a distinctive

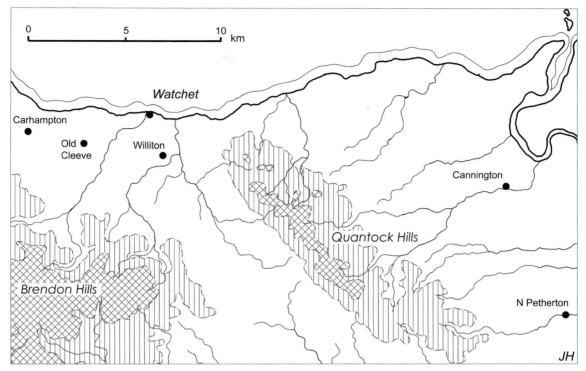

Fig. 8.10 Watchet and its area, in relationship to the royal manorial centres of Carhampton, Old Cleeve, Williton Cannington and North Petherton. North to top.

feature of the landscape in 878–9. There are two possibilities which could characterise this relationship. Firstly, the earlier hilltop fortress at Daws Castle could have been reused by Alfred as a temporary fort, as was clearly the case with Pilton and Halwell in Devon, and others such as Bredy (South Dorset), Chisbury (Wiltshire), Burpham (Sussex) and Eashing (Surrey). The development of Watchet could therefore be seen as resulting from the replacement of the hilltop *burh* at a later date, a process which can be recognised in the replacement of Pilton by an urban *burh* at Barnstaple and Halwell by urban *burhs* at Totnes and Kingsbridge (Haslam 1984a, 259–75), Chisbury by Marlborough (Haslam 1984b, 94–102) and Eashing by Guildford (O'Connell and Poulton 1984, 46). This creation of new urban *burhs* as replacements for non-urban temporary fortresses has been argued by the writer as taking place in the later ninth century as a response to the new Viking incursions of the 890s (Haslam 2005, 137 n. 103; Haslam 2009, 103–4), rather than in the 930s in the reign of Athelstan, as argued by David Hill (2000).

The inclusion of the named *burh* at Watchet in the Burghal Hidage would suggest, however, that the hillfort at Daws Castle was not used in the new Alfredian system of 878–9, but that the new *burh* of this date was located at Watchet itself. The archaeological evidence of the phase 1 defences at Daws Castle shows that these primary defences had not been refurbished at any time before the early eleventh-century phase of burh-

building suggested above, but had been allowed to degrade naturally (Haslam 2011a). In logistical terms, the provision of adequate defences for a new *burh* on the hilltop would have been a much more expensive process, in terms of the utilisation of available human resources, than providing for the defence of a somewhat smaller site at sea level. The garrisoning of the defences of the new *burh* at Watchet would have been made immeasurably easier by virtue of the fact that it would have been provided with a resident population. By analogy with Langport, it seems probable that the present settlement at Watchet would have functioned as a royal market and port for sea-borne trade supported by, and serving the interests of, the royal centres of Carhampton, Williton, Old Cleeve, Cannington and North Petherton at a period rather earlier than the 870s, possibly acting as a coastal emporium for sea-going trading, which would have been controlled by these royal sites throughout the middle Saxon period (Aston 1986a, 49–54). This would place in context its choice as the site of the fortified *burh* of the new system put in place by King Alfred in 878–9 in order both to enhance the security of the adjacent seaboard and to facilitate the control of this trade by the king. It is likely, however, that the earlier defences and the hilltop site at Daws Castle would have been used on a temporary basis in association with the garrisoned *burh* below as a look-out post and signalling station, a function which can also be reasonably postulated in the use of the hilltop site at Langport.

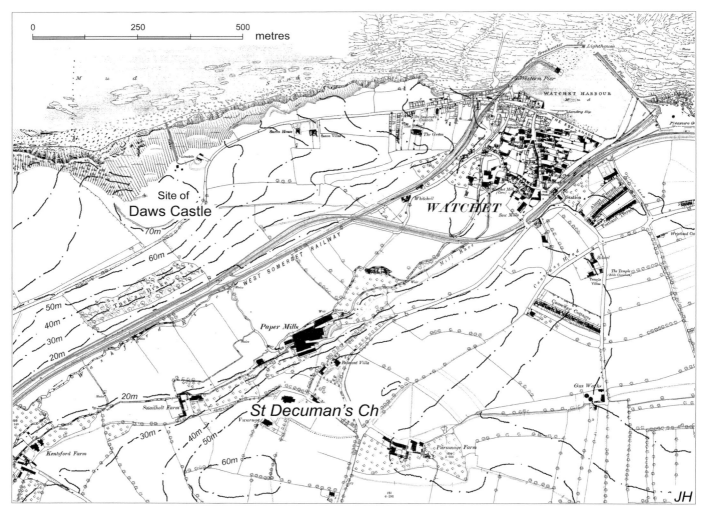

Fig. 8.11 Watchet and Daws Castle in relation to the parish church of St Decuman. Extract from OS 1:10,560 map of 1884. North to top. Contours in metres above OD.

The existence of a *burh* at Watchet, while indicated by the arguments given above, is not however so easily inferred from the surviving topography of the town (Fig. 8.12). Though Dunning has implied that Swain Street, the main spinal street of the town, grew from the medieval market place at the northern end of the town (Dunning 1985), most commentators are agreed that Swain Street marked the central street of the *burh* on the crest of a low spur of land marked by the river Washford to its west (Aston 1984, 192–4; Hill 1996, 223–4; Gathercole 2003, 6–7). The break of slope along this line is indicative of the existence of defences here. Various episodes of coastal erosion, known to have occurred from the late medieval period onwards (Dunning 1985, 146–7), have however destroyed some, if not most, of the *burh* as originally laid out (Gathercole 2003, 6), as of Daws Castle.

Ilchester (Figs 8.13, 8.14)

I have given reasons elsewhere for considering that the former Roman town of Ilchester would have formed part of the system of *burhs* which was set out in the Burghal Hidage (Haslam 2013a). It is suggested that this was omitted from the original manuscript which formed the progenitor of the two extant versions which have survived, just as various other places were omitted in different versions of these later copies (Rumble 1996, 37–8). There are two significant strands of evidence from which this can be inferred. The first is that the addition of the hides of the burghal territory of the missing *burh* would be necessary to bring the total number of hides in the Burghal Hidage into line with those in the Domesday shire (the latter being greater than the former). The reasoning for this is discussed elsewhere (Haslam 2013a). The second is its heterogeneous tenure shown in Domesday, in which it is

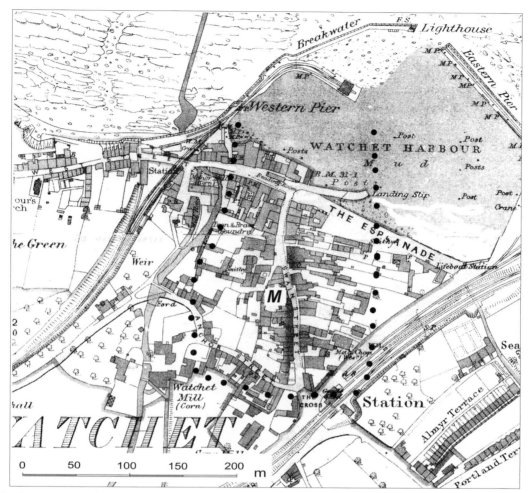

Fig. 8.12 Watchet – suggested area of burh, with possible central market area, now infilled. Extract from the OS 1:2500 map.

clearly shown to have been a market settlement dependent on the royal site of Milborne Port. Milborne Port also had its own market, and to it pertained 107 burgesses 'in' Ilchester who paid 20s. This relationship has clear functional and spatial parallels to the *burh* at Axbridge, where there were 32 burgesses under the entry for Cheddar who paid 20s 'in' Axbridge (Thorn and Thorn 1980, 1,2), and the royal manor of Somerton, which had 'a borough which is called Langport in which 34 burgesses live who paid 15s' (*ibid.*, 1,1).

Of significance for the present thesis is that there are clear indications in the archaeological and historical evidence relating to Ilchester for the development of central place and marketing functions of the site in the century or more prior to its likely inclusion as a *burh* in King Alfred's system of *burhs* which is otherwise listed in the Burghal Hidage. The early development of the nearby minster at Northover, on the site of a large well-organised Roman cemetery of late fourth-century date to the north of the former Roman town (Dunning, 1975, 44–6; Leach 1994, 10; Richardson 2002, 9, 11; Costen 2011, 148–9) would, as Costen has emphasised, have played a key

role in the maintenance of Ilchester's status as a central place throughout the middle Saxon period (Costen 2011, 148–9). In strategic terms, a *burh* at Ilchester would have provided a defence of eastern Somerset, including the royal centres at Bruton, Frome and Yeovil (Barker 1986).

Discussion and conclusions

An important outcome of the reassessment of the evidence relating to these five places in Somerset has enabled new solutions to be put forward concerning the layout and location of their defences, which to some extent clarifies their function within the development of the historic landscape, in ways which are susceptible to further testing by archaeological and other means.

It has also been the intention to show that the relationship of the *burhs* both to the physical and built topography of their sites and to the wider landscape can give insights into two main aspects of developments of the period. Firstly, some aspects of the sites and name-forms of these *burhs* open a window

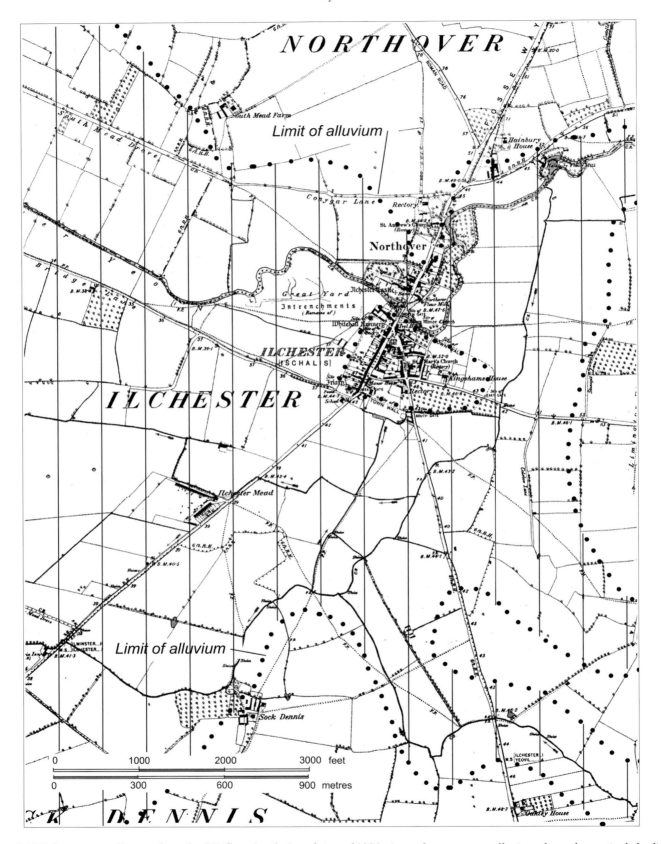

Fig. 8.13 Ilchester area. Extract from the OS 6" to 1 mile 1st edition of 1891. Area of quarternary alluvium shown by vertical shading.

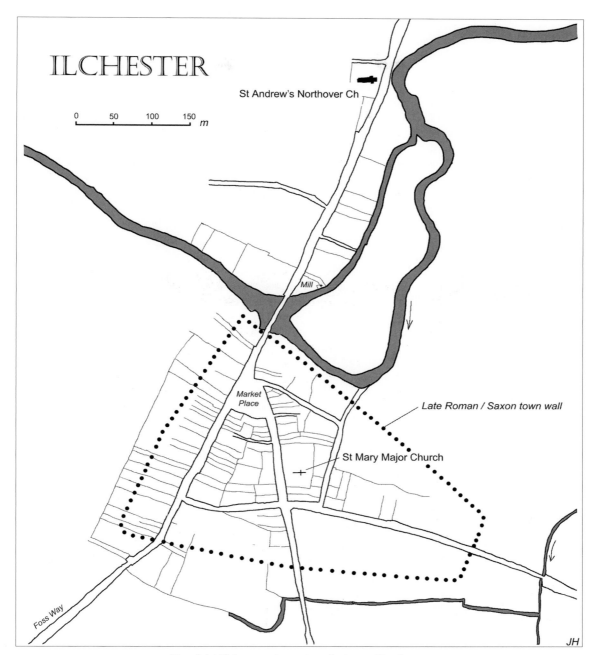

Fig. 8.14 Ilchester, shown in relation to Northover.

into a landscape organised for strategic purposes before the creation of the new burghal system by King Alfred in 878–9. There can be discerned in this evidence the outlines of a programme involving the development of hillforts to provide rudimentary local defences and to create lookout and signalling posts or beacons, in association with bridges and causeways which were designed to facilitate movements of military levies. Some elements of these would undoubtedly have been newly constructed for the purpose by means of a system of public

obligations for work on bridges and fortifications and for garrison duty. The existence of causeways and bridges which had a military or defensive function in the middle Saxon period, which may be reasonably seen as forming part of a coherent system of which the forts were a part, can be inferred at both Athelney/Lyng and at Langport, while the existence of an early causeway and bridge is clearly indicated at Axbridge. An early fort or ungarrisoned *burh* appears to have been newly constructed at Daws Castle near Watchet, arguably also as an element in such a system. I have discussed the provision of such defensive measures at this period elsewhere (Haslam 2011a), and similar points have been made by John Baker and Stuart Brookes (2011, 106–8).

The association with royal estate centres shown by all the *burhs* of the late ninth century discussed here – either singly (Axbridge with Cheddar, Ilchester with Milborne Port), as pairs (Langport with Somerton and probably Curry Rivel, Lyng with South Petherton and also possibly Curry Rivel), or with several (Watchet, as a centre for a large estate comprising Carhampton, Williton, Cannington, North Petherton and Old Cleeve) – which is shown clearly in the evidence from Domesday (see Fig. 8.2), is also of some significance for the interpretation of their wider economic and social functions within the landscape. Recent work suggesting that the redistribution of food renders brought to royal estate centres played a large part in the economy of large royal *wics* in the middle Saxon period (Cowie 2004) emphasises the equivalent importance of these royal estate centres to the development of smaller inland marketing or redistribution sites such as the places under discussion. The development of markets at other royal centres in Somerset, recognisable as boroughs at the time of Domesday (such as Frome, Bruton, Crewkerne and others), appears to have extended this pattern over much if not most of the shire. This pattern is also repeated in other areas of Wessex. This carries the implication that 'rural' – or possibly quasi-urban – markets in the eighth and ninth centuries developed as redistributive centres under the control of the king on sites which bore a close relationship to these royal centres, either at these centres or nearby. The complexities of this pattern are illustrated by the relationship of Axbridge to a newly-established royal site at Cheddar, which is seen as a new development of the 880s in which royal control was consolidated in a new way over a landscape which was already organised for a strategic response to the defence of a vulnerable river system.

The *burhs* discussed here may be considered as likely sites of such royal markets at which these functions had already developed to an extent by the time they were chosen for their strategic potential as defensive locations in 878–9. This is clearly indicated by the name-form of Langport, which suggests the development of a *port* by that time at a site which would have been of regional importance, both strategically and economically, in being sited near an important crossing of the River Parrett. Ilchester/Northover appears also to have acted in the same capacity at the head of the Parrett river system. Similarly at Lyng, a probable early market site of the same type appears to have developed in close relationship to the royal 'citadel' and putative 'productive' site of Athelney, and to other neighbouring royal estate centres, including Curry Rivel and North Petherton. Axbridge was sited at another nodal position in relation to the royal estate centre at Cheddar in that it commanded access across the Levels, as well as along the foot of the Mendips. It may well have been involved in the redistribution of silver and lead produced by the royal

exploitation of mines on the Mendips. The development of Watchet as such a marketing site can be inferred from its nodal position on the coast and its central relationship to the four royal estates which covered the coastal area of the western part of Somerset shown in Domesday, for which it may have acted as a coastal trading outlet or *wic*, possibly from the eighth century.

The choice of these sites reflects not only their strategic significance but also their regional accessibility, which would have enabled and facilitated the distribution of commodities controlled from these royal estate centres. The development of these market functions well before the establishment of the burghal system, with its new system of fortified markets and new towns, seems to be implied in the reform of the coinage by King Alfred in the mid-870s (Blackburn 1998), which suggests that already by this time Alfred was taking active steps to exert control over marketing and the redistribution of commodities, as well as of taxation. The same network of communications is likely therefore to have also served in a military capacity, and to have been supported as public works by the system of obligations already mentioned.

While this model may lack substantive evidence in the form of concentrations of (or even single) artefacts of the period from excavated contexts (apart from the evidence from Athelney), the choice of these sites as *burhs* in King Alfred's provision of a defensive system for the whole of Wessex, described in the contemporary Burghal Hidage (which I have argued as having been put in place in the years 878–9; Haslam 2005, 129–33) can be seen as being in part a development and consolidation of earlier defensive arrangements for the region. Although these *burhs* can best be seen as elements in a new *system* which was created at this time, the evidence described here also suggests that this system incorporated and built upon an earlier raft of defensive measures which had been put in place from at least as early as the middle of the ninth century, which may well have been conceived and set out in a more-or-less systematic way. It can be argued, as already indicated, that the choice of these sites as *burhs* also reflected the need of the king to provide a defence for sites where marketing or redistributive activities were concentrated.

It is perhaps significant that in Somerset these new defended *burhs* (with the exception of Bath which filled a gap in the northern part of the shire) were not created at those 'marketing' sites associated directly with the centres of early royal estates, such as Frome, Crewkerne and others, which in a middle Saxon context would have been of equivalent importance in the local economy. The placing of these new *burhs* of the Burghal Hidage system at points which were most accessible to routeways which had strategic potential, illustrated particularly clearly in the case of Ilchester, would also have been a factor in the function of these sites in the flow of goods around the countryside, as well as in the provision of renders to support these centres. The function of the *burhs* can therefore be understood both in terms of further enabling and concentrating the control of these functions in the king's hands, as well as countering movement by hostile forces.

An important and often overlooked aspect of the *burhs* in the Burghal Hidage system is that the new *burhs* became – or rather were created as – the centres of a nexus of tributary relationships by means of which the king was able to enforce the provision of services by the holders of land within the burghal territories which had been created around each *burh* for its upkeep. This would of course have included work on the construction and maintenance of the *burhs* themselves. For this reason, I have elsewhere called these 'territories of obligation' (Haslam 2012). In a more general sense, the system of which they were components would thereby have been a significant instrument by which the king would have consolidated the political control of his kingdom, an aspect which I have explored in detail elsewhere (Haslam 2012, chapters 8 and 9; Haslam 2013b; see also Abels 1988, 138–41). As can be shown in the cases of the burghal territories of Wiltshire and Hampshire (Haslam 2012, chapters 3 and 4), and those of Oxfordshire, Berkshire and Buckinghamshire (Haslam 2012, chapter 11) as well as Devon (Brooks 1996, 138–41), it would be expected that the hidages recorded in the Burghal Hidage would represent a record of the extent of these burghal territories. The delineation of these burghal territories within the envelope of the shire in Somerset, which in general would have been based on the extent of already existing royal, possibly hundredal, units, would be a major step forward in the elucidation of the landscape organisation of the period. It is hoped, however, that this will be explored on another occasion.

Note

1 The archaeological information in this paragraph is taken from a preliminary report on excavations by Time Team in 2002, prepared on behalf of Somerset Co. Council, in advance of full publication. I am grateful to Johanna Zetterstrom-Sharp of L-P Archaeology for providing me with a copy of this report. For the Time Team excavations, see http://www.channel4.com/history/microsites/T/timeteam/2003_athelney.html .

9

The Mints of Anglo-Saxon and Anglo-Scandinavian England, 871–1066

Martin Allen

The publication of David Hill's *An Atlas of Anglo-Saxon England* was a landmark in the development of Anglo-Saxon studies. The coinage was not neglected in this groundbreaking survey of the history, economy and administration of Anglo-Saxon England (Hill 1981, 126–30). Hill provided nine maps of the English mints from Alfred's accession in 871 to 1066, showing the great increase in the number of mints over this period. Tables of the mints known in each reign or coin type revealed the intermittent or ephemeral nature of the activity of many of the mints. A map originally developed for the Æthelred II millenary conference in 1978 used the numbers of moneyers known at each mint between Edgar's reform of the English coinage in about 973 and 1066 as a measure of the relative sizes of their outputs, demonstrating the dominance of London and a few other major urban centres, particularly in the southern and eastern parts of England (Hill 1978, 214–17; 1981, 126, 130). The contents of the Chester (Pemberton's Parlour) hoard (*c.* 980) were used to examine the integration of the coins of various mints into the currency a few years after Edgar's reform, drawing upon Michael Metcalf's work on this subject for the 1978 conference (Hill 1981, 126; Metcalf 1978, 168–9).

More than three decades have now passed since the publication of Hill's *Atlas* and during that time our understanding of the Anglo-Saxon and Anglo-Scandinavian coinages issued between 871 and 1066 has been revolutionised by major new coin-finds and archaeological discoveries, and by considerable research in this field. It is the purpose of this chapter to review these developments. I shall begin with the coinages of Wessex and Mercia in the last three decades of the ninth century before reviewing the many recent advances in our knowledge of the Anglo-Scandinavian coinages of the Danelaw, and finally turning to the coinages of the Anglo-Saxon kings in the tenth and eleventh centuries.

The reign of Alfred and the origins of Anglo-Scandinavian coinage

The publication of three important papers by Mark Blackburn and Simon Keynes on the coinage of Alfred and his Mercian contemporaries in 1998 constituted a major step forward in our understanding of the monetary and political history of the period (Blackburn 1998; Keynes 1998; Blackburn and Keynes 1998). Blackburn and Keynes used the evidence of the coinage to propose that London did not fall under Danish control in 877 when the kingdom of Mercia was divided between the English and the Danes, as had been the general assumption of historians of the period. In the second half of the 870s the Cross-and-Lozenge coinage was minted for Alfred and Ceolwulf II of Mercia in London, Winchester and possibly other places, and for Alfred and Archbishop Æthelred in Canterbury (Keynes 1998, 16–18; Blackburn 1998, 114–16; Blackburn 2003b, 212–14, 216–17). In this construction of the evidence Alfred had authority over London after Ceolwulf II's disappearance from the scene in *c.* 879, and his London Monogram type was part of a monetary reform in about 880 and not a special issue celebrating the occasion in 886 when he 'occupied' or 'established' (*gesette*) London, according to the *Anglo-Saxon Chronicle* (Plummer 1892–99, I, 80–1). A Viking force was ejected from London in 883 after a siege, but they had not been there since the late 870s, and Keynes interpreted the 'occupation' of 886 as a relocation of the existing commercial settlement of *Lundenwic* west of the Fleet to Alfred's new *burh* inside the old Roman walls (Keynes 1998, 19–34). Jeremy Haslam (2009) has argued that Alfred founded the new *burh* in 879–80, shortly after Guthrum's Vikings retreated to their independent kingdom in East Anglia and the Viking army based at Fulham moved to the Continent, but this is far from certain.

The monetary reform of *c.* 880 involved an increase in the weight of the penny to a new standard of some 24½ grains (*c.* 1.6g) and the introduction of the Two-Line or Horizontal type, with mint-signed issues at London (the London Monogram type), Canterbury, Exeter, Gloucester, Oxford and Winchester, and possibly other mints not named on the coinage, while the old *c.* 21 grain standard was perpetuated by Anglo-Scandinavian mints in the Danelaw (Blackburn 1998, 107–12; 2003, 206–8). Blackburn analysed the extensive coinage of light-weight imitations of Alfred's Two-Line type from the Danelaw, which may have been struck at a number of mints in East Anglia and the east Midlands, with some thirty named moneyers and possibly others working anonymously (Blackburn 1989a, 16–18, 20–1; 1989b, 342–8; 2001, 128–30). In 1984 the Ashdon (Essex) hoard provided 102 fragments of some sixty-five to seventy Two-Line pennies, deposited *c.* 890–5, and Blackburn (1989a) found that twenty-eight of the thirty-four identifiable coins were Danelaw imitations in the name of Alfred, with one official coin of Alfred, five coins of Guthrum and a unique coin attributed to Guthfrith, king of York (*c.* 881/83–95). Blackburn also published comprehensive studies of Guthrum's Two-Line coinage (Blackburn 2005, 30–3, 38–42) and of the earlier East Anglian coinages of the 870s and early 880s in the names of Guthrum, Æthelred and Oswald with blundered inscriptions (Blackburn 2001, 125–7; 2005, 22–30, 34–5, 36–8; 2011, 371–2, 375).

In the mid-890s the St Edmund coinage took the place of imitations of Alfred's Two-Line type in East Anglia and the east Midlands. The Manningtree (Essex) hoard of *c.* 1995 and the 'Baldwin' parcel of *c.* 1993 greatly increased our knowledge of the late phase of this coinage (*c.* 905–17/18), showing that it effectively replaced the coins of the early phase in a homogeneous local currency (Blackburn 2001, 132–4; Blackburn and Pagan 2002). The Morley St Peter (Norfolk) and Brantham (Suffolk) hoards have demonstrated that after the extension of Edward the Elder's authority to East Anglia and the east Midlands in 917–18 the St Edmund coinage was quickly superseded by local variants of Edward's Portrait and Horizontal types, the latter perhaps principally minted in Stamford (Blackburn 2001, 138; 2006, 206–8).

Danelaw imitations of Alfred's London Monogram type, some of which have a monogram reading *Lincolla* for Lincoln, seem to have been produced in the Five Boroughs in the 880s. They were present in the Stamford hoard (*c.* 890), but not in the Ashdon hoard (*c.* 895), and there are no recorded single finds of these imitations further north than Doncaster, on the northern border of the Five Boroughs (Blackburn 2004, 327). The unique penny of King Halfdan ('VLFDENE RX'), combining a London Monogram reverse with an earlier Two Emperors reverse, and the also unique Two-Line halfpenny of '+ALFDENE RX' can no longer be attributed to Halfdan, the first Scandinavian king of York, but they may instead provide evidence of an otherwise unrecorded king in the Five Boroughs in the 880s (Blackburn 2004, 327–8), or alternatively they might be connected with a Viking king killed during a raid across the Midlands in 910 (Williams and Archibald 2011, 47–8, 65). The early coinage

of the Five Boroughs probably also included imitations of Alfred's Two-Line type and the unique coin of Guthfrith of York (Blackburn 2001, 131; 2006, 215). Blackburn (2004, 328–9) suggested that the Orsnaforda imitations of Alfred's Ohsnaforda Oxford coinage, imitations of the DORO coinage of Alfred and Archbishop Plegmund from Canterbury (*c.* 895–99), and the extensive series of coins combining a York 'Cnut' obverse with a reverse copied from Frankish coins of Quentovic were probably struck in the Five Boroughs or the northern Danelaw. The finding of an Orsnaforda imitation corroded together with a St Edmund penny at Little Chesterford (Essex) in 2008 led Blackburn (2011, 373–4) to offer the alternative suggestion that the Orsnaforda coinage may have been from the south or south-east Danelaw, south of the Five Boroughs and west of East Anglia. The coins of Earl Sihtric (Sitric Comes) struck by the moneyer Gundibertus at Sceldfor, probably in the 890s, have been attributed to a mint at Little Shelford in the Outer Danelaw (later in Cambridgeshire), but this is by no means certain (Blunt, Stewart and Lyon 1989, 101–2; Hart 1995; Williams and Archibald 2011, 48).

York and the Five Boroughs

The York regal coinage of Sigeferth (*c.* 895–900) and Cnut (*c.* 900–05) has been well known since the finding of more than 3,000 specimens in the Cuerdale hoard in 1840 (Blackburn 2004, 329–32; Williams and Archibald 2011, 43–7). The most important addition to our knowledge of this coinage since the publication of Hill's *Atlas* in 1981 has been provided by the discovery of the Silverdale hoard in September 2011. This hoard, which was deposited *c.* 900–10, had ten arm-rings, two finger-rings, fourteen ingots, six bossed brooch fragments, one hundred and forty-two pieces of hack-silver and twenty-seven coins, including the first coin of an otherwise unknown king apparently named Harthacnut ('AIRDE CONVT') (Boughton, Williams and Ager 2012; G. Williams 2012). The hoard also included a penny of 'ALVVALDVS', of the type attributed to Æthelwold, the West Saxon prince who was accepted as a king in Northumbria after the death of Alfred in 899 and who died leading an East Anglian army against Edward the Elder in 902 (Blunt 1985; Blackburn 2004, 329).

The York regal coinage of *c.* 895–905 was succeeded by the St Peter coinages, which were issued from *c.* 905 to *c.* 927, interrupted by the coinage of Ragnald I (*c.* 919–20/1). Ian Stewart and Stewart Lyon have reviewed the evidence for the chronology of the St Peter coinages, with a corpus of known specimens and a die study (Stewart and Lyon 1992). They established beyond doubt that the coins without a sword should be dated before the reign of Ragnald, and that the coins with a sword belonged after Ragnald, in the 920s. The explicit dedication of the coins to St Peter, without the name of a king, has naturally prompted the suggestion that this is an ecclesiastical coinage (Rollason 2004, 313–14), but this has been firmly rejected by Blackburn (2004, 332–5).

Mint	Edward the Elder (899–924)	Athelstan (924/5–39)	Eadmund (939–46)	Eadred (946–55)	Eadwig (955–59)	Edgar pre-reform (957–c. 973)
Barnstaple					N	
Bath	N	N	U		N	N
Bedford	U?		N?, U		N	N
Bridport		N				
Buckingham						N
Cambridge						U?
Canterbury	U	N, G	U	N		N
Chester	U	N	N	U	U	N
Chichester	U?	N, G				N
Cricklade						N
Darent	U?	N				
Derby		N	N	U	U	N
Dover		N	U			
Dorchester		G				
Exeter		N, G	U		N	N
Gloucester		N				
Hastings		G				
Hereford		N	U			
Hertford		N	U?		N	N
Huntingdon			U?		N	N
Langport		N	U?			
Leicester		N	U			N?
Lewes		N, G	U			N
Lincoln				N	U	N
London	U	N, G	U		N	N
Lympne		N				
Maldon		N	U?			
Malmesbury						N
Newark						U
Newport (Pagnell?)					N	N
Northampton	U?		U		N	N
Norwich		N	N			U
Nottingham		N				
Oxford	U	N	U	N	N	N
Rochester		N, G				
Shaftesbury		N, G	U			N
Shrewsbury	U	N	U			
Smierl		N				
Southampton	U	N, G	U		N	N
Stafford		N	U			N
Stamford	U?					U
Tamworth		N				N
Thetford						N?

Mint	Edward the Elder (899–924)	Athelstan (924/5–39)	Eadmund (939–46)	Eadred (946–55)	Eadwig (955–59)	Edgar pre-reform (957–c. 973)
Totnes					N	N
Wallingford		N	N		N	N
Wareham		N, G	U?			
Warwick		N?	U			N
Weardburh		N	U?			N
Wilton						N
Winchester	U	N, G	U		N	N
Worcester		N?	U?			
York		N	N	N	U	N

Fig. 9.1 Mints from Edward the Elder to Edgar's reform, 899–c. 973. Key: N = mints named on the coinage; G = mints in Athelstan's Grately code; U = uncertain.

In the 920s the St Peter Sword coinage was the inspiration for similar coinages outside the northern Danelaw. Blackburn argued, on the basis of hoard evidence and moneyers' names, that the Sword/Cross type of Sihtric Caoch (920/1–27) and the Anonymous Sword types of the same period were struck south of the Humber in the Five Boroughs, probably in Lincoln, down to Athelstan's taking of York in 927 (Blackburn 2001, 137; 2006, 209–15, 222–5; 2011, 380–2). Stewart (1982, 111–14) had previously suggested that the Sihtric coinages were from north-east Mercia, with at least some of them coming from Lincoln, in succession to the St Martin coinage of Lincoln. The hoard evidence for the area of origin of Sihtric's Sword coinage is no longer as clear-cut as it used to be thought to be however, because examples of it have occurred in two hoards from beyond the northern boundaries of the Five Boroughs: the 2005 Flusco Pike (Cumbria) find and the 2007 'Vale of York' hoard (Williams 2008c, 231–2, 234; 2008b, 43; 2011, 147, 153). The 617 coins in the Vale of York hoard included one of a new Sword type with 'rORIVA (alternatively hORIVA or SORIVA) CASTR' on the obverse and a continental Germanic moneyer's name ('OTARD MOT') on the reverse. Gareth Williams has argued that this coin may be from a previously unknown mint at Rocester in Staffordshire, which was the site of a Roman fort at a strategic location (Williams 2008a, 43–6; 2008c, 231; 2011, 149, 153; Ager and Williams 2011, 143). Two coins of Sihtric's Sword type known before the discovery of the Vale of York hoard, from a reverse die reading '+CASTDAEQRT', might be from Lincoln or some other place with a Roman fort or town (Blackburn 2006a, 213, 215, 223).

The Vale of York hoard was deposited soon after the termination of the St Peter and Sword coinages by the extension of Athelstan's authority to the Five Boroughs and the northern Danelaw in 926/7. It included thirty-six pennies of Athelstan's Church type (twenty-two of them with a York mint signature), which seems to have been the first coinage of the northern Danelaw after the death of Sihtric between January 926 and

July 927. There is also one coin of Athelstan's Rex To(tius) Brit(anniae) type, which is assumed to have been issued after the kings of northern Britain and Wales submitted to Athelstan at Eamont Bridge near Penrith on 12 July 927 (Williams 2008c, 229–31). This period of transition is also illustrated by the spectacular finds from the excavations at Coppergate in York in 1976–81, which provided unparalleled evidence of die-making and minting activities (Pirie with Archibald and Hall 1986, 20–2, 33–43, 54–7; Blackburn 2004, 338–41). The Coppergate finds included an obverse die of the St Peter Sword type; a broken obverse die-cap of Athelstan's Rex To Brit type; a fragment of a lead trial-piece with an impression from a reverse die of Athelstan's Church type (moneyer Adelbert); and a lead trial-piece from an Athelstan reverse die of the moneyer Regnald. A lead strip with impressions from irregular dies of Eadwig, in the name of the Chester moneyer Frothric, was from a much later period (955–57). In addition, there were pottery crucibles, many with metallic waste still adhering; complete and fragmentary stone moulds for casting ingots; lead ore (galena, which was a source of silver); and iron slag from smithing.

After the death of Athelstan in 939 his successor Eadmund (939–46) temporarily lost control of the northern Danelaw and the Five Boroughs. The arrangement of the Anglo-Scandinavian coinages of York in 939–44/5 has been clarified by the realisation that some of the coins attributable to Anlaf Guthfrithsson (939–41) or Anlaf Sihtricsson (941–44/5) came from mints in the Five Boroughs, before this area of the Danelaw was reconquered by Eadmund in 942: Derby, probably Lincoln and perhaps Stamford (Blunt, Stewart and Lyon 1989, 216–19; Blackburn 2004, 337). A round halfpenny allegedly found near Neston (Flintshire) in 2005, which was originally interpreted as a coin of Anlaf Guthfrithsson or Anlaf Sihtricsson from an old reverse die of Ragnald I probably minted at Derby, has been shown to be a modern forgery, along with a second specimen from a different die (Blackburn 2006, 218–20; 2011, 378).

The final period of Anglo-Scandinavian coinage between 947 and 954, which was restricted to York, is not as well understood as some earlier coinages. There are two possible chronologies: either the coinage of Eric belongs to two separate reigns in 947–48 and 952–54, interrupted by the rule of Eadmund's successor Eadred (946–55) in 948–50 and Anlaf Sihtricsson in 950–52, or one reign of Anlaf in 947–50 was followed by Eric in 950–52/4 (Sawyer 1995; Blackburn 2004, 337).

Mints of the Anglo-Saxon kings, 899–*c.* 973

The mints of the Anglo-Saxon kings from the accession of Edward the Elder in 899 to Edgar's reform of the English coinage in *c.* 973 have been reviewed in *Coinage in Tenth-Century England* (Blunt, Stewart and Lyon 1989). Lyon (2001) has surveyed the coinage of Edward the Elder (899–924), and Christopher Blunt's classic study of the coinage of Athelstan (924/5–39) (Blunt 1974) is still of fundamental importance for the reign. Blackburn (1996) has analysed the references to mints in Athelstan's Grately decree of *c.* 925–30, connecting the expansion of the mint network under Edward the Elder and Athelstan with the establishment of *burhs*. The publication of the British Museum's coins from Athelstan to Edgar's reform (Archibald and Blunt 1986) was the occasion of a survey of the English coinage in this period by Stewart (1988). Hugh Pagan (1995) has surveyed the mints of the west Midlands in the reign of Eadmund (939–46), and the pre-reform coinage of Edgar.

After Edgar's reform all English coins name their mint, but before the reform this practice was by no means general. Figure 9.1 summarizes the mints of the Anglo-Saxon kings from 899 to Edgar's reform, listing mints that are named (N), the mints specified in Athelstan's Grately code (G), and un-named mints the existence of which has been inferred with reasonable certainty (U) or only tentatively (U?). Un-named mints have been identified from similarities of moneyers' names on coins with and without mint names and from the style or elements of the design of the dies used.

Three mints named on the coinage of Athelstan have so far defied identification. *Weardburh* (Blunt 1974, 103–4) was a west Midlands *burh* established by Æthelflæd, lady of the Mercians, in 915, and Stewart (1988, 206–7) has suggested that it may have been in Worcestershire. *Darent*, which is named on two coins reading 'DARE.NT.VRB', might be Totnes or somewhere else in its vicinity (Blunt 1974, 75–6), and the location of *Smierl* is quite uncertain (Blunt 1974, 78–9). Coins of the moneyer Monthegn at *Veri* in the coinage of Athelstan might be from Warwick or, less likely, Worcester (Blunt 1974, 102–3). Pagan (1995, 139 n. 1) has suggested that the unique coin tentatively attributed to Thelwall by Blunt (1974, 101–2) is actually a coin of Chester. Since the publication of *Coinage in Tenth-Century England* in 1989 three mints have been added to the corpus in Edgar's pre-reform coinage: Cricklade, Lewes

and Lincoln (Blackburn and Leahy 1996; Pagan 2008, 196, 199; Allen 2012, 16 n. 102).

Kenneth Jonsson (1987b) has published an important monograph on Edgar's reform, which includes surveys of the pre-reform coinage and the mints and moneyers of Edgar's Reform type, Edward the Martyr (975–78) and the First Small Cross type (978–*c.* 979) of Æthelred II. With Gay van der Meer he has also compiled an invaluable series of tables listing the types issued by each moneyer active between Edgar's reform and 1066 (Jonsson and van der Meer 1990), and up-to-date tables of the mints active in each reign have been published by the author of this paper (Allen 2012, 385–95). The coinage of Edward the Confessor (1042–66) has been the subject of a monograph by Anthony Freeman (1985). Freeman's attempts to distinguish between 'established' moneyers and 'single-type' moneyers, and his concept of an Anglo-Saxon 'mint' as a coherent institution transcending the reality of a collection of individual moneyers in their own workshops, have been criticized by Michael Metcalf (1987), but his surveys of the activity of each mint are of immense value. More recently Pagan has published comprehensive studies of Edward the Confessor's Pacx type (Pagan 2011) and the coinage of Harold II (Pagan 1990).

Since the publication of Hill's *Atlas* only two places have been added, tentatively, to the lists of mints between Edgar's reform and 1066, both in Æthelred II's First Hand type: Grantham and Melton Mowbray (Jonsson 1987a; Blackburn 2000). The identification of Melton Mowbray as a mint followed the discovery of a penny with the mint name Metheltu(n) ('MEÐELTV') from the same dies as a fragmentary coin previously attributed to Peterborough (Medeshamstede) by Michael Dolley (1952–54).

Ten mints have been the subject of published studies since the 1980s: Aylesbury (Clarke and Symons 2007), Bury St Edmunds (Eaglen 2006), Cambridge (Jacob 1984), Huntingdon (Eaglen 1999; 2002), Ipswich (Sadler 2010; 2012), Lydford (Allan 2002), Reading (Freeman 1983–85), Wallingford (T. Williams 2012), Winchester (Biddle 2012) and Worcester (Symons 2003; 2006).

The recently published book on the Winchester mint (Biddle 2012) is particularly notable because this was one of the most important mints of Anglo-Saxon England. David Hill (1978, 214–17; 1981, 126, 130) used the numbers of moneyers at the mints to rank their activity, which is a method also applied to the coinage of Edward the Confessor by Freeman (1985, 55–8, 527–8) and Eaglen (2001), but Metcalf has shown that numbers of coins in Scandinavian museum collections and English single-find data are much more satisfactory bases of mint rankings and estimates of relative sizes of outputs at each mint (Metcalf 1978, 173–87, 206–12; 1980, 31–5, 49; 1981, 52–5, 68–85; 1998, 18–21, 293–301). Metcalf has also used regression analysis of single-finds of coins from seven of the most active mints (London, Winchester, Thetford, Norwich, Canterbury, Lincoln and York) to argue that there were zones of monetary circulation in late Anglo-Saxon England, although coins of London penetrated East Anglia, Wessex and the south-west in relatively large numbers (Metcalf 1998, 42–7, 49, 51, 53, 55). Rory Naismith (2012) has recently extended this form of analysis to 1,852 single-finds of coins of *c.* 973–1100, more than three times the number of finds (588) analysed by Metcalf. If single-finds and discoveries of hoards continue at the rate of recent years, further great advances in our knowledge of the English mints between 871 and 1066 can be confidently expected.

10

'Sudden Wonder': Urban Perspectives in Late Anglo-Saxon Literature

Mark Atherton

David Hill was a great promoter and encourager of dialogue between scholars working in different disciplines. When I first met him in the 1990s – when I came to work for two years on the *Fontes Anglo-Saxonici* project at Manchester University – I was impressed by his matter-of-fact statement that he had walked the circuit of every single Anglo-Saxon town in the country. That is a good corrective for anyone who works in the world of texts, in Old English language and literature, a reminder of what still exists to see and visit. For the background to this paper I did some travel in the world outside the text. I went to the city of Winchester and walked around its perimeter, saw the pattern of the Anglo-Saxon streets and the many water-courses, looked at the gates, the walls, and saw the outline of the Old and New Minsters where they once stood on the cathedral precinct opposite the site of the Anglo-Saxon royal palace. In this respect, there is a definite Hillian inspiration to this paper.

Introduction

As archaeologists and historians such as David Hill and others have shown, the revival of urban life in early medieval England goes back to the late ninth and the tenth centuries, to the refortification of the former Roman settlements and the construction of the aptly named *burhs* of southern and central England. The question this chapter seeks to address is the extent to which these new and radical transformations of the landscape and economy are reflected in the more 'imaginative' or 'creative' literature of the period, that is to say in the Old English and Anglo-Latin poems and prose narratives – and occasionally also their accompanying illustrations. The chapter will consider views of the city in the following late Anglo-Saxon texts: the poems *The Coronation of Edgar* and *Durham* – both in their different ways concerned with celebrating a contemporary city – the Anglo-Latin Lives of Saint Swithun written at Winchester, the Illustrated Old English Hexateuch done at Canterbury, and the anonymous tenth-century prose *Legend of the Seven Sleepers of Ephesus*. The new city was a

cause of celebration in many of these literary texts, but there is also a note to be heard of 'sudden wonder' tinged with fear or anxiety, and this adds further interest to the picture.

Words for 'City' in Old English

Before we continue, some orientation is needed with regard to the urban vocabulary available in Old English to designate towns and settlements and to translate the Latin terms for city: *urbs* and *civitas*. First it may be useful to exclude two terms from our discussion. The Old English word *tun* (pronounced with the same vowel as present-day English 'moon'), which eventually became the modern word *town*, did not in fact mean 'town'; Henry Sweet in his *Anglo-Saxon Reader* derives it from a word meaning 'enclosure' and glosses it as 'farm, village' (Sweet 1922, 296). And as the standard textbooks on place names will show, *tun* was mostly used to denote an estate or farm in the administrative documents of the period. For example, there is the familiar pattern of various estates situated to the north, south, east and west of a larger settlement and given the common designations 'Norton', 'Sutton', 'Easton', and 'Weston' (Cameron 1996, 143–44). Similarly 'Kingston' originally meant a royal estate, *cynges tun* in Old English, but only Kingston upon Thames acquired special status as a royal centre where kings were consecrated and crowned.

A second word to be excluded is the term *wic* (the letters *i* and *c* in the digraph *ic* were nearly always pronounced 'itch' in standard Old English). This is another place name element, seen in names such as (in their modern spelling) Droitwich, Greenwich, Northwich, Norwich, Sandwich; here *wic* appears to denote a large trading centre or emporium, as in *Hamwic*, the old name for the great emporium at Southampton. This is the meaning adopted by historians as a technical term when discussing the emporia or *wics* of earlier Anglo-Saxon economic history. In literature the word has a more general application. For example, in *Beowulf* the word can appear in a plural form *in wicun* or *in þæm wicum* meaning apparently 'in the dwelling-places'. Interestingly neither of these two poetic examples refers to a town. The first occurs at line 1304a in the context of the consternation felt by the people who have been sleeping at King Hrothgar's hall and its surrounding outer buildings (the whole complex is too small to be a city or town) after the murderous night attack by Grendel's mother (Dobbie 1953, 41). The second *in þæm wicum* at line 1612a refers to her cave, which Beowulf abandons unplundered after overcoming her in a desperate hand-to-hand fight (Dobbie 1953, 50). Both *wic* and also *tun* seem to assume this general sense in literary contexts and it is evident that the two nouns do not normally denote the concepts of 'town' or 'city'.

This leaves three urban terms: the native *burh*, and the two Latin imports into the language, the loanwords *ceaster* and *port*. Of the three the last is perhaps the most surprising to the budding student of Old English, for it was taken into the language from Latin *portus*, a port or harbour, and may even bear that meaning, as for instance in the account of the Voyages of Ohthere and Wulfstan in the Old English *Orosius* (Bately 1980, 13–18, at 16, line 2; trans. Treharne 2010, 24–31). There is no doubt, however, that the word *port* was used to mean 'town', as in the modern place-name Port Meadow on the edge of Oxford. Numerous documents mention *port*, and the Anglo-Saxon official who was given administrative duties over a town was entitled a *port-gerefa* or 'town-reeve'; while important roads were sometimes known as the 'port-way', Old English *portweg*, an example being the Roman road running to the south-west of Oxford (Blair 1994, 88).

The second term for an urban settlement is *ceaster*, pronounced in the West Saxon variety of Old English roughly as 'chaster', and commonly found in modern place-names as the second element -*chester*, -*caster* and -*cester*. Again the word is Roman in origin (from Latin *castra*), and towns with this second element in their names are invariably Roman in origin, often with their base structure intact (the outline of the city walls and the usual four entrance gates), a classic example, as we will see, being Winchester, Old English *Wintanceaster*, from Latin *Venta Belgarum* (Biddle 2000, 289).

The word *burh*, alternatively spelt *burg* (the final *h* and *g* were both pronounced as a fricative akin to Scots 'ch' in *Loch Ness*), also appears in the form *byrig* (pronounced 'bury'). For reasons of -i-mutation, as Campbell states in his *Grammar* (1959, 252–253, paragraphs 624–5), this noun is grammatically irregular and changes its shape in the oblique cases and in the plural; the varying forms of the word are listed in full in the glossary of Mitchell and Robinson (2007, 354), and may be tabulated as follows:

	SING.	PLURAL
Nom	burh	byrig
Acc	burh	byrig
Gen	byrig	burga
Dat	byrig	burgum

Examples in place names abound, from Bamburgh in the north to Banbury in the south, the first example preserving the nominative form, the second the dative form of the word. In origin and meaning, *burh* is a derivative of the verb *beorgan* 'to protect, defend, preserve, save' (Healey 2007; cf. Clark Hall 1960, 42), and accordingly one meaning of *burh* is 'fortified enclosure, fortification' hence also the meaning 'fortified dwelling, estate, manor' (Healey). It is this latter meaning of the word that is found in the text of 'Cynewulf and Cyneheard', the famous annal in the *Anglo-Saxon Chronicle* for the year 755, where king Cynewulf is trapped inside a small building at the estate of *Merantun* (note the *tun* 'estate' element in the name) by his rival, the atheling Cyneheard. The king's house is small but clearly defensible, and the fighting takes place at the door or the gates of the building (755A; Bately 1986, 36–8; trans. Swanton 1996, 46–8).

The alternative meaning of *burh* is 'fortified town; generally, town, city' (Healey 2007). A city, like a fortress, is surrounded by a wall for protection and it is this feature that yields to the semantic broadening of the term *burh*. This use of *burh* occurs in traditional Old English poems, but it becomes particularly relevant as towns developed or re-developed in the later Anglo-Saxon period, not only for economic reasons but also for purposes of defence against Viking attack in particular. With this development came a different legal status attached to a *burh*, as implied in the list of towns known as the Burghal Hidage (Robertson 1939, 246–249) This document calculates the number of hides of land needed to support the men who man the walls in times of emergency (Hill 1996b) and so allows us to calculate the length of the defensive walls for nearly every *burh* with accuracy, as David Hill's *Atlas* shows (Hill 1981 fig. 149). Many of the *burhs* listed in the Hidage later became flourishing towns. The Anglo-Saxon *burh* in this sense was a precursor of the later medieval borough, the citizens of which paid higher taxes but enjoyed burgage tenure and certain privileges in return (Beresford and Finberg 1973, 26–8).

The urban landscape of England was certainly changing by the tenth century. Seen archaeologically, the earlier pattern of minsters, *wics* and shifting rural settlements had given way to towns. A good example here is the pattern at London: the earlier site was *Lundenwic* on the area of the Strand, a typical *wic* or trading emporium (see Tyler and Beard, both in this volume, pp. 37–40, 41–5 respectively); then came the Viking incursions, and the population moved to *Lundenburh*, the old Roman *Londinium*, in fact the present-day City, the epitome of the walled city of the later Anglo-Saxon period (Pryor 2007, 165 and 170, figs 27 and 29). By the 980s, when many of our texts were being written, urban life was on the increase, with shire administration, highly regulated royal mints, and markets centred on towns. Their populations had grown, and their leading citizens were taking a prominent role in the political life of the country (Fleming 1993).

'Views from afar' in Old English poems

From the perspective of the elegiac poems of the tenth-century *Exeter Book*, however, there was no urbanisation: in these traditional texts the urban landscape is merely a reminder of the past, of the long-gone Roman empire. For these poets, city ruins serve as potent symbols of transience and decay. There is for example the poem of exile and hard-gained wisdom *The Wanderer* (Krapp and Dobbie 1936, 134–7; trans. Treharne 2010, 56–61). Here the poet or lyric speaker at one point (lines 58–62) meditates on *eorla lif* 'the life of warriors'; the expression is traditional and even archaic, since *eorl* in an eleventh-century context was coming to mean 'earl' or 'governor of a region'). In the same context, the poet also calls such men 'courageous retainers' *modge maguþegnas*, and again the expression is archaic-poetic. Inevitably, in an elegy of this kind, the poet's mind grows dark as he contemplates their swift passing, and he observes how this is the way of the world, which 'droops and falls' *dreoseð and fealleþ* (line 63b). It follows then that a 'wise man' or 'counsellor' (the term *wita* covers both meanings) must acquire appropriate virtues, until in his wisdom he will perceive the transience of earthly dwellings – described by the speaker in terms of wasted wealth, of wind-blown walls, snow-covered buildings and toppled wine-halls (lines 73–7), with their inhabitants long gone or fallen in battle *wlonc bi wealle* 'proud by the wall' (line 80a). All this, thinks the speaker, is the action of Providence:

> Yðde swa þisne eardgeard ælda Scyppend
> oþþæt burgwara breahtma lease,
> eald enta geweorc idlu stodon
> (*The Wanderer*, lines 85–7; Krapp and Dobbie 1936, 136)

> The Creator of men thus laid waste this earth
> until deprived of the joy of its inhabitants,
> the ancient work of giants stood empty (trans. Treharne 2010, 59).

Line 87 *eald enta geweorc* the 'ancient work of giants' serves here as a poetic expression for the great men of the past: the 'giants' are the *burgwara* or 'city-dwellers', *i.e.* Romans who built the cities which once, long ago, flourished across the whole of southern Britain but which now (so the poet declares) stand empty and uninhabited.

Another equally striking example of urban wasteland is found in the *Exeter Book* poem *The Ruin*, which opens as follows:

> Wrætlic is þes weallstan, wyrde gebræcon
> Burgstede burston, brosnað enta geweorc (*The Ruin*, lines 1–2; Krapp and Dobbie 1936, 227–9).

> Splendid is this wall-stone which the fates broke.
> The city-buildings fell, the works of giants crumble.
> (my translation)

Here the element *burg* appears in the form *burgstede*, and here again is the formula *enta geweorc*, which places this skilfully

wrought poem at the very centre of traditional Old English verse making, as Andy Orchard (2008) has shown. The dominant image in the text is clearly one of transience: the whole poem contemplates the past splendours of a large old city that has now been reduced to a set of crumbling ruins. Paradoxically, however, the anthology in which this poem appears was being copied in an important scriptorium at the very time when the new urban renewal was taking place. Scholars are divided on the question of where the manuscript was made (though it is clear that Leofric, bishop of Exeter, held it in his library in the 1070s), but it seems unlikely that the scribe of the *Exeter Book* would have recognised the city so depicted in the text, for by the late tenth century all English cities had been cleared and their walls restored. Exeter itself, for instance, had been given a new street plan within the old Roman walls, and its minster refounded as a Benedictine monastery in 968 (Henderson and Bidwell 1982; Allan *et al.* 1984). As for Bath, ostensibly the crumbled splendour pondered in *The Ruin*, by the time the scribe was copying the poem in the tenth century this city was in fact a reformed Benedictine abbey complex within a new urban power centre (Cunliffe 1984; Hill 1996b, 190–192). Either the *Exeter Book* poets wrote in an earlier period before the urbanisation began, when the now buried Roman baths were still visible, or alternatively they chose to employ given themes and images rather than describing what they could actually see all around them.

One other poem of the tenth century deals with Bath, and here scholars are in no doubt as to the identity of the town, for it is named twice within the text itself. In the clearly contemporary poem *Edgar's Coronation* that constitutes the entry in the *Anglo-Saxon Chronicle* for 973 the poet celebrates the city (Bately 1986, 76–7):

> Her Eadgar wæs, Engla waldend,
> corðre micelre to cyninge gehalgod
> on ðære ealdan byrig, Acemannesceastre;
> eac hi igbuend oðre worde
> beornas Baðan nemnaþ. Þær wæs blis micel
> on þam eadgan dæge eallum geworden,

> Here was Edgar, lord of the English,
> before a great multitude consecrated as king
> at the ancient city, Akemanchester;
> which island-dwelling men also call
> by the other word Bath. There great joy
> had come about for all on that blessed day …

Though he does not provide any actual physical description of Bath itself the writer probably thought that Edgar had good reasons for having his coronation *on ðære ealdan byrig* 'in this ancient city', with its two names, the one probably based on the *aqua* element in its Roman name *Aquae Sulis*, the other a more modern descriptive toponym like the present-day name Bath. Rather than being a symbol of transience, as in *The Ruin*, the city in this *Chronicle* poem has become an index of imperial power, part of a Benedictine Reformist ideology in which both Church and State are unified under the tutelage of the sanctified king (Salvador-Bello 2008).

Another Old English poem in a manuscript of the *Chronicle* also raises questions about changing urban perspectives. In the poem *Maxims II*, copied with another poem immediately before the *Chronicle* in BL Cotton Tiberius B. i (O'Brien O'Keeffe 2001, 11–13; Dobbie 1942, 55–7), the poet opens with a perspective on cities and their place in the scheme of things. 'Cities', he says (the word used is *ceastra*), 'are seen from afar, the cunning work of giants'. At first sight the *enta geweorc* or 'work of giants' seems to be the familiar trope of transience and admiration of past splendour. But on closer scrutiny it will be seen that despite the ready-made formulas these cities are still in existence on the earth in all their glory: their construction is *orðanc* 'cunning' and their stone walls *wrætlic* 'splendid'. This poem is often cited as a characteristic example of traditional verse, but its theme is arguably 'modern' (in terms of the eleventh century), and although the relevant section is only short, nevertheless the cities to which it alludes are far from ruinous and stand tall and prominent in the landscape.

A specific example of a splendid city 'seen from afar' is found in *Durham*, recorded in a twelfth-century manuscript, and often regarded as one of the last Old English poems in the traditional alliterative metre (Lerer 1999, 18–22). The context is clearly that of another monastic renewal, that of the late eleventh century (Knowles 1963, 158–71), the movement which sought to revive the golden age of Northumbria as it had been in the age of Bede. Possibly the poem was written on the occasion of the translation of St Cuthbert's relics to Durham in 1104 (Kendall 1988). It opens with the uncompromising value judgement that 'this city is famous', the term used being the traditional *burh*, here spelt *burch*, clearly meant to convey the idea of a city literally of great standing (Dobbie 1942, 27; trans. Hamer 1970, 31–3). The description that ensues, though brief, captures some of the salient features of the city seen at a distance: its height and dominance, and its great stone walls, rather unusually described as 'wondrously grown', almost as though they had an organic life of their own. Next the poet delineates the surrounding features of the city, with its running river filled with fish, and its secure enclosing woods with 'deer in deep dales'. Unlike the elegies the view of the past in *Durham* is wholly affirmative, there is no sense of regret for times gone by. In this medieval Christian monastic context the past is a cause for celebration, and the second half of the poem emphasises that Durham is the home of a multitude of saints. In an enumerative list, the poet names first and foremost the 'pious and blessed' St Cuthbert, and mentions also 'the lion of the English' St Oswald, as well as Bishop Aidan, and 'the noble companions' Eadbert and Eadfrith, among others. His conclusion is clear: the continual presence of St Cuthbert and of the other saints' relics in the cathedral accounts for the many miracles that take place there. As has been pointed out (Schlauch 1941), the poem belongs in the poetic tradition of

encomium urbis, in which the city or *urbs* is the focus of praise and celebration (see also Appleton forthcoming).

Celebrations of the city in Anglo-Latin

As a number of recent large-scale editions reveal, Winchester is relatively well served for documentation and literature in the late Anglo-Saxon period. The city had burgeoned under Alfred, declined a little under Athelstan but then flourished again under Edgar and his son Æthelred, becoming an important royal centre in the reign of Cnut (Biddle and Hill 1971; Yorke 2000). Edgar of course gave access to the monastic reformers, granting them permission both to clear away the old clerical housing and to expand the three minsters. As the documentation reveals, any disputes between these three foundations were settled by the king:

> Her is geswitulod on ðysum gewrite hú Eadgar cining mid rymette gedihligean het þa mynstra on Wintanceastræ syþþan he hi ðurh godes gyfe to munuclife gedyde.7 þet asmeagan het þet nan ðera mynstra þær binnan þurh þet rymet wið oðrum sace næfde

> Here in this writing is declared how King Edgar ordered that the monasteries in Winchester should be given privacy by means of a clearance, after he, through the grace of God, had turned them to the monastic life, and that he ordered it to be devised that none of the monasteries within that place should have any dispute with another because of the clearance … (Rumble 2002, 140–3).

The charters and other texts edited by Alex Rumble in his anthology *Property and Piety in Early Medieval Winchester* are of added interest for the occasional sporadic detail they reveal of the urban scene; they mention the many Winchester water-courses and water-mills, and they even give the names of streets and the owners of particular houses within the city. Such documents can be read usefully in conjunction with poems and prose associated with the cult of St Swithun, the ninth-century bishop of Winchester who was regarded as a saint by later generations; this material is now conveniently gathered together in a new masterly edition and parallel translation (Lapidge 2003). The lives of St Swithun were written by tenth-century writers who were or who had been monks at Winchester, Lantfred and Wulfstan, and by the anonymous eleventh-century hagiographer who wrote the *Vita S. Swithuni Episcopi et Confessoris* (the *Life of St Swithun, Bishop and Confessor*). The latter *Life* has been attributed (Sauvage 1888) to Goscelin, the foreign cleric present in England during the reigns of both Edward the Confessor and William the Conqueror, who in his anglophile enthusiasm and hatred of Norman innovation set about recording for posterity the lives of the English saints whom he so admired. However, the more recent editor of the poem is cautious about attributing the poem to Goscelin, though he has argued on the grounds of style that the author also wrote the *Miracula Sancti Swithuni*

(Lapidge 2003, 612). Despite the length of time that separates the anonymous author from the subject of his hagiography it is clear that he knew some local traditions regarding this bishop (Yorke 2000, 109); here is an example:

> Vnde factum est ut, necessitate exigente, de spiritualibus ad forinseca exiens, utilitati communi ciuium sicut semper et aliquando prouideret, pontemque ad orientalem portam ciuitatis arcubus lapideis opera non leuiter ruituro construeret.

> Whence it happened that he turned from spiritual matters to those of the outside world under constraint of necessity, he attended to the common welfare of the townspeople, as he did always and at any time, and built a bridge at the East Gate of the town, constructed of stone arches so that it would not easily collapse (Lapidge 2003, 634–5).

This information appears in chapter 6 of the *Vita*, in which the author recounts a miracle that took place during the construction of this bridge. A certain woman living in great poverty was carrying a dish of saleable eggs across the building site when she was 'grabbed by the wantonly playful workmen' (*ab operariis lasciuientibus et ludentibus miseram apprehendi*). Her eggs were all broken, but the distraught woman was led before the bishop, who restored her eggs with a blessing. The story points to a tradition that Bishop Swithun was very concerned to restore the ruined churches of the city (ch. 7), and that he also organised other building projects in the city (ch. 6).

As Yorke (2000, 109) argues, the egg miracle is an authentic ninth-century anecdote, perhaps confirmed by the existence of a Latin poem on the same subject. In an archaeological survey of the development of the city in the Anglo-Saxon period, the archaeologist Martin Biddle drew attention to the following highly appropriate passage from this late eleventh-century poem (Biddle 2000, 308, citing Locke 1912, 124–25):

> Gratuletur et exultet felix urbs Winthonia
> Que uirtute tanti patris meritisque rutilat
> Cuius sacra fouet ossa sentit et miracula
> Incessanter illi plaudat odas cum letitia.

> May the blessed city of Winchester rejoice and exult, which shines through the excellence and merits of so great a father whose sacred bones it cherishes, which indeed experiences miracles, ceaselessly commending him in joyful odes.

The similarity of this passage to the theme of *Durham* will be immediately apparent. Like Cuthbert in *Durham*, this poem, *Unum Beati Swithuni Miraculum* (now re-edited by Lapidge 2003, 793–6), celebrates a city and its saint, in this case its former ninth-century bishop, St Swithun. However, the poem is otherwise rather different from *Durham*, more obviously anecdotal than descriptive, for it also tells the story of Swithun's egg miracle as in the anonymous *Vita*. The text of this poem appears in BL Royal 15 C. vii, fol. 125v; it was written in

the second half of the eleventh century, possibly at Sherborne (Lapidge 2003, 364).

Unlike the author of the *Vita*, the two tenth-century biographers found their subject, Bishop Swithun, a highly elusive character. For Lantfred in his Preface, his work was not so much a biography since so little was known of the life of the bishop, who had lived in the previous century to the time of writing and whose deeds had not been written about at the time (Lapidge 2003, 250–1). Instead Lantfred deals with the posthumous cult of the saint named Swithun: his translation into the Old Minster at Winchester and the subsequent miracles that were performed there. In many respects, the real protagonist of the texts of Lantfred and Wulfstan is the city itself and its streets, and above all the Old Minster where Swithun's mortal remains are located. In the many anecdotes that make up these two works, Winchester is a magnet that constantly draws people. Often it is the towers of the Old Minster that are seen from afar, and these are described literally in glowing terms as travellers use them as a landmark on their journeys. There is for instance the case of the man who escapes from the stocks by the saint's assistance in chapter 27 (Lapidge 2003, 314–15), or the man cured of blindness in chapter 29:

> suspiciens haud longe Wintoniam conspexit, quam toto mentis ardore paululum ante desiderebat uidere

> he looked up and saw Winchester not far off, which he desired to see with all his heart a short while before (Lapidge 2003, 318–19)

The pilgrims, penitents and cure-seekers all journey towards the city in these narratives, and all the miracles take place in sight of the city or within its walls.

In the detailed descriptions in Wulfstan's *Narratio Metrica de S. Swithuno*, the Old Minster is huge and impressive, with a mighty church organ operated by bellows (Lapidge 2003, 385–7). Wulfstan sees the building programme of Swithun's tenth century successor, bishop Æthelwold, as unprecedented since ancient times:

> He built all these dwellings with solid walls; and he also covered them with new floors, and rejoicing adorned the monastery with decorations of all kinds. And to this place he conducted pleasant streams of water abounding in fish; and conduits from a watercourse penetrate the inner recesses of the buildings, cleansing the entire monastery with their murmuring flow. Æthelwold also rebuilt the building of the Old Minster with lofty walls and new roofs, strengthening it on its southern and northern sides with solid side chapels and arches of various kinds. Similarly he added numerous chapels to house holy altars; these disguise the entrance of the main doorway so that, if someone were to walk through the interior of the church with unfamiliar steps, he would not know whence he came, nor how to retrace his steps, because in every direction open doorways may be seen and there is no route apparent to him. Stopping,

he casts his wandering eyes around here and there and marvels (as it were) at the Daedalian structures of Greece, until an experienced guide comes to him and leads him to the threshold of the one remaining door [*i.e.* the entrance once again]. Here in amazement he signs himself with the Cross – and in this astonished state he still does not know how he can get out! (Lapidge 2003, 375–7)

The church is so large according to Wulfstan of Winchester's account that people can lose their way and need a guide to locate the door. It worthy of note that this Latin passage must be the first account in English literature of someone becoming lost in a city. As such it is an index of the enormous impact that such large urban buildings must have had on the contemporary people who first experienced them.

An illustrated Benedictional owned by Æthelwold gives a visual equivalent of the descriptions to be found in Wulfstan and Lantfred. On folio 118v there is a picture of a bishop (probably Æthelwold himself) reading a blessing to a company of monks (Withers 2007, 166, fig. 72). The bishop stands under a round arch, while the monks stand under a square roof-shaped structure; such architectural features are intended by the artist to convey the idea that the bishop and monks are inside a building, here clearly a church, and most likely the Old Minster. Above the rectangular roof, a large belfry tower with two bells and a weathercock helps further to identify the building, while in the background of the picture we see the distant towers of the city walls, other churches and the roofs of houses: an iconic representation of the *felix urbs* – the blessed city of Winchester. We are a long way here from the *eald enta geweorc* of *The Ruin*.

The country and the city: the story of Joseph and his brothers

Perhaps inspired by Prudentius or Psalter illustrations was an eleventh-century artistic project with a Canterbury connection, the illustrated Old English Hexateuch (BL Cotton Claudius B. iv). Its designers aimed to provide a set of connected narrative illustrations to the translation of the first six books of the bible. From the point of view of the city, the coloured drawings which accompany the Genesis portion of the illustrated Hexateuch are particularly informative. In particular there is the story of Joseph, Genesis chapters 39 to 50, which we know from other manuscripts was a popular text in eleventh century England (Richards 2000). As Daniel Anlezark has shown in a detailed study (2006), the story of Joseph was regarded as a kind of saint's life; it was extracted from the context of the full Hexateuch, lightly reworked, and it then circulated as a separate text.

In the earlier part of the narrative there is no representation of the landscape as such; all the focus is on the interaction between characters. For example, Jacob sends his son Joseph from the vale of Hebron to meet his brothers tending the herds in Sichem. On his way he encounters an unknown man who tells him that his brothers have moved on further to Dothain (Genesis 37, 14–17). In the biblical text this scene involves a protracted dialogue between Joseph and the man at Sichem. The narrative function of this dialogue is to delay the action of the plot and give more time to the narration. The brothers are able to see Joseph approaching them at a distance – and they have space and time to discuss their next course of action: whether to kill him or not (Genesis 37, 18–22). This episode is represented in the illustrated Hexateuch by two images linked by blocks of text over two facing pages of the manuscript. The illustration on folio 53v shows Joseph in his special coat talking to a bearded man, who appears to be a nobleman of rank with a cloak and shoulder brooch, holding a spear. The background to this framed picture is empty of all detail. Both figures point to the right across to the facing full-page illustration (fol. 54r) depicting the brothers and the subsequent events in this episode, as told in the intervening block of text (Genesis 37, 23–36). In this drawing, various events in time coalesce: from left to right we see the brothers looking into the distance at the approaching Joseph while others stand arguing as two of them force Joseph into a deep pit, the waterless well of the biblical text; below we see in some detail the large herds of sheep on rolling lines of what must be imagined as open hill country (Withers 2007, 235, fig. 96). The point here is that almost no landscape details are given and there is no trace to be seen of buildings or even tents: the emphasis is wholly on the human figures in the drama.

Later, however, the scene switches to Egypt, and the story culminates with the protagonist's appointment as great regent of the whole country, second only to Pharaoh the king. Unrecognisable now to his family, Joseph receives his suppliant brothers, the pastoral herdsmen who in the years of famine that follow the years of plenty come seeking food and grain from the Egyptian cities where it has been stored. In the translation of the biblical text, the word for these cities is *burh*, here rendering the Latin *urbs*, and *burg* seems to mean 'city' rather than its other meaning of stronghold or fortress (for the text, see Crawford 1969). Unlike their previous practice in telling the story of Joseph, it is only now that the artists begin to include background buildings in their illustrations. In each illustration, the stylised iconic towers and roofs are clearly meant to indicate a large city, while the arch under which characters converse is clearly a stylised means of showing a scene taking place indoors, inside a building within the city. There are many examples of these cityscapes, to be seen in the two published facsimiles (Dodwell and Clemoes 1974; Withers 2007. For a full-colour digital facsimile of the Hexateuch, the sharpest images are available via the British Library Manuscript Viewer: http://www.bl.uk/manuscripts/ FullDisplay.aspx?index=0&ref=Cotton_MS_Claudius_B_IV)

The following are worthy of mention. On fol. 60r the picture shows how the king appoints Joseph as reeve over all Egypt while in the background on the left a stylised city complex is to be seen (Withers 2007, 244, fig. 100). On fol. 60v Pharaoh presents Joseph with a wife; here the Old English text explains the etymology of her father's city: he is priest 'of þære byrig þe is genemned Eliopoleos, þæt is on Englisc, 'Sunnan Buruh' (the priest, of the city that is called Eliopoleos, that is in English 'Sunbury'); again the stylised towers and roofs of a city complex are seen on the left of the picture (Withers 2007, 245, fig. 101). Subsequently on fol. 63r we see Joseph waiting for his brothers' second visit and standing at the entrance to the city pictured as two towers and a gate; over the page on fol. 63v he gives formal reception to his brothers, provides a feast in hall, and retires to another chamber to avoid showing his emotions in public and revealing his true identity. On the next page in another illustration set against an urban backdrop we see Joseph ordering his reeve to meddle with his brothers' grain bag. The text under the picture emphasises the fact that he waits for his brothers to leave the city before he sends out his patrol to search and accuse them (his motivations are mixed, but above all he wants to test their reactions and draw the rest of the family to him). More cityscapes appear in the illustrations as the brothers return; the artist now uses his sense of space to dictate movement and significant location. First the brothers are outside the city on the right; but then they are drawn into the architectural frame as the reconciliations start to take place (Withers 2007, 253, fig.105).

The familiar story of Joseph is thus told in a combination of interactive word and image, and the visual medium adds further meanings to the text. As the artists picture it, the narrative begins in a bare landscape of sheep and shepherd and ends in a cityscape of arched halls, towers, roofs, walls and gates. The artist-illustrators clearly reflect their differing views of Canaan and Egypt in these illustrations, for while the earlier scenes set in Canaan show human figures against a blank background, in the later dramatic scenes in Egypt many architectural details are now added (Withers 2007, 248–55). The change seems to be deliberate, suggesting the move from the country to the city, which is surely one of the themes of the story. The brothers in the story are compelled by their own need and that of their families to go up to the city, and yet they are reluctant to do so, for the city is a strange place, with its rules and regulations and its awe-inspiring and rather wilful ruler, who puts them to the test for (as it seems to them) no apparent reason.

The Old English *Legend of the Seven Sleepers*

The anonymous Old English *Legend of the Seven Sleepers of Ephesus* is a kind of novella or short story that nods to its originative genre, a saint's life, but shows a remarkably expansive narrative style. This manner of writing can seem almost modern in terms of the psychological interest that the author adds to the given plot of the legend. Its editor Hugh Magennis (1994) dates the Old English text for various reasons to the late tenth or early eleventh century, and he elsewhere discusses its departures from normal hagiographic style

(Magennis 1985 and 1991). Historians are now alerted to the historical evidence that this tale provides for the workings of the law in an urban setting (Whitelock 1961; Cubitt 2009) and it is clear that the Old English legend deserves further work and a wider audience. With regard to its portrayal of a working city the story is remarkable for its focus on the fears and anxieties of the reluctant visitor, drawn against his will into its legal procedures.

Behind the plot is the classic folklore wonder-tale of the man who returns to his hometown after a brief journey or night away, only to find that years or centuries have passed in his home and everything has changed. In the *Seven Sleepers* legend, which goes back to the late Roman world in its older Latin versions, the seven young men fall asleep in a cave outside Ephesus to escape an anti-Christian persecution. The pagan emperor, the villain of the piece, has the cave walled up, and two soldiers, secretly Christian, leave a message in the cave for posterity, telling of the martyrdom of the seven heroes. In the morning (in fact three hundred and seventy two years later) the seven men wake up and send their steward Malchus into the city in disguise to buy food and gather news. Malchus is arrested at the market place when he tries to buy bread with ancient coins. Taken before the town consul and the bishop they finally believe his story and summon the emperor (the present emperor is now of course a Christian) to witness this miracle and proof of the doctrine of the resurrection.

My previous research (Atherton 2013) followed Whitelock (1961) and Magennis (1985, 1991, 1994), who showed that the Old English version is an expansion and modernising of the Latin. With their work as a starting point I argued for three major modernisations in the Old English text. First, the emphasis on the revaluing of the coins reflects tenth-century royal policy, especially from the time of King Edgar, to regulate and control the English currency. Secondly, the merchants depicted in the story as willing to vouch for Malchus before the law represent a new force in the economy of the country, which various lawcodes sought to channel and regulate, so that trading could only take place in towns and cities where it could be properly monitored. Thirdly, the hearing before the city consul in the Latin becomes a meeting of the *portgerefa* and *burhgemot* or city assembly in the Old English. Legal terminology similar to that found in accounts of lawsuits suggests that Malchus has to put forward his claim or *talu* and summon witnesses to the assembly who will *betellan i.e.* 'support his claim' before the law. A recent study (Cubitt 2009) confirms the contemporary relevance of the depictions of legal procedure in this story.

The crime that Malchus has committed is serious, in Anglo-Saxon terms; it seems that he is accused of using counterfeit or out-of-date coinage, and of trading outside the confines of the city. Two extracts from tenth-century law-codes have obvious relevance to the story. The first clause of I Edward reads as follows:

And ic wille, ðæt gehwilc man hæbbe his geteaman; and nan man ne ceapige butan porte, ac hæbbe þæs portgerefan gewitnesse oððe oþera ungeligenra manna, ðe man gelyfan mæge. (Attenborough 1922, 114–15)

And my will is that every man shall have a warrantor [to his transactions] and that no one shall buy [and sell] except in a market town; but he shall have the witness of the 'portreeve' or of other men of credit, who can be trusted.

A similar line is taken in the Latin of IV Æthelred, clause 7; note here that the Latin word for 'town' is *portus*:

Et diximus de mercatoribus qui falsum et lacum afferunt ad portum, ut advocent si possint. (Robertson 1925, 76–7)

And we have decreed with regard to traders who bring money which is defective in quality and weight to the town, that they shall name a warrantor if they can.

As stated in the laws of tenth-century kings, all transactions were supposed to take place within the confines of the city or market town, under the eyes of the royal reeve whose job it was to supervise trade and coinage. This aspect of everyday commerce and crime in contemporary Anglo-Saxon society is reflected here in the story, in the modernisations added to the core narrative when it is translated, paraphrased and retold by a late Old English writer.

Hugh Magennis has shown that the style of this writer promotes a fast-moving narration in which the thoughts, feelings and perceptions of the characters are highlighted. In the rest of this discussion we will consider some of the psychological additions of the Old English writer to the major episode: the story of Malchus's arrival at the city.

As Malchus sets out on his expedition and leaves the cave there is a nice touch of psychological authenticity in the Old English. In the Latin version, when Malchus sees the scattered stones at the cave entrance he feels astonished (*miratus*) and then becomes afraid of discovery. In the more complex Old English, Malchus is preoccupied:

he healfunga þæs wundrode, þeah na swiðe embe þæt ne smeade, ac he forht of þære dune mid miclan ege nyðereode (Magennis 1994, 448–9).

Seeing the stones lying about he 'half wondered at this but did not dwell too much on it', so anxious is he to get down the mountain and carry out his task. The word I have here translated as 'dwell on' is 'smeagan', a term traditionally associated with pondering, meditation and depth of thought. The Old English author makes clear that subconsciously Malchus has registered the first of the many changes that have taken place in the new world in which he has arrived; but his preoccupations prevent him from realizing its significance.

Having failed to heed the evidence before him, Malchus is brought suddenly face to face with the brave new world in which he has landed. The writer effects the abrupt incredulous amazement that Malchus experiences by a series of repetitions:

And Malchus, as he went up very close towards the town gates he looked towards them and saw the sign of Christ's holy rood fixed with honour above the town gates; and he was seized by such wonder, and at the sight of it he stood with wondrous astonishment, and he stood and beheld, and it seemed wondrous to him; and he looked on all sides, and he stared at the rood, and it all seemed wondrous to him, and he thought in his mind what this was supposed to be. (My translation)

In the original Old English, deliberately repeated phrases, words, parts of speech, alliteration and assonance all hammer home the series of shocks:

And he þa Malchus, þa he ful gehende wið ðæs portes geate eode, þa beseah he þiderweard, and beseah to þære halgan Cristes rode tacne hwær heo uppan þam portgeate stod mid arwurðnysse afæstnod; and hine þær gelæhte syllic wundrung, and on þære gesihðe hine gestod wundorlic wafung, and he stod and beheold, and him wundorlic þuhte; and he æghwider beseah on æghwile healfe, and he hawode on þa rode, and hit him eall wundorlic ðuhte, and he þohte on his mode hwæt hit beon sceolde (Magennis 1994, 454–60).

Although such techniques are put to use by near-contemporary writers Ælfric and Wulfstan, they are no less effectively employed here, and for a different purpose – the didactic style of these two writers contrasts with the more purely realist-narrative purposes of the author of the *Seven Sleepers*. In the next few lines Malchus's bewilderment continues to be presented (461–8). Baffled, Malchus runs around the city from gate to gate full of *wundrunge and wafunge* 'wonder and amazement' (line 464). He sees that the city is 'on oþre wisan gewend on oþre heo ær wæs' (lines 464–5): it has been transformed in a manner very different from what it once was, and now all the buildings are built in a different style from what they once were. It is like a dream, the writer comments, following his source (467–8), but adds: 'Malchus could recognise about as much of the city as a man who had never seen it before with his own eyes'. He now resorts to divine assistance, and as he says in the prayer, it is *eall ... færlices wundres* (478) 'all ... of sudden wonder': he cannot tell whether it is true or simply a dream. Clearly still worried that he will be recognised by Decius's men, he pulls on a beggar's disguise and hurries into the city.

At the marketplace in the city there are more sudden wonders, for here the men are all making their deals and transactions in the name of Christ. 'La, hwæt þis æfre beon scyle þæt ic her wundres gehyre?' exclaims Malchus (485–6): 'Whatever can this mean that I hear such a wonder?' Only just now, he says to himself, he *saw* a great wonder and now he is *hearing* an even greater one. Yesterday, no one even dared mention Christ's name, while today his name is continually on every man's tongue (485–9). The rhetorical contrast highlights Malchus's ever-increasing bewilderment. It also verges on comedy. Almost we are in the world of illusion and mistaken identity presented to great comic effect in another story of Ephesus, Shakespeare's *Comedy of Errors*. Malchus now pauses for thought, wondering, as he puts it, 'what his truth is' (497). Asking a passer-by in a convincingly polite and hesitant manner for the name of the town, he learns that this place really is Ephesus.

Such comic error and bewilderment has its dark side. The longer the character Malchus is denied the explanation for his experiences, the more he begins to suspect that he is not after all dreaming; and the more he realizes this, the more he begins to doubt his own sanity. Gradually, as it begins to involve more and more of the local citizens the comic situation threatens to turn very dark indeed. Like the servant sent to fetch rope in the *Comedy of Errors* only to find himself beaten with it by his own master, here similarly Malchus, who (it should be recalled) was sent to buy bread and to make sure he did not skimp on the portions, falls quickly foul of the non-comprehending market-traders and citizens.

The traders and merchants are a new breed of city inhabitant: nominally Christian in the way they speak, they are also rough and colloquial, and their main motivation is money. Ironically, given that Malchus has been wondering 'what his truth is', they are excessively confident that they know what the truth is:

> Without doubt it is the truth that we all see here, that this unknown young man has found an old gold hoard from ancient times and has kept it hidden secretly for many years.

Characteristically for the psychological realism of this story, Malchus immediately misunderstands the reason for their excitement. He begins to quake and tremble at the thought of them delivering him into the hands of Decius. He decides to abandon his errand. 'Keep the coins and the bread', he blurts out, for he wants none of them. In their turn, suspecting him of deliberate deception 'with your smooth words' ('*mid þinan smeðan wordan*') the traders lay hands on him and insist that he tell the truth, so that they can all share out the proceeds; and they even are willing to act as his *midsprecan i.e.* his advocates or co-witnesses – presumably at the city assembly – when the town-reeve (or *portgerefa* as the consul is called in Old English), will investigate this coinage, as he is required to do by late Anglo-Saxon royal legislation.

Conclusions

The fact of urbanisation in the tenth century is one that history and archaeology have gradually pieced together. The traditional poems of the *Exeter Book* do not record this trend, for they depict cities as ruined landscapes, emblems of transience. As is to be expected, however, those poems that can be firmly dated to the tenth century confirm the picture as we have it from archaeology. In the two Old English poems discussed above, a city like Bath is a place of royal consecration, under the tutelage of the established Church, and a city like Durham is famous for its saints and wonders. Anglo-Latin literature takes this further: Winchester is a *felix urbs*, as the many descriptions only confirm. These texts are paeans of the city.

But not everyone was content under the new dispensation. A careful reading of the story of Joseph and his brothers in BL Cotton Claudius B. iv, which is told through the mixed medium of word and image, of text and illustration, suggests that the city is a nexus of political power to which country people must turn only with trepidation. In the *Seven Sleepers* this theme is even more acute, for here we are presented with the character of the fearful and anxious steward Malchus, accused as a trafficker of false money and hauled before an insecure and irritable *portgerefa* (town-reeve) and the town assembly, all in a brave new post-Edgarian world of city gates and wily merchants. The author of the *Seven Sleepers* is a skilled writer, who expands on the Latin not only to anglicise the setting of the story but also to explore the protagonist's emotions of confused wonder and anxiety as he is confronted with his familiar birthplace transformed into a strange city. To use a parallel from archaeology: *Lundenwic* has become *Lundenburh*. In the Old English *Seven Sleepers*, Malchus becomes a figure of the returning exile, a tragic-comic figure facing change, an individual forced to come to terms with a newly urbanised and regulated society.

PART THREE

Topography

Bursting the Bounds of the Danelaw

Gillian Fellows-Jensen

It was the appearance of David Hill's *Atlas of Anglo-Saxon England* in 1981 that opened my eyes to the vast potentialities offered by map-making to the student of settlement history and it was many later encounters with David Hill 'live' in Manchester that really made me conscious not only of the three-dimensional landscape but also that time is a factor not to be forgotten. I am therefore delighted to offer this contribution to the conference volumes in his memory.

Introduction

It was a very flat map that influenced my first serious forays into settlement history. This was the one entitled 'The Scandinavian Settlement' that Hugh Smith published in connection with his pioneering work *English Place-Name Elements* (1956, map 10). The striking feature about it is the way in which it seems to show the effectiveness of the southern boundary that was drawn up between King Alfred and the Danish king Guthrum in the 880s (Whitelock 1955, 380–1). Smith's map has been reprinted time and time again since 1956. There are several factors to be remembered about the map, however. First and foremost, Smith does not include in it all names of Scandinavian origin but only parish names. Secondly, he omits from the map a number of place-names reflecting Scandinavian influence because they occur well south and west of this boundary. Thirdly and most seriously from the point of view of a study of Viking settlement, he omits all the relevant names in the Isle of Man and across the border in Scotland.

Nevertheless, even the most casual glance at the map will show how efficiently the southern boundary of the Danelaw functioned as a convenient demarcation between English and Danish territory in the ninth and early tenth centuries. The document in question is, of course, referred to in both surviving versions as a *frið* or 'peace treaty'. Smith's map certainly seems to show that apart from a few names in Northamptonshire and Warwickshire and a single one in Bedfordshire, Danish settlement was confined to the north and east of the boundary. In northern England, however, Danish place-names clearly

continued to spread out from the original areas of Danish settlement, while, although not shown by Smith, some few Nordic or nordicised names also made appearances south of the boundary, as can be seen, for example, on the 1973 Ordnance Survey map of *Britain before the Norman Conquest*. I shall therefore show here some sketch maps that can reveal how a few name-types have been disseminated at varying periods and in different directions and give some tentative explanations for the development of these distribution patterns.

The Grimston-type names

I shall begin with the Grimston hybrids, *i.e.* the English place-names in *-tūn* the specifics of which are personal names of Nordic origin. It was David Hill's maps showing the itineraries of King Cnut 1018–25 (Hill 1981, no. 163) and the extensive earldom of Svein Godwine's son in 1045 (Hill 1981, no. 184) that helped to explain the significance of the occurrence of such names in south-western England. That the estate of East Garston in Berkshire (*Esgareston* 1182) commemorates Esgar the Staller, the grandson of Tófi the proud, one of the most powerful followers of King Cnut, was pointed out over a hundred years ago by Sir Frank Stenton (1911, 26–7). At some time between 1086 and 1180 the hybrid name must have replaced the earlier name of the estate, *Lamborne*, which survives as the name of the parish and the hundred (Gelling 1973, 12; 1974, 330). The dates of formation of the other Grimston-type names in the south-west vary. A few of them are first recorded in Domesday Book, others in the twelfth to fourteenth centuries, but it seems most likely that all these names were formed during the reigns of Cnut or his successors. The group of six names in Herefordshire (Arkstone (*Arnketil*), Durstone (*Thorrøth*), Rowlston and Rowlstone (*Hrolf*), Swanstone (*Svein*) and Thruxton (*Thorkel*)) is striking and seems certain to date from the early years of Cnut's reign, probably around 1016, when three earls with Nordic names, Hákon, Eilíf and Hrani, were appointed to the earldoms of, roughly speaking, Worcestershire, Gloucestershire and

Herefordshire respectively (Keynes 1994, 80). Hákon Eiríksson was the son of Cnut's sister Estrith, and Eilíf Thorgilsson the brother of Cnut's brother-in-law Ulf Thorgilsson, while it was the less well known Hrani, also one of Cnut's trusted followers, who was assigned Herefordshire (Keynes 1994, 58–62). Something similar may have happened with the Grimston-type names in Staffordshire and Warwickshire but in these counties bordering on the Danelaw the names may be older than from Cnut's reign. Rolleston [rəʊlstən] (on Dove) in Staffordshire, for example, is recorded in the form *Roðulfeston* in a thirteenth-century transcript of a document dated 942 (S 479 and Sawyer 1979, no. 5) and in other eleventh-century documents and may well have received its name in the tenth century (Fig. 11.1).

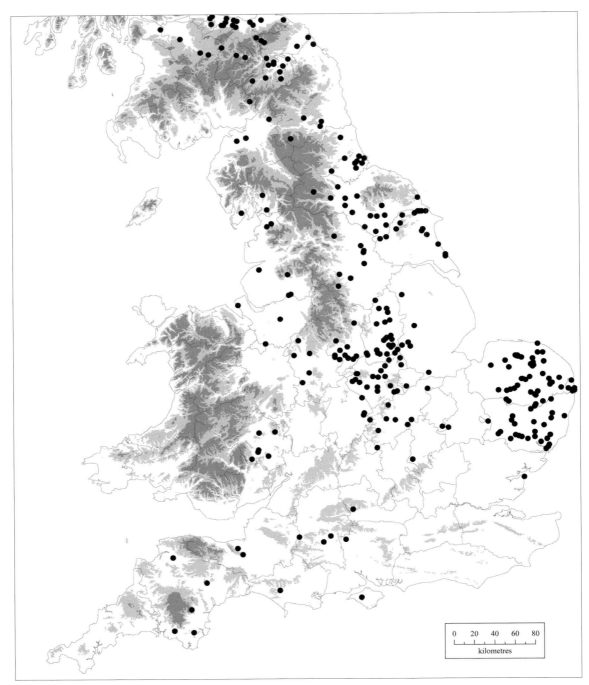

Fig. 11.1 The distribution pattern of the Grimston-hybrids recorded before c. *1500 (Drawn by the author with the aid of GenMap UK).*

In northern England there are ten possible Grimston-type names in Durham and the personal names involved suggest that they reflect settlers with Danish names who had moved north from the Danelaw. There are also a few examples of such names in Northumberland but what is really surprising is the spread of the Grimston-type names across the border into Scotland, where there are no fewer than twenty-eight names in south-east Scotland and the Central Lowlands (Nicolaisen 1967, 223–44). Almost all the Nordic personal names involved are also of frequent occurrence in Yorkshire and it seems likely to me that the names were brought to Scotland from the Danelaw together with settlers introduced there by the Scottish kings or other great lords. Two Nordic names that would seem to have become particularly popular in Scotland are *Dolgfin* and *Orm*, for they both occur four times in Grimston-type names, *e.g.* Dolphinton in East Lothian and Ormiston in Lanarkshire. With the exceptions of two Bonnytons in Angus that may contain the Nordic loanword in Scots *bond*< *bóndi* 'husbandman' rather than the related personal name (Kreis 2003, 314), the Grimston-hybrids do not spread any further north, naturally enough as such names only occur in areas where English was spoken. In Scotland they are, in fact, to be looked upon as Scots-English formations rather than Nordic ones.

The *býs*

The second group of names to be discussed are those containing the generic -*bý*, which is the most commonly occurring Nordic element in English place-names and had a fairly general meaning that would be appropriate for all kinds of habitations. I have noted at least 880 documented instances in Britain. After some initial uncertainty on my part as to its significance I finally came to the conclusion that it was generally bestowed by the Danes in England on pre-existing settlements and that this process can have taken place at different periods in various parts of the country. I had already reached the conclusion that the dissemination of the name-type began to spread out from the areas where the Danes settled after the original partitions of land when I presented a map showing the spread of the *bý*s in 1986 (Fellows-Jensen 1988, map 10f). This was after I had noted that most of the names in -*bý* in England that lie outside the Danelaw proper must reflect a penetration across the Pennines, moving in particular along the Eden valley towards Carlisle and spreading north from the Carlisle plain into Scotland and south from Carlisle along the coastal plain to near the present Maryport and across the sea to the Isle of Man and perhaps back from there to southern Lancashire and Cheshire (Fig. 11.2).

The most striking feature about the distribution of the *bý*s, however, is their comparative rarity of occurrence in East Anglia with the exception of the marked cluster on the island of Flegg in Norfolk, where there are no fewer than thirteen. I have been inclined to believe that an enclave of Danish settlers must have remained behind in Flegg after the English had regained control of East Anglia in 917 and that it was only because of the density of Danish settlement there and the isolated situation of the island that so many Nordic names survived (Fellows-Jensen 2007, 96–9). Other explanations are possible. Tom Williams (1993, 108) considered that Viking peasant immigrants may have been deliberately encouraged to settle in this remote area or that the names in Flegg are borne by settlements established at a late date when the elite in Norfolk may have been Scandinavian speakers. James Campbell (2001, 18–21) has suggested that Flegg may have been a fortified Viking base, while Lesley Abrams and David N. Parsons (2004, 418) looked upon Flegg as having had a strategic role in protecting commercial traffic between Norwich and the continental markets. These suggestions all have attractive features, although I hardly feel that the *bý*s were coined by a tenth-century Norfolk elite.

The dating of the formation of the *bý*-names in the Danelaw is uncertain but I am inclined to think that the *bý*s containing common nouns, for example Derby, Danby and Sowerby, pointing to the presence of deer, Danes and sour land, were among the earliest examples, resembling in type *bý*-names in Denmark, while *bý*s containing personal names of Nordic origin reflect the splitting up of great estates into smaller units of land that passed into the ownership of individual Danes at a slightly later date. Names containing personal names that had been introduced by the Normans, for example *Grimald* in Grimoldby in Lincolnshire and *Folkward* in Fockerby in the West Riding of Yorkshire, are unlikely to antedate the eleventh century. It is noticeable that there are no such names in East Anglia, only three in Lincolnshire and six in Yorkshire, while in Cumberland there are no fewer than nineteen *bý*s containing personal names that must have been introduced by the Normans, for example *Alain* in Allonby and *Robert* in Robberby and across the Scottish border in Dumfriesshire there are eight, for example *Lochard* in Lockerbie (Fellows-Jensen 1985, 15). These names reveal that the element *bý*, which would seem to have dropped out of use in England by the time of the Norman Conquest, must have remained in currency in Cumberland and Dumfriesshire, not to mention further afield in Scotland, for in addition to a few names in -*bý* that straggle along the coast in Galloway, for example Bagbie in Kirkcudbrightshire, there are several in the Central Lowlands. Most of the specifics in these names are not personal names but common nouns and adjectives of the type found in *bý*s in Denmark and in the early period in the Danelaw. The late names would seem to be analogical formations, recalling the *bý*-names in Yorkshire, for example *buski* 'shrubbery' in Busby in Renfrewshire and *hund* 'dog' in Humbie in Midlothian (Fellows-Jensen 1991, 83–4). It must also be analogical names inspired by immigrants from the Danelaw that account for the scattered *bý*s in Wales and the many in the Isle of Man, while the very scattered names in northern Scotland and the Northern and Western Isles were probably coined by Norwegian settlers. It should be noted that the *bý*-element would not seem to have spread to Scotland through Northumberland, where the element is completely absent.

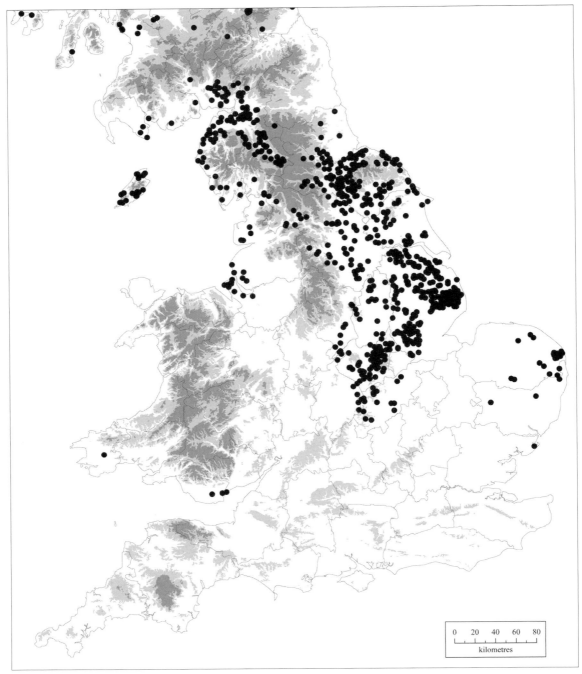

Fig. 11.2 The distribution pattern of place-names in -bý *recorded before* c. *1500 (Drawn by the author with the aid of GenMap UK).*

The *thorps*

The third dissemination pattern I shall discuss is that of the element *thorp*, which denotes some kind of secondary settlement and is the second most frequently occurring Nordic element in England (Fellows-Jensen 2009, 43–5). There are at least five hundred and seventy instances in England, and their distribution pattern is similar to that of the *bý*s in the Danelaw proper, although *thorp*, unlike *bý*, has made hardly any inroads west of the Pennines or across the southern boundary of the Danelaw. The most significant fact about this distribution pattern is that the *thorp*s cluster along or close to the two prominent ridges of high ground that run in the shape of two crescent moons in broad sweeps from the Yorkshire Moors down towards south-west England – the chalk ridge to the east and the ridge further west of oolitic limestone. The situation is complicated by the fact that at least fifty-four names contain the cognate Old English element *throp*, most of which form a kind of attenuated tail to the *thorp*-names. These English *throp*s mostly occur in the limestone Cotswolds (Gloucestershire 15, Oxfordshire 5) and Salisbury Plain (Wiltshire 10). The most recently published discussion of the *throp*-names, that by Cullen, Jones and Parsons (2011, 29–31 and fig. 2.6), has suggested modifying the line drawn by Alfred and Guthrum's treaty to exclude the greater part of Essex from the Danelaw and prefers to treat several of the names considered by Hugh Smith to be *thorp*s as *throp*s. This seems to me a rather drastic revision to make, even though it is true that the treaty-boundary was neither firm nor impenetrable. It is surely not surprising to find some uncertainty as to the choice between *thorp* and *throp* in areas close to boundaries such as Essex and the West Riding of Yorkshire. It now seems to me that all we can say with certainty is that on cretaceous and limestone upland the map shows the combined distribution pattern of *thorp* and *throp* (Fig. 11.3).

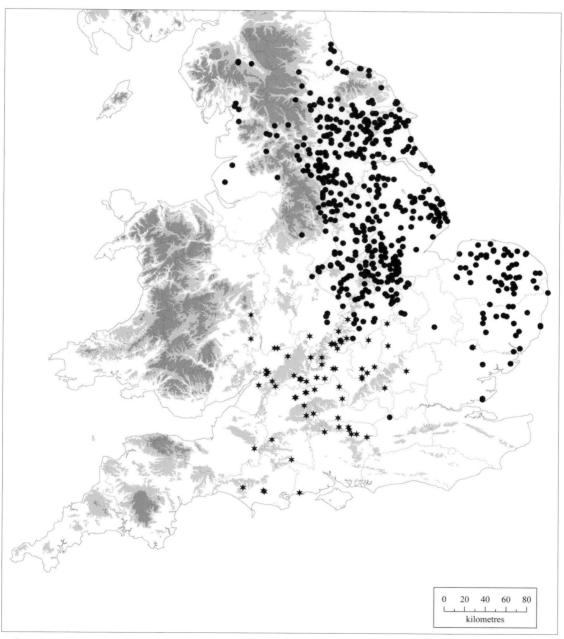

Fig. 11.3 The distribution pattern of place-names in -thorp (circles) and -throp (stars) recorded before c. *1500 (Drawn by the author with the aid of GenMap UK).*

Many years ago my good friend and Danish colleague Niels Lund wrote 'The absolute dominance of personal names as Danish first elements [in the *thorp*-names] suggests that the names do not signify the colonization of unused land, but rather a take-over of existing villages already called something + *thorp*, just as the Grimston hybrids were formerly called something + *tūn* (Lund 1976). I was rather shocked by this at the time but I have gradually come round to a somewhat different way of thinking because I have noted that although the Danes on the one hand were probably responsible for coining the *thorp*-names which have Nordic specifics, some of the simplex names in *Thorp*, as well as the compound names with English specifics, may simply reflect nordicisation of earlier English names. As an experiment, I produced two maps of names in *-thorp* in the East Midlands, one showing all the *thorp*-names and the other only those with Nordic specifics (Fellows Jensen 1978, 253, 256, maps reprinted in Fellows-Jensen 2009, 49–50). In spite of the possibility that *throp* may earlier have been current in a much larger area of England than the south-westerly regions where *throp*-names still survive, however, I still consider the numerous *thorp*-names in England to be largely the result of Danish influence, although I agree with Karl Inge Sandred (1994, 135) that they can hardly be relied upon as a basis for mapping Danish settlement. There seems no reason to look upon *thorp* as an element that made major inroads across the Danelaw boundary in England.

The *tofts*

There are only two other Nordic generics with a habitative significance that occur in fairly substantial numbers in settlement names in England. These are *toft*, denoting 'a curtilage, a plot of land on which a building stands' and *thveit*, denoting a clearing. The only serviceable distribution map that I had of names in *toft* was taken from Bengt Holmberg's thesis (1946, Karta 12). This showed that as far as England is concerned the distribution pattern of the *tofts* is with very few exceptions concentrated in the Danelaw area and no general movement of the element would seem to have taken place. The only marked exception is the single township-name *Toft*, with its earliest record as *Tofte* in the twelfth century (Dodgson 1970, 81). This Cheshire *Toft* lies in Bucklow Hundred and now consists of little more than a great house and a nineteenth-century church. From my own experience I know that the majority of the *toft*-names in England seem to be comparatively young, with comparatively few of them recorded in Domesday Book. They are most numerous in Lincolnshire. Interestingly enough, field-names containing the element are particularly frequent in the Holland division of that county, where early settlement names are rare (Cameron 1978, 82–3). It seems clear that the field-names containing the element reflect the fact that *toft* entered at an early date into the English language. Many of the settlement names and field-names are consequently English formations. As an element for forming settlement names *toft*

would not seem to have moved far out of the Danelaw. Peder Gammeltoft has for many years now been engaged on a study of *toft*-names in England and has found over 280 of them so far in eastern and northern England, and even a few in Gloucestershire, and he considers there are more to be found (Gammeltoft 2003, 43–63). I hope that he will soon be able to produce an up-to-date map.

The *thveits*

The last distribution group is one containing the element *thveit*, which originally denoted a clearing produced by cutting down trees or shrubland but was subsequently used in place-names of the settlements established on the sites. I have located 267 names in *-thveit* in England and Scotland and I consider that *thveit* is probably the best indicator of areas that were first fully exploited by the Vikings. The generic is certainly of Nordic origin. The pattern of distribution is very different from that of the other elements I have discussed, however. Nevertheless it seems likely that the element must have been more widespread in the early Viking period than suggested by the map. The reason why there are so few *thveits* to be seen in the southern Danelaw area is probably because the element dropped out of use at an early date there. Even as early as the time when Domesday Book was written the scribe found some difficulty with spelling the word and for later scribes in Norfolk it had become unrecognisable. Although its earlier presence in the county has been proved by its presence in several lost field-names there, it would not seem to have survived in the local dialect. In compound place-names in Norfolk English words were substituted for *thveit* as generic, for example *wīc* 'dairy farm' and *wiht* 'bend' in Crostwick, Taverham Hundred (*Crotuuit* and *Crostueit* in Domesday Book, *Crostwic* '1291) and Crostwight, Tunstead Hundred (*Crostwit* in Domesday Book), Guestwick (*Geghestueit* in Domesday Book, *Geystwight* 1482). The generic element remains clearly identifiable, however, in the two still surviving simplex names Thwaite (with Alby) and Thwaite (St Mary), probably because the monosyllable naturally bears the stress. Karl Inge Sandred (1990, 316) noted the fact that in Norfolk several of the *thveits* are found close to names in *-bý*, on which they may well have been dependent. Moving north into the East Midlands we find only a single name in *-thveit* in Northamptonshire, none at all in Leicestershire or Rutland, and only one in Lincolnshire, while there is a cluster of *thveits* in the well-wooded parts of Nottinghamshire and Derbyshire (Fellows-Jensen 1998, 101–06). There are many *thveits* in Yorkshire, particularly in the Pennine areas, and they are even more frequent in Cumbria and northern Lancashire, as well as southern Dumfriesshire (Fig. 11.4).

Most of the *thveit*-names are not recorded in early sources, only eleven in Domesday Book, four in Norfolk, five in Yorkshire and one each in Lincolnshire and Nottinghamshire. Most of the other names are found in much younger sources and in more northerly areas, where the generic *thveit* entered

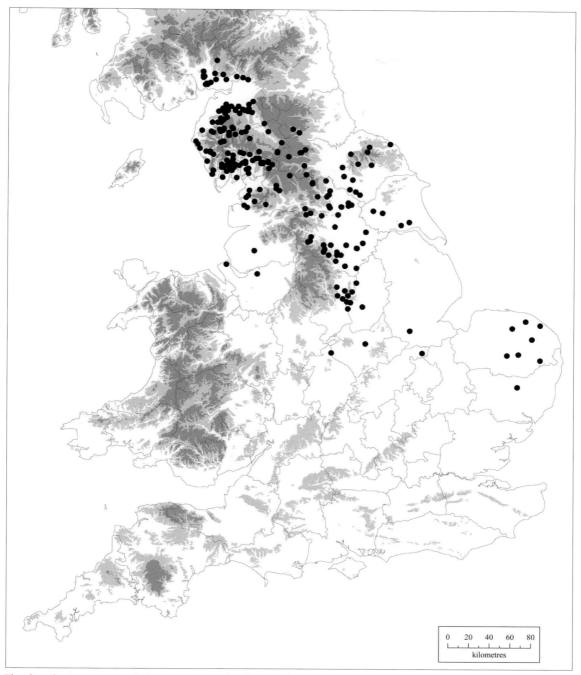

Fig. 11.4 The distribution pattern of place-names in -thveit recorded before c. 1600 *(Drawn by the author with the aid of GenMap UK).*

into the local dialects. Harald Lindkvist (1912, 97) pointed to a semi-appellatival use of the Scandinavian word with a perhaps fossilised plural ending in a twelfth-century Latin charter referring to land in Ireby in Cumberland: *Langethweit, et Stalethweit, et alios Thweiter qui pertinent ad Langethwest.* This would suggest that the Nordic element was current in the local dialect then. That a Nordic language was still being spoken quite generally at a relatively humble level of society

in the early twelfth century in north-west England has recently been argued persuasively by David Parsons (2011, 138) in his discussion of the background for the so-called Hiberno-Norse inversion compound names found there.

In parts of the area, for example the Furness Fells in northern Lancashire, I have noted the presence of several compound names in *-thveit* containing Nordic specifics, for example *íkorni* 'squirrel' in Ickenthwaite, *logn* 'calm' in

Loanthwaite and *sætr* 'shieling-hut' in Satterthwaite (Fellows-Jensen 1985, 348–57, map 18). Even though some of these names were first recorded after 1500, it seems likely that it was Nordic-speaking people who first established these clearings in woodland, presumably to increase the area of arable land available. That these names may represent the exploitation of new land in the Viking period is perhaps suggested by the fact that pollen diagrams in these areas indicate a decline in the amount of tree pollen at that time (Franks 1957, 2–10). On the other hand, many of the *thveit*-names in northern England may simply reflect the fact that long after Danish had ceased to be spoken in the Danelaw proper, that language continued to be used by humble people in the more isolated areas and that it was in these areas that the word *thveit* was absorbed into the English dialects. This means that what we are observing in the distribution pattern of the *thveit*s is on the one hand a general if limited use of *thveit* as a current naming-element in the Danelaw in the Viking period and on the other hand both the survival into the twelfth century of Nordic as a spoken language and a subsequent transference of the Nordic common noun *thveit* into the more northerly of the English dialects so that names containing this element continued to be formed.

Conclusions

The spread of the Grimston names reflects the spread of Nordic forenames and not of place-name elements. The occurrences of the Nordic forenames in south-western England show the influence of King Cnut and his successors and their followers. From the Danelaw proper the hybrid names spread northwards through Durham and Northumberland to south-eastern Scotland in the post-Conquest period together with an English language that had undergone marked Danish influence.

The *by*s are spread more densely than the Grimstons over the Danelaw with the exception of East Anglia. There would seem to have been a movement of *by*s from the Danelaw across the Pennines, spreading out from Carlisle south along the coastal plain to Man and perhaps back to southern Lancashire and Cheshire, and north into Dumfriesshire and the Central Lowlands. The settlers in Scotland must have brought the name-fashion north with them from the Danelaw.

The *thorp*s did not spread out of the Danelaw, only within it. It would seem that the *thorp*s and the cognate English *throp*s eventually ran together in a shared pattern reflecting the kind of land suitable for arable farming.

The *toft*s like the *thorp*s seem almost only to have spread within the Danelaw and much of the spread seems to have been at a rather later date than that of the *by*s.

The distribution pattern of the *thveit*s shows that in the south the element *thveit* dropped out of use at a very early date, while in the north it seems clear both that Nordic remained in common use after the end of the Viking period proper and that the element *thveit* later entered the English vocabulary there, where it was used frequently in connection with assarting, that is the grubbing up of trees and bushes in woodland to convert it into land suitable for arable cultivation.

Acknowledgements

I am deeply grateful to Alex Rumble for reading the paper at the conference when I could not be present and for making some helpful suggestions about the text. To Bo Nissen Knudsen I am indebted for turning my illustrations into a more preferable format. A slightly revised version of the paper in Danish translation is forthcoming in the series *NORNA-rapporter*.

Note

In this text place-names are located to the English and Scottish counties that precede the pre-1974 reorganisation.

'A Hill by Any Other Name': Onomastic Alternatives in the Anglo-Saxon Bounds of Taunton, Somerset

Alexander R. Rumble

I have two reasons for choosing this topic in memory of David Hill. Firstly, because it relates to the Anglo-Saxon history of Taunton in Somerset where David went to school, up the railway line from where he lived as a child and youth on the coast at Watchet. Secondly, because it relates to Anglo-Saxon estate-boundaries and makes me recall hearing David lecture, before I became a colleague of his at Manchester, when he was directing a weekend course on the Anglo-Saxon landscape for the department of Extra-Mural Studies at the University of Oxford in 1979. I was impressed then and often later by David's infectious enthusiasm both for mapping everything and for seeing the Anglo-Saxons as living figures in the landscape.

The early history of Taunton

Taunton in north-west Somerset was a major Anglo-Saxon estate-centre, with a minster church, situated in the valley of the river Tone between the Blackdown and the Quantock Hills (Fig. 12.1; Aston 1984, 189–92; Darby and Finn 1967, 202–4 , 214–16 with figs 35, 48 and 50). It was built by King Ine of Wessex as a fortification against the West Welsh and is mentioned in the *Anglo-Saxon Chronicle* under the year 722 as having been destroyed ('towearp') by Ine's wife Queen Æthelburh, apparently during a dynastic conflict involving an ætheling called Ealdberht (Bately1986, 34; with Greenway 1996, 226–7; Kirby 1991, 131). According to Winchester tradition (Luard 1865, 6; Deedes 1913–14/1924, 609), Taunton was given to the church by a Queen Frithugyth (probably the wife of King Æthelheard, Ine's successor)[1] *de suo patrimonio* 'from her patrimony', a gift subsequently augmented and confirmed by Kings Æthelheard, Æthelwulf and Eadred (S 254, 310–11, 521; OMW 4, 20–1, 85; CW 119, 128, 117, 57). However, since elsewhere Frithugyth is associated several times with Forthhere, bishop of Sherborne, the western of the two West Saxon dioceses which had been created by an

ecclesiastical division of *c.* 705 (Colgrave and Mynors 1969, 514–15), it has been thought 'most unlikely' (Finberg 1964, 217) that she would have granted such an important estate, which was within Forthhere's bishopric, to the eastern diocese of Winchester.[2] The charters relating to these particular alleged grants and confirmations of Taunton to Winchester all appear to be forgeries from the late tenth/early eleventh century. While it is probable that the bishops of Winchester at some point obtained control of the minster of Taunton with its landed property,[3] it is likely that they lost possession of the estate during the first half of the tenth century and that it returned to the royal fisc. The earliest believable records of permanent episcopal possession of the whole estate relate to the reign of Edgar (S 825; OMW 144; CW 29; Rumble 2002, no. V (xiv). Also S 1242; OMW 180; CW 61). The tenure of the estate by Bishop Ælfsige of Winchester (951–8) appears to have been only temporary, on a lease from King Eadwig to whom it was returned in the bishop's will (S 1491; Whitelock 1930, no. 4). Legal and fiscal rights which later belonged to the hundred of Taunton appear to have been acquired from Edgar and were enjoyed by the bishop of Winchester in 1066 and later (S 825; OMW 144; CW 29; Rumble 2002, no. V (xiv). GDB, fol. 87v; Thorn and Thorn 1980, entries 2:2–4. Pelteret 1990, no. 144; Robertson 1939, appendix i.4; Darby and Finn 1967, 203). The bishop had a castle there by 1138 (Luard 1865, 51) and held both the forinsec hundred and the hundred of the borough in the reign of Edward I (London, The National Archives, S.C. 12/18/28, recto; *Inquisitio quo warranto*). It is clear that Taunton, apparently once a royal administrative and defensive centre,[4] was one of the most important assets of the late Anglo-Saxon and medieval bishopric of Winchester.

Taunton's queenly connection is of interest in passing, as it includes not only the alleged actions of Æthelburh and Frithugyth in the eighth century, but also Edgar's queen Ælfthryth, who gave testimony in 995 × 1002 concerning the tenure of Ruishton, one of Taunton's dependencies (S

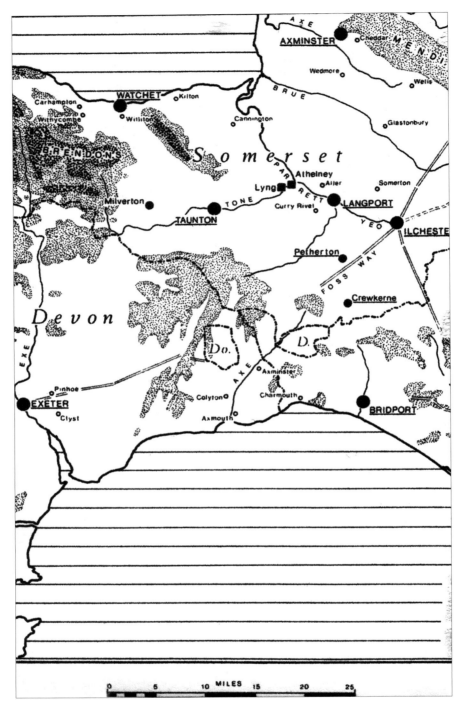

Fig. 12.1 The Location of Taunton (Extracted from D. Hill, An Atlas of Anglo-Saxon England, Oxford, 1981, p. 135, map 227. Reprinted by permission of the publishers Wiley-Blackwell and University of Toronto Press). Enlarged to approx. 106%.

1242; OMW 180; CW 61; Harmer 1952, no. 108. GDB, fol. 87r: Thorn and Thorn 1980, entry 1:26). We may note also that the neighbouring estate of Milverton had been held by Edith, queen of Edward the Confessor, before her death in 1075 (GDB, fol. 87r; Thorn and Thorn 1980, entry 1:26). She appears to have previously granted it to Giso, bishop of Wells, in 1061 × 1066, perhaps on a lease (S 1240; Harmer 1952, no. 70; Kelly 2007, no. 39).

Anglo-Saxon estate boundary-descriptions

Both texts discussed in the present paper are examples of estate boundary-descriptions.[5] An Anglo-Saxon wishing to describe the boundary of a unit of land could make use of three different categories of information:

(i) Reference to discrete places on the periphery of the land-unit

References of this sort are preceded by a preposition (such as *to, in, on, into*) and normally consist of one of the following constructions:

- *an article + a simplex noun*: 'a/the ford'
- *a compound of adjective + noun*: '(the) stony ford'
- *a compound of pers.n. + noun*: 'Wulfric's ford'
- *a pre-existing place-name + noun*: 'thorn-tree valley's ford'
- *the genitive of a folk-name in* 'ingas'/'waru' + *noun*: 'x-inga' or 'x-wara ford'
- *a longer descriptive phrase*: 'the valley which is called Wulfric's combe'; 'the thorn-tree which stands at the ford'

(ii) Use of the four cardinal points

The cardinal points are used in the following ways:

- to fix the limits of each of the four sides of the estate: 'on the north side *x*', 'on the east side *y*'
- to indicate the relation of one peripheral place to another: 'to *x* to the west of *y*'
- to specify the particular part of a named place: 'to the north part of *x*'; also, by inference, 'to the middle part of *x*'
- to control the direction of travel around the boundary: 'then onwards south to *x*'

(iii) A description of the line taken between peripheral places

Such descriptions of the perambulation associate the line of travel with a significant landscape feature by the use of adverbs which give modulations in height (*up, adune*) or directness (*on geriht, þweors*), or the use of prepositions which describe the route along, through or past the feature (*andlang, þurh, be*).

Different combinations of these three categories of information formed a text which was usually subdivided into sections introduced by words such as *þonne, þonon, þæt* or *swa*. Such a text could delimit for legal purposes the complete circumference of any size of land-unit. It would originally have been articulated in oral form during a perambulation of the particular boundary. Written versions of such descriptions delimiting estates of bookland survive both as integral clauses within royal Anglo-Saxon diplomas and as separate undated documents. The overall majority of these surviving texts are written wholly in the vernacular and followed, at least by the tenth century, a fairly consistent pattern. There are however a small number of boundary-descriptions which are mainly written in Latin with a scattering of Old English descriptive terms or names within them. The dating of these Latinate texts is not always clear: some are late eighth- or early ninth-century and pre-date the use of vernacular descriptions in a particular kingdom (Kelly 1998, 8; Kelly 2000–1, 34; Kelly 2007, 196), some others are later medieval texts. Among the later ones we must include the fifteenth-century Latin translations in the *Liber Abbatiae* of Hyde Abbey (BL MS Additional 82931), which occur in the manuscript immediately after their Old English models and counterpart Middle English translations, though their latest editor (Miller 2001) has removed the Middle English and Latin versions to an appendix in his edition.

The Taunton boundary-descriptions

In the case of Taunton we have both a boundary-description written wholly in Old English and one which is mainly in Latin. A comparison between the two texts allows some suggestions to be made about their relationship and date. Certain sections of the vernacular version also call into question a recent theory about the precision of Old English topographical terms.

Amongst the various documents surviving in the Old Minster archive which concern Taunton and its dependent settlements is a file which contains both a group of boundaries and a memorandum about early tenth-century leases. This file is represented by a group of seven consecutive texts copied into *Cod.Wint. I*, the earliest part of the *Codex Wintoniensis*, in 1129 × 1139 (BL MS Additional 15350, fols. 27v and 28r; S 352(1), 1819, 1571, 311(2), 254(2) *bis* and 1572; CW 64–70).[6] One of the documents in this file is the undated Old English version of the Taunton bounds (S 311(2); OMW 215; CW 67). These delimit the hundred of Taunton Deane and ran clockwise around the valley of the River Tone (Finberg 1964, no. 410; Darby and Finn 1967, figs 35, 48, 50; Grundy 1927, 7–22), starting and finishing in the east and crossing a large number of tributary streams. Some of the Taunton landmarks are also used in surviving boundary-descriptions for other estates in this part of Somerset, in particular Pitminster to the south (sections 14–16, 19, 21–2, 24–6) and Ruishton to the east (sections 1, 5, 15, 19–20, 72; S 440, 310) (OMW 65, 20; CW 72, 128),[7] while the 'gemot leah' 'meeting clearing' (in section 56) also occurs in the respective bounds of Bishops Lydeard, Cothelstone and *Cyricestun* (S 380, 1571, 345; Kelly 2007, 205).

A Latin version of the same Taunton boundary also survives but is not part of the file mentioned above. It is found within a grant by King Æthelwulf claiming to date from 854 but probably forged in the late tenth/early eleventh century (S 311(1); OMW 21; CW 117).

As was already realised in the sixteenth century by the antiquary John Joscelyn, who made two marginal notes in the *Codex Wintoniensis* to that effect,[8] we thus have alternative Old English and Latin forms for the locations named in most of the seventy-two discrete sections of the Taunton boundary. Not all of these alternative forms are of the same type however.

Thus in section 2 there is an example of full translation: *inde ad uetus fraxinum*, 'þanon to þam ealdan æsce' ('then on to the old ash-tree'), but in section 15 only partial translation, giving a hybrid form in the Latin *hinc usque ad collem ringpoldes* where the vernacular text has 'spa forð to ringpoldes hylle' ('so forwards to Ringwold's hill'). In section 13 we have the translation of a longer clause including reference to the line of the boundary: *hinc contra riuulum usque ad caput fontis*, 'þanon up agen stream oð hit cumð to ðes pulles heafde' ('then on up against the flow until it comes to the head of the stream'). In section 40 an extended descriptive phrase is used in the Latin but does not appear in the vernacular: *hinc ad uadum qui pettes ford dicitur* as opposed to 'ðanon to pyttes forda' ('and then to [the ford which is called] ford at the pit').

There is clearly an Old English text of some sort behind the Latin version. There is at least one error of translation in the Latin: *ad duram portam* for 'to heardan geate' ('to the hard gate' for 'to Hearda's gate') in section 25. There is also one apparent equivalency which I am as yet unable to explain: Latin *ad uiam publicam* ('to the public way') as against OE 'to þam ambran pege' ('to the ? favourable way')[9] in section 7, repeated in *usque ad ueterem uiam publicam* for 'oð ðone ealdan ambran peg' in section 49.

However *blaambroc* in section 20, a miscopying of 'blacanbroc', is probably an error on the part of the twelfth-century cartulary scribe. It may indicate that his exemplar was in an imitative script which contained a Half-Uncial or Hybrid Minuscule *a* (which looks like a double *c*), causing *ca* to be misread as *a*.[10]

But there are also copying errors in the vernacular version. Thus, there was a duplication after section 60 of section 68 'þanon on hægelstal cumb' due to eyeskip by a copyist. Also 'leollesces cumb' in section 65 is a mistake for *leolles cumb*. Elsewhere 'brigc cumbe' was written in section 64 for *byrig cumb*, due to confusion of OE *brycg* and *burg* (dat. sg. *byrig*), and in section 72 'on beaddincgbeorh' was written for *in beaddingbroc*, due to confusion of OE *beorg* and *brōc*.

In section 50 there is a variation between the two texts where it is not certain which is the more correct: the Latin has a directional command to the west (*hinc ad occidentalem partem uallis qui trus cumb nominatur*) while the vernacular has one to the north ('7 spa on norð healf trus cumbes') so it is not clear where the boundary lies in relation to 'trus cumb'.

Despite its peculiarities, it is probable that the Latin version is the primary written text of the boundary. We should note in particular the presence of a large number of extended descriptive clauses in the Latin version which utilised verbs of naming, several of which have their counterparts in the Old English.[11] Examples of these are:

[43] *... ad originalem fontem riuuli qui pillite nominatur*
'... to ðere frym pylle þe man pyllite namð'
'to the stream-source named Willett'

[46] *... usque ad occidentalem partem illius gronne qui pulluces mor nominatur*

'... oð ða peast healfe ðes mores þe man het pulluces mor'
'as far as the west side of the marsh called Wulluc's marsh'

[69] *... ad locum qui stan tor dicitur*
'... to þære stope þe is gehatan stan torr'
'to the place called stone rock'

Such phrasing would be unnecessarily wordy in a monoglot Old English context where the language of both the topographical term and the surrounding text is the same. It would be more natural to say 'to Willett'; 'to Wulluc's marsh'; 'to stone rock' instead of using a defining word with a subordinate clause. We should note Janet Bately's view that naming-constructions of this sort in Old English belong to a 'literary, not a colloquial, register' and reflect translations from a Latin source (Bately 2006, 357–8). Because the vernacular Taunton text thus appears to be a translation from the Latin one (and includes some copying errors) it cannot be seen as an exact representation of a primary Old English oral description taken down 'in the field'. It is a twelfth-century copy of a written exemplar which itself was at least two removes from the oral original.

The Latin text and its dating

The first written Latin record of the Taunton boundary was probably made at some time in the late ninth or tenth century, but not necessarily especially for inclusion in the charter of Æthelwulf into which it was subsequently copied (and from which the cartulary-copy was made), which is a forgery of the late tenth/early eleventh century. Although we should note the survival of some sequential Latin boundary-descriptions from Wessex which are dated to the late eighth and early ninth centuries,[12] two of which relate to estates in Somerset, the Taunton text is dissimilar in its vocabulary. It is unlikely that the Taunton text is so early. Its Latinity is not easy to date, but one word in particular suggests that the text is more likely to be from the late ninth or the tenth century. The noun *gronna* meaning 'a marsh or swamp' which occurs in sections 44, 46 and 67 is Late Latin, perhaps from Gaulish (Latham and Howlett 1975–97, 1108). It is found once in Nennius, *Historia Brittonum*, and also once each in the pertinence clause of two diplomas: one is the dubious foundation-charter of Thorney Abbey of alleged date 973 (S 792; Birch 1885–99, no. 1297), but the other is an apparently authentic diploma of Æthelred II dated 1002 concerning an estate in Sussex but possibly drafted in Kent (S 904; Kemble 1839–48, no. 707; Keynes 1980, 132–4). More significantly, the noun was used twice in Asser's *Life of King Alfred*, on both occasions in connection with the marshes around the minster at Athelney (caps 92, 97; Stevenson 1904, 80, 84, 255–6), some eight miles east of Taunton. An adjectival form *gronnosa* (neuter plural accusative) was also used by Asser to describe the same marshy Somerset landscape when King Alfred took refuge in it from the Vikings (cap. 53; Stevenson 1904, 41).[13] This may reflect the use of Asser's *Life* as a source of information about this part of Somerset by the draftsman of the Latin text of the Taunton bounds, although Taunton itself was not named by Asser. Alternatively, it may perhaps indicate that both Asser and the draftsman of the Taunton text acquired this possibly continental Latin word from a member of the community of the minster at Athelney, founded by King Alfred, a number of whom, as Asser stated (cap. 94; Stevenson 1904, 81), had come from Francia, probably as refugees from the Viking attacks in the 880s (Keynes and Lapidge 1983, 272, note 232).

Another Latin word is of interest in the context of any discussion of boundary-descriptions, although it is not so unusual in charter-texts as *gronna*. This is the noun *plaga*, used with a directional adjective such as *septentrionalis, orientalis, occidentalis* and either *australis* or *meridionalis* to refer to the side of something in relation to one of the cardinal points. It occurs ten times in the Taunton bounds (in sections 11, 14, 26, 28, 33–4, 39, 43, 48 and 63). The same word is also found in several places in the Vulgate version of the Old Testament, also with a directional aspect. For example, in Genesis (4:16. Gryson 2007, 9) it refers to the dwelling-place of Cain *ad orientalem plagam Eden* 'at the east side of Eden'. In Ezechiel (47: 15, 17–20 and 48: 1–8, 16, 23–8, 30, 32–4. Gryson 2007, 1338–40) it is used in connection with the recording of landmarks both in the setting of the borders of Israel and the division of the land between the twelve tribes of Israel. The usage in the Taunton bounds is slightly different, however, being used as part of a command to turn 'to the east, west, *etc.*'.

The Old English version and topography

The Old English version has certain features which may be of significance to those interested in current theories about topographical elements in English place-names. The wording of some of the extended descriptive sections in the vernacular version may call into question the claim of great specificity for such elements put forward in 1984 by Margaret Gelling in her book *Place-Names in the Landscape*, in the introduction to which she wrote:

> The general picture which emerges from the study [of Anglo-Saxon landscape terms] is of a people in possession of a vast and subtle topographical vocabulary ... [which] includes many groups of words which dictionaries treat as synonyms. My study has convinced me that they were rarely, perhaps never, synonyms to the Anglo-Saxons. Just as the Arab has many words for 'camel' and the Eskimo has many words for 'snow', the Anglo-Saxon peasant farmer had many words for 'hill' and 'valley' (Gelling 1984, 7).

This thesis was considerably expanded in 2000 in the collaborative and illustrated publication which the same author published with Ann Cole entitled *The Landscape of Place-Names* (Gelling and Cole 2000). In the introduction to this study of topographical settlement-names we find the argument even more forcefully put:

> Study of topographical names in relation to the actual landscape has made it clear that groups of words which

can be translated by a single modern English word such as 'hill' or 'valley' do not contain synonyms. Each of the terms is used for a different type of hill, valley or whatever, and many of the words have connotations which are not simply geomorphological. Valleys called **cumb** offered totally different prospects as settlement-sites from those called **denu**; a hill called **dūn** was likely to be the site of a large village, while one called **beorg** might have a single farm or be the site of a church (Gelling and Cole 2000, xiii).

Bearing these statements in mind, it is noteworthy that among the extended descriptive clauses in the OE version of the Taunton boundary we have some instances where the translator of the text from Latin has clearly not considered that the pairs of topographical words *cumb* and *denu*, *dūn* and *beorg*, *dūn* and *cnoll*, *holt* and *bearu* were different from each other. Thus, we find:

[5] '... to þere dene þe man het orcerd cumb'
  'to the valley (*denu*) called orchard valley (*cumb*)'

[63] '... on midnepeardne del þære dune þe man hæt beorg nemð'
  'to the middle part of the down (*dūn*) named heath hill (*beorg*)'

[60] '... on middel del þære dune þe man middel cnol nemð'
  'to the middle part of the down (*dūn*) named middle knoll (*cnoll*)'

[11] '... on norð healf ðes holtes þe man duddincg bearu nemð'[14]
  'to the north side of the wood (*holt*) named Dudda's grove (*bearu*)'

According to the Gelling/Cole thesis of topographical specificity, the paired words in these sections should not be employed as synonyms. The words for valley are thus sharply differentiated: *cumb* is a 'short, broad valley, usually bowl- or trough-shaped with three fairly steeply rising sides'(Gelling and Cole 2000, 103); but *denu* is 'mostly used of long, narrow valleys with two moderately steep sides and a gentle gradient along most of their length'(Gelling and Cole 2000, 114). Likewise, the word *dūn* is defined by the same authors as 'a low hill with a fairly level and fairly extensive summit ... ' and as 'whale-backed' (Gelling and Cole 2000, 164, 166), *beorg* is said to refer to an eminence with 'a continuously rounded profile' and is sometimes 'a rounded knob on the end of a ridge' (Gelling and Cole 2000, 145, 148), while *cnoll* is the 'summit of a hill' (Gelling and Cole 2000, 157). When it comes to the woodland terms, the contrast between *holt*, a 'single-species wood', and *bearu* 'a small wood' may not seem so remarkable, but the use of *holt* as the more generic term here is noteworthy.

The usage of these words in the Old English version of the Taunton bounds seems to call into question the current theory about topographical terms. The terms *denu, dūn* and *holt* appear to be employed as generic descriptions rather than as words designating highly-specific landscape features. However, as I hope to have demonstrated, we should remember that we are dealing with a translation rather than a primary Old English text here: a translation following, particularly closely in the extended descriptive clauses, the Latin written version of the boundary and one perhaps made by a monk whose first-hand experience of the niceties of the rustic landscape was limited due to his cloistered existence. His attitude to some at least of the inhabitants of that landscape may be judged by his comment on the 'holy ash-tree' in section 37: *ad quendam fraxinum quem imperiti sacrum uocant*, 'to a certain ash-tree which the ignorant call holy'.

Conclusion

One general conclusion to be drawn is that some surviving Old English boundary-descriptions may not be as close to the spoken word as we might expect. Other records of this sort, besides the Taunton one, may have been mediated, at least in part, through earlier written Latin versions which we do not now have. A hill by any other name may *not* be just as steep, but the Taunton texts suggest we cannot always tell this from the written boundary-descriptions.[15]

Notes

1   A doubt was raised by R. R. Darlington, in Fryde *et al.* 1986, 22. However, Frithugyth appears as Æthelheard's queen in S 1677 (Finberg 1964, no. 382).

2   On one occasion she travelled with Forthhere to Rome (*Anglo-Saxon Chronicle, s.a.* 737; Bately 1986, 35).

3   Immunities for the minster at Taunton, together with the church itself, were granted in 904 by Edward the Elder to Bishop Denewulf of Winchester and his community as part of an exchange in return for estates in Somerset and Wiltshire (S 373, 1286; OMW 44–45; CW118, 62; with Asser, bishop of Sherborne, witnessing S 1286 but not 373). This grant was also referred to in S 806; OMW 130, 130a; CW 58, 60 a forged charter of King Edgar dated 978 ?for 968.

4   It was not, however, mentioned in the Burghal Hidage, *temp.* Edward the Elder. The Somerset fortifications were Langport, Lyng, Watchet and Bath (Hill 1996, 206, 209, 223–4 and 190–2).

5   For a general survey of the surviving material, see Reed 1984.

6   For the date, see Rumble 1981, 163–4.

7   Note also in Ruishton S 310 (but not in the Taunton bounds) *to offa dic*, apparently a doublet of Offa's Dyke, a major research interest of David Hill's.

8   BL MS Additional 15350, fol. 27v: 'this description is also in latyne. fol. 57 where this note is. [*nota*]'. This note links with another example of Joscelyn's distinctive *nota* on fol. 59r, the location of S 311(1); OMW 21; CW 117. He also underlined most of the Old English words in the latter text. For Joscelyn's interest in Old English words, see Graham 2000, especially 121, note 76.

9   Following Turner (1953, 124): 'A weak form of OE *ambyre*, "favourable, fair", is a possibility to be considered'. Cf. also the comments on *ambyrne wind* (*Orosius* I.i), with various connotations of usefulness or suitability, noted by Bately (1980, 193).

10 For charters in imitative scripts, see Crick 2011. Two of Crick's examples (discussed on pp. 11, 14, 16, with figs, 1.3–4) are from the Old Minster archive (S 376 and 540; OMW 50 and 90); she dates S 376 to 'the last Anglo-Saxon century' (p. 14) and says that S 540 was 'possibly by the same scribe'(p. 16).

11 See sections 1, 5–6, 8–9, 11–12, 17, 19–20, 22, 30, 32–3, 37, 40–1, 43, 46, 50, 60, 62–4, 67, 69–71. Note that the sections 62 'to þere riðe þæt man negles cumb clypiað' 'to the stream called "Nægl's valley"' and 67 'on east healf þæs mores þe man hafoc ford nemð' 'to the east side of the marsh called "hawk ford"' are elliptical in connection with places called 'Nails[bourne] combe stream' and 'hawk ford [marsh]'.

12 S 262, King Cynewulf ?774 (Kelly 2007, no. 27; land on the River Wellow, Som.); S 264, King Cynewulf 778 (BL Cotton Charter viii.4; Birch 1885–99, no. 225; Little Bedwyn, Wilts.); S 267, King Beorhtric 794 (Finberg 1964, 118–20; land on the River Parrett, Som.); S 268, King Beorhtric 801 (Kelly 2000–1, no. 7; Crux Easton, Hants). Cf. also S 230, King Cædwalla 680 (?improved in the tenth century) (Kelly 1998, appendix 2A; Pagham, Sussex).

13 A further substantival form was also used by Asser in relation to the metaphor of the scholar ceaselessly collecting diverse extracts of Holy Scripture, like a bee collecting [pollen from] the flowers of the surrounding marshes (*gronnios*, masc. acc. pl.: cap. 88; Stevenson 1904, 74). The simile is Aldhelmian, see Lapidge 1979, 61–2.

14 A further example may be 'to þam ðyfele þe man het bradan ðorn', 'to the bush called "broad thorn-tree"'(section 6) although the word *ðyfel* probably always has a more general connotation than the species-specific *ðorn*; see respectively Smith 1956, ii. 223 and 204–5. The section 'to ðæm beorge ðe mon hateð æt ðæm holne', 'to the tumulus/hill called "at the holly-tree"' in the mid-ninth-century bounds of the South Hams, Devon (within S 298; OMW 16) is not similar, however, since *beorg* and *holegn* do not belong to one single category of terms.

15 Since delivery of my paper at the memorial conference in June 2012 I have come across Kitson 2008 which criticises the over-prescriptive attitude of Gelling and Cole in relation to usage of *beorg* and *dūn* in OE and which independently has reached the same conclusion as me with respect to dating of the Latin and OE versions of the Taunton bounds.

Appendix:

Latin and Old English Bounds of Taunton, Somerset

BL MS Additional 15350, fols 27v (Old English) and 59r (Latin); here divided into 72 sections, with Modern English translation from the vernacular text. Note that I have translated OE *healf* as 'side' when (*e.g.* in section 41) it is matching *pars* in the Latin text (and is followed by a boundary feature referred to in the genitive case). I have left it untranslated when it matches *plaga*, where the sense is of a more general directional instruction (*e.g.* in section 28). A full discussion of the topography will appear in Rumble forthcoming. I have only identified here watercourses and the settlement-names Wiveliscombe (38) and 'Lydeard' (45).

1. *In primis ubi riuulus qui beaddingbroc nominatur in fluuium tan ingreditur*
   'Æræst þer beaddincbroc scyt innan tan'
   First where *Beaddingbroc* goes into the Tone

2. *inde ad uetus fraxinum*
   'þanon to þam ealdan æsce'
   then on to the old ash-tree

3. *sic trans montem in alterum fraxinum*
   'spa ðpyres ofer dune to þam oðrum esce'
   so crosswise over the down to the second ash-tree

4. *hinc tendit ad occidentem usque quo ueniatur ad spenam*
   'spa pestpeard þæt hit cymð to spænan'
   so westwards so that it comes to the place where shingles are got (*spænan*)

5. *hinc ad uallem qui orcer cumb nominatur*
   'þanon to þere dene þe man het orcerd cumb'
   then on to the valley called 'orchard valley'

6. *hinc directo termino trans montem ad fruticem quę lata spina uocatur*
   'ðanon on gerihta ofer dune to þam ðyfele þe man het bradan ðorn'
   then straight on over the down to the bush called 'broad thorn-tree'

7. *inde ad uiam publicam*
   'þanon to þam ambran pege'
   then on to the ? favourable way

8. *hinc ad locum qui pidecumbes heafod uocitatur*
   'þanon to pidecumbes heafde'
   then on to the head of wide valley

9. *hinc per riuuli decursum ad uadum quod æartancumbes ford nominatur*
   'ðanon andlang riðe to eartancumbes forda'
   then on along the stream to ford of the valley of the Yarty

10. *hinc ad latum fossatum*
    'þanon to þere pidan dic'
    then on to the wide ditch

11. *hinc tendit ad occidentalem plagam in aquilonali parte nemoris quod duddincg bearuðu <nominatur>*
    '7 spa hit strecð pestperd on norð healf ðes holtes þe man duddincg bearu nemð'
    and so it extends to the west to the north side of the wood named 'Dudda's grove'

12. *hinc a lato quodam fossato ad uadum quod oteri ford nominatur*
    'þanon of þere pidan dic to oterigc forda'
    then on from the wide ditch to ford on the Otter

13. *hinc contra riuulum usque ad caput fontis*
    'þanon up agen stream oð hit cumð to ðes pulles heafde'
    then on up against the flow until it comes to the head of the stream

14. *hinc ad aquilonalem plagam usque in piðig cumb*
    'þanon on norð healf oð hit cumð to piðig cumbe'
    then on to the north until it comes to willow-tree valley

15. *hinc usque ad collem ringpoldes*
    'spa forð to ringpoldes hylle'
    so forwards to Ringwold's hill

16. *hinc usque ad uiam paldanes*
    'þanon to paldanes pege'
    then on to *waldan*'s way

17. *hinc ad campum qui oxena feld dicitur*
    'spa to oxena felda'
    so to open land of the oxen

18. *hinc ad caput snelles cumb*
    'ðanon to snellescumbes heafde'
    then on to head of Snell's valley

19. *hinc directe ad lapidem qui gregan stan nominatur et ad occidentalem partem collis qui man hille nominatur*

   'spa forð on gerihta to gregan stane 7 on pest healfe man hylle'
   so forwards straight on to grey stone and to the west side of common hill

20. *hinc ad fontem riuuli qui blaambroc dicitur*

   'þanon to blacanbroces pylle'
   then on to spring of Black Brook

21. *sic per riuuli decursum in rubro uado*

   'spa nyðer andlang streames on ðone readan ford'
   so down along the stream to the red ford

22. *sic ad occidentem per quoddam nemus usque ad riuulum qui scitere dicitur*

   '7 spa pest þurh þone holt oð hit cymð to scytere'
   and so west through the wood until it comes to *Scytere*

23. *sic per riuuli decursum in uetus uadum*

   'andlang scyteres on þone ealdan ford'
   along *Scytere* to the old ford

24. *hinc ad occidentalem in profundum uadum*

   'þanon on peast healf on þone deopan ford'
   then on to the west to the deep ford

25. *hinc ad duram portam*

   'ðanon to heardan geate'
   then on to Hearda's gate

26. *hinc dirigitur ad australem plagam in riuulum bænnan cumb*

   'þæt on suð healfe on bennascumbes riðe'
   then to the south to stream of Benna's valley

27. *hinc deorsum in riuuli cursum*

   'spa nyðer on ðere riðe forðryne'
   so down in the flow (*forð-ryne*) of the stream

28. *a torrente illo ad occidentalem plagam usque ad fures leage*

   'of ðere burnan on pest healf oð hit cymð to fyres leage'
   from the stream to the west until it comes to furze-covered clearing

29. *hinc ad columbarem uallem*

   'ðanon to culfran dene'
   then on to valley of the dove

30. *hinc ad locum qui fidu scaga dicitur*

   'þæt forð to ðere stope þe man het fiduc scaga'
   then forwards to the place called Fiduc copse

31. *hinc trans campum ad occidentalem partem in hafuc halras*

   'spa ðpyres ofer ðone feld on pest healfe on hafuc alras'
   so crosswise over the open land to the west to hawk alder-trees

32. *hinc directo termino usque ad amnem qui tan nominatur*

   'þæt on gerihta oð hit cymð to tan ðære ea'
   then straight on until it comes to the River Tone

33. *hinc ad occidentalem plagam usque ad riuulum qui mælænburna dicitur*

   'þanon on pest healfe to melenbeorge burnan'
   then on to the west to 'Melbury-bourne'

34. *hinc ad aquilon<al>em plagam usque ad ceappan leage*

   'spa norð oð cyppan leage'
   so north as far as Cyppa's wood/clearing

35. *hinc ad mæleburnan*

   'þanon to melenburnan'
   then to 'Melbourne'

36. *hinc ad canum spinum*

   'spa to þam haran ðorne'
   so to the grey thorn-tree

37. *hinc ad aquilon<al>em partem et sic ultra campum tendit ad occidentalem partem usque quo ueniatur ad quendam fraxinum quem imperiti sacrum uocant*

   'þæt norð ofer ðone feld pestpeard oð hit cymð to ðan halgan æsce'
   then north over the west part of the open land until it comes to the holy ash-tree

38. *sic ad occidentalem dirigitur in flumine iuxta terminos pifeles cumb*

   '7 spa pest on þa ea pið pifelescumbes gemere'
   and so west to the river towards the boundary of Wiveliscombe

39. *item ad aquilon<al>em plagam per flumen dirigitur usque uetustum ac terminalem fossatum*

   'þæt eft norð be ea oð ða ealdan gemerdic'
   then again north by the river as far as the old boundary-ditch

40. *hinc ad uadum qui pettes ford dicitur*

   'ðanon to pyttes forda'
   and then to ford at the pit

41. *hinc ad occidentalem partem montis <qui> lufan dun nominatur*

   '7 spa on peast healf lufes dune'
   and so to the west side of Luf's down

42. *hinc ad aquilon\al/em partem in ueteri strata*

'þæt norð on ða ealdan streat'

then north to the old paved road

43. *et sic per aquilonalem plagam tendit ad originalem fontem riuuli qui pillite nominatur*

'7 spa ðurh ðone norð del on gerihta to ðere frym pylle þe man pyllite namð'

and so straight on north to the stream-source named Willett

44. *sicque ad orientem usque ad albam gronnam*

'spa east on ðone pitan mor'

so east to the white marsh

45. *inde ad lidegeard*

'þanon to lydegeard'

then on to grey ridge/'Lydeard'

46. *hinc ad aquilonalem partem usque ad occidentalem partem illius gronne qui pulluces mor nominatur*

'þanon norð oð ða peast healfe ðes mores þe man het pulluces mor'

then on north as far as the west side of the marsh called Wulluc's marsh

47. *et sic tendit usque ad aquilon<al>em partem usque ad amnem*

'7 spa on gerihta norð on ða ea'

and so straight on north to the river

48. *sic contra amnis decursum ad occidentalem plagam usque ad longam spinam*

'þæt up ongen stream on norð healf oð ðone langan þorn'

then up against the stream to the north as far as the tall thorn-tree

49. *hinc ad aquilon\al/em partem ultra campum usque ad ueterem uiam publicam*

'þæt norð ofer ðone feld oð ðone ealdan ambran peg'

then north over the open land as far as the old ?favourable way

50. *hinc ad occidentalem partem uallis qui trus cumb nominatur*

'7 spa on norð healf trus cumbes'

and so to the north side of brushwood valley

51. *hinc in publicam uiam usque ad breuem fossatum*

'spa on ðone ambran peg oþ þa sceortan dic'

and so to the ?favourable way as far as the short ditch

52. *hinc ad orientalem partem in rugan beorh*

'spa on east healf on rugan beorg'

so to the east side to rough hill/tumulus

53. *ab hoc loco in aquilonalem partem æsc holtæs in hors paðes uadum*

'of ðere stope on norð healf esc holtes on horspaðes ford'

from that place to the north side of ash-tree wood to horse-path ford

54. *hinc ad australem partem ad sordidum uadum*

'þæt suð on ðone horegan ford'

then south to the dirty ford

55. *hinc in hean pylle*

'spa on hean pille'

so to deep spring

56. *hinc in gemot leage*

'þæt on gemot leage'

then to meeting clearing

57. *hinc dirigitur usque ad dun dic*

'spa on gerihta oð dun dic'

so straight on as far as down dic

58. *hinc in piscis fontem*

'þæt on fisc pylle'

then to fish stream

59. *sic ad elle pylle*

'spa to elle pylle'

so to elder-tree spring

60. *hinc ad mediam partem montis qui middel cnol nominatur*

'spa on middel del þære dune þe man middel cnol nemð'

so to the middle part of the down named 'middle knoll'

<68 duplicated here in the Old English text>

61. *et sic in mæccan fen*

'7 spa on meccan fen'

and so to Mecca's marsh

62. *sic ad riuulum qui negles cumb nominatur*

'þæt to þere riðe þæt man negles cumb clypað'

then to the stream called 'Nægl's valley'

63. *hinc ad orientalem plagam in mediam partem monticuli qui hæð beorh nominatur*

'spa east on midnepeardne del þære dune þe man hæt beorg nemð'

so east to the middle part of the down named 'heath hill'

64. *sic in summitate uallis quę byrig cumb dicitur*

'7 spa be ufepeardum brigc cumbe'

and so by the upper part of bridge [*for* fort] valley

65. *hinc in leolles cumb*

    'þanon on leollesces cumb'
    then on to ?old man's beard valley

66. *deinde in pennan stan*

    'spa on þeannan stan'
    so to ?Weanna's stone

67. *hinc in orientalem partem illius gronne qui hafuc ford nominatur*

    'þæt on east healf þæs mores þe man hafoc ford nemð'
    then to the east side of the marsh named 'hawk ford'

68. *inde on hegsteldes cumb*

    'þanon on hægelstal cumb'
    then on to bachelor's valley

69. *et sic ad locum qui stan tor dicitur*

    '7 spa to þære stope þe is gehatan stan torr'
    and so to the place called 'stone rock'

70. *hinc ad sæchbroc*

    'þæt to secgbroce'
    then to sedge brook

71. *et sic in flumine quod tan nominatur*

    '7 spa on ta þa ea'
    and so to the River Tone

72. *et sic per aluei decursum quoadusque perueniatur iterum in beaddingbroc*

    '7 spa be eastreame oð hyt cymð eft on beaddincgbeorh'
    and so by the river-stream until it comes back to *Beaddingbroc*

13

The Early Medieval Dykes of Britain

Erik Grigg

I first met David Hill at a conference on Defence in the Viking Age at University College London in 2007. His advice as I was embarking on a PhD on medieval dykes has proved invaluable.

Introduction

This paper discusses early medieval dykes, what an older generation might call linear or travelling earthworks. There seems to have been a rash of them built in the early Anglo-Saxon period, roughly AD 400–850, and though many of us are aware of the work David Hill did on Offa's Dyke (Hill 1985; Hill 2000; Hill and Worthington 2003), how many other early medieval dykes could we name? While there have been thorough surveys on individual earthworks and comprehensive reviews of other aspects of Anglo-Saxon life such as coinage, burial practices, poetry, law or literature, there has been no

general survey of these dykes. This means scholars have focused on the better-known, larger earthworks like Offa's Dyke, but this is extremely atypical among early medieval dykes (Fig. 13.1). Even if we only count the continual central section (which is about 95 kilometres long), Offa's Dyke is thirty-two times longer than the average length of other possible early medieval dykes. It is like generalising about motor vehicles based on Formula One cars or thinking the Flying Scotsman can tell you how tank engines shunted goods in the 1930s. It is surprising not only that no-one had systematically studied these dykes, but also how many there were.

The adjective 'possible' is used quite deliberately when discussing early medieval dykes as they are notoriously hard to date since there is no associated buried domestic refuse. For some dykes there are OSL and radio-carbon dates from ditch

Fig. 13.1 Offa's Dyke (Photograph: Erik Grigg).

Dyke	Date range	Median
Becca Banks (Radiocarbon)	559–674	637
Scot's Dyke (Optically Stimulated Luminescence)	420–600	510
Clawdd Mawr, Llanfyllin (Radiocarbon)	630–710	670
Crugyn Bank (Radiocarbon)	650–780	715
Giant's Grave, Powys (Radiocarbon)	340–530	435
Short Ditch, Powys (Radiocarbon)	410–590	500
Upper Short Ditch (Radiocarbon)	540–660	600
Wat's Dyke (Radiocarbon)	268–630	449
Wat's Dyke (Optically Stimulated Luminescence)	792–1002, 747–927 and 742–952	897, 837 and 847
Fleam Dyke (Radiocarbon)	340–640	490
Devil's Ditch, Garboldisham (OSL)	660–980 and 650–930	820 and 790
Harrow-Pinner Grim's Ditch (Radiocarbon)	60–340 (Possibly residual material)	200
East Wansdyke (Radiocarbon)	890–1160 (Possibly material dumped after the abandonment of the earthwork)	1025

Fig. 13.2 Dates from excavations of dykes.

deposits, but for most, other evidence is necessary (Smith and Cox 1986, 20–1; Malim, Penn *et al.* 1996, 65–7; Wheelhouse and Burgess 2001, 144; Hankinson and Caseldine 2006; Bates, Hoggett *et al.* 2008; Bowlt 2008; Hayes and Malim 2008; O.A.N. 2008; Fig. 13.2). If, for example, an earthwork cuts a Roman road it is probably post-Roman, and if an Anglo-Saxon charter records the dyke or it has an Anglo-Saxon pagan burial inserted into the ditch it undoubtedly existed in the early medieval period. If there is good evidence that it is early medieval the term *probable* early medieval dyke is used; if there is no dating evidence, and we also cannot prove it is not early medieval, it is termed a *possible* early medieval dyke.

The division of groups of dykes and intermittent earthworks can be rather arbitrary, but a search of various lists of monuments (including the National Monuments Record and the county Sites and Monuments Records) and consultation with county archaeologists suggested about 137 separate possible candidates. Nineteen were dismissed as a mixture of roads, natural features, prehistoric dykes and later medieval earthworks, which left eighty-five possible early medieval dykes, twenty-four probable examples and nine prehistoric dykes possibly either rebuilt or reused in the early medieval period (not reused as mere hedgerows or somewhere to bury the dead, but reused as a dyke; Figs 13.3–13.6). That is potentially 118 early medieval dykes, stretching 449km or 279 miles, approximately the distance from Manchester to Dieppe. These are actual built structures; this study does not include sections where a river links two parts of an earthwork or possible lost sections that may only ever have existed in the imagination of

Aves Ditch

Berks Downs Grim's Ditch

Bucks-Herts Grim's Ditch

Cranborne Chase Grim's Ditch

Deil's Dyke

Devil's Mouth

Double Banks

Foulding Dykes

Grim's Ditch (Leeds)

Hug's Ditch

King Lud's

King's Wicket

Miles Ditches

Reading – Coombe Bank

Reading – Oxford Road

Riddlesdown Dyke

Roman Rig

Senghenydd

South Dyke

South Oxfordshire Grim's Ditch

Tisted cross valley dyke (n)

Tisted cross valley dyke (s)

Whitford Dyke

Fig. 13.3 Prehistoric or later medieval dykes.

Aberbechan	Crookham Common earthworks	Minchinhampton
Aber-Naint	Dane's Dyke	Mount Pleasant dyke
Bank Slack	Devil's Ditch Doles Wood	New Ditch
Bardon Mill	Devil's Ditch Pepper Hills Firs	Nico Ditch
Bar Dyke	Devil's Ditch Wonston	Offa's Dyke in Herefordshire
Battery Banks	Dodman	Offa's Dyke in the Wye – English Bicknor
Beachley Bank	East Tisted-Colemore	Offa's Dyke in the Wye – St Briavel's
Bedd Eiddil	Faesten Dyke (Kent)	Panworth
Bedwyn Dyke	Festaen Dyke (Hartley Witney)	Park Pale near Topcliffe
Black Ditch Snelsmore	Ffos Toncenglau	Pen y Clawdd
Bolster Bank	Fron Hill Dyke	Ponter's Ball
Broomhead Dyke	Froxfield Long Dyke	Red Hill
Bunns' Bank	Froxfield short dyke A	Shepherd's Well
Bwlch y Cibau (west)	Froxfield short dyke B	Stepper Point
Bwlch y Clawdd	Froxfield short dyke C	Surrey-Kent Dyke
Bwlch yr Afan	Froxfield short dyke D	Swaledale Hodic
Calver Dyke	Fullinga Dyke	Swaledale middle group north
Catrail (Picts' Work Ditch)	Giant's Grave	Swaledale Ruedic
Catrail proper	Giant's Hedge	Swaledale southern dyke
Cefn Eglwysilan and Tywn Hywel dykes	Gilling Wood	Swaledale western group
Cefn Morfydd	Grim's Bank Padworth	Tor Clawdd
Cefn-y-Crug	Hayling Wood	Tor Dyke
Clawdd Llesg	Heriot's Dyke (Greenlaw)	Tyla-Glas
Clawdd Mawr (Dyfed)	Heriot's Dyke (Haerfields)	Ty Newydd
Clawdd Mawr (Foel)	High Dyke	Vervil Dyke
Clawdd Mawr Glyncorrwg/Bwlch Garw	Horning	Wallace's Trench
Clawdd Seri	Inkpen Dyke	Wantyn Dyke (northern)
Clawddtrawscae	Lower Short Ditch	
Cowlod	Military Way	

Fig. 13.4 Possible early medieval dykes.

Aelfrith's Ditch	Devil's Ditch	The Rein
Becca Banks	Fleam Dyke	Rowe Ditch
Bica's Dyke	Fossditch	Rudgate Dyke
Bokerley Dyke	Giant's Grave	Short Ditch
Bran Ditch	Grey Ditch	Upper Short Dyke
Bury's Bank	Heronbridge	Wansdyke (East)
Clawdd Mawr (Llanfyllin)	Offa's Dyke	Wansdyke (West)
Crugyn Bank (inc. Two Tumps)	Pear Wood	Wat's Dyke

Fig. 13.5 Probable early medieval dykes.

Bichamditch

Black Ditches Suffolk

Black Dyke

Bwlch y Cibau (north)

Combs Ditch

Devil's Ditch Garboldisham

Harrow-Pinner Grim's Dyke

Launditch

Scot's Dyke

Fig. 13.6 Rebuilt or reused prehistoric earthworks.

an antiquarian. Despite their differences in length they were all surprisingly similar in design: they usually had a single bank and single ditch. The ditches were about as deep as a grown man, they are often ignored by parish boundaries and most are found around the fringes of Mercia (but not within Mercia).

They can be subdivided into different categories termed by this study Sinuous, Route-blocker, Reused Prehistoric, Peninsula, Marker Boundary, Multiple and Large, though most fit into more than one group. Although a few look like mere estate boundary markers (two probable and three possible early medieval dykes classified as Marker Boundaries), the majority are obviously something more. Compared to other pre-Modern earthworks they are huge; after calculating the volume of earth moved it became obvious that only Roman engineers eclipsed them (Fig. 13.7). Estimates for the number of workers needed to build these dykes have used a variety of formulas and the results have varied. Wormald claimed Offa's Dyke could have been built with just 5,000 men if it was spread over the four decades of Offa's reign, Hill claimed 125,000 men could build it in two summers, while Reynolds suggested the building of Wansdyke required over 15,000 labourers (Wormald 1982b, 122; Hill 1985, 142; Hill and Worthington 2003, 113–19; Reynolds and Langlands 2006, 41). To produce a far more accurate estimate of the number of labourers required, many different digging rates (from experiments using prehistoric techniques, accounts of nineteenth-century navvies, estimates used in the building trade and figures provided by archaeologists) were studied (Hanson and Maxwell 1983, 132; Bachrach 1993, 67; Dixon 1993, 147; Ashbee and Jewell 1998, 491; Breeze and Dobson 2000, 82; Spain 2001, 5; Erskine 2007, 98; Anon. 2008, 9-1-1 and Nick Higham personal communication; Fig. 13.8). Where the source gave an hourly rate a daily rate was extrapolated and *vice versa* to make them comparable. From these figures it was calculated a man in the early medieval period could move 0.25 to 0.3m³ of soil per hour, with a daily rate of 1.5 to 3m³ (the range depended of on whether they worked a 6- or 10-hour day). This would mean the largest early medieval earthworks

would have required a workforce of just a few thousand and for most early medieval dykes a mere one hundred men could have dug it in a summer. This is far fewer than the estimates of most previous studies. If Offa could raise *tens* of thousands of men as others have speculated, he probably would not have bothered digging a dyke, but instead would have annihilated the Welsh.

Functions of dykes

The original primary function of these dykes has long been a mystery. Scholars once thought they marked fortified borders between Anglo-Saxon kingdoms or where the Britons held back the onslaught of the Anglo-Saxons (Taylor 1904; Godsal 1913; Sumner 1931). Fox challenged this belief, claiming that Offa's Dyke in particular was an agreed frontier marker (Fox 1955). More recently scholars have linked dykes to the rise of kings and kingdoms, seeing them as manifestations of imperial pretensions, assertions of power in the landscape, methods of unifying/defining a heterogeneous kingdom and ways of creating a sense of 'us and them' (Squatriti 2002; Wileman 2003; Reynolds and Langlands 2006; Tyler 2011). It is necessary to explore the main theories in turn, considering whether the dykes had a military function, were frontier markers, or were manifestations of regal power; but first some other ideas must be briefly discounted. These dykes are not trade barriers: there is simply not enough trade in this period to justify building such huge structures to control it. They are too large to be agricultural and do not enclose areas like an estate or a park boundary. They are not religious: clerics barely mention them and none seems to demark a sacred space.

We need to clarify what kind of evidence would we expect if a theory of a particular function was valid. If they were border markers they should obviously mark borders and large sections would continue to do so both in Anglo-Saxon charters, and even on early Ordinance Survey maps, as borders have a great continuity in the English landscape. If they were a border they would have a title like 'border dyke' or be named after the kingdom that built it. If they were manifestations of royal power they might also be named after kingdoms or at least the king that built them. The king would publish boasts about them on, say, coinage, inscriptions and in the written literature. If they were military and were garrisoned we would expect to find living quarters and forts which would yield signs of occupation.

The idea that dykes were manifestations of royal power perhaps sounds the most elegant and seductive theory. However, apart from one line in Asser's biography of Alfred where he (inaccurately) says Offa's Dyke ran from sea to sea, which may be an echo of Mercian boasting, there is nothing in the literature, on any coin or even a single inscription where a king boasts about a dyke (Keynes and Lapidge 1983, 71). If the dykes took tens of thousands of people to dig, this was surely beyond the organisational skills of all but the mightiest of kings

Name	Volume in m³	Length in metres
Car Dyke	3300000	92000
Hadrian's Wall (wall and vallum)	3000000	120000
Offa's Dyke	798000	95000
Antonine Wall (ditch and bank)	569835–955000	63000
Devil's Ditch	550800	12000
Wat's Dyke	453120	59000
East Wansdyke	244800	20400
Silbury Hill	239000	158
Fleam Dyke	234000	5200
Dorset Cursus	116970	10000
(Average dimensions of probable early medieval dykes)	113742	10323
Bokerley Dyke	95310	5295
West Wansdyke	89100	13500
Becca Banks	65520	4200
Fossditch	60480	9000
Thetford Castle motte	52000	100
Bran Ditch	35100	5000
Rowe Ditch	28125	3750
The Rein	22344	1900
(Median dimensions of probable early medieval dykes)	19272	3235
Bury's Bank	16200	1500
Crugyn Bank (inc. Two Tumps)	11750	2720
Ladle Hill hillfort (if completed)	11000	750
Grey Ditch	9504	1200
Aelfrith's Ditch	4350	5000
Heronbridge	3654	350
Pear Wood	2462	400
Great Barrow at Knowlton Rings	2318	38
Upper Short Dyke	1575	500
Clawdd Mawr (Llanfyllin)	1215	450
Short Ditch	1152	640
Camps Top hillfort near Morebattle	900	1000
Giant's Grave	780	250
Rudgate Dyke	261	100
Bica's Dyke	216	400

Fig. 13.7 The size of probable early medieval dykes and other large ancient earthworks.

and they would be manifestations of royal might, a way of extracting tribute in a largely coin-less society through labour from the marginal areas of a kingdom. However, the estimates of the number of labourers needed in this study suggests most dykes were undertakings less on the scale of the Olympics and closer to the building of a youth centre. Only two dykes are named after kings; none are named after kingdoms and only one (The Rein near Aberford in Yorkshire) has a name that may mean 'boundary' (Smith 1961, 230). Only 26% of the total length of probable early medieval dykes is contiguous

Study	Type of equipment	Hour rate in m³	Day rate
Overton	Prehistoric	0.14–0.17	[0.84–1.7]
Pitt-Rivers	Prehistoric	0.25	[1.5–2.5]
Erskine	Roman	0.75–1.5	10–20
Bachrach	793 *i.e.* Charlemagne's workers	0.3	[1.8–3]
?Navvy	Nineteenth-century	[1.53–2.55]	15.3
Rawlinson	Nineteenth-century	[0.61–1.02]	6.1
Dixon	?	0.5	[3–5]
Spon's	Modern	0.3	[1.8–3]
Royal Engineers	Modern	0.3	[1.8–3]
Overton	Modern	0.48	[2.9–4.8]
Higham	Modern	0.4–1	[2.4–10]

Fig. 13.8 Estimates of digging rates.

with parish boundaries, exactly the same percentage as the nine prehistoric dykes in this study, and the figures for contiguity with county, national and diocese boundaries are tiny. When dykes are cited in boundary clauses of Anglo-Saxon charters they seem to be landmarks not borders. Some Anglo-Saxon estate boundaries cut straight across dykes, others merely touch the dyke before changing direction, while some seem to deviate from their natural course to run along the dyke for a short distance before leaving the earthwork. This makes the border theory as unlikely as the regal power theory. Historians who have tried to match dykes to early medieval borders, like the southern frontier of Northumbria, have tied themselves in knots (Blair 1955; Hart 1977, 53; Higham 1993a, 142–4; Higham 1997, 151; Rollason 2003, 25–8; Higham 2004b, 405–8). If Wansdyke did not exist it is unlikely any historian would suspect the Mercian-Wessex border ran through the middle of Wiltshire. However, if the only solution left is the military one then we would need to account for the total lack of evidence of forts and a permanent garrison.

David Hill postulated that Offa's Dyke was a stop line set back from the border where locals rallied to thwart raiders penetrating the heart of the kingdom. If this theory was accurate for all dykes we would not expect gateways or forts and these features are indeed absent. They should be set back from borders (which they are) so that the locals could gather their weapons and assemble during times of stress before the dyke was overrun. Almost all early medieval dykes cut either Roman roads, ancient ridgeways, or trackways described in Anglo-Saxon charters as a *herepaþ* or army path. During fieldwork, dykes are often hard to locate even with a good Ordnance Survey map, yet there are invariably panoramic views either from the dyke or an adjacent prominent hill. Perhaps beacons surmounted these hills. Pollen samples from early medieval

dykes suggest they were dug across open grassland which would accord good views (Crampton 1966; Green 1971, 138; Nenk, Margeson *et al.* 1992; Malim, Penn *et al.* 1996, 78–95; Wheelhouse and Burgess 2001, 141; Squatriti 2004). There is some evidence from a couple of dykes of turves placed onto the bank; this may have been to stabilise the earthwork but would also camouflage it (Green 1971, 132–3; Hill and Worthington 2003, 54, 81 and 101). If these earthworks were designed to promote the power of kings they should not be hidden.

While there is almost no evidence of dykes as symbols of regal power, there are references in Welsh poetry to fighting on dykes and references in the *Anglo-Saxon Chronicle* to fighting near dykes (Evans 1915, 113–14; Williams 1935, 3 and 42; Kirby 1977, 32; Bately 1986, 25 and 33; Jarman 1988, 38; Pennar 1988, 70; Nurse 2001, 3; Irvine 2004, 22 and 35). Some dykes have names that suggest a military function like Burghdyke and Festean Dyke. Even the size of the banks and ditches suggest a barrier to movement. Some scholars have summarily dismissed a military use, asking where is the archaeological evidence for battles at the dykes (Muir 1981, 155–60; Squatriti 2002; Wileman 2003, 63; Squatriti 2004; Tyler 2011, 161), but there are numerous examples of weapons and burials with signs of injury from dyke excavations. In Cambridgeshire at Bran Ditch, over fifty burials, some of which had no heads, were found (Fox, Palmer *et al.* 1924–5; Lethbridge and Palmer 1927–8; Reynolds 2009, 57 and 106–8). Shield bosses, swords and spear heads have been found on different occasions at the Devil's Ditch and the High Dyke in Cambridgeshire (Lethbridge 1938, 309; Phillips 1948, 9; Lethbridge 1957, 1–2; Biddle 1962–3; RCHME 1972, 147; Webster 1973; Hope-Taylor 1975–6, 124; Reynolds 2009, 217). There are two mass graves from dykes on the Welsh borders plus reports of skeletons 'slain

Dyke	Labourers needed to build it in a single season	Range of estimates by other scholars
Offa's Dyke	2660–5320	5000–76000
Devil's Ditch	1836–3934	1000
Wat's Dyke	1510–3237	100–36875
(East and West Wansdyke together)	1113–2385	15000
East Wansdyke	816–1749	1000
Fleam Dyke	780–1560	
Becca Banks [through rock]	655–1092	
Average for early medieval dykes	397–785	
Bokerley Dyke	318–635	
West Wansdyke	297–594	20
Fossditch	202–403	
Bran Ditch	117–234	
Rowe Ditch	94–188	
The Rein	74–148	
Median for early medieval dykes	64–128	
Bury's Bank	54–108	
Crugyn Bank (inc. Two Tumps)	39–78	
Grey Ditch	32–63	
Aelfrith's Ditch	15–29	
Heronbridge	12–24	
Pear Wood	8–16	
Upper Short Dyke	5–11	
Clawdd Mawr (Llanfyllin)	4–8	
Short Ditch	4–8	
Giant's Grave	3–5	
Rudgate Dyke	1–2	
Bica's Dyke	1–2	
Total	9099–18199	

Fig. 13.9 Estimates for the number of people needed to build various probable early medieval dykes.

in battle' from Bedwyn Dyke in Wiltshire, as well as reports of weapons or bodies at three other dykes (Bray 1783, 206; Burne 1950, 403; Fox 1955, 204–5; Hill and Worthington 2003, 150–52; Reynolds 2009, 59). Some may be later victims of the Vikings, disturbed pagan furnished burials, or criminals buried in a convenient ditch, as we know the Anglo-Saxons inserted burials into older features and buried executed criminals at prehistoric dykes (Hinchcliffe 1975, 126–28; Reynolds 2009, 130–31). Hill postulated that the Bran Ditch burials indicated a typical execution site from AD 900 to 1080, a suggestion Malim thought 'very sensible' despite the fact that the associated finds date to the fifth or sixth centuries (Hill 1975–6; Malim, Penn *et al.* 1996, 111); unless they were executed for being extremely out of fashion the idea is untenable. Apart from the mutilated burials and weapons, there are no other early medieval finds from any early medieval dyke apart from one cattle jawbone from a dyke in Yorkshire (Wheelhouse and Burgess 2001, 144): no coins or pottery, just spearheads, shield bosses, knives, swords and mutilated bodies.

Dykes and defence

Undoubtedly the idea that dykes are manifestations of royal power sounds more sophisticated than a theory that has people hacking bits out of each other with lumps of sharpened metal, but David Hill once wrote that a model should grow out of the evidence; we must not start out with a model and bludgeon the information into the approved shape (Hill 1988, 10). If we create a theory on the basis of no evidence, or even worse, in defiance of the available information, we are no better historians than Geoffrey of Monmouth. This study concludes that dykes were designed to prevent or counteract raiding. However, recent studies of dykes have displayed a reluctance to accept that they fulfilled such a military function despite the evidence all pointing to this conclusion; but why is this so? Historians from Gildas and Bede onwards have never really liked or understood warfare, and this pacification of the past is not confined to studies of the early medieval period (Armit 2001). Modern historians dismiss the military theory by simplistically asking why the invaders did not simply outflank the defenders by going round the ends of the dyke (Muir 1981, 158–9; Wileman 2003, 63), but that is very easy to answer. Early medieval warfare was probably characterised by localised raiding, not mass invasions or set-piece battles with flanking movements that can be reproduced on a table top using lead soldiers. The location of these dykes clearly demonstrates they were designed with raiding in mind. They are set back from borders and on a hit-and-run raid you might not know about the earthwork until it was too late; as you rode into the heart of an enemy kingdom along a road it would suddenly come into view, lined with locals protecting their lands and families. A dyke would give locals levies somewhere to stand firm as uncontrolled flight is a common and disastrous problem with non-professional troops. The raiders would not have an Ordnance Survey map. If they did go round the ends they would probably enter the woods, marshes or heathland that seem to mark the ends of many dykes, this is where the locals hunted and the raiders would now be the game. As they were picked off, the leader of the attackers would have to decide whether to leave the wounded or further deplete his forces by allocating men to help them. Meanwhile the hue and cry would bring more defenders and the raiders would be outnumbered. Even if they carried on, the raid would be doomed: raiders need a quick getaway to drive their captured slaves and cattle home, not an extensive detour through hills, woods, marshes or moors pursued by angry defenders.

Groups from across the globe have used raiding as a significant tactic in war: the Maoris, the tribes of the Amazon, the Native Americans of the plains, slave raiders of East Africa, the soldiers who carried out trench raids in World War I, the tribes of Indonesia, the commandos of World War II (Halsall 1989; Brown 1991, 191–217; Nunneley 1998, 46–8; Ashworth 2000, 176–203; Phillips 2000, 15–20). All these groups called off their raids when the alarm was raised and did not creep round fortifications once they were spotted. Raids are quick, furtive and confused affairs. Often early medieval dykes occur in groups: creep round one and there is another. Only when the Vikings started to raid did it become impossible to predict the route raiders would take and dykes were superseded by *burhs*. Some early medieval dykes have single large postholes and others decapitated skeletons. These are not gallows sites as hanging does not sever the neck; perhaps heads of defeated raiders were displayed on stakes to scare off others or decapitated unsuccessful defenders buried where they fell (Lethbridge and Palmer 1927–8; Palmer, Leaf *et al.* 1930–1; RCHME 1970, 313–14; Youngs 1981, 184).

An exception

On that grim note we should end, but perhaps it is worth adding a postscript on Offa's Dyke. This earthwork dates to the twilight of the 'Dyke Ages' as we could dub them, it *is* named after a king and it is too big to ambush an unsuspecting raider. Perhaps it was a grandiose white elephant. Offa may have taken a widespread practical utilitarian military structure and build a 'supersized' version as a response to Welsh raids. Perhaps this is the one dyke that *was* built to reflect the power and pretensions of a king and unite a disparate kingdom in opposition to the foreigners or *wealas* to the west. If so David Hill's theory that it was built as a stop line against Welsh raids was the right theory, but applied to the one dyke that was the exception that proved this rule.

Reflections upon the Anglo-Saxon Landscape and Settlement of the Vale of Pickering, Yorkshire

Dominic Powlesland

D. Hill D. Phil, as he was known to many friends, was a remarkable scholar, a gifted teacher and passionate believer in the need both to challenge and understand the Anglo-Saxon past. His method was through the study and mapping of the text resources and the physical remains. In his own words he was 'less interested in undertaking excavation than in using the results'. He also surrounded himself with those who were zealous about different aspects of research. He taught thousands of Extra-Mural students about the methods, delights and returns of scientific field archaeology while at the same time entertaining both undergraduates and Extra-Mural students with his intimate understanding of Anglo-Saxon England and its role in post-Roman Europe.

David's underlying shyness was coloured by an unjustifiable insecurity related to his unconventional academic career. This contributed to his boisterous lecturing style, most often described as brilliant, which had a considerable influence on my own approach to public lecturing. He was an inveterate 'borrower' of cigarettes and 'cadger of lifts', both actions being linked to intense, exciting, incisive and humorous discussion. I count myself to have been lucky to know David as a friend, a teacher, mentor and colleague; he knew more about Anglo-Saxon England than anyone I have ever met and anyone who was put off by his occasional use of 'Bollocks' to start a lecture failed to appreciate how much knowledge and dedication underpinned every 'performance' as his lectures were. While David, in his own words, was not an ardent excavator this did not stop him from successfully training many hundreds of Extra-Mural students to excavate and record to high standards and engage them in the reasoning behind every trench opened. I worked with him on numerous excavations on Offa's and Wat's Dykes, excavations which for the most part could solve a question in a weekend. The 'Doris' trenches on the Wat's Dyke for instance, consistently revealed that 'gaps' in the Dyke described by Cyril Fox as areas covered with 'Forests so Dense' or as David said one day after a couple of

pints 'Doris-so-Fence' were in fact not gaps at all, implying that we need be careful about populating gaps in our data with woodland (Fox 1955). It is of considerable interest to note that these areas described by Fox as covered with woodland seem all to be located remotely from the public houses in which Fox stayed when carrying out his fieldwork.

I remember well the day when the idea to create the *Atlas of Anglo-Saxon England* (Hill 1981) was put forward, over lunch in the Manchester University staff bar, and the excitement of drawing up with David the first few maps before I left Manchester to work at West Heslerton; that memory is of David at his most inspiring, and I shall always carry it.

Introduction

I have worked in the Vale of Pickering in North Yorkshire for nearly thirty-five years. My departure from Manchester for West Heslerton was triggered by the discovery of the early Anglo-Saxon cemetery during sand extraction (Powlesland *et al.* 1986, Powlesland and Haughton 1999). A request for appropriate staff to take on the excavation was made to the Department of Archaeology at Manchester. David put me forward and the rest, as they say, is history. From my own point of view the interest in West Heslerton was greatly enhanced by the suggestion that other discoveries at Cook's Quarry, West Heslerton, included evidence of contemporary settlement. In the short term this turned out to be untrue as the settlement situated to the north of the Anglian cemetery was in fact of Late Bronze/Early Iron Age date (Fig. 14.1), but by the time this was discovered we had already started work and the chance to engage with a supposedly 'empty' landscape was too absorbing to miss. Work with David provided a fine foundation for the ideas that developed during the early years at West Heslerton, in particular the need to engage with the archaeology at a landscape scale.

The chance discovery of an early to middle Saxon cemetery could have been followed by a simple salvage excavation and

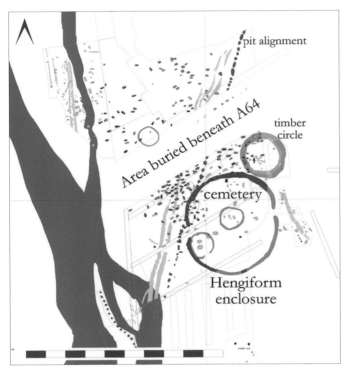

Fig. 14.1 West Heslerton, plan of the Neolithic and Bronze Age monument complex and overlaying Early Anglo-Saxon cemetery.

summary report, adding to the corpus of Anglo-Saxon burials, but not much more. However, it was recognised that the cemetery was located within an established prehistoric monument complex. It was also realised that the parts immediately threatened by quarrying did not cover the full extent of the cemetery which was being badly damaged by ploughing beyond the limits of the quarry; equally important evidence of activity from other periods was similarly under threat elsewhere within the approved planning permission for the quarry. More significantly, although the Vale of Pickering covers an area of more than 500sq km, with the exception of Star Carr, associated sites around the edge of the former Lake Flixton, the late Bronze/early Iron Age palisaded enclosures at Staple Howe and Devil's Hill, the Roman Fort and *vicus* at Malton, a few Anglo-Saxon *Grubenhäuser* at Wykeham and Seamer and a handful of medieval castle and monastic sites, it appeared at the time to be largely an archaeological distributional blank (Clark 1954; Brewster 1963,1981; Corder and Kirk 1928; Moore 1966; Pye 1976, 1983; l'Anson 1913). In contrast, numerous barrows situated on the uplands of the Wolds and Moors overlooking the Vale had been the subject of multiple investigations by antiquarians, evidence taken to reflect both intensive and extensive activity in the upland areas (Greenwell 1877; Mortimer 1905; Manby 1975). Both in terms of visible distribution and the pattern of earlier investigation an impression thus existed that while the Yorkshire Wolds and North York Moors were landscapes of major archaeological significance, the Vale was an area where little had happened.

The discovery of a 'new' early Anglo-Saxon cemetery at West Heslerton thus raised important questions about the scale and distribution of post-Roman population and offered substantial new analytical opportunities such as the recovery of mineral replaced organic materials and textiles and early research into trace elements and archaeological DNA (Montgomery 2006). Amongst the first studies of Anglo-Saxon DNA, research was undertaken on the Anglian burials by a PhD student at UMIST, Christine Flaherty, who sadly was unable to complete her research but was able to indentify male burials with conventionally female grave assemblages and female weapon burials. As such the cemetery excavation could be justified on the basis of the production of new knowledge, and this could only be properly appreciated if it was contextualised.

The need for a landscape perspective

The initial work at Cook's Quarry revealed that the cemetery and surrounding landscape had been extensively affected and influenced by deposits of blown sands which had gradually built up, preserving archaeological deposits in a way very rarely found in Europe. These blown sands had buried fragile old ground surface deposits, protecting them from plough damage but at the same time reducing the sensitivity of the buried features to crop-mark formation. Areas of exceptional preservation had thus been lagged against discovery through air photography on account of the thick blanket of blown sand limiting crop-mark growth, giving an impression of absence where in fact there was outstanding presence. Whilst excavation proceeded in the area of the cemetery and over many hectares of ground due to be quarried to the north, it was realised that the blown sands preserved an effectively unique landscape record showing extensive, intensive and multi-functional as well as multi-period use of the landscape. Such evidence directly contrasted with the established view of a landscape of minimal archaeological potential. In order to try and gain some understanding of the discoveries at Cook's Quarry a programme of more intensive air-photography was begun in tandem with the rescue excavations to try to secure evidence that would enable us to place the substantial evidence in a broader landscape. The air photography programme relied largely upon the generosity of local farmers with aeroplanes, in particular Carl Wilkinson from Knapton whose runway was in the adjacent parish, about 3km away, who was happy to report the visibility of crop-marks as they formed and take advantage of local conditions to go aloft at short notice. The aerial surveys were mostly conducted during the summer, and autumn excavation seasons were targeted primarily at a small 10 × 20km area covering south eastern parts of the Vale of Pickering and the northern edge of the Yorkshire Wolds (Powlesland 1980). This area was repeatedly visited, enabling us to build up a picture of crop-mark evidence. What this showed was that past activity on the southern margins of the Vale had been more extensive than on the Wolds.

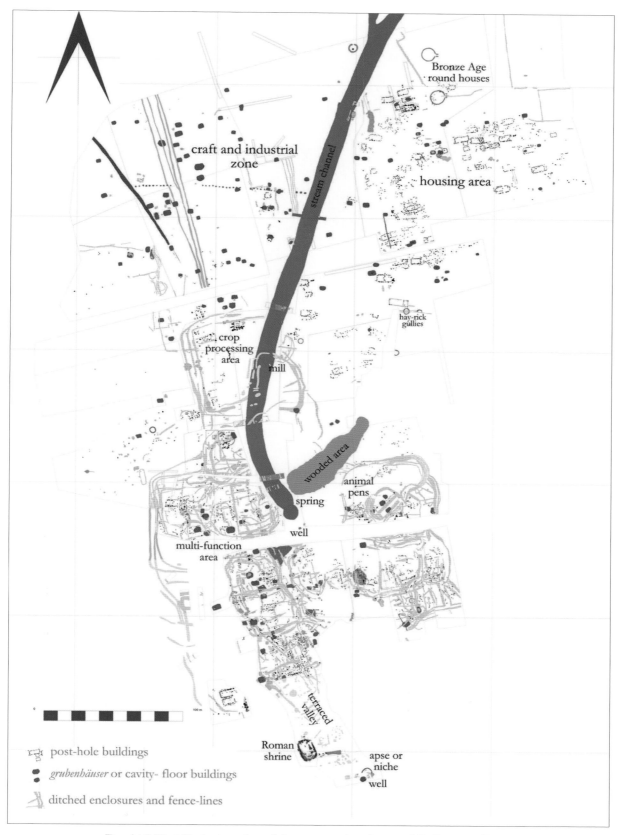

Fig. 14.2 West Heslerton, plan of the excavated early to middle Saxon 'village'.

Fig. 14.3 A large cluster of Grubenhäuser *situated to the south of a section of Iron Age and Roman period 'ladder settlement' near East Heslerton; notice the large concentration of tiny ring-ditch features between these two groups on the western side.*

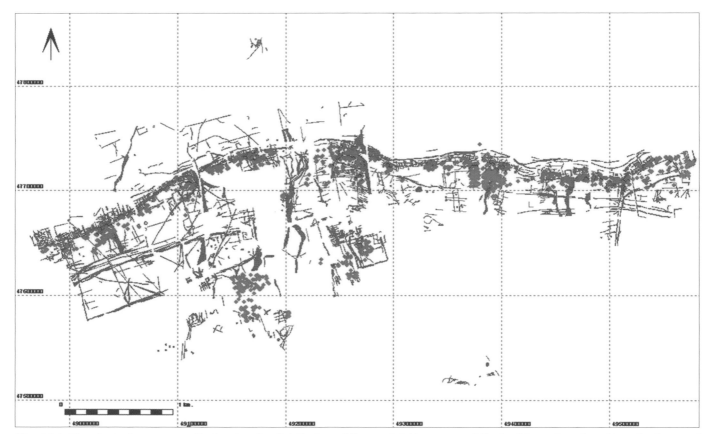

Fig. 14.4: Geophysical survey results showing the distribution of 'barrowlets' in green and Grubenhäuser *in red against a background plot of other features in grey, the line of the 'ladder settlement' is very clear following the edge of the wetlands.*

Fig. 14.5 Crop-mark showing the 'D-Shaped' enclosure and internal features in Sherburn taken in 2010.

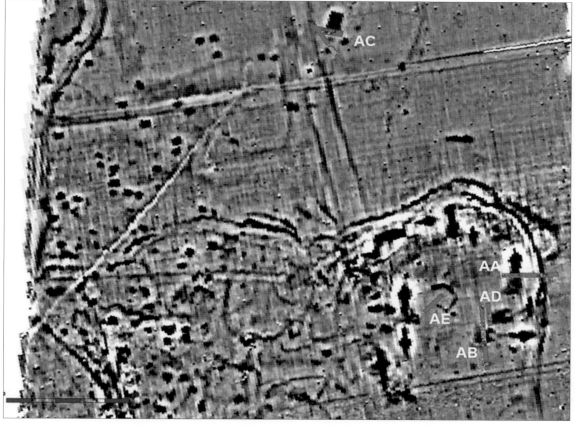

Fig. 14.6 Geophysical survey results showing the enclosure and sample trench locations.

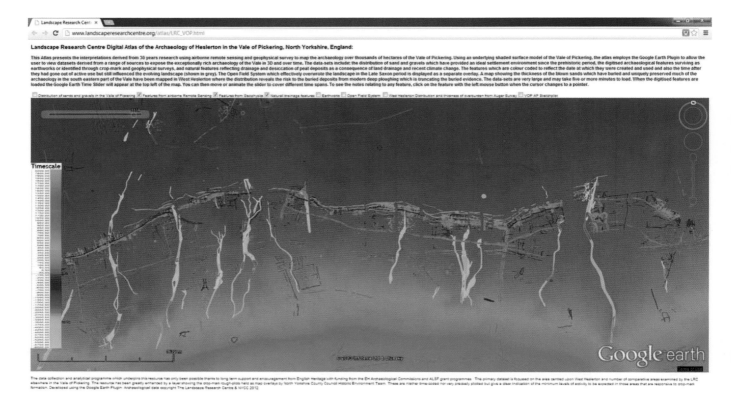

Fig. 14.7 The landscape Research Centre Digital Atlas, which brings together the results of a very long term remote sensing programme supported by English Heritage to identify the scale, nature and quality of the buried archaeology in the hinterland of the major excavations undertaken at West Heslerton.

The initial impetus behind the aerial survey programme was to seek the location of any settlement that might be contemporary with the cemetery and other evidence which might throw light on the ongoing prehistoric discoveries at Cook's Quarry. Evidence for the presence of Anglo-Saxon settlement was not identified at first. Initially it appeared either that the established view of a sparsely settled post-Roman landscape was true, or that we were simply trying to identify cemeteries and settlements with inappropriate tools, or alternatively that such sites were situated in areas that had not been observed. Meanwhile other evidence proliferated, revealing complex 'ladder settlements' from the late Iron Age and Roman periods laid out following the edge of the former wetlands in the centre of the Vale and ploughed out or buried barrows and other prehistoric features dominating the landscape between the wetlands and the foot of the Wolds. Other crop marks indicated intensive use of former islands in the peaty wetlands that predominate in the centre of the Vale. These islands had been used both for settlement and for burial, including one large cemetery that had apparently been in use at least from the Neolithic until the late Iron Age.

Chance discoveries of early Anglo-Saxon burials elsewhere in the Vale of Pickering had been made at Staxton with other

Anglian burials reported, if not confirmed, at East Heslerton and Sherburn (Brewster 1957; Anon [Otago Witness] 1866). Fragmented and limited Anglo-Saxon settlement evidence had been identified during development and quarrying at Seamer and Wykeham (Moore 1966; Pye 1976, 1983). Numerous early Anglo-Saxon burials had been excavated by antiquarians; particularly J. R. Mortimer on the Wolds and more recently at Sewerby Hall where Rahtz had excavated a cemetery containing fifty-nine graves (Hirst 1985). However, these additions did not seem substantially to modify the received picture of a sparsely settled early Anglo-Saxon landscape. Indeed, they rather seemed to corroborate the then-prevailing view of a thinly settled landscape with small shifting farmsteads and small cemeteries – a view which in turn fitted the notion of Dark Age contraction following the departure or failure of the Roman administration (Jones 1973; 1974; 1980).

In the early 1980s further areas of the West Heslerton Anglian cemetery were examined in ploughed fields to the south of the quarry. A broad strip of land sealed by the A64 trunk road bisects the cemetery and could not be examined, but the rest was excavated in its entirety. The cemetery appears to have been established during the late fifth century AD, and was located in and around a Neolithic and Bronze Age monument complex. It continued to receive burials until the mid-seventh century, during which time between 300 and 400 individuals were interred in what appear to have been clusters of graves that may have related to individual families. The size of the cemetery was in contrast with the established impression that early Anglo-Saxon presence hereabouts had been negligible. This alerted us to the need to try to locate any associated settlement.

West Heslerton; the Anglian Settlement

Intensive aerial prospection and surface collection survey failed to give any hints. A programme of trial trenching was accordingly undertaken in 1984, the trenches being located in areas which on other grounds could be assessed as suitable for settlement. Trial trenching some 400m to the south of the cemetery at once revealed Anglo-Saxon structural evidence, although the distribution of the cuttings did not give an indication of the true scale of the settlement and suggested that it was quite small, confirming the established view. The excavation of the Anglian settlement at West Heslerton followed from 1986 to 1996, its publication being delayed by events that could not have been predicted. The excavated cemetery at West Heslerton is the most completely examined example of its type in northern England. The settlement, the association of which is given some support by the recovery of cast copper alloy wrist clasps both from the cemetery and the settlement, is likewise the only fully excavated example in the north, and on present evidence seems to be only the second example examined in its entirety, the other being Mucking in Essex (Jones 1974; 1979; 1980; Hamerow 1993).

At the time of discovery the research strategy for the excavation of the settlement was influenced by an assumption that the settlement covered no more than 25 acres, that the *Grubenhäuser* were sunken floored buildings with dedicated functions such as weaving sheds, and that they may have been used for housing. According to the then-prevailing model the settlement should be seen not as a single entity but as a gradually shifting group of farmsteads that were being replaced at intervals. In other words, this was not a village but a kind of evolving neighbourhood. It was also expected that the material evidence recovered from the *Grubenhäuser* would allow the structures to be dated and that reliable dating could be derived from the ceramics. All these assumptions turned out to be incorrect. Although some avenues of research proved fundamentally flawed, the excavation transformed our understanding and potential research strategies with reference to early Anglo-Saxon settlement studies (Powlesland 1998a;1998b; 1999; 2000).

The excavations were undertaken as a rescue excavation, on behalf of English Heritage, to recover as much evidence as possible within an area of active plough damage and as such the excavations were framed within a research strategy with a specific but broad set of research questions. The scale of the settlement at West Heslerton was far larger than could have been predicted and the degree of deliberate organisation quite unanticipated. Although there is some evidence that the settlement changed overall shape during its life, the model of small shifting farmsteads proposed for Mucking is not supported by the evidence recovered at West Heslerton. This may seem to be a radical departure from the established view of settlement development in this period but owes most to a new understanding of the site formation and de-formation processes and the realisation that the deposits that fill the *Grubenhäuser* very rarely incorporate primary deposits (Tipper 2004). Where this can be proven this seems to reflect late deposition in the depressions in the top of these filled-in structures rather than primary discard in the base of the features. There was no evidence to support the view that the material in the base of the *Grubenhäuser* comprised material that had accumulated from material falling between the planks of the raised timber floors as suggested by Stanley West for West Stow (West 1985). West's suggestion that some of these structures had raised timber floors was confirmed, although this appeared always to be the case. In those cases where oven-bases *etc.* were found in the base of the filled in features these were quite clearly secondary and represent the use of the pit following the abandonment of the building formerly standing over the pit. It is possible that ovens were deliberately sited in the bases of abandoned *Grubenhäuser* where it may have been easier to control the flow of air through the flue. The case made for gradually shifting small farmsteads proposed for Mucking owes most to the use of a very small number of 'dateable' objects recovered from a tiny percentage of features (Hamerow 1993). If the material recovered from these features is within a secondary or tertiary deposit then these dated objects have neither a secure relationship with the use of the features and associated structures nor any necessarily useful chronological relationship; they may have lain within a midden or other deposit elsewhere for a long time before incorporation within the filling of the abandoned feature.

Some of the material found in *Grubenhäuser* at West Heslerton appears to have been derived from turves, which the evidence suggests were used in the construction of the buildings; although this is obvious in the case of discrete prehistoric lithic assemblages this may also include earlier Anglo-Saxon debris buried or incorporated within the active turf/topsoil subsequently used for construction purposes. Analysis of the ceramic assemblages from West Heslerton seems to indicate that the approach to early middle Saxon ceramics has also been over-simplified, particularly with reference to chronological sequencing; while some fabrics do seem to reflect middle Saxon activity, those fabrics and forms most often classed as early Anglo-Saxon seem to have continued in production until the site was abandoned in the ninth century.

One is tempted to suggest that many of the problems that relate to aspects of continuity and dating with reference to early

Anglo-Saxon settlement arise out of a subconscious expectation that the archaeological evidence is somehow 'medieval' in character; relatively well-ordered and sequenced. In fact the physical evidence from the early Anglo-Saxon period, up until about the middle of the seventh century, has much more in common with the archaeology of the late Iron Age. Clearly there are aspects of the Anglo-Saxon settlement (most obviously the architecture) that are very different from that found in Iron Age contexts but, from an excavator's point of view, it might be easier if we adopted the continental approach and viewed what is conventionally seen as the early Anglo-Saxon phase of activity as the post-Roman Iron Age. The very limited number of extensively excavated settlement sites of this period make generalisation problematic, particularly at a time when 'regional variation' can be so easily invoked to emphasise differences in the observed archaeological record; however, the most striking feature of early Anglo-Saxon settlements in the east and south-east of England is their similarities rather than their differences. Approaches to the study of early Anglo-Saxon archaeology have frequently been framed within historical perspectives drawn from middle or late Saxon texts, such as the *Anglo-Saxon Chronicle*, inscribed several hundred years after the events taking place; this has led to a preoccupation with issues such as invasion or mass migration and continuity from Roman to Saxon which at best are exceptionally difficult to detect in the archaeological record.

The excavation of the settlement at West Heslerton was driven by a research agenda that addressed a number of different stand-alone primary research questions. Evidence was gathered in a way that was sensitive to analysis that could be used to test some of the established interpretations rather than simply maintain the *status quo* and accept the 'known' and build upon it. The latter approach may well have been intellectually easier but might have done little to improve our understanding of this difficult period of our past. In contrast with the well-dated, stratigraphically and materially very rich archaeology of the Roman or medieval periods, early Anglo-Saxon settlement archaeology is characterised by open settlements with limited stratigraphy and low frequency of artefacts, of which the majority are re-deposited or in residual deposits and are, in any case, rarely dateable with any precision. The relative absence of enclosing features, a lack of construction in stone, the slight nature of the post settings in the timber-framed buildings, the gathering of refuse in middens and the limited precision with which most of the finds can be dated combine both to limit the site visibility and also to make excavation and interpretation particularly challenging. Surface collection surveys at West Heslerton failed to reveal even a hint that a huge settlement lay beneath the ploughsoil, frequent air photographic sorties over the area likewise failed to reveal any crop-marks with the exception of the relict stream channel which bisects the 'village', and the successful discovery of the site through trial trenching owed most to luck (had the trenches been repositioned by 5 metres in any direction, most likely nothing would have been found).

Besides covering an area about twice the size of that predicted after the initial trial trenching programme, the evidence recovered indicated a radically different arrangement and evolution of the settlement from that which had been anticipated, with a life-span that outlived the use of the excavated cemetery by about two hundred years (Fig. 14.2). In contrast with the interpretations offered for the settlements at Mucking and West Stow, there was no convincing evidence to support the theory of small shifting farmsteads. Although the excavations of the northern portion of the settlement indicated that, with the exception of a range of different Neolithic and Bronze Age activities the site appeared to represent a *de novo* creation, established on open ground, the evidence in the southern part of the site revealed that this was not the case; here the settlement had apparently been placed upon or re-used a small sacred complex including at least one shrine which appears to have functioned as some sort of religious centre from some time in the Iron Age. Some sort of processional way was established, running uphill from the natural spring situated in the centre of the later Anglian settlement through a small dry valley which appears to have been terraced in the Roman period when a small structure with apses at both ends and a possible colonnade along one side was set back into the side of the dry valley. The upper part of the dry valley seems to have been deliberately left unsettled or open during the life of the Anglian settlement although the presence of a middle Saxon strap-end just outside the robbed remains of the shrine may signify that this part of the site continued to function in a special way as late as the early ninth century (Powlesland 1998a).

One of the more intractable challenges facing any research into settlement in the post-Roman period relates to continuity; whether with reference to population or landscape, this is made more problematic by the changes in the nature and architecture of early Anglo-Saxon settlement as opposed to late Roman settlement which in itself was radically changed or changing during the fourth century at the latest. It is worth pondering what exactly we would need to prove continuity, and what we mean by continuity. In the case of West Heslerton, although the settlement site partially uses ground formerly used for some sort of shrine complex there is no indication that the settlement was built on abandoned land; had this been the case we might have expected to find blown sand deposits separating Roman from early Anglo-Saxon deposits. Whilst there is plentiful evidence for continuity of same site occupation from the middle of the Iron Age to the end of the Roman period, this sort of settlement continuity does not seem to be a feature of early Anglo-Saxon settlement development. This need not reflect a discontinuity of population and may reflect changes both in land tenure, at a time when an increasingly wet climate had made the locations preferred during the Iron Age and Roman periods less attractive, and a change in the economic and probably social structure of settlement itself. It appears that in the Vale of Pickering settlement locations established during the Iron Age continued to evolve during the Roman period and continued in use even when ground conditions reflecting a rising water-table had declined seriously because of issues relating to land tenure, which meant that there was no land 'available' for new settlement cores to be established. Rising late Roman ground water-levels observed in small excavations in Sherburn in the Vale of Pickering show declining ground conditions which would logically have prompted people to move their settlements to new drier locations, and yet they did not. Evidence from aerial and geophysical surveys suggest that the immediate landscape was fully in use, and thus one is tempted to see that the land was controlled at a high level and it was only possible to move once the Roman administration had completely collapsed (Powlesland *et al.* 1997). Whatever the case there is nothing to suggest that the landscape in which the early Anglo-Saxon settlements evolved was anything less than fully in use and under management (Powlesland 2009; 2011). As such, the dense forests supposedly covering most of lowland Britain and articulated through the Ordnance Survey map of Britain in the Dark Ages belong with the myth of the 'Dark Ages', in which the Anglo-Saxon population eked out a living in small, widely-distributed farmsteads, a view presented in the majority of publications until very recently.

One of the primary research objectives in the excavation of the Anglian settlement at West Heslerton was to recover the full plan of the settlement; particularly to be sure that the limits of the settlement were covered even if they were not articulated by enclosures or identifiable fences. At West Stow in Suffolk it is clear that the limits of the settlement lay beyond the limits of excavation, and with the exception of Mucking the majority of excavations of early Anglo-Saxon settlements have otherwise failed, for understandable reasons determined by the context of rescue excavation, to recover a secure picture of the true scale of each settlement. In the case of West Heslerton it is clear from the ground plan that the settlement comprises a number of contrasting zones; that these different areas supported different activities is demonstrated through variations in the material culture and environmental evidence (Fig. 14.3). This spatial patterning alone suggests that an unsophisticated picture of a small number of frequently shifting farmsteads is not supported by the evidence, and although one can argue for a change in the shape and extent of the active settlement over time this seems to reflect a gradual reorganisation of the 'village' when enclosed areas were defined in the southern two thirds of the settlement, probably in the seventh century.

The overall structure of the settlement seems to reflect elements of deliberate planning or aspirations towards deliberately establishing something with a structure we might appreciate as a village, rather than simply a cluster of farmsteads. Most distinctive are the areas marked as 'craft and industrial zone' and 'housing area' in the northern portion of the settlement; these are separated by an active stream and it is difficult to interpret the differences in the two areas in terms of farmsteads, unless one wishes to see the two

areas as chronologically or even socially different, with the *Grubenhäuser* representative of a different status from the post-setting structures to the east of the stream. Similarly the area in the centre of the settlement which was devoted to agricultural functions such as crop processing, probably milling and animal management, seems to have served communal activities rather than a single high status property or farmstead. The southern part of the settlement with an extensive complex of ditched and fenced enclosures, some of which appear to have originated during the Roman period, may have had the greatest level of continuity and emerged as the primary settlement core, but there is no reason to believe that the northern third of the settlement was completely abandoned.

West Heslerton has been described as 'atypical in many ways' (Wickham 2005, 503n.159). However one needs to be aware that the 'typical' (in terms of totally excavated early Anglo-Saxon settlements in England) would at present appear to be the single example of Mucking. The excavations at Mucking seem to have encompassed the limits of what has been interpreted as a single settlement shifting over time, but may alternatively represent two separate but adjacent and broadly contemporary settlements.

Beyond the West Heslerton Anglian Settlement

Whilst the evidence recovered in the excavation of the Anglian settlement challenges the established view of early Anglo-Saxon settlement development on a number of fronts, we need to be aware of the very limited sample of sites and the intellectual context within which the established interpretation is framed (Hamerow 2002; 2012). The excavation at West Heslerton has revealed problems in the nature of the evidence which exposed the need, for instance, for much more comprehensive scientific dating programmes, but at the same time has exposed tremendous similarities in the domestic architecture and evidence of long-distance trade which reveal a far more connected early Anglo-Saxon England than we might otherwise appreciate (Powlesland 1999). The massive air and geophysical survey programme that has been undertaken by the Landscape Research Centre over the last thirty-five years was conceived to try to identify the context of the various excavations in progress and to try to develop a detailed understanding of a large block of landscape where the true scale of the archaeological resource could be identified. The results of this research have been extraordinary and have transformed both our understanding and the identifiable research potential of the Vale of Pickering, an area in which the sheer scale of the observed resource coupled with exceptional preservation gives the area unique qualities. With reference to our understanding of the Anglo-Saxon landscape the research has exposed a pattern of activity that no one could have predicted (Powlesland 2009; 2011).

The excavated settlement at West Heslerton is neither exceptional in terms of scale nor isolated; rather it forms one of many similar settlements situated between the northern scarp slope of the Yorkshire Wolds and the edge of the former wetlands in the centre of the Vale of Pickering. Repeated air survey over the same ground, multiple times per year, and over more than thirty-five years has revealed changes in the visibility of crop-marks over time which seem to reflect the result of intensification of agriculture with deeper ploughing, changes in the cereal crops in particular and climate change which have changed the nature and timing of the returns from air photography over the last decade rather than reduce them as we had assumed would be most likely. Thus areas which had been frequently flown in 'good crop-mark' conditions in the 1980s and shown little, now regularly produce detailed crop-marks showing the distinctive plan of *Grubenhäuser*. By the mid 1990s, when it appeared that the number of new discoveries was rapidly diminishing, it became clear that an alternative approach was needed which was less sensitive to the vagaries of crop type, variation in subsoil and short-term climate patterns, as well as being more consistent. Gradiometery had been used to tremendous effect during the last seasons of the settlement excavation and a project was developed with English Heritage designed to assess the potential of large area surveys to reveal features both in areas that had produced crop-marks and also those with a more limited crop-mark record. The first stages of this project were so successful that further projects followed, focussed upon the aggregate resources that had provided the perfect setting for prehistoric and later settlement. By 2010 a single contiguous block of geophysical survey covering more than 1000 hectares had been undertaken revealing many thousands of new features of all periods and including thirteen clusters of *Grubenhäuser* within a strip of land some 11km long. Whilst the distinctive crop-marks resulting from the presence of *Grubenhäuser* are subject to the vagaries of crop-mark formation, the almost ubiquitous filling of these features with domestic refuse gives exceptional and consistent results when surveyed using magnetic methods, results that are not compromised by the weather conditions or the time of year that they are surveyed. The exceptional returns from the geophysical surveys in the Vale of Pickering have revealed nearly 1,350 *Grubenhäuser*, the identification and interpretation of which has been tested and confirmed in four of the newly discovered clusters. It is easy to think that the combined surveys are revealing everything, but this is not the case. The resolution of much of the gradiometer data gathered during the period until 2005 was insufficiently dense, with readings taken at 0.25×1.0m intervals, to reveal smaller features; even since then surveys undertaken with a sampling resolution of 0.10×0.5m only rarely allow us to identify potential post-holes, and where this has been the case they have related to prehistoric round houses rather than the distinctive rectangular but generally very slight arrangements of post-settings that characterise early Anglo-Saxon structures.

Two of these clusters, one at East Heslerton and another at Sherburn, are larger than the excavated example at West

Heslerton, the remainder showing a remarkable distribution with groups of *Grubenhäuser* spaced at roughly 800m intervals following the southern edge of the late Iron Age and Roman period 'ladder settlement' that followed the edge of the former wetland. In the case of Sherburn the survey results indicate continuity of settlement in the same location from the middle of the Iron Age to the present village, in the case of East and West Heslerton the Anglian settlements seem to have been abandoned in favour of new settlements; in the case of West Heslerton this seems to have occurred in the mid-ninth century, whilst a single date from one of the *Grubenhäuser* immediately to the south of medieval East Heslerton indicates that settlement had already been established here by the mid-seventh century. If one of the strengths of the combined surveys is that they show the scale, distribution and density of *Grubenhäuser* over a large area of landscape, in relation both to the Roman and medieval settlement patterns, a weakness is the fact that the distribution includes more than about 1,350 *Grubenhäuser* which, with the exception of a number of examples at West Heslerton, one from East Heslerton and one from Sherburn, are undated.

Any ideas we may have had about a thinly-spread population occupying small farmsteads are unsustainable on the basis of the survey evidence. When examined against the intense Iron Age and Roman occupation of the 'ladder settlement', where large farmsteads linked by a continuous track-way seem to have a regular distribution occurring at an interval of *c*. 250m, the clusters of *Grubenhäuser* just to the south of the earlier settlements could arguably represent the emergence of more focussed settlements combining the populations of multiple large farmsteads. It should be noted here that the scale of these farmsteads has more in common with the medieval manor farms that dominated medieval villages rather than the small groups of buildings we might first identify with the term farmstead.

Amongst the thousands of features identified in the combined surveys an unusual and previously unidentified class of feature, comprising very small ring ditches we have termed 'barrowlets', cluster along the southern edge of the late Iron-Age and Roman period ladder settlement; these features have been interpreted as funerary monuments, tiny mounds as small as two metres across, where we believe cremations were inserted into the mound, although this interpretation has yet to be confirmed. If these are indeed late Iron Age and Roman period burial features (possibly succeeding the use of Square Barrows for burial) then it might explain the complete absence of identified Roman burials in a landscape that is clearly intensively used at this time. A small exploratory trench where geophysical survey had revealed two of these features revealed ten examples in the same area, indicating that the survey is showing as little as 20% of the total number of these monuments. Across the survey area more than 1,250 have been identified, and if the same limitations apply then a total of more than 6,000 barrowlets indicates a considerable population as indicated by the density of activity in general.

The discontinuous distribution and grouping of these features along the line of the ladder settlement may be indicative of small cemeteries associated with each farmstead. It may be of more than passing interest that the upstanding cemetery at Petty Knowes just outside the Roman Fort at High Rochester in Northumberland includes more than one hundred very small mounds which in plan would look not unlike the groups of ploughed-out barrowlets found in the Vale (Charlton and Mitcheson 1984). Whatever the case, the impression given by the combined survey evidence is that the landscape, or at least the 1–2km wide strip between the foot of the Yorkshire Wolds and the edge of the wetlands in the centre of the Vale of Pickering, was intensely settled and utilised no less than is indicated for the early middle Saxon period as is effectively demonstrated by comparing the distribution of identified barrowlets and that of the *Grubenhäuser*.

It is tempting to suggest that the smaller clusters of *Grubenhäuser* along the southern edge of the ladder settlement may represent a first phase of Anglo-Saxon settlement, followed by nucleation leading to the creation of the large settlements at East and West Heslerton and Sherburn, but on present evidence this would merely be speculation. Whilst it would be easy to speculate regarding the settlement sequence spanning the period from the Roman until the late Saxon, such speculation would not improve our understanding in an environment where a well-designed research project, supported by an extensive carbon-fourteen dating programme, would resolve the sequence and arguably give insight into the sequence we might anticipate in other valley landscapes in the south and east of England. What is certain is that the intensive and long term programme of research centred on Heslerton has generated an unparalleled evidence base in which the odd individual *Grubenhaus* may well have been overlooked but for the first time we have a map reflecting the true distribution of Anglo-Saxon settlement over more than 2000ha extending for nearly 12km along a well-defined block of landscape. There is no reason to believe that the density of settlement reflects anything more than the elevated and long-term level of research undertaken in the Vale of Pickering, particularly in the light of recent discoveries of multiple clusters of *Grubenhäuser* indicating a similar density of settlement in the Great Wold Valley only 7km to the south. In the latter case these discoveries are a very dramatic reflection of increasing returns from aerial photography during the last five years, in areas previously intensively flown which are now regularly the setting for exceptional crop-marks occurring as a consequence of many combined factors which include climate change, increasingly aggressive deep ploughing and changes in the crops themselves; these factors in combination have also led to much earlier crop-mark formation than we have experienced in the past. The 'new' discoveries in the Great Wold Valley show the need for increasing vigilance and continued regularly repeated aerial reconnaissance at more times of the year if we are not to be lulled into believing that we have 'mapped everything'.

Much of what has been said above may be considered by some to be speculative or in detail untested; this is a function of the scale both of the research undertaken and the response needed properly to evaluate the discoveries made through remote sensing. Much of this work has also been focussed upon the early to middle Saxon period rather than the middle to later Saxon period, the point at which I would argue that Anglo-Saxon England as an entity begins to emerge. During the seventh century, the kingdom of Deira, of which the Vale may have formed the heartland, emerges as a distinct entity with a high density of early ecclesiastical foundations established in and around the Vale of Pickering.

A middle Saxon Royal or Monastic centre at Sherburn

The village of Sherburn, situated 5km to the east of West Heslerton, is the largest of the villages that lie at the foot of the Wolds in the south-eastern part of the Vale of Pickering. At Domesday Sherburn was the setting for two churches, only one of which survives today. The surviving church, which was almost completely rebuilt during 'restoration' between 1909 and 1912, incorporates a number of fragments of late Saxon/Viking Age sculptural stone in the present fabric and sits in a dominant position at the northern end of the present village. Archaeological research by the Landscape Research Centre over the last three decades has included extensive air-photographic survey and, more recently, large-scale geophysical survey around the present village. The geophysical survey in particular reveals that Sherburn has a settlement history that extends back into later prehistory, and that during the Anglo-Saxon period the settlement extended over more than 30ha, larger than the excavated village at West Heslerton, with a considerably larger number and greater density of *Grubenhäuser*. To the east of the present village a crop-mark of a 'D-Shaped' enclosure measuring nearly 100m across, seen from the air after the field was first ploughed in modern times in 1981, has produced increasingly clear crop-marks, reflecting ongoing plough damage during the last few years. This enclosure, and what appears to be a rectangular structure aligned east-west just outside it to the north, appears with great clarity in the crop-mark record; geophysical survey has shown that the field in which it is situated contains a vast amount of archaeological evidence (Fig. 14.5). The enclosure is unusual and internal details, visible in the crop-mark, geomagnetic and electronic resistance surveys, indicate that it is exceptional. Very strong magnetic anomalies, possibly indicative of burnt structures, are situated just inside the ditch that defines the enclosure in a situation that is not dissimilar to the distribution of industrial structures in early Irish monastic enclosures (Fig. 14.6).

The enclosure is situated in what is now a very large field where a number of burials, apparently aligned east-west in a single grave-pit, were discovered in a sand-pit in 1850, somewhere on the western boundary of the present field; these were examined by a group of antiquarians including Canon Greenwell in 1866 and reported in newspapers as far afield as New Zealand (Anon. 1866). Greenwell identified the burials as of late Saxon date. The location of these burials has now been lost but the suggestion that they were rapidly buried in a single grave which, from the description, was cut into the blown sand which is a feature of the area, may suggest that these burials relate to a single event, perhaps, if the enclosure is monastic, a consequence of Viking activity. A series of small trial excavations were conducted with volunteers in 2011 to secure dating evidence and examine some of the features identified through the remote sensing programme (Powlesland 2012b). One of the features inside the perimeter ditch proved to be a remarkable and very large grain drier, which was probably the source for a 5m thick deposit of ash completely filling a *Grubenhaus* measuring *c.* 10 × 6m a few metres to the south-east; the ash deposit must have been derived from the processing of hundreds of tons of grain, primarily rye, rather than from the burning of a building as we had perhaps hoped when it was first identified. Two carbon-fourteen dates were secured: one from a wattle from the clay vault which had covered the grain drier was between AD 605 and AD 674 (95.4% probability), the second, from charcoal from a post-hole within a second *Grubenhaus*, gave a date between AD 772 and AD 952 (95.4% probability). A third and very large *Grubenhaus* situated some 90 metres to the north of the enclosure proved to be nearly one metre deep with what appeared to be a sill beam setting just below the upper edge of the pit; this feature is yet to be dated. The very large *Grubenhäuser* at Sherburn are exceptional and I am aware of no excavated parallels from middle Saxon sites; the presence of internal timbering within the sub-floor pits may indicate that these structures are of some sort of hybrid design, but the excavations were very limited in scale and more extensive excavation will be required if the buildings are to be understood. The significance of the grain-drier and the ash deposit indicate the exceptional nature of this site and neither confirm or disprove the possibility that the enclosure relates to monastic activity. An alternative interpretation, that this site represents part of a royal manor and tithe rendering centre, is no less interesting, particularly given the date of the grain drier. The huge faunal assemblage recovered from the excavation of the settlement at West Heslerton, with nearly a million fragments recovered, may infer the removal of livestock through the payments of tithes since market-age cattle are heavily under-represented. Within the context of the middle Saxon period we have to assume that considerable wealth was raised through some sort of taxation in order to fund the construction in stone of the many early churches around the Vale.

In the case of Sherburn the remote sensing evidence indicates that the village in broad terms reflects continuity of settlement in the same location since the late Iron Age,

perhaps reflecting the unusual topography with the surviving church situated on a raised spur, a former moraine, which juts out into the area of former wetlands. The precise nature and extent of the 'village' at any one time is difficult to determine with so much of the current village envelope built over; the geophysical surveys show *Grubenhäuser* immediately to the north, east and west of the village in addition to Roman and probably Iron Age enclosures apparently extending beneath the northern and eastern portions of the village. In the case of East and West Heslerton settlement shift does seem to have occurred; in the case of West Heslerton the early Middle Saxon settlement was abandoned during the ninth century and it is assumed that the present village was then established in a less overlooked setting. It appears that the area of the earlier settlement was quickly overwritten with rig and furrow and there is no reason to suggest that this did not happen soon after the settlement was abandoned, although this would be exceptionally difficult to determine through excavation. Whatever the case, the division of the land into rig and furrow, which probably represents the largest single direct impact by humans on the British landscape since the large-scale clearance of forest in the Neolithic and Bronze Age, cannot have happened piecemeal and as such reflects a very deliberate restructuring of the whole agrarian landscape, overwriting for the first time whole tracts of landscape. It is possible that the entry in the annal for 876 in the *Anglo-Saxon Chronicle* referring to Halfdene 'dividing up the land of Northumbria' may provide a context for the introduction of rig and furrow; with Halfdene as king in York the reference to 'Northumbria' may more precisely be referring to southern Northumberland or alternatively Deira (Swanton 1996).

The landscape on the web: a resource for the future

Remote sensing suggests that, rather than being a constantly re-written palimpsest of overlapping features, the landscape has developed through the continual use and accumulation of features, many of which were retained within the structure of the landscape long after their primary function had passed. This can be viewed dynamically using the Landscape Research Centre Digital Atlas of the Archaeology of Heslerton in the Vale of Pickering (Fig. 14.7) which uses the Google Earth plug-in to display and animate a time-coded map of the evidence recovered from the massive remote sensing programme which has evolved over the three decades of work in the Vale of Pickering (Powlesland 2012a). This exposes the density and distribution of Anglo-Saxon settlement evidence against the prehistoric and Roman landscape that preceded it, and it must be acknowledged that it is the resource and the lifetime spent researching and creating that resource that is exceptional, rather than the landscape within which it is based. It is difficult, even allowing for regional variation, to argue that what has been discovered in the Vale of Pickering is not likely to reflect the general situation in other valley landscapes in southern and eastern England.

Reflecting now on the time spent working and researching within the Vale of Pickering, the vast majority of which has been hand-to-mouth, whilst former colleagues and fellow students from the department went on to forge academic or other similarly aligned careers, I am confident that D. Hill D. Phil would have loved the results, despite the fact that it is very much the product of the computer age rather than the lovingly hand-drawn maps on which he wore out his rapidograph pens.

'Ploughing Old Furrows Afresh' – the Importance of the Practical in the Study of the Anglo-Saxon World

Christopher Grocock

As its title suggests, this paper involves a fresh look at old ground – the land holdings of the monasteries of Wearmouth and Jarrow – and celebrates the importance of everyday and sometimes mundane aspects of early medieval society for a better understanding of the ways in which early medieval society functioned. These can be platitudes for some. David Hill's work over a lifetime countered any such vacuous shallowness. I remember from my first meeting with David Hill back in the 1990s that we shared a passion for the practical; it has a value. The devil is in the detail; the ordinary underpins everything. Without them, we may use terms and concepts without any real content, depth or understanding.

Introduction

Many years ago in presenting a paper on this topic at the Institute of Historical Research as a means of exploring the question 'how were the monasteries funded' I was met with the comment from a member of the audience to the effect that 'we already know how they were funded – from their rents'. The problem with such an approach is that it is not an answer at all – it just replaces one term with another, leaving many questions unaddressed. Of what did these rents consist? How much land was needed to provide them (or how much income could be got from the land areas without reducing the workers to utter penury – and would such an approach fit with the ethics of a Christian foundation)? Who worked the lands? The peasant farmers left *in situ*? Lay brothers? Slaves? How much work did the monks get involved in themselves? I will return to the question of slaves later, but let us make a start with the evidence about Wearmouth-Jarrow's land holdings as it is provided by our primary evidence – the *History of the Abbots (HA)* and the anonymous *Vita Ceolfridi (VC)* or *Life of Ceolfrith*.[1]

The land-holdings of Wearmouth-Jarrow

The *History of the Abbots* begins with this very theme:

HA 1 The pious servant of Christ Biscop, also called Benedict, was inspired by the grace from above and built a monastery in honour of Peter, the most blessed prince of the apostles, next to the mouth of the river Wear on the northern bank. Ecgfrith, the venerable and most dutiful king of that people, assisted him and gave him land.

More detail is provided in subsequent chapters:

HA 4 Benedict at last went back to his native people, to Ecgfrith king of the region beyond the Humber, turning his steps towards the land where he was born. Once there he related all he had done since he left his homeland as a youth, and did not conceal the religious devotion with which he burned. He explained what church and monastic practice he had learned at Rome and elsewhere, and showed how many divine books and relics of the blessed apostles and martyrs of Christ he had brought back. He received such a great and gracious welcome from the king that the latter immediately endowed him with seventy hides of his own land and instructed him to build a monastery there to the first pastor of the church. This was done, as I also recalled in the prologue, at the mouth of the river Wear, on its north bank, in the six-hundred-and-seventy-fourth year from the Lord's birth, in the second indiction, and in the fourth year of king Ecgfrith's reign.

There was thus a grant *in toto* of seventy hides for Wearmouth; but there is no indication of the numbers supported by that land, for the time being at least. *VC* 7 has a more verbose account which does not limit the grants to Ecgfrith:

VC 7. Now they began to build a monastery by the mouth of the river Wear in the six hundred and seventy-fourth year since the Lord's incarnation, in the second indiction, and in the fourth year of the reign of king Ecgfrith. They received land from him, fifty hides at first, though later on the monastery was made larger through giving both by him and by other kings and noblemen.

Wood (2010, 87) notes that the discrepancy may be solved by assuming (as we do in *Abbots of Wearmouth and Jarrow*) that the anonymous *Vita Ceolfridi* was written later than Bede's *Historia Abbatum*: 'the anonymous author was simply being more precise than Bede'. We may compare these texts to the inscription from St Paul's Jarrow, recording a foundation some 8 years later in 681/2, which is worded as follows: DEDICATIO BASILICAE SCI PAULI VIIII KL. MAI ANNO XV ECFRIDI REG CEOLFRIDI ABB. EIVSDEM QQ ECCLES. DEO AVCTORE CONDITORIS ANNO IIII (Grocock and Wood 2013, frontispiece; Cramp 2005, 144, 365; Wood 2008, 2). It makes use of indictions and dating *anno domini* which are similar to the wording in the anonymous *Life of Ceolfrith*, but not to Bede's practice in the *History of the Abbots*.

Ian Wood also remarks that Hild had once had a monastery on the north side of the Wear, which is mentioned in Bede's *HE* IV. 23 (Grocock and Wood 2013, xxvi). Could this have been on the site later given to Wearmouth? At any rate, it is clear that Wearmouth was built on royal land. This in turn raises questions about the sort of royal gift it was, and whether it should be compared with the land-grants described by Bede in the *Letter to Ecgbert*.

It looks as though Wearmouth was established in 673, to judge by the comments on Biscop's abbacy that follow, though the actual building work seems to have started a year later, in 674. This is not surprising, given the need which Bede stresses to obtain specialist workmen from overseas, and in fact the building programme may have extended for more than this, as building programmes tend to do. In all this, Bede stresses that Ecgfrith was the instigator; this may be a suggestion that the king was trying to tie Biscop down. It might also be the case that by emphasizing the royal origin of the foundation of the monastery Bede was seeing off any counter-claims of jurisdiction over it, for example from Wilfrid (Foot 2013, 29–30; Grocock 2013, 105–7). Gunn (2009, 44) stresses the importance of Ecgfrith's involvement at Wearmouth, though Ian Wood fairly points out that 'by not stressing the distinction between Wearmouth and Jarrow, she overestimates royal interest in the earlier foundation' [*i.e.* Wearmouth] (Grocock and Wood 2013, 31, n. 41 on *HA* 4).

What is interesting is the stress which Bede makes not only here in his *HA* account, but also in the *Homily* i. 13 on Benedict Biscop, that

> secular rulers too became aware of his devotion to virtue, and took pains to grant him a site for building a monastery, and that not taken away from any of the lesser persons but given from their own property.

Wood (2010, 87) comments 'clearly there were some who did not accept that the lands on which Wearmouth was founded had come directly from the pool of land we know to have been held by the king, but believed it to be rather from property that had already been granted out to others.' This view is supported by Campbell (2010, 31–2). However, the endowments given to Jarrow were on a smaller scale:

> King Ecgfrith was thoroughly pleased with the good qualities, hard work and devotion of the venerable Benedict. He took pains to increase the land which he had given to him to build the monastery, because he saw that he had given well and fruitfully, and granted him ownership of a further forty hides. Benedict sent some monks there, a good seventeen in number, with the priest Ceolfrith over them as their abbot, and a year later, by the decision and indeed by the command of the said king Ecgfrith, built the monastery of the blessed apostle Paul, on the basis that a single peaceful harmony and the same friendship and grace should be maintained in each of the two places in perpetuity, so that just as (to use an illustration) the body cannot be torn from the head, through which it breathes, and the head cannot forget about the body, without which it does not live, so no man should try by any attempt to split these monasteries of the first apostles, joined as they are in their brotherly fellowship, apart from one another. (*HA* 7)

There are a number of issues raised by this passage which are discussed in the commentary on these passages in *Abbots of Wearmouth and Jarrow*. Here it is sufficient to note *en passant* the very emphatic stress on the original unity of the two sites – which sounds very much like Bede 'protesting too much' – and for our purposes, the size of the grant given – forty hides (Wood 2008, 12–13; Grocock and Wood 2013, xxix). This is supported by *VC* 11:

> Eight years after they had begun to found the aforementioned monastery, it pleased king Ecgfrith for the redemption of his soul to give another forty hides of land to the most reverend abbot Benedict, on which the church and monastery of the blessed Paul was to be built; and it was not to be separated from the community of the first monastery, but joined to it in all respects in harmonious brotherly love. Ceolfrith very energetically carried out this task, which was committed to him; he received twenty-two brothers, ten of them tonsured and twelve still awaiting the grace of the tonsure, and came to the place.

Again, this passage raises a number of issues not relevant to our discussion of the size of grants given, which are discussed in the commentary to *Abbots of Wearmouth and Jarrow*. The key point is that the *Life of Ceolfrith* confirms the grant of forty hides. If we accept twenty-two as the correct number of monks, we may begin to develop a simple argument to the effect that in the case of Jarrow, twenty-two monks were supported by an endowment of 40 hides; in theory then *pari passu* there would be something like a maximum of 22 × 70/40 monks at Wearmouth … This equates to thirty-nine; the total community (assuming Wearmouth and Jarrow *are* one community; though for the sake of the simple arithmetic it makes no odds) might then number 39 + 22 = 61 by the time that Jarrow was founded. These numbers, it has to be said, may only have been a core for a larger community, as will become clear later.

Later, a little more land was granted through exchange:

> Among other items he also brought two cloaks of pure silk, whose workmanship was without equal; afterwards he used them to obtain three hides of land *to the south of the Wear near the mouth of the river* from king Aldfrith and his thegns, for he found on his return that Ecgfrith had already been killed. (*HA* 9, my italics).

Land on the estates of Bishopwearmouth is clearly indicated here: Bede is being very specific in his wording 'to the south of the Wear near the mouth of the river.' The silk cloaks mentioned in *HA* 9, a product of Benedict Biscop's fifth journey, were clearly valuable trading commodities, desirable by the royal household, and perhaps unsuitable for monastic use. It is possible that, as with the *codex cosmographiorum* mentioned below, they were acquired by Benedict Biscop because he knew how valuable a gift they would be.

Later, even more carefully negotiated transactions are recorded:

> With the gift of a volume of cosmographies, of marvellous workmanship, which Benedict had purchased at Rome, he also obtained for the possession of the monastery of the blessed apostle Paul eight hides of land along the river Fresca from king Aldfrith, who was very learned in the scriptures. So long as he still lived Benedict himself had placed great weight on negotiating its purchase with the same king Aldfrith, but he died before he was able to complete it. Later, when Osred was king, Ceolfrith exchanged this land, and a worthy sum of money besides, for twenty hides of land in the place which is called in the local language Elder Farm, because it seemed nearer to that monastery. (*HA* 15)

A number of interesting points arise from this. First of all, it seems that the negotiations had been fairly protracted – they had begun before Benedict Biscop's death, some time before, it seems; we might ask why there was so much delay, and on which side there was unwillingness? We might also wonder what the king wanted with this book, and how he intended to use it. It might have been classed as a beautiful gift like a piece of jewellery as much as a work of learning.

It was worth the investment it seems, despite the comments about the alienation of gifted property stressed by Benedict Biscop in his departure speech in *HA* 11:

> He directed that the very splendid and well-stocked library he had brought from Rome, and which was needed for the teaching of the church, should carefully be preserved intact

and not spoiled through lack of attention or divided up all over the place.

The letter of privilege given by Pope Agatho in *HA* 6 was intended to protect the monastery from interference *from outside*; as is obvious from Bede's acerbic comments in the *Historia Abbatum* about a 'fleshly brother' in *HA* 11 there might also have been a danger of interference from *inside*; it is possible that the negotiations conducted by Benedict Biscop and Ceolfrith were the result of a policy intended to ward off such interference (Wood 2008, 16–17).

The second point which arises is that the land acquired at first seems to have been 'kept in reserve' and used (together with a financial sum, unspecified) in exchange for a larger amount of land which was closer and therefore more valuable to the monastery itself. Bede makes it clear that proximity to the monastery certainly seems to have been uppermost in the mind of Ceolfrith – perhaps for ease of management – and Blair (2005, 251–7) notes the importance of the management of resources in early medieval minsters, but it may also indicate that some monastic labour was employed on lands owned by the monastic house. Foot (2010, 62) notes that:

> Poverty lay at the heart of the monastic ideal, yet in order for monasteries to survive economically, they had necessarily to acquire sufficient lands and material wealth to liberate their members from the mundane grind of subsistence agriculture in order to devote themselves to prayer.

Wearmouth and Jarrow's monastic holdings were almost complete. A final gift is recorded in *HA* 15:

> In those days the aged and devout servant of Christ Witmer, a man as learned in the knowledge of worldly subjects as of the scriptures, committed himself to the monastery of the blessed apostle Peter which he ruled over, and gave ten hides of land located near the farm called Daldun (usually identified with Dalton-le-Dale) whose ownership he had received from king Aldfrith to that same monastery to own lawfully in perpetuity.

Thus we can arrive at a pretty specific number in *hides* for the total monastic holdings of Wearmouth and Jarrow: 70 (Wearmouth) + 40 (Jarrow) + 3 (the silk cloak) + 20 (the *cosmographium* and a sum of money) + 10 (Witmer) = 143 hides in total. This is *not quite* supported by *VC* 33:

> He left in the monasteries a company of soldiers of Christ more than six hundred in number, with a good one hundred and fifty hides of land according to the way the Angles measure it.

The phrase 'a good one hundred and fifty' (Latin *familiarum ferme centum quinquaginta*) has a nice ring to it, at any rate. The size of the grants made to Wearmouth-Jarrow is interesting and significant, too: from charter evidence, other grants vary between ten hides (Osuiu's grant of twelve such endowments in 654/5) and 124 hides and nine *sulungs* given over to Minster-in-Thanet, while Blair (2005, 87) notes that 'estates of 300 hides are mentioned at the Isle of Wight, Chertsey, Gloucester, Pershore, and Eynsham.' In Wood's view 'neither Wearmouth nor Jarrow was spectacularly rich in the extent of their estates. They do not, for instance, seem to have possessed as much land as Wilfrid's foundations', and he goes on to suggest that other revenue might have accrued to the monastery from 'rights relating to the habour that lay at the very gates of the monastery' (Wood 2010, 93). As is well known, the Old English term 'hide' refers to an area of land which might vary in size from place to place, as it produced enough *surplus* to provide for a family, hence Bede's regular use of the Latin *familia* to translate it (Wallace-Hadrill 1988, 33; Charles-Edwards 1972; Fowler 2002, 318) through Ryan (2011, 210–11) notes that 'a range of terms such as *cassatus*, *manens*, and occasionally *tribunarius*, *familia*, *mansa* and *mansio* are found in Latin charters from the pre-Viking period, and Bede's regular preference for *familia* may be a hall-mark of Wearmouth-Jarrow house style.

Can we get anywhere near identifying the extent of these holdings using more modern measurements? One way of doing this is suggested by Fowler (2002, 261–4), who draws on landscape evidence from West Overton, Wiltshire, and its entry from Domesday, to infer 'how people saw their land and … some idea of what they were looking at' (*ibid.*, 261). Blair (2005, 154) comments on the gifts made by Osuiu and Æthelbald of Mercia that 'these kings or their servants must have known where the lands lay, what ten hides amounted to, and how the food-renders from them could be split off from the rest and assigned to new recipients.'

The effort is worth making, I think; any steps which get us closer to having a good conceptual model are worth exploring. As I said at the start, such an endeavour might enable us to avoid the charge that we are using terms in an airy-fairy way without knowing what they mean or having any real grasp of them. I cannot see that David Hill would have stood for that. Some attempt, however hedged about with caveats, could be made to use them.

Place-names and historical sources

Secondly, a historical approach may also be attempted, with the usual necessary caveats. In her magisterial survey of Wearmouth and Jarrow, Cramp (2005, 37–8) has followed earlier scholars in using later historical sources to try to reconstruct the size and location of Wearmouth-Jarrow's holdings, and for lands south of the river Wear she refers to Athelstan's grant of lands in South Wearmouth: '*Weston*, Westoe; *Ufferton*, Offerton; *Sylceswurthe*, Silksworth; *duas Reofhoppas*, the two Ryhopes; *Byrdene*, Burdon; *Seham*, Seaham; *Seton*, Seaton; *Dalton*, Dalton-le-Dale; *Daldene*, Dawdon; *Heseldene*, Cold Hesleden. Fulwell and Southwick, which were part of the Wearmouth estate in the medieval period, could also have been part of the medieval grant.'

For Jarrow, Bishop Walcher's grant of 'appurtenances to the newly refounded monastery at Jarrow … are a compact group and may have been part of the original holdings. They are *Preoston*, Preston; *Munecatun*, Monkton; *Heathewurthe*, Hedworth; *Heabyrme*, Hebburn; *Wivestou*, Wivestow; *Heortedun* … it is clear that the initial Wearmouth/Jarrow endowment must have swallowed up a large amount of land in what may once have been a large royal estate bounded on the west by the main Roman road north, on the north by Gateshead on the Tyne, on the south by *Cunecacestre*, Chester-le-Street, on the Wear, and on the east by the sea' (Cramp 2005, 37). Wood (2008, 31) concurs that 'the Tyne as a whole was a major cultural and political zone … This is a cluster of royal sites which almost stands comparison with those in the Merovingian heartlands of the Île de France, and is indeed much more compact.' Figure 15.1 shows the terrain of the area, and the dependent vills identified by Cramp (2005, 37–39); it is hardly surprising that the lands owned by Wearmouth-Jarrow lie below the 400′ contour as these are likely to have been more suitable areas for agriculture; it is also worth noting that all the vills lie south of the Tyne, and those south of the Wear are clustered in the coastal area between the East Durham Plateau and the sea; none are more than ten miles distant from Jarrow. Proximity seeems to have been an important factor, allowing direct involvement in physical work on the land by members of the monastic community.

Indications of population density

A third issue might be explored: that of possible populations. Could we make any estimates here? How large was the monastic community? How great a population existed to support them? We have already seen that seventeen (or twenty-two) brothers formed the core of the new community at Jarrow. (see *HA* 7 and *VC* 11, cited above, p. 125). But we are told that when Ceolfrith left Wearmouth-Jarrow in 716 on his final journey to Rome

HA 17 He crossed the river, bowed to the cross, got on his horse, and left, leaving behind a good six hundred brothers in his monasteries.

The 'river' may be a symbolic feature of the journey, but the monastery owned land on both sides; what is more important is that a population in terms of *brothers* of six hundred was supported by/involved with/worked on one hundred and forty-three (or about one hundred and fifty) hides. This is of course, and perhaps unsuprisingly, considerably more than the figure of sixty-one at which we arrived earlier. However, there is a place where we have an indication of land measurement in both early medieval and modern reckoning – the island of Iona. In *HE* III.4, Bede says of it *neque enim magna est, sed quasi familiarum quinque, iuxta aestimationem Anglorum* ('neither it is large, but is of about five hides, in English reckoning'). Now of course in the present day we *do* know how big Iona is, and what its topography is like; a simplified

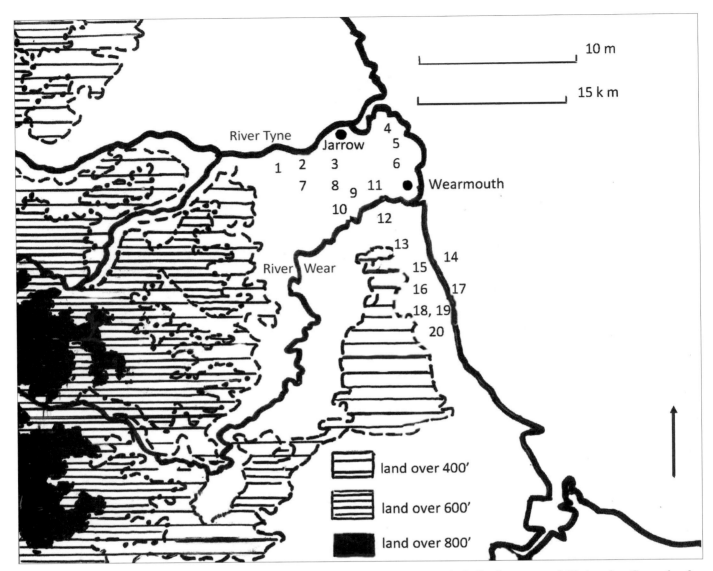

Fig. 15.1 North-East England, showing Wearmouth, Jarrow, and their dependent vills (Sally Grainger and Christopher Grocock, after Cramp 2005).

Key to the vills: 1. Gateshead; 2. Hebburn; 3. Monkton; 4. South Shields; 5. Westoe; 6, Harton; 7. Heworth; 8. Hedworth; 9. East Boldon; 10. Hilton; 11. Fulwell; 12. Suddick; 13. Silksworth; 14. Ryhope; 15. Burdon; 16. Seaton; 17. Seaham; 18. Dalton-le-Dale; 19. Daldon; 20. Heselton.

illustration showing the main features of the island may be found in Fig. 15.2. The vallum which enclosed the monastery on Iona is said to have enclosed an area of 8ha (Ritchie and Fisher 2001, 23). By comparison, the one at Baliscate, just across the bay on the Isle of Mull, had an enclosure for its main chapel of 1.37ha (Wessex Archaeology 2010). The extent to which the terrain of Iona is dominated by rough ground is clearly shown in Fig. 15.2; it is also worth noting that the highest point of the island, Dùn I, is no more than 100m/330 feet above sea level.

There is also a significant amount of relevant data from earlier periods about Iona. MacArthur (1995, 49) notes that

The earliest surviving estate map for Iona is dated 1769, but the pattern of land use it carefully recorded matches any earlier written descriptions. There is no logical reason why the general layout will have changed substantially since the medieval period or even before.

The maker of the map, William Douglas, marked out the arable and hill land with comments such as 'sandy soil with a mixture of black earth' or 'green pasture with a mixture of meadow.' Along the island's eastern edge and right around the northern shore to Calva; across its central belt and right around the northern shore to Calva; across its central belt and

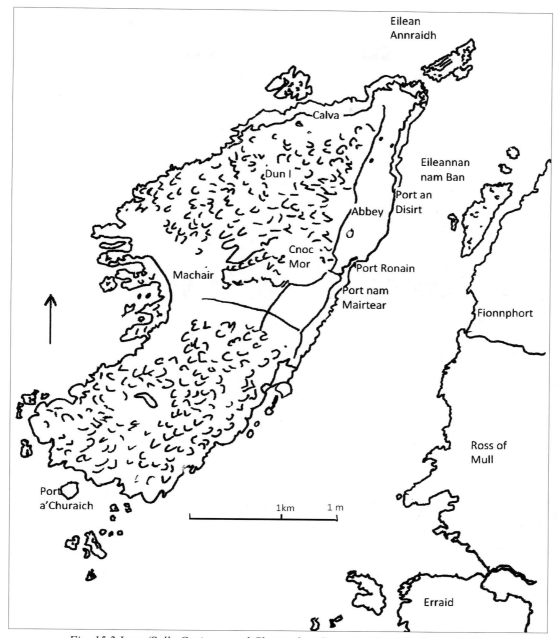

Fig. 15.2 Iona (Sally Grainger and Christopher Grocock, after MacArthur 1995).

over a broad swathe of the present Machair; from Creann na Creige to beyond Dùn Bhuirg, Douglas indicates land under cultivation. Some of this will have been worked too during both the earlier periods of monastic settlement. Adomnán tells us that the Columban monks tilled the soil of the 'western plain.' More may have been put under the *cas-chrom* or foot-plough as the population grew. On sheltered slopes and crannies all over the island are patches of rig-marks, now smooth and green, silent testimony to the toil of former generations.

There are various air photographs in earlier publications, though much more detail can easily be identified using Google

Earth: for example, the image at 56° 20′ 06″ N, 6° 23′ 34.60″ W (accessed 4 November 2012) shows numerous small rigs and enclosures no longer in use; unfortunately a band of cloud obscures the area immediately south of the monastery, at Baile Mór, in the imagery dating from 1/1/2010.

Current estimates for the resident population of Iona vary from ninety to one hundred and twenty-five (explore-isle-of-iona 2012, sacred-destinations.com 2012) but its population in earlier times was far greater. According to Thomas Shuttleworth Grimshaw (1829, 256), the Rev. Legh Richmond had noted that late in the eighteenth century it was capable of supporting some four hundred and fifty people, and was exporting grain and cattle from an economy of a pre-Agricultural Revolution type, which may have been more productive than that of the early medieval period, but perhaps not much. MacArthur (1995, 57, 63, 70, 74) notes that Iona had a population of 'eighty families' in 1688, two hundred and forty-nine individuals in 1779, had grown to three hundred and eighty-four by 1804, and 'reached probably its highest figure of 521 in 1835' – just before the arrival of the devastating potato famine, which had inevitable effects on mortality and emigration, though after 1867 'the population remained stable for the remainder of the nineteenth century, and in 1891 stood at 247.' According to James Boswell, who accompanied Dr Johnson on his celebrated tour of the northern parts

> Icolmkill [Iona] is a fertile island. The inhabitants export some cattle and grain; and I was told, they import nothing but iron and salt. They are industrious, and make their own woollen and linen cloth; and they brew a good deal of beer, which we did not find in any of the other islands (Boswell 1785, 11).

Sir Walter Scott was to note the effects of economic hardship a short while later: Mitchell (2006, 60) states that 'On Iona in 1810 he saw the wretched state of poverty of the inhabitants and records "We were surrounded on the beach by boys and girls, almost naked, all begging for charity and some offering pebbles for sale," and returning in 1814 he commented "my eyes, familiarised with the wretchedness of Zetland (Shetland) and the Harris, are less shocked with that of Iona."'

MacArthur (1995, 8) supports the view that Iona was attractive and fertile over a long period – certainly during the period in which Bede was writing:

> Without doubt people had come and gone from Iona more or less continuously over a thousand years in pre-Columban times. After that, this was 'ayne faire mayne isle … ifruitful of corne and store and guid for fishing.' Not enough had changed, in climate or topography, to make this substantially less true for the sixth century than for the sixteenth. It was an attractive place to settle.

If its early medieval population was similar, then we can arrive at a figure of about eighty to one hundred people (all ages and both genders) per hide, taking all levels of the 'economic pyramid'. On this basis, using the lower figure, we might estimate the population of the Wearmouth-Jarrow estates at $143 \times 80 = 14400$ – a huge difference from the 'six hundred brethren'. Even halving the total gives a ratio of 1:10 of brothers to peasantry (or whoever) as a whole. 1:20 seems a much more likely ratio. Whichever figure is chosen, the brothers are a tiny minority of the whole population. In a second example, at Mayo, the monastic rath encompasses twenty-eight acres. It seems very unlikely that this could have been cultivated by the original thirty monks who accompanied Colman in his exile from Lindisfarne via Iona (though Bede says in *HE* iv. 4

that by his own day 'it has now become very large' (Colgrave and Mynors 1969, 347–9). Sadly Bede gives no details of the extent of the monastery in terms of hides.

Who did the work?

There was clearly *some* involvement in manual work on the farms owned by the monastery: the classic example of this is that of Eosterwine, whose activity is recorded in *HA* 8:

> he remained so lowly, and so very like the other brothers, that he rejoiced to work cheerfully and obediently at winnowing and threshing with them, at milking the ewes and the cows, in the bakehouse, in the garden, in the kitchen and in all the work of the monastery.

We know from Bede's warm words about the Anglo-Saxon foundation in Ireland at Mayo that labour was valued:

> This monastery is still occupied by Englishmen; from small beginnings it has now become very large and is commonly known as *Muig éo* [Mayo]. All these monks have adopted a better Rule and it now contains a remarkable company gathered there from England, living after the example of the venerable fathers under a Rule, having an abbot elected canonically, in great devotion and austerity and supporting themselves by the labour of their own hands' (*HE* IV.8: Colgrave and Mynors 1969, 349).

But was this wishful thinking? Was Eosterwine the exception that proved the rule? And did slaves do any of the necessary work? The issue has been discussed (Franzen and Moffat 1994; Pelteret 1995), though it has to be said that slaves get no mention in any of Bede's work; he does not refer to the status of those who work the land at all, and it may well have varied, with a 'mixed economy'; where Bede does make mention of local inhabitants, in the *Life of Cuthbert* or the *EEE* for example, he regards them as parishioners in need of pastoral care – though that was no doubt not their only role or function in the landscape, as they clearly provided some, if not most, of the labour to farm the land. While it is possible in this case that 'absence of evidence not evidence of absence', in the *EEE* Bede certainly gets worked up and expresses himself very freely; if slaves were used (and perhaps their use might have met with some disapproval?) he might easily have mentioned them there and discussed their status and treatment. In addition, one of Bede's complaints in *EEE* 7 is that *tributa* and *pecunia* are given to bishops by villagers who never see them. This sounds like the acts of free (if poverty-stricken) peasantry. Pounds (1994, 51) thinks that the practice of using slaves on a large scale had died out by the early years of the ninth century on the Continent. The situation of dependent vills shown in Fig. 15.1 would suggest that monastic labour could be employed on quite a lot of the lands owned by the twin houses.

There are also clues which we can glean from continental parallels. It seems clear that by the ninth century, a little later than our period, a system of demese land – *mansus indominicatus* – had come into being; it was cultivated on behalf of the monastery by lay peasantry, who worked their own land. Perhaps a similar system was in place in these ex-royal lands given to Wearmouth-Jarrow. Pounds (1994, 501–4) helpfully notes that on the Continent, land was measured in *bonniers*, which equated to just over a hectare, or 2¾ acres, and a *mansus* was as a general rule the amount of land needed to support a fairly well-to-do family (similar to a hide). He cites the polyptique of the abbey of Saint-Amand, near Lille, which gives an idea of how the system worked:

> In the villa of Businiacas is a demesne *mansus* with a house and sixteen other buildings, as well as a garden, an orchard and a chapel. Sixteen *bonniers* (= 20 hectares/45 acres) of cropland belong to the demesne. Of these, five *bonniers* are sown in autumn with 20 *modii* (= 40 gallons) and six are sown in spring with 35 *modii*. There are four *bonniers* of meadow, from which 30 loads of hay can be taken. There are three *bonniers* of copse. There is a mill which yields 20 *modii* a year.
>
> There are eleven *mansi*, each paying 10 *modii* of malt and 2 *modii* of hops and as a relief (*pro leuamine*) a denarius, and also a pig. They journey to the vineyards in every other year, or pay a solidus instead. Every seventh year they each pay a solidus for military service (*pro hostelico*). They each provide a pound of flax, a chicken and five eggs. They make (*wagtas*). They work two days a week with an ox, and for a third day they provide manual labour.

In addition to this, Pounds (1994, 51) adds that ten other *mansi* gave labour services and dues of slightly different kinds; in addition, there were 28 *ancillae* who each gave a solidus, and the demesne possessed enough woodland to support ten pigs. Saint-Amand provides an indication of what kind of income in money and in kind could be provided by land held by a monastery (and perhaps money income of this kind was the source of the funds Ceolfrith was able to draw on to buy the 20 hides at *Sambuce* or 'Elder Farm').

The information here is in terms of *yield*; documentary evidence such as this, and indeed from any period which pre-dates the Agrarian Revolution, might be useful in indicating what sort of revenues in kind and money might have been available to support the activity of a monastic centre. Estimated yields might also draw on the findings of experimental archaeology, though such data needs to be established over a long term, and checked in more than one site.

The practical labour requirements of a given *area* of land are much more complex: the ratio of individual labourers/workers to acreage will vary considerably from season to season (the tail end of the demands made by the harvest still linger on in our academic calendars) and from land-types; seasonality plays a part, and so does the type of farming activity envisaged (arable; pasture; woodland management).

Conclusion

This paper may not have taken us much further in a quest for a deeper understanding of what the countryside which supported a monastery like Wearmouth-Jarrow actually looked like, or how it functioned; but the quest is worth pursuing. In the case of Wearmouth-Jarrow, a start has been made by looking at place-names, (Cramp 2005, 37–8), and there has been much exploration of the term *hide* and what that may have indicated, translated as it were into modern terms (Fowler 2006, 261–4; Ryan 2011).

We may never get to a universally-accepted estimate in *modern* terms of what these early medieval land-holdings were; but that should not stop us trying. Combining available data with recent innovations in mapping techniques might permit us to refine our understanding of areas of land with greater precision. The result might be no more than an 'intelligent guess' of what different areas might have been used for in the early medieval period, but coupled with place-name evidence and boundaries, archaeobotany, and even *current* land use (which may vary greatly – but farming was innately conservative until very recent times) it may help us grasp what kind of activity was likely where in the monastic past. There will always be objections to any experimental work or estimates based on theory; the key is not to avoid the enterprise altogether but to refine the parameters and produce baselines which can be justified, even in general terms, and also to produce variants. As I learned from a retired bank manager some years ago, there are times when you simply have to 'take a view' and run with it until fresh evidence enables us to sharpen that view, adapt it, or abandon it in favour of something better.

Note

1 All translations from these are taken from Grocock and Wood 2013, which contains texts, translations and commentary of Bede's *History of the Abbots* and the anonymous *Life of Ceolfrith*, as well as *Homily* i. 13 and the *Letter to Ecgbert Bishop of York*.

The Late Anglo-Saxon Landscape of Western Cheshire: Open Field, Ploughs and the Manor within the Dykes

N. J. Higham

My friendship with David Hill dates back to 1974, when I had only recently begun doctoral study in archaeology at Manchester. Soon after, I began teaching evening classes for the Extra-Mural Department in both history and archaeology, helping out on Offa's Dyke and running study visits and day schools. When, in 1977, I took up the initially temporary and part-time post of Staff Tutor in History in the same department, I shared an office with both David and John Smith (the Senior Staff Tutor in Local History) and we worked closely together for over thirty years. There were considerable successes, including the jointly organised conference on Edward the Elder in 1999, the papers from which we published two years later (Higham and Hill 2001). Along with this whole volume, my paper is dedicated to David's memory, and offered in thanks for the stimulus which he invariably brought to my work.

Introduction

In 1977 Rhys Williams, the county archaeologist for Cheshire, was keen to strengthen archaeological oversight of development of the visitor potential of the Old Hall complex at Tatton Park. He approached David with a view to his undertaking the work. David was, of course, very fond of Tatton Park; in recent years he enjoyed holding his birthday celebrations there. Back then he responded by taking Extra-Mural students to observe, record and evaluate the shallow trenches which had been dug preparatory to erection of an early modern threshing barn which the County Council were re-locating to the site. He was not, however, much inspired by the archaeology he encountered, which included the regular planting trenches of an early twentieth-century tree nursery, and preferring to focus his Extra-Mural training digs on things Anglo-Saxon he suggested that I take on the work at Tatton instead. So was born the Tatton project, which ran from 1978 until 1988. As a training dig it was lodged securely within the overall umbrella of David's programme. Extra-Mural students participated,

often for years, and, of course, we used the same precious cache of tools as had been bought for work on the dykes. At Tatton, we began by excavating inside and immediately around the Old Hall (Higham 2002), then switched attention to the recording and excavation of a substantial part of the deserted medieval village which lay outside the Old Hall precinct (Higham 2000), one of the few DMVs then known in Cheshire. We ended up exposing a large slice of the DMV, exploring an Early Mesolithic flint-napping site on the Mere's edge (Higham and Cane 1999) and examining various other pre- and post-medieval sites. It was only in the last two years of the programme that we identified a probable late-Anglo-Saxon element in the medieval settlement to place alongside the single piece of late-Anglo-Saxon 'Chester Ware' which we had found earlier. The long delay certainly vindicated David's initial unwillingness to commit to the site, but this project gave birth to my own interest in medieval settlement and field systems in Cheshire, from which stems the programme of work discussed here.

Cheshire's Late Anglo-Saxon Landscape: Problems and Approaches

Today the Dee is the principal boundary of western Cheshire, with only relatively small areas beyond the river, immediately west of Chester, within England. In 1066, in contrast, both sides of the Dee valley lay within *Cestrescire*, with the thinly settled hundreds of Atiscross and Exestan lying entirely west of the Dee, and Dudestan, although predominantly on the east bank, inclusive of Eaton, Pulford, Poulton and Eccleston beyond the river (for general discussion, see Thorn 1991). The Dee valley in its totality was, therefore, the very edge of late Anglo-Saxon Mercia.

Alongside Offa's and Wat's Dykes, one of David's particular interests towards the end of his life lay in Anglo-Saxon farming, in particular the mechanics of the later Anglo-Saxon plough (as Hill 2010a). It is clear from Domesday Book that the heavy plough with a large plough-team was by 1086 standard in Cheshire; occasional references to ploughing with fewer oxen make the point, as at Robert of Rhuddlan's small estate of Cuddington, where the bordars had only two beasts (DB 264c: Erskine 1988). However, Cheshire's medieval fields were neglected by early researchers (White 1995, 15–17), who found there few of the manorial court rolls, extents, enclosure awards and early modern estate maps which underlay their work elsewhere, preferring instead to concentrate on the less opaque and simpler systems characteristic of the Champion Country of the East Midlands (as Gray 1915; Orwin and Orwin 1938). While this focus has only been challenged on the national level in recent years (Rippon 2008; White 2012), there has been a strong current of regional studies. Dorothy Sylvester initiated research in the region in the late 1940s, exploring medieval field systems and settlements via tithe, estate and early Ordnance Survey maps cross-referenced with published cartularies (1956, 1969), and her lead was followed by others, initially using similar types of evidence (as Chapman 1953; Higson 1993). Later researchers introduced aerial photography, survey and archaeological excavation (Williams 1984; Wilson 1987) resulting in multi-disciplinary local studies (Thompson *et al.* 1982; White 1995; Higham 2000; 2004a).

What has emerged locally is recognition of a distinctive pattern of both settlement and land use in the Middle Ages. Settlement tends to be dispersed; while field name and other documentary evidence implies that open fields were commonplace across the Cheshire lowlands, they were generally small in scale and interspersed with closes, woods and meadows in a complex landscape quite unlike the Champion Country, where open fields characteristically extended across the bulk of each manorial territory. However, major difficulties remain. It has proved problematic to date ridge and furrow and the settlements associated with it; much of which still survives as earthworks may be post-medieval in date. Excavation has been held back both by the difficult of identifying early sites on the ground, and then by problems of dating. 'Chester Ware' was entering the region in the late Anglo-Saxon period, but these vessels have a very restricted distribution outside Chester itself; with only a handful of exceptions (as Tatton, above), 'Chester Ware' is only very rarely identified in the countryside, which was to all intents and purposes aceramic from the fourth century, when the deposition of Roman pottery died away, until the early thirteenth, when medieval pottery made its appearance.

In consequence, it has proved difficult to build up a picture of the development and history of medieval farming in the region. Our understanding of late Anglo-Saxon settlement and land-use rests far too heavily for comfort on the Domesday descriptions of manors, and the absence of Anglo-Saxon charters, combined with the lack of pottery of the period, has stifled attempts to drill down to the Middle Anglo-Saxon period. The main approach right across the West Midlands has

been to divide place-names into the categories of 'settlement' (principally -*tūn*, *burh*) and 'woodland' (largely -*lēah*), and map them against the drift geology. By doing this Margaret Gelling (1976, 205–10; 1988, 126–8; 1992, 7) was able to show that settlement-type names generally dominate the better drained terrain, particularly in the main river valleys, while woodland names are common on poorly drained clay and the interfluves; but applying this to Cheshire has its own difficulties, since many flat claylands have settlement type names and some sites with woodland-type place-names seem to have been occupied early. In general, though, Cheshire's medieval landscape probably originated with clusters of settlements on the better-drained agricultural land surrounded by more wooded terrain on intractable clay soils, which were cleared later and long used as pasture, for gathering timber and fuel and/or hunting (Higham 2000, 62–4). When this type of data was then mapped against the Domesday hundreds, the resultant patterns implied that across much of Cheshire these tenth- and eleventh-century sub-divisions of the shire had been based on smaller, older territories. Particularly in central and northern Cheshire, hundreds seem to have been formed by the amalgamation of two pre-existing units, still recognisable as parishes, between which a line of woodland place-names mark the earlier divide (Higham 1993b, 146–60). This is an ancient landscape, therefore, which bears the imprint of settlement and land-use strategies from at least the eighth century, but it is not one which it is easy to bring into sharp focus.

Ridge and Furrow in the Dee Valley

This paper concentrates on an area immediately south of Chester, in the parishes of Chester St Oswald, Eccleston, Aldford, Coddington and Malpas (Fig. 16.1), and focuses on excavation and photographic evidence relating to medieval ploughing. In and around the Dee valley, there was a hierarchy of settlements visible on the early nineteenth-century tithe maps (Chapman 1953, 37; White 1995), with a minority of substantial villages but more numerous townships characterised by hamlets and/ or dispersed settlement. The Domesday settlement pattern was similar, though the larger sites were not always the same as on the tithe. By local standards, large populations were listed in Domesday Book for Eaton (ten households), Aldford (the more northerly of the two manors therein named Farndon: fourteen households), Saighton (ten households) and Tilston (fifteen households: DB, 236d, 266d, 263b, 264b: Erskine 1988); both Aldford and Eaton have small earthwork castles and were the centres of early Norman baronies and all of Aldford, Eaton and Tilston were held in 1066 by Earl Edwin of Mercia. The presence of fisheries at Eaton and Aldford and mills at Aldford and Tilston underline the status of these manors in a landscape where such assets were almost exclusively sited on the estates of the political elite (Higham 1993b, 196–7).

At Eaton the medieval settlement is now lost beneath the later mansion and gardens, but the creation of an extensive deer

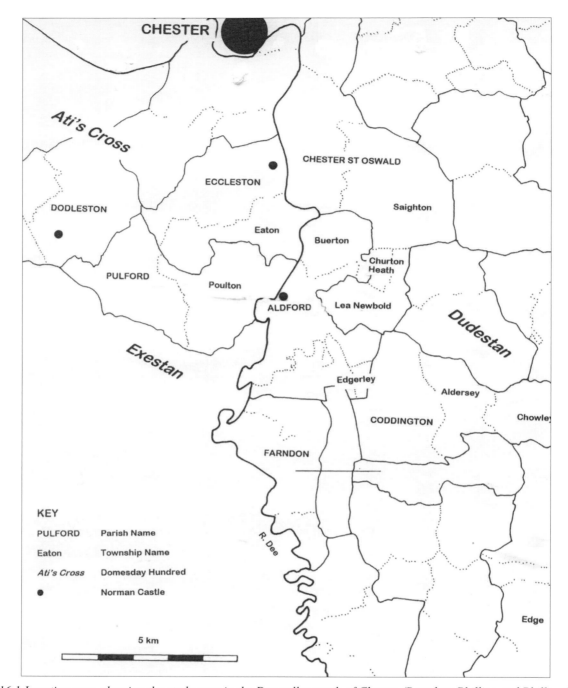

Fig. 16.1 Location map, showing the study area in the Dee valley south of Chester (Based on Phillips and Phillips 2002).

park has conserved the broad ridge and furrow far better than in neighbouring townships, where much has been ploughed out in recent years. Ridge and furrow covers virtually the entire northern end of the park, and although the remains are far from dramatic there is a very low ripple effect on the surface, with the better preserved ridges a mere 15cm above the furrow bottom and a width varying from 5.5m to 7m. Test pitting and subsequent observation (in 2011) during large-scale excavations for a new ha-ha cutting across these ridges revealed a plough-soil depth on average marginally less than thirty centimetres, above a very variable but uniformly clay subsoil. The thinness of the topsoil clearly limited the height which ridging could achieve. There was a parallel impact on the clayey subsoil, which had a slight undulation mimicking the surface ridge and furrow, demonstrating that ploughing had affected the full depth of the soil.

Besides a variety of land drains (in general see Phillips 1989), glazed pottery, bricks and slate, all of the eighteenth or nineteenth centuries, there were no finds so no way of estimating the chronology of this ploughing beyond the fact that it had ceased before, or at latest when, the deer park was established. That date is unfortunately unclear, though it was certainly parkland by the later eighteenth century. Where precisely the two ploughlands noted in Domesday Book lay is unknown, but a substantial and well-organised field system developed here; west-east ridging ran for up to 400m away from parallel headlands on both sides of the Roman road running southwards through the park, the surface of which was revealed by trenching beneath an eighteenth-century carriage road (Buchanan *et al*. 1975).

In 1066 Earl Edwin of Mercia held the more important manors in the Dee valley and was arguably the patron of all other landholders in the area. The only other figures of any real status were ecclesiastical, but both were very close to Edwin: the bishop of Lichfield was ex-abbot of the earl's family monastery at Coventry and the abbot of St Werburgh's, at Chester, seems

to have been operating in close association with Edwin and his brother Morcar (Higham 1988). Saighton was the first of St Werburgh's manors named in Domesday Book; although it was only lightly hidated it had eight ploughlands, with a single plough in lordship, and nine villeins with five ploughs. The abbots retained a manor house here across the Middle Ages, the fifteenth-century gatehouse of which still survives, while the strongly nucleated village is today surrounded by vestiges of an extensive open-field system. The modern enclosure system includes a series of near concentric hedges which delimit the ridges (Fig. 16.2), and while these might be interpreted as evidence of expansion during the Middle Ages they could equally reflect progressive abandonment of the outer furlongs, as land was enclosed and converted to pasture in the later Middle Ages. There is a regularity to this field system, however, which invites comparison with England's Central Province.

Aldford had a similarly extensive open field system, with ridging to the east of the village still widely visible in the 1940s, but here it was far less symmetrically organised. The village probably initially occupied a triangular area to the south of the

Fig. 16.2 Saighton village and its hinterland to the east, where ridge and furrow survives in concentrically arranged furlongs. Millfield Lane is visible diverting round old furlongs (RAF Aerial Photographs from Operational review (1945–1948): © UKaerialphotos).

136 N. J. Higham

Norman castle and the church and west of the Roman road. By the late twelfth century, though, construction of Aldford's bridge and the establishment of the line of the B5130 road east of the Dee had provided an alternative to the Roman road southwards from Chester, perhaps in response to collapsing English control of north-east Wales (from the 1130s onwards). Once the new road was established the settlement expanded eastwards to form a near-square plan (Fig. 16.3). Although since destroyed, broad ridge and furrow was still visible in the 1940s between the triangular core of the village and its later expansion to the east. It seems unlikely that this area would have been ridged after the new area of settlement had become established, when closes and crofts can reasonably be expected to have been laid out behind the tofts on the roadside, so these ridges arguably became ossified comparatively early. The Roman road southwards from Chester is sealed by this ridge and furrow, suggesting that this route had already fallen out of use when the ridges were created.

Excavation in 2012 preparatory to the erection of a new timber-framed barn close to the Roman road revealed an upper plough soil containing artefacts dating from the sixteenth to the twentieth centuries, with a concentration associated with Aldford's re-building as an estate village in the 1880s. Beneath was a very different cultivated loam entirely devoid of pottery, suggesting an agricultural soil which had already been abandoned before artefactual deposition resumed in the period 1200–1500, so this was probably last cultivated earlier than the thirteenth century.

Beneath this putatively early plough soil was found a probable ditch, running east-west, which was also devoid of artefactual material. A second, parallel ditch was clearly later since it cut the lower plough soil. This was probably one of the boundaries visible on the Tithe Map of the late 1830s and the RAF vertical from the 1940s, which were removed in the late 1980s when the area was converted to amenity space; but these parallel ditches of very different periods suggest an

Fig. 16.3 Aldford village: the early village probably centred on the triangle of roads on the west side, then spread eastwards with the development of a new North-South route. Ridge and furrow was ossified within the enlarged settlement and its tofts (RAF Aerial Photographs from Operational review (1945–1948): © UKaerialphotos).

enclosure system which retained its basic shape over many centuries but underwent internal processes of change, with boundaries discontinued but replaced by others. That the croft boundaries are parallel with the ridge and furrow is clear from Fig. 16.3, so supposing this ridge and furrow does pre-date the westward expansion of the village then the ditch which it seals is unlikely to be later than the central medieval period, and could be far earlier.

The Aldford field system has predominantly east-west ridge and furrow, providing drainage towards the Dee. The area where 'town-field' field names were located in the early nineteenth century lies south of the village (White 1995) but ridge and furrow here has since been ploughed out; however, there are on the east side of the main settlement a variety of small parcels of ridges aligned across the main west-east axis. Such are a common feature of ridge and furrow in the Dee valley, where there are often compact blocks of ridges laid out in a very different direction from their neighbours.

This is particularly frequent away from the main settlements, among the minor manors listed in the eleventh century. In the far north of Aldford Parish, in Buerton township, there is a complex of very small blocks of ridges adjacent to a moated site within the hamlet of Bruera (Fig. 16.4). Buerton lay between the Dee and two townships with names distinctive of late clearance – Lea Newbold and Churton Heath – and was also perhaps a well-wooded area in the Anglo-Saxon period, despite the settlement-type name. Ploughed land later expanded as colonisation occurred in the twelfth and thirteenth centuries associated with a dispersed pattern of settlement. The photographic record supports the identification of a small DMV at Bruera, immediately adjacent to the moated site (Medieval Village Research Group Records, number 108, RCHME 1994).

Similar processes of colonisation arguably lie behind the group of small manors named *Lai* (Lea) in Domesday Book (263d, 266d: Erskine 1988), all of which occupy a poorly drained, flat area of clay-land east of the Dee. Old English *lēah*

Fig. 16.4 The shrunken hamlet of Bruera, with adjacent ridge and furrow: a moated site (top right) lies at the north end of the medieval settlement remains, with pronounced areas of ridge and furrow to the west and south (RAF Aerial Photographs from Operational review (1945–1948): © UKaerialphotos).

is the commonest woodland place-name in Cheshire, occurring both as a suffix (as Buckley) but also as the simplex place-name Legh or Lea. Margaret Gelling (1988, 126–9) considered that where it occurred in clusters it should be translated as 'clearing' but in isolation as 'wood'. Here three manors bearing the name had been created by 1066 around the Aldford Brook but there is little mention of woodland by 1086, so this was arguably cleared land.

Identifying the three manors named *Lai* in Domesday Book is problematic, but the most substantial, held by Earl Hugh in 1086 and valued in 1066 at 30s with 4 ploughlands and ten households, should almost certainly be identified with Lea Hall Farm in Lea Newbold, where a small DMV is detectable on the vertical photograph immediately south of the hall, associated with extensive ridge and furrow covering the bulk of the early modern township (Fig. 16.5). The other *Lai* manor which Hugh held in 1086 was waste and had only one ploughland; this was probably 'Newbold', a name first recorded in 1287 (Dodgson 1972, 120) and meaning 'the new house', lying at the northern

extremity of the township. That township was created in the early modern period for purposes of civil government by the agglomeration of these two estates, one large and one small, into a single unit, initially named 'Lea cum Newbold', now Lea Newbold.

The third *Lai* manor was held in 1086 by Bigot of Loges and occurs in Domesday Book immediately after Bigot's manor of Farndon (*i.e.* Aldford: DB 266d: Erskine 1988); Ansgot held it in 1066 as a hide with two ploughlands, 2 bordars and 1 acre of meadow, valued at a mere 2 shillings. That Lea Manor Farm is the only one of the three surviving *Lai*-named settlements to lie in Aldford makes it the strongest contender for this identification. While we cannot be certain, therefore, it seems likely that the two Lea manors held by the earl in 1086 eventually formed the basis of Lea Newbold township, while that held by Bigot and his immediate descendants, who constructed the castle at Aldford, comprised land between the Plowley Brook and Aldford Brook which was subsequently retained within Aldford. This almost detached, eastern portion

16.5 Lea Hall Farm: a small DMV can be seen south of the Hall, adjacent to meadow and marshland skirting the Aldford Brook. Extensive ridge and furrow lies above the marshland, extending across much of the rest of the township (RAF Aerial Photographs from Operational review (1945–1948): © UKaerialphotos).

of Aldford township now dominated by Lea Manor Farm may therefore approximate to a small late-Anglo-Saxon and early Norman manor, even though there is little now visible on the site earlier than a farmhouse of the 1820s. The land around was under cultivation during the medieval period, since shallow, broad ridge and furrow is detectable on 1940s aerial photographs in several of the surrounding fields (Higham 2004a, 57), but has since been destroyed by ploughing. As late as the nineteenth century the approach track from the north twisted between interlocking furlongs of ridge and furrow. A recent programme of test pits in the paddock east of the farmhouse confirmed headlands on both sides of this access way, which implies that this approach dates to the Middle Ages, but otherwise the blocks of ploughing seem to run straight onto each other, often at ninety degrees. That the farm lies on a medieval settlement is confirmed by the finding during re-development in 2013 of later medieval building materials and ceramic wares, including a sherd of imported glazed pottery of the period 1250–1400 from one of the test pits excavated in 2012. Early Roman pottery and building materials were also found. This site was clearly occupied in the late first to early third centuries AD, suggesting a complex and multi-phase settlement history.

Other small manors abutted the three Domesday estates named Lea. To the south, for example, were the three manors of Coddington, held severally by Ernwy, Ansgot and Dot, responsible jointly for only two hides and with only four ploughlands between them; Earl Hugh had control of these manors in 1086 but the presence of a Frenchman, a radman and the earl's own demesne, associated with five villeins and a cottar, implies that the three-fold division survived. Hugh's own manor, with the bulk of the manorial tenants, should probably be located at the later dispersed settlement of Coddington itself, in the west of the medieval parish and, given his priority in the names listed, this was probably Ernwy's portion in 1066. The lesser Coddington manors were probably Beechin, in the far north, and Aldersey in the centre of the parish, which later became a separate township; both have woodland place-names and dispersed settlement patterns typical of what had been well-wooded landscapes.

While the minority of larger and higher-status settlements – as Eaton, Aldford or Saighton – are associated with ridge and furrow which can be interpreted in terms of comparatively large open fields, the smaller Domesday manors exhibit rather different landscapes. That is not because there is any shortage of ridges, for in many cases these cover the bulk of the territory; rather, it is a matter of the arrangement of ridges, their length and overall patterning and ways in which the arable was sub-divided. While classic open field systems are generally characterised by long parallel ridges in large blocks, these small Cheshire manors exhibit a wide variety of ridge length, including numerous very short sections in small often interlocking parcels. Take, for example, the strip of land between the Roman road – visible on Fig. 16.6 as a long,

straight hedge running approximately north west/south east – and the Plowley Brook, which runs approximately parallel to the east of it and serves as the western boundary of Edgerley, a tiny township in Aldford parish. Both features, obviously, were already present when these ridges were formed, but although the fields between them vary in width (west-east) from marginally less than 300m, at the north end of Edgerley, to less than 100m in the south, in every case the ridge and furrow runs from the road-line to the brook. The need to drain the land was, therefore, the key issue here. Although the ridge widths vary, suggesting that some may be post-medieval, much is broad ridge and most exhibit the reverse 'S' shape characteristic of medieval ploughing, caused by the need to begin turning the plough team before the end of the furrow has been reached, and the modern hedges follow this same alignment. The basic patterning, therefore, is medieval. These short ridges are not just a consequence of the close proximity of two existing landscape features, for similar length ridges are commonplace throughout Edgerley and its immediate environs, at Bruera and at Lea Newbold. Rather, short ridges are typical of this landscape. Another characteristic is the small parcels into which such ridges are often grouped, often intermingled with others on different alignments, resulting in groups of ridges abutting each other, at an angle or sideways on. This is well-illustrated at Bruera (Fig. 16.4), where numerous sets of short ridges interlock around the medieval settlement. Some parcels of ridges are less than 100m in length and a mere 80m in width, such small parcels of ridging concentrating particularly around hamlets and small villages, as the DMVs at Bruera and Lea Hall Farm.

The question arises as to what form these sets of ridges took in the Middle Ages, when they were being ploughed. Today, fields are mostly larger than the smaller parcels, several of which may often be identified within one modern enclosure, but although some farms clearly had their fields re-organised in the modern period, most seem to have developed organically from what went before. While hedges that cut ridge and furrow are not uncommon, it is far more frequently the case that the modern hedgerow serves as the boundary of the medieval furlong. Observation of the tithe maps demonstrates that the fields that we see today are in many cases larger than in the 1830s. The enlargement of fields by hedge-removal has been a common-place, therefore, although not on the scale which has occurred in much of eastern England. Many of the now-lost boundaries visible on tithe maps, for example at Bruera, demarcated the parcels of ridge and furrow identified from the air in the 1940s. Assuming therefore that the tithe maps represent only a snapshot within a longer process of field enlargement associated with settlement desertion and the consolidation of farming into ever fewer units, it seems reasonable to suppose that at an earlier date hedges served to mark even more of the boundaries of the parcels of ridge and furrow that we see today.

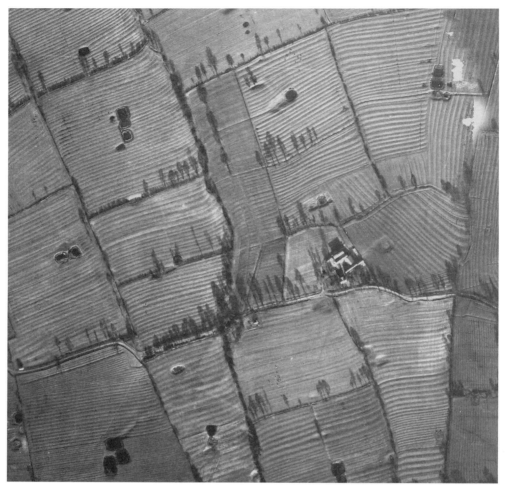

Fig. 16.6 Edgerley Farm lies at the approximate centre of the tiny township of Edgerley, with the wooded line of the Plowley Brook as its western side. The straight hedge running from the north-west corner of the plate marks the line of the Roman Road southwards from Chester (RAF Aerial Photographs from Operational review (1945–1948): © UKaerialphotos).

Dating Enclosure

We must conclude, therefore, that this landscape has been heavily enclosed, even more so than is currently apparent, but when this occurred and how this process related to the working of ridge and furrow is less clear. Specifically, it is difficult to ascertain the extent to which hedge boundaries were present while the ridges were under cultivation. On the one hand, we might argue that it would have been extremely difficult to use a mould-board plough and its plough team within these small parcels of land when they were enclosed, implying that the ridging occurred predominantly in a more open landscape which was later hedged as part and parcel of the shift from arable to pasture. On the other hand many field names referring to crofts and similar on record in the thirteenth and fourteenth centuries suggest numerous enclosures at an early date. One way of testing this issue is the incidence of headlands – the strip of land used to turn the plough at the

end of a group of ridges. Such do occur in this landscape, as in Eaton Park and at Lea Manor Farm (above), but there are far more instances where ridges run right up to modern hedges, or to neighbouring parcels of ridge and furrow within a modern field. The comparative scarcity of headlands implies that it was common practice to turn the plough and team on neighbouring parcels of ridge and furrow, in which case many of these small blocks of ridges were necessarily unenclosed when ploughing was occurring. Once ploughing ceased and the land was put down to grass, the furlongs determined the division of the land as pasture. Conversion to grazing seems to have begun well within the Middle Ages, leading to an increasingly enclosed landscape, but the process was still underway in the 1830s, when occasional open field strips are still visible on the tithe maps (White 1995).

An alternative interpretation of some ridges is prompted by Sir James Caird's study in the mid-nineteenth century (1852,

252), which notes that ridging was undertaken to improve surface drainage at the point when arable was converted to permanent pasture. Instances of this have been reported in Huxley (Thompson *et al.* 1982, 61, 67). Clearly that must be acknowledged as a possible source of some of the ridging visible on the RAF verticals, but the majority exhibit features which are incompatible with this explanation, even when they are bounded by modern hedge boundaries. There is a high incidence of the reverse 'S' shape, for example, which seems difficult to envisage being formed in the process of ridging merely to drain pastureland and numerous parcels exhibit the tapering off and even discontinuation of some ridges where space becomes limited, which seems equally unlikely in the context set out by Caird. Again, some ridges are cut by field boundaries; while Caird's interpretation is arguably valid in some instances, this is not a satisfactory explanation of the bulk of the broad ridge across large parts of Cheshire.

Conclusion

A high proportion of western Cheshire exhibited ridge and furrow until the widespread destruction caused by post-War ploughing, and recent excavations at Eaton and Aldford have revealed something of the nature and chronology of the ridges. It is clear that they were both formed and farmed at a period when very little artefactual material was being deposited on the fields; none at all was found at either of these sites. Focusing away from these major centres onto the numerous minor settlements which lay adjacent allows us to take a fresh look at the agricultural systems with which they were associated. Small furlongs containing comparatively short ridges are an important component of this landscape, forming many of the units that were the basis of its management. While there were clearly numerous closes in the Middle Ages, many of these small furlongs were not permanently enclosed while the ridges were under cultivation, allowing the plough and team to be turned on adjacent land, in that sense ploughing in the open field tradition. In other respects, however, this was a landscape which looks very different from the Champion Country, where holdings consisted of numerous very long but narrow parallel strips in several large open fields. In Cheshire, open fields were generally small; selions lay within parcels of ridges or butts containing only a few acres, which often interlocked with one another in a way which contrasts with the open fields of, for example, Nottinghamshire. Clearly some land was never ploughed for environmental reasons, as the wetlands around the Aldford Brook at Lea Hall Farm (Fig. 16.4), so this was available variously as meadow and grazing; elsewhere, however, most of the land surface was ridged, though only a small proportion need have been ploughed in any one year.

The decline of arable in the fourteenth century led to the hedging of parcels of ridges, as these became permanent pastures. Enclosure was barely an issue locally by the sixteenth century, having very largely already occurred by consent, though the process remained incomplete well into the modern period.

The evidence offered here is very local, although I am confident that the pattern that I am recording recurs widely elsewhere in Cheshire, if not elsewhere. It is important, though, to recognise at the close that there were other local landscapes dependant largely on physical factors. Travel just a few miles east from the Dee and you reach the Central Cheshire Ridge and townships such as Edge, near Tilston but in the parish of Malpas; here modern settlement is highly dispersed and was so already in the Middle Ages. Domesday Book (264b, 264c: Erskine 1988) records two manors, both held by a thegn named Edwin in both 1066 and 1086, though at the later date as a sub-tenant of Robert of Rhuddlan. These manors owed tax on only two hides between them, with just two ploughlands, and three slaves manning a plough at the larger of the two. Both had small woodlands but the entry for the larger included the succinct comment, *morae sunt ibi* – 'there are moors here'. As its name implies, Edge lies on the Central Cheshire Ridge, a sandstone outcrop today largely topped with heather and conifers. It is noticeable just how thin settlement is even today and there is a notable absence of ridge and furrow. While the heavy mouldboard plough could be used to cultivate the better tracts of the poorly drained claylands of the Dee valley, even this technology was incapable of bringing much of Edge into cultivation, compelling farmers to locate themselves on the periphery of such upland townships.

While the ridge and furrow that can still be seen today is, of course, the product of many different periods of ploughing, enough remained in the early post-War period to make it possible to explore the nature of arable cultivation in the Middle Ages and so to reach out towards the data on ploughlands and ploughs recorded in Domesday Book. David Hill was a keen and expert field-archaeologist throughout his long career; it is my belief that he would have enjoyed viewing and discussing the evidence that I have presented in this paper. I have not, unfortunately, had the benefit of that input, but his long shadow lies across this study, as much else of my archaeological and landscape interests.

Acknowledgements

My thanks to Moya Watson and her colleagues at Cheshire Historic Environment Record and to Tom Samuels of UKaerialphotos for their assistance in accessing the RAF vertical photographs used here.

Mapping Late Anglo-Saxon Manuscripts and Documents

Donald Scragg

I was closely associated with David Hill academically from 1984 when the Manchester Centre for Anglo-Saxon Studies was formed. David was an Associate Director and long-time member of the Management Committee, where he proved a most valuable colleague. He was always full of imaginative ideas for day-schools and residential conferences, and he it was who first suggested the interdisciplinary, part-time MA in Anglo-Saxon Studies, taught by members of the Centre. A number of successful students taking that degree went on to study for PhDs in Anglo-Saxon subjects, and many more continue to support the Centre at papers and conferences to the present day.

This paper is also dedicated to Mary Syner who was secretary to the Centre for many years, and who died at Easter 2012.

Introduction

Today we live by maps. True, many of us have route planners on our mobile phones or satellite navigation in our cars and find our way from a to b by means of a voice in the sky, but we still all have maps in our heads that tell us where India stands in relation to Australia. This was borne in on me the first time I taught the history of the English language in America and found that undergraduates in the Mid-west had no more idea where Poland stands in relation to Portugal than British students have in placing Maryland in respect of Minnesota. Maps are very necessary to us. But the Anglo-Saxons had no maps before the eleventh century, and we had no reliable maps of Anglo-Saxon England until relatively recently. It is true that the mapping of Anglo-Saxon England began in the sixteenth century, but the apotheosis of mapping the period was achieved only in 1981 with the appearance of David Hill's *An Atlas of Anglo-Saxon England*. David was an inveterate cartographer, still drawing maps until very late in his life, and planning a second volume of the Atlas thirty years after the publication of the first. Nonetheless, invaluable as what we already have is and without wishing in any way to denigrate David's very considerable achievement, I would like to suggest that there is

still room for much more in the field. In my recently published *Conspectus of Scribal Hands* (Scragg 2012a) I included, where possible, amongst the information gathered about each of the scribal hands described, an indication of the location of the writer. There is also a summary of that information in a map at the end of the Introduction, a map of what I have called the location of scribes (and therefore of the manuscripts and documents that they produced). It is a map which is remarkably similar to that of the Benedictine Houses shortly before the Conquest produced by David in his *Atlas* (Hill 1981, map 246), and the coincidence is hardly surprising since the survival of those houses through the later medieval period means that most of the books and documents that have been preserved for us are associated with monasteries. But the careful reader of my *Conspectus* may also have noted that, again in the introductory matter, I observe that location is the most uncertain element of my description since 'scribes were mobile and the distinction between where a document or book was made [its origin] and where it spent its early years [its provenance] is both a fine one and ultimately incapable of proof' (Scragg 2012a, xv). Helmut Gneuss, in private discussions I have had with him, agrees with this, saying that he too was uncertain about this element of his *Handlist of Manuscripts Written or Owned in England up to 1100* (Gneuss 2001) and he even went so far as to doubt if some of the manuscripts now on the Continent should have been included in his list because of the uncertainty about who wrote them and where.

Neil Ker in his *Catalogue of Manuscripts Containing Anglo-Saxon* (1957) discusses the origins of many of the manuscripts that he includes, but by definition his *Catalogue* does not deal with single-page documents (see also Ker 1964). In the standard catalogue of such single-page material, Peter Sawyer (1968) gives no information on the location of their scribes.[1] We can, however, make certain assumptions about charters. Where one is written in favour of the house in which it has been preserved, we might reasonably assume that it was written there, but this falls far short of proof. In the case of royal charters (by far the largest number to survive), the royal chancery may have produced them, and that was probably peripatetic. But we can at least be certain in the case of the large number of eleventh-century forgeries, since, where a document survives in the house that benefitted from the forged instrument which itself was written many years after the time that it purports to relate to, it is clear that only the house itself could have produced it. Taking charters and manuscripts together, it happens that, of more than a thousand scribal hands writing English whose work survives from the last century or so of the Anglo-Saxon state, little more than half can be located even imprecisely, and of those, only a suggestion for the location of a great many can be made. Hence in my *Conspectus*, the location of a large number of hands is accompanied by a question mark. For those who like statistics, of the 1,063 hands that I identify, 417 are reasonably certainly located and a further 241 more possibly so. 405 remain unlocated. Should further scholarship find more (or fewer) hands, it seems unlikely that the proportions will be altered appreciably.

Scribal notes

It is rarely easy to locate a scribal hand, as may be seen from a simple marginal annotation in a Latin manuscript of saints' lives, now Dublin, Trinity College 174. On the recto of a flyleaf, late in the eleventh century, someone wrote *of searbyrig ic eom* 'I am from Salisbury'. The assumption is that the comment refers to the book itself (see Webber 1992), but even so there can be no assurance that the note was written at Salisbury since as long as the book remained in Salisbury's library there would be no obvious reason to write such an ascription. However, if the book was on loan somewhere, the comment would certainly be fitting, and it might in that case have been written anywhere. Likewise in the unlikely instance that the comment is a doodle rather than an ascription and refers to the writer, it might again have been written anywhere. Consequently, in my *Conspectus*, I have left this marginal note without a location. More certainty comes from indirect evidence. In a double volume of homilies in English written at the end of the tenth century or the very beginning of the eleventh, Oxford, Bodleian Library, Bodley 340/342, a blank space at the end of the final leaf was filled half a century later with a note on St Paulinus, the bishop of York who converted King Edwin and who became bishop of Rochester after Edwin's defeat in 633. The note talks of the establishment of Paulinus at a bishopric in Kent in terms of *þes stede* 'this place', and states that he remained there until his death when he was buried *her* 'here'. Clearly the note was written in Rochester. It is possible, of course, that such a note, incomplete as it is, might have been copied from another manuscript, except that two early library catalogues from Rochester mention a double volume of homilies in English (Sisam 1953, 151–2). The evidence that this note was made in Rochester seems unambiguous. It is less likely that the double manuscript was written there, given the relative poverty of the establishment at Rochester.

Also uncertain is the origin of material on two additional quires added at some time in the eleventh century at the end of the manuscript, following the page on which the Paulinus note was written. Palaeographically it would seem that they were actually written before the note, and they contain four items, all from Ælfric's First and Second Series of Catholic Homilies. The first pair are incomplete items, the first lacking its beginning and the second ending in mid-sentence in mid-line halfway down a page, the rest of which is left blank. It would appear from this that these two quires were once part of an incomplete book consisting of more quires, a book which, for some reason now irrecoverable, was left unfinished. Where this lost book was made cannot be determined. The quires appear to have been added to the Bodley 340/342 homiliary not for the interest in these incomplete items but for the second pair of items, both on St Andrew and from Ælfric's First Series. Since Andrew was the patron saint of Rochester, they may have been written there, or they may of course have been commissioned from elsewhere in the south-east, presumably Canterbury.

Colophons

Although considerable doubt in locating the majority of manuscripts and documents will always in all probability remain, that should not prohibit us from trying to locate them. We can approach the subject in a number of ways, beginning with those that are firmly located. One of the most useful means of locating material is by the use of colophons, whereby the scribe signs himself, usually at the end of his writing stint. Such a colophon occurs, for example and most famously, in the Lindisfarne Gospels, BL, Cotton Nero D. iv, where we are told in English on fol. 259r, at the end of the Gospel of St John, that the Latin text was written by Eadfrith, bishop of Lindisfarne 698-721, and glossed (and the colophon written) by one Aldred who describes himself as *presbyter*. It is clear from palaeographic evidence that Aldred also glossed part of a service book, now Durham, Cathedral Library A. IV. 19 (the Durham Ritual). Palaeographically, Aldred's writing can be dated to the second half of the tenth century, and consequently it seems likely that he was working at Chester-le-Street where the monks from Lindisfarne were housed from 883 to 995. Linguistic evidence makes it clear that Aldred himself composed and wrote the gloss in the Lindisfarne Gospels, rather than it being copied from elsewhere (Ker 1957, 216). Another manuscript with a colophon, Cambridge, Corpus Christi College 140 + 111, pp. 7, 8 and 55–6, contains the four Gospels in eleventh-century English. The scribe of St Matthew identifies himself in Latin as being one *ælfricus* writing the Gospel in the monastery of Bath. The identification with Bath is confirmed by a number of legal documents which are entered on opening and closing leaves and which relate to Bath. The copying of documents which a community wished to be preserved is not infrequent in Bibles, including those in English, just as families until very recently copied significant notices into their Bibles.

Not all evidence from colophons can be relied upon as definitive, however. A single scribe working at Worcester in the second half of the eleventh century created a double volume of homilies, Oxford, Bodleian Library, Hatton 113 and 114, usually assumed to be for the use of Wulfstan, bishop of Worcester 1062–95, and also a book of penitentials and canons (many of them composed by Archbishop Wulfstan the homilist), Oxford, Bodleian Library, Junius 121. Further scribes added other material at the end of both Hatton 114 and Junius 121. But in the middle of the original scribe's work in Junius 121 (fol. 101r) there is a Latin colophon which identifies the writer as Wulfgeat, and although the rest of the page is left blank (a mere five lines), the next page continues with similar material, and it is doubtful if Wulfgeat was the immediate copyist of Junius 121 but rather a predecessor whose work was copied (together with the colophon) into the surviving manuscript.

Diocesan association

It is possible to localise a number of manuscripts in the second half of the eleventh century by virtue of their association with a particular diocese (Ker 1957, lvi–lx). Leofric, bishop of Devon and Cornwall 1046–72, transferred his sees from Crediton and St Germans to Exeter in 1050, and developed a scriptorium there in which a large number of books were copied by a group of scribes who can be identified by their distinctive style of handwriting. Many of these books survive. Likewise, Wulfstan, the bishop of Worcester identified in the last paragraph, had a series of manuscripts created for his own use (Hatton 113/114 and Junius 121, again identified above), and although these were originally copied by a single scribe, additional items were added by more than a dozen further hands, and there are many other additions and corrections in the margins. This means that it is possible to identify a considerable body of scribes working at the Worcester scriptorium in the last decades of the eleventh century.[2] Some of them also wrote in other manuscripts, thus increasing our knowledge of Worcester books, and a few of these scribes can even be named, especially Hemming who wrote English in five books and a charter (Scragg 2012a, hand 172) and Coleman who wrote marginalia in six manuscripts (*ibid.*, hand 87). Late in the eleventh century, scribes at Christ Church, Canterbury, developed a distinctive writing style. Although there may be no further existing manuscripts and documents that can be matched to these distinctive scripts in terms of handwriting, we might associate other surviving Old English with them through a careful study of language.

Location through language

We now know that although most of late Old English (*i.e.* from the end of the tenth century and through to 1100) is written in what used to be called the late West Saxon dialect and is now more usually and correctly known as Standard Old English (Gretsch 2001), there are varieties within that form of written language, just as there are variations today between, for example, written British and written American English, in such words as *honour* where the spelling with or without u has nothing to do with pronunciation but has more to do with the chauvinism of the eighteenth-century American lexicographer Noah Webster. So it may be possible to link surviving examples of Old English linguistically. The tenth-century Vercelli anthology of religious prose and poetry has now been firmly established as a Kentish book, principally on the basis of linguistic forms found occasionally in the work of its scribe (Scragg 1973). For another example worthy of investigation, there are two related manuscripts of the immediate post-Conquest period, BL Cotton Faustina A. x which contains a copy of Ælfric's grammar of Latin written in English, and Oxford, Bodleian Library, Hatton 115 which, in its earliest form before it was much altered in the later eleventh and twelfth centuries, consisted of three booklets, each containing a collection of homiletic and related pieces, again all of them by Ælfric. On the basis of script, Ker assigned these two to the same scriptorium (Ker 1957, 196). The Ælfric editor John Pope assumed that 'almost certainly' they were written by the same scribe (Pope 1967–7, I.58), which may be overstating the case, but the point in any case is irrelevant to the locating of the scribe or scribes. The important thing is that the two undoubtedly formed a programme of preserving a collection of Ælfric items in a single library. Where that library was is unknown at present. But the collection of items in the two manuscripts is so large (the grammar itself is one of the longest texts in Old English) that a full examination of the language of them might reveal something of the patterns of usage or training of their scribe or scribes.

The difficulty involved in a linguistic exercise of this sort is that the items in Hatton 115 appear to have been drawn from a variety of different source-books, and thus linguistically may reflect the practices of earlier copyists. This might be avoided to some extent by choosing a much smaller sample of Old English, such as the single-page fragment which was preserved as a pastedown attached to the binding of a book published in 1601, and thus is very fragmentary indeed. It has the distinction of being the only passage of eleventh-century English now found in Switzerland, Geneva (Cologny-Genève), Bibliotheca Bodmeriana, Bodmer 2 (see Scragg 2012a, 345). It consists of a mere twenty-four lines on each side, transcribed and published by Neil Ker some fifty years ago (Ker 1962). It contains part of a homily by Ælfric from his Second Series. In terms of transmission, it is related to the version sent by Ælfric to Sigeric, archbishop of Canterbury, in 991, that archbishop whose trip to Rome around 990 was revisited by David Hill nearly a quarter of a century ago (see Higham, this volume, 4). The text of the First and Second Series of homilies sent by Ælfric to Sigeric is represented now by a group of manuscripts copied in Canterbury (*e.g.* Clemoes 1997, 67–8). Of its language, Ker concludes that it 'agrees with manuscripts from the south-west of England in its spellings' (he cites the use of *i* for *y* and vice versa) 'and in the use of *þæge* for the relative and demonstrative pronouns' (Ker 1962, 79). Now although consistent substitution of *y* for *i* or alteration of *i* to *y* may be a south-western feature – although the evidence for that is incomplete – simple variation between the two letters is very widespread in the second half of the eleventh century and far from confined to the south-western area. When Ker wrote fifty years ago, the comment might have been valid, but today we have enough evidence to say that it is quite wrong. Moreover, Ker's comments were based on the collation that he made with the copy of the text in Bodley 340, whereas my own collation with the copy in Cambridge, Corpus Christi College 162 shows that Bodmer 2 agrees with the latter in every case. Since CCCC 162 is a south-eastern manuscript, almost certainly made *c.* 1000 in St Augustine's, Canterbury, the south-western provenance of Bodmer 2 is unproven on the grounds of its use of *i/y* alone. Furthermore, at the end of the original homiliary in CCCC 162, a nearly contemporary hand added the beginning of an additional homily on St Augustine of Canterbury, and this includes the word *þæge*. Thus none of Ker's argument for placing the Bodmer fragment in south-western England stands.[3]

Lastly, in terms of linguistic study, there is the question of the location of scribes. In many ways this is even more difficult than the location of manuscripts, because scribes, like that which they wrote, are mobile. Even when we know (or believe we know) where a manuscript was written, there is no assurance that the scribes are from the same place. Take the case of BL, Royal 7 C. XII which contains the earliest surviving copy of Ælfric's First Series of homilies, and which is widely believed to have the author's own annotations in the margins, making changes to the text as he looked over an early draft. If so, this places the manuscript squarely in Cerne Abbas in Dorset around 989 where Ælfric was in charge of teaching the novices. In a recent paper (Scragg 2012b) I have shown that the work of the many scribes of this manuscript, but particularly that of the two principal ones, shows a variety of linguistic forms, both within the stints of individual scribes and between them. Now the possible reasons for this are manifold, but one is that they were not trained together at the same school. If we look at the dating more closely, however, we see that 989 when the manuscript was written is very close to the date of the founding of Cerne Abbas by Æthelmær, son of Ealdorman Æthelweard, in 987. It is most unlikely that the professional scribes engaged in copying this manuscript were trained in the place at which they wrote it. Like Ælfric himself, they were sent to the new monastery at the time of its foundation. In other words, scribal practice in itself may not be particularly useful in placing a manuscript. The scribes may simply be reflecting the usages of wherever they were trained.

It is also true that any external information that we have – or think we have – about the whereabouts of the writing of a manuscript needs to be looked at closely. It is often assumed

that the Royal Psalter (BL, Royal 2 B. V), written in Latin in the tenth century and with an English gloss between the lines written by the same scribe, is to be associated with Winchester, on the basis of what is now its opening quire (Ker 1957, 320). This first quire contains matter other than the Psalter, which itself begins on the first page of Quire 2. But on the first page of the psalter proper – fol. 8r of the manuscript – there are a number of sixteenth-century signatures of ownership, first, Thomas Cranmer, King Henry VIII's archbishop of Canterbury at the dissolution of the monasteries, who presumably found the manuscript in Canterbury at the time of the dissolution, then the Earl of Arundel who obtained it after Cranmer's execution under Queen Mary I, and lastly John, Lord Lumley, who later owned the manuscript, and who gave it to his tutee, Prince Henry, King James I's eldest son, and thus it came into the Royal collection, now in the British Library. The significant thing is that its sixteenth-century owners all signed the book on folio 8. Why would you do this? Only, I suggest, if, at the time the signatures were added, that very folio was the first in the manuscript. The opening quire, in other words, on which association of the Psalter with Winchester is based, may not have been part of the original manuscript, and perhaps was not associated with it until the sixteenth century, very possible by Lord Lumley.[4]

A way forward

Let me turn finally in this brief paper to another way in which the subject of the location of books and documents might be approached and that is through the physical characteristics of the parchment used. Archaeologists are rightly excited about recent discoveries of material objects from the Anglo-Saxon world, but amongst the largest collection of physical objects that we have from the period is the books and documents that survive. Each of the larger books that remain is made up of the skins of quite literally hundreds of animals, and Helmut Gneuss in his *Handlist* of books written or owned in Anglo-Saxon England lists a thousand books. That in itself constitutes a lot of skins. But we also have many hundreds of single-page documents. Commentators disagree about whether the skins are from calves (properly vellum) or from sheep (parchment), but all agree that we are dealing with the remains of domestic animals.[5] If we take sheep as an example, we may suspect that there were many regional varieties during the period. Even today, Norfolk sheep are very different from those found in the Lake District, and although these are now different breeds, they were developed to suit the conditions of different environments and different grasses. These days, DNA analysis is very sophisticated, and it should be possible to combine analysis of manuscript skins with that of bones from archaeological digs. Far be it from me to suggest that we might snip a small corner from a page of each and have it analysed, since librarians in their drive for conservation might well be reluctant to allow this. However, analysis of DNA is now so sophisticated that less than a pinhead might reveal much, and most surviving manuscripts have some material from which the tiniest sample of parchment might be spared without any material damage to the book. For example, although the majority of manuscripts from the period consist of quires each of four double sheets folded into two and fastened down the fold, hence eight sheets making sixteen pages, a large number of books have the occasional quire with one or more half sheets in the middle which is held in place by being slightly wider than a normal half sheet would be, with a flap folded over and sewn into the centre fold. The overlapping parchment thus serves no purpose other than that of fixing the sheet into place, and losing a pinhead of parchment from this would hardly lead to the detriment of the whole. With single-page documents, which are frequently written leaving little space on the front, the dorse is usually blank, or has simply an inscription. This leaves ample opportunity for a very small sample of material to be scratched from the surface without harming the whole. Thus it might be possible, with the cooperation of sympathetic librarians, to build a comprehensive database of the DNA of surviving manuscripts and documents, and perhaps ultimately achieve that most desirable goal, the true and full mapping of the writings of Anglo-Saxon England.

Notes

1 For the latest information on single-page documents, see the electronic Sawyer: http://www.esawyer.org.uk .

2 The work of two novice scribes is described in Scragg 2005.

3 In a recent introduction to a facsimile of Bodmer 2, McGowan (2012, 27) simply repeats Ker's argument of fifty years ago, without any apparent attempt to check the findings.

4 Another Lumley signature appears on what is now fol. 1, suggesting perhaps that this was independent of the Royal Psalter in Lumley's collection. Lumley is known for the rearrangement of books in his collection, as is Sir Robert Cotton.

5 Goatskin may also be described as parchment, but although goats were no doubt widely kept since (like pigs) they could forage for food cheaply in the widespread woods, there is little mention of them in the surviving records. Sheep, on the other hand, are to be found in accounts of the estates of kings and the aristocracy. Perhaps goats were kept by the poor (Finberg 1972a).

18

Mapping the Anglo-Saxon past

Simon Keynes

David Hill's *Atlas of Anglo-Saxon England* was published by Basil Blackwell in 1981.[1] One might guess that part of the inspiration for the distinctive view of the subject represented by this book should be attributed to a sense of place and landscape which originated with David's upbringing in Somerset. He would have acquired useful skills in the 1950s as a surveyor's apprentice for the Minehead Urban District Council, and during his two years of National Service with the Royal Artillery in Germany. These skills must have been complemented by his own historical interests, and extended by his archaeological and surveying work for Martin Biddle at Winchester; and no doubt it was this work, furthered by his studies with Peter Addyman at Southampton, in the later 1960s, that led among other things to his paper on the 'Burghal Hidage', published in 1969. He was presumably preoccupied thereafter with his duties in the Department of Extra-Mural Studies, at Manchester; and it must have been in the midst of performing these duties that he started work on the *Atlas*. I have a distinct memory of David clutching an early version of the book at the conference on Æthelred the Unready which he organized at Oxford in 1978; and it was apparent then that Patrick Wormald was closely involved as encourager and advisor. When the *Atlas* was published, in 1981, it made an immediate impression as a work of a kind which had never been seen before, and it must come high among David's most original and enduring contributions to the field. It is, of course, far more than a collection of historical maps; for it is about the many *different* ways of processing, representing and conveying information about the Anglo-Saxon past. I described it in a review as a 'remarkable series of 260 maps, charts and diagrams which illustrate many aspects of Anglo-Saxon history and enable the reader to see at a glance what otherwise he might never have seen at all'.[2] I have admired it and used it ever since.

The organisation of the Anglo-Saxon past

One can only guess how those living in the seventh, eighth or ninth century *imagined* Britain in physical terms, without recourse to a map (let alone ready access to google.earth): the disposition of peoples and places in relation to each other; how to get from one place to another; or even what lay beyond the horizon. The 'world map' copied at Canterbury in the mid-eleventh century, but which belonged to a much earlier Roman tradition, is a reminder that maps of a certain kind were available for certain purposes.[3] So far as one can tell, however, the English of the Anglo-Saxon period made do largely with imagining, verbalizing and *writing* their maps of Britain and latterly of England (Howe 2008). The names given to peoples and their kingdoms suggest how from the outset the inhabitants of Britain were imagined in relation to each other (Northumbrians, West Saxons, East Angles, South Saxons). Anyone might have known what lay further up or down Watling Street, or further up or down the river Thames; and when in the early 670s Archbishop Theodore and his episcopal colleagues laid down that church councils should be held once a year, at *Clofesho*, those expected to attend might soon have become familiar with the route. In charters of the same period (the last quarter of the seventh century) we read of estates whose boundaries were so well known that they did not need to be described (for the benefit of those who knew them already); and if one ventured further afield, and lost one's way, one could always shout, or blow one's horn, as recommended in the Kentish law-code of Wihtred and in the West Saxon law-code of Ine.[4] The boundary-clauses found in royal diplomas of the tenth and eleventh centuries suggest that land surveying, for such purposes, soon developed conventions of its own and became a skill practised widely across the land. Many people would live out their lives within a small area, but there were at all times others who had occasion to travel much greater distances. A map of meeting-places known to have been used for royal assemblies, in the tenth and eleventh centuries, serves as a reminder of the widening of horizons as we pass from the pre-Alfredian into the post-Alfredian part of the period, when bishops, abbots, ealdormen and thegns were regularly if not constantly on the move (Keynes 2013, 34). Perhaps all that was needed was a basic knowledge of tracks, roads, rivers, estuaries, and landmarks, plus a sense of direction and a readiness to ask questions of those with local knowledge; of course, guides were also available, and for longer journeys a traveller might have been able to refer to a written itinerary.[5]

The 'Anglo-Saxon' antecedents for David Hill's *Atlas of Anglo-Saxon England* are of a different kind. In 730, or thereabouts, Bede became the first in a long line of historians who saw it as some part of their proper business to bring information under control: explaining dimensions, locations and distances, as well as describing relationships, providing lists (whether by borrowing them from elsewhere, or by reducing his own knowledge to such a form), and arranging events in a relative and where possible in an absolute chronological order; and in these ways first reaching and then conveying a better understanding of the past, for whatever purposes he had in mind. Bede acknowledges the help provided by Abbot Albinus, in Kent; and one imagines that among the records which came to him in this way would have been lists of bishops and kings. The so-called 'Anglian' collection of episcopal lists and royal genealogies, compiled perhaps at Canterbury, *c.* 800, represents the sort of thing we might have in mind; and it travelled in association with information of other kinds (Keynes 2005; Dekker 2007). It is clear that the compilers of the so-called 'common stock' of the *Anglo-Saxon Chronicle*, *c.* 890, and their successors in the tenth and eleventh centuries, enjoyed access to later and updated versions of such material; indeed, it is a mid-eleventh century version which also includes the world map. We move forward from there to the late eleventh- or early twelfth-century dossier or digest of information copied at the start of the principal surviving manuscript of the 'Worcester Latin Chronicle', attributed to Florence and/ or John of Worcester.[6] The information brought together in this compendium also descends from the 'Anglian' collection of episcopal lists and royal genealogies (Dumville 1976); but in this manifestation of it an attempt is made to display the information in graphic form. The details of episcopal succession for each diocese are clearly displayed in columns, kingdom by kingdom; and the compiler then devised a way of representing the details of royal succession, for each of the kingdoms, with wiggly lines indicating family relationships. The overall effect is illustrated by the page covering the dioceses in the extended kingdom of the Mercians, and by the page covering the line of the kings of Mercia.[7] Whether David Hill knew it or not, the tables for episcopal succession are in fact the direct ancestors of the last two tables in his *Atlas of Anglo-Saxon England* (Hill 1981, 165–6 (nos. 259–60); see also Lapidge *et al.* 2014, 177–8, with Appendix II). In the same way, the diagrams for royal genealogies are themselves the ancestors of the tabular genealogies of the kings of the Mercians, the West Saxons, and all the rest, which remain so crucial to this day in explaining the unfolding course and internal dynamics of dynastic politics.[8]

One could say more about the ways in which the perception of the Anglo-Saxon past developed during the late eleventh,

twelfth and thirteenth centuries, and thereafter, not only as stories multiplied, and were improved, but also as those with reason or inclination to write about the past practised their respective skills and in so doing put the past to new and different purposes. One thinks, for example, of Eadmer of Canterbury, Simeon of Durham, William of Malmesbury, Henry of Huntingdon, Ralph de Diceto, Walter Map, Roger of Wendover, and Matthew Paris. It was Matthew Paris, monk of St Albans in the mid-thirteenth century, who deserves particular credit for developing the role of graphic design in the representation of the past. His circular diagram representing the seven kingdoms of Anglo-Saxon England, with King Alfred at the centre of its component parts, was an effective way of showing how (in his view) Alfred was the first ruler of all the English (Cambridge, Corpus Christi College, MS 26, fol. iv verso: see Lewis 1987, 165–74; Keynes 1999, 231–2, with plate VII*a*). Matthew also developed a form of annotated and animated genealogy, using pictures as well as words, inside roundels joined by lines, to represent the lines of descent.[9] Matthew Paris was followed in both respects by the genealogical rolls which originated in the later thirteenth century and which proliferated thereafter.[10] The originator of the tradition picked up the basic ideas from Matthew Paris, and ran – or rolled – with them. The circular diagram of what would come to be known as the 'Heptarchy' provided the story with a comfortable and comprehensible beginning, which could then lead via some more colourful characters to the Norman Conquest, after which the story was clear, and could be put to good contemporary purposes. Similar ideas would be adopted in the second half of the sixteenth century, when the study of Anglo-Saxon England was first brought together with the making of maps.

Laurence Nowell

Laurence Nowell (1530–*c*.1570) is renowned as a pioneer in Anglo-Saxon studies, who in the 1560s moved in the circles of Sir William Cecil, 1st Lord Burghley (1520–98). I dwell on Nowell because he was the first to combine an interest in Anglo-Saxon England with an involvement in the making of maps, and because David Hill made a close study of Nowell's work – assembling material in the form of a substantial A4 booklet which was in some sense 'published' in connection with a lecture he gave on the subject in November 1992.[11] Nowell was without question an enthusiastic maker of maps, but he comes across none the less as more of a scholar than a surveyor, and the question is how he managed to bring the two pursuits together.[12]

The systematic mapping of England began during the reign of Henry VIII, and was taken significantly further in the reign of Elizabeth I (Tyacke and Huddy 1980; Barber 1983a; Tyacke 1983; Shirley 1991; Black 1997). Some of the surveying work was carried out in the 1550s, by John Rudd (*c*. 1498–1579), who seems to have been expected by the Queen to complete the task in 1563. In June of that year, perhaps eager to take over, Nowell

Fig. 18.1 Laurence Nowell, Map of Ireland and England (c. 1563). BL Add. 62540, fols 3v–4r (British Library Board. All Rights Reserved).

wrote to Sir William Cecil, the Queen's principal secretary, proposing that he might produce a comprehensive map of England, complemented by more detailed maps of the separate counties.[13] It was seemingly in this connection that Nowell presented Cecil with a small but most attractive and stunningly detailed map of Ireland and Britain, with the adjoining coast of northern France and Flanders, apparently to advertise his credentials as a map-maker.[14] The map was drawn, inscribed, coloured and decorated on a single bifolium (Fig.18.1), and is still contained within its original limp vellum binding. Most charmingly, we see in the lower left corner a representation of Nowell himself, resting his head on a pedestal, which bears a quotation in Greek,[15] and the initials L.N. (Fig. 18.2*a*); the drawing is balanced in the lower right corner by an image evidently of Cecil himself (Fig. 18.2*b*). The dynamic between the two men seems clear enough. Nowell looks disconsolate, dangling what is plainly and pointedly an empty purse from his knee, indicating his need for employment. To make matters worse, a barking dog holds him at bay, symbolizing one of the hazards faced by the (would be) land surveyor.[16] Cecil, on the other hand, sits bolt upright with his arms firmly folded, having put down a couple of books by his feet on the floor; he looks as if he is a man waiting to be impressed, and the fact that he sits on an hour-glass, shown already mid-way through its course, acknowledges that he was short of time.[17] An interesting aspect of Nowell's map is the (relative) accuracy of its outline, at least in comparison with what had gone before. Cornwall and Devon may be elongated, and England's backbone needs straightening up; but the representation of Cardigan Bay, in Wales, marks a significant improvement, even if the west coast of Ireland still looks like a vague approximation. The line is remarkably similar to a map published by Gerard Mercator in 1564, to an extent which is indicative of a relationship between the two. Mercator is said on good authority to have used a map sent to him from England; and unless it came from Nowell himself, the most likely explanation is that both drew from the same source, perhaps in the circle of Cecil.[18]

For all that he might have needed to make a living from more useful skills, Nowell was at heart an Anglo-Saxonist. It was at Cecil's town house, on the Strand, that he is known to have transcribed several Old English texts, from a composite manuscript which itself passed subsequently into the Cottonian library and was all but destroyed in the fire of 1731.[19] Nowell's transcript of the contents of this manuscript passed much later to the British Museum (BL MS Additional 43703), and now forms the basis for our knowledge of an important mid-tenth century manuscript of the Old English Bede, the G manuscript of the *Anglo-Saxon Chronicle*, and a version of the Burghal Hidage.[20] In another paper volume written at about the same time (in the early 1560s), which also came into the Cottonian library but which survived the fire in 1731, Nowell entered a series of maps covering Ireland, Scotland, and England.[21] The pages which cover England build up in a series of openings, working across from west to east, then up a bit and across

another section of the country. The first sequence of four openings, making 8 pages from left to right, form the lowest level of the map, covering southern England from Cornwall in the west to Kent in the east (fols 110v–114r); the next three openings cover in six pages the section of land from south-west Wales across to Essex and the Thames estuary (fols 114v–117r); the next three openings cover in six pages the section of land from north-west Wales across to north Norfolk (fols 117v–120r); two openings above them make up 4 pages at the level of the Humber estuary (fols 120v–122r); and finally a single opening at the top makes 2 pages for the northernmost part of England, up to the Forth (fols 122v–123r). These pages seem at first sight to form a detailed and ambitious map of Anglo-Saxon England, of which just a small part can be shown here (Fig. 18.3); but the appearance is deceptive. The maps use what is essentially the same outline of Britain as that used for the diminutive coloured map presented to Cecil; but while the names are given in pseudo-'Old English' spelling, and written in Nowell's pseudo-Anglo-Saxon script, the selection is again 'modern', *i.e.* sixteenth-century, rather than determined by Nowell's reading of particular Anglo-Saxon texts. In effect, therefore, Nowell was constructing Old English forms, and in so doing necessarily avoiding 'Norman' or later names. The exercise as a whole represents the dressing-up of sixteenth-century England in Anglo-Saxon costume: the atlas is an affirmation of a strong connection between the Elizabethan present and the Anglo-Saxon past (of which Archbishop Parker would have approved), but it is not yet an attempt to *recreate* that past in cartographic form.

In 1567 Laurence Nowell left England, to travel on the Continent. He had entrusted his books and papers into the safe-keeping of his friend and fellow Anglo-Saxonist William Lambarde (1536–1601); but he would appear to have died *c.* 1570, in Austria or Germany. In the 1570s, and thereafter, John Rudd's young apprentice Christopher Saxton (*c.* 1542–1611) was with Cecil's, or from 1571 the 1st Lord Burghley's, patronage able to bring Rudd's earlier project to fruition. Saxton's famous series of English county maps made its first appearance in 1579, followed by a wall-map of the whole of England (on 20 sheets) in 1583 (Tyacke and Huddy 1980, 24–39). In the 1590s, also with Lord Burghley's patronage, John Norden (*c.* 1547–1625) was able to improve the maps for several counties.[22] The county maps of Saxton and Norden, with their little mountains to represent high ground and little trees to represent woodland, have done as much as Shakespeare to determine the enduring image of Elizabethan England.

Maps of the Anglo-Saxon 'Heptarchy'

Laurence Nowell's work as a cartographer, and as an Anglo-Saxonist, led directly to the emergence of a series of maps depicting the Anglo-Saxon 'Heptarchy', which had a significant influence on the perception of the Anglo-Saxon past in the late sixteenth century, throughout the seventeenth century, and long thereafter. The concept of an organized combination of seven kingdoms, which had originated probably from a reading of Bede's *Historia ecclesiastica*, had been promoted in the twelfth century by Henry of Huntingdon, and soon entered into the mainstream of English historical tradition (Lapidge *et al.* 2014, 238); but it was the way it lent itself to expression in cartographic form that guaranteed its impact in the longer term.

The earliest (early modern) manifestation of the theme is the map included in William Lambarde's edition of Anglo-Saxon law-codes (*Archaionomia*), printed and published by John Day in 1568 (Fig. 18.4).[23] The outline used for the map was derived directly from Nowell's cartographic work. The map itself bears no heading or title; and its only 'historical' feature, apart from the context of its publication, is that each of the seven kingdoms (Wessex, Sussex, Kent, Essex, East Anglia, Mercia and Northumbria, with their boundaries indicated by dotted lines), is named on the map in Latin and in Old English, and numbered from 1 to 7. On the two pages of explanation (in Latin), which follow the map, Lambarde introduces the term 'Heptarchia', rehearses the historical background, and remarks on each of the kingdoms (and its component counties), ending with an allusion to the laws observed in them. Soon afterwards, Lambarde began work on his pioneering history of Kent, in which context he would need to accord the county its place as one of the heptarchic kingdoms. In his manuscript draft, written in 1570, Lambarde copied out his map of the seven kingdoms, as published in 1568, still without heading or title, but now furnished with an expanded version (in English) of his explanatory text, headed 'The xposition of this mappe, of the Inglishe Heptarchie, or seven kingdomes'.[24]

In 1573 Lambarde sent a copy of his unpublished work to Matthew Parker (1504–75), archbishop of Canterbury (1559–75), for him 'to peruse, to correct and amend'; whereupon Parker sent a transcript of it to William Cecil, Lord Burghley, knowing that he too would be interested.[25] It is from the covering letter to Lord Burghley that we learn that Parker had in his service at this time 'drawers and cutters, painters, limners, writers, and bookbinders'; and it was with their help, in the early 1570s, that he was undertaking various historical projects and publications (Hind 1952, 12–17). This programme soon led to the appropriation and development of Lambarde's map of the 'Heptarchy'. In 1574 Richard Lyne (*fl. c.* 1570–1600), one of the 'drawers and cutters' in Parker's service, and Henry Bynneman, one of the printers used by Parker, were responsible for the engraving and production of a composite design (for want of a more appropriate term) representing the course of British and English history from Brutus of Troy to Elizabeth I (Fig. 18.5).[26] The design as a whole is headed 'Regnum Britanniæ tandem plene in Heptarchiam redactum [*sic*] a Saxonibus, explusis Britonibus' ('The kingdom of Britain at length fully reduced by the Saxons into a Heptarchy, once the Britons themselves had been driven out'); but it also took the story onward from the Heptarchy to the present day. The train of thought starts, in the lower left segment, with

the succession from Brutus of Troy to the last of their line in the seventh century, with chronology expressed by A.M. and B.C. The main intention of the argument behind the design, however, is to show how the component parts of the Anglo-Saxon heptarchy were resolved into the unified kingdom of England. The seven crowned roundels across the main part of the design denote each of the seven kingdoms. In each case, the name of the founder of the dynasty is given first (in a roundel), followed by the first king who was a Christian, and then the last in succession; the diagonal lines indicate how in time six of the kingdoms were absorbed into the central line, itself representing the seventh, which was the kingdom of Wessex and which became the kingdom of England. The process of unification seems on this understanding of the story to have come to an end with the submission of Northumbria to King Eadred (946–55). There follow separate roundels first for a series of English kings (Eadwig to Edmund Ironside), then for the Anglo-Danish kings (Swein to Harthacnut), and finally for Edward the Confessor and Harold. At this level on the diagram the names are given of all the dioceses and counties which pertained to each kingdom; then the 'Normans' arrive, and the sequence of rulers is taken further from William the Conqueror (1) to Elizabeth (23). In the lower right segment, we find Lambarde's map, now headed *Angliæ Heptarchia*, and adorned with the royal arms (featuring an English lion and a Welsh dragon as supporters), as well as heraldic badges for England (with Wales), France, Ireland and Man (Fig.18.6).[27] The overall effect, therefore, is to suggest that Queen Elizabeth was heir to one and all. The engraving is signed and dated, bottom left, by Richard Lyne ('Richardus Lyne Seruus D. Matthæi Archiepi Cantuar: sculpsit. Aº 1574'); the monogram, bottom centre, is that of the printer, Henry Bynneman.

This composite design has long since passed into oblivion (except so far as the map, bottom right, is concerned); but it deserves resurrection and recognition in its own right as a graphic manifestation of the position so famously adopted within Archbishop Parker's immediate circle, and even as a symbol or product of Parker's agenda in the promotion of Anglo-Saxon studies. It is not immediately clear who might have been responsible for the design's conception and content, or for what kind of use it was intended. The engraved plate generated a print of fair size (*c.* 390mm × 280mm), and one might imagine that impressions were kept safe, in a drawer, or framed, on a wall. Most importantly, Lyne's engraving was one of a pair. Another separate engraving, of very similar dimensions, headed 'Regum genealogia a conquestu 1067' ('Genealogy of kings from the conquest 1067'), shows the line of genealogical descent from William I to Elizabeth (with the monarchs themselves numbered from 1 to 23, as in Lyne's engraving). It also incorporates, in the top right segment, a diagram representing the *Linea Franciæ*, juxtaposing the Valois line and the English line, and encapsulating the deep rooted claim to France. In this case, the engraving is signed by Remigius Hogenberg, another of the 'drawers and cutters' who

Fig. 18.2 (a) Laurence Nowell (and a dog), and (b) William Cecil. BL Add. 62540, fols 3v–4r, details (British Library Board. All Rights Reserved).

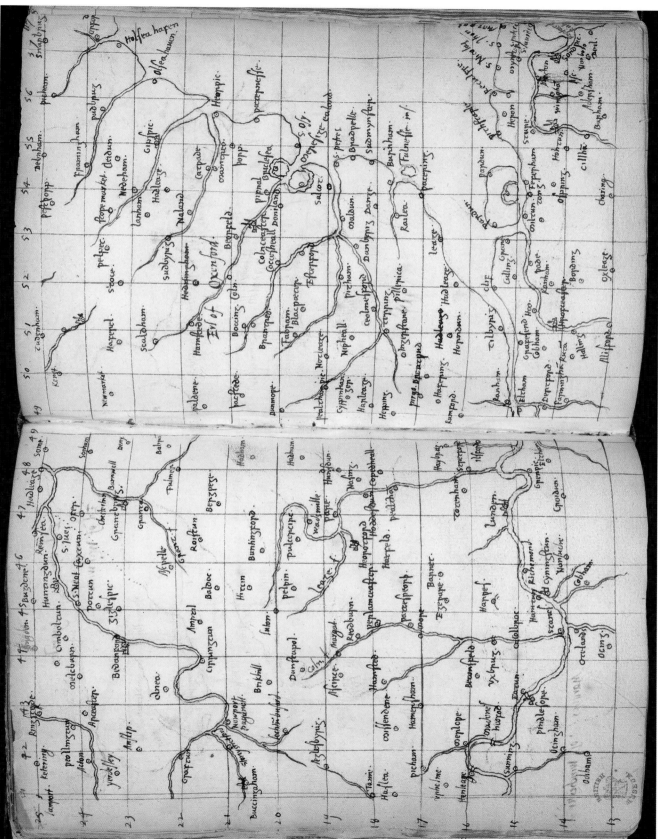

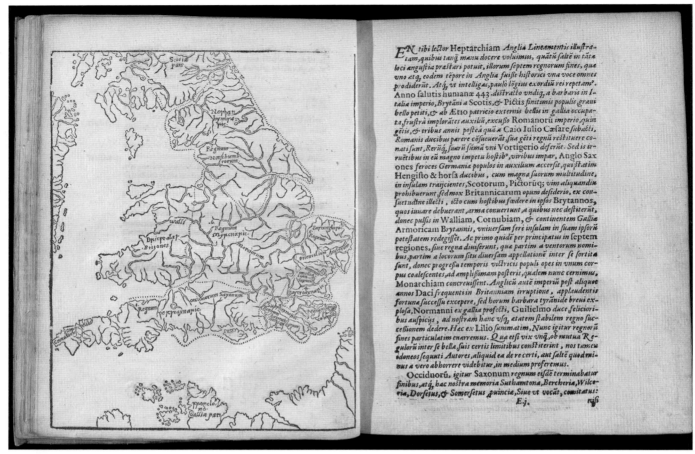

Fig. 18.4 [Nowell-Lambarde], The Anglo-Saxon Heptarchy, from Archaionomia *(1568). Cambridge, Trinity College Library, VI.1.75 (The Master and Fellows of Trinity College, Cambridge).*

worked for Archbishop Parker, using precisely the same form of words: 'Remigius Hogenbergius Seruus D: Matthæi Archiepi Cantuar: sculpsit. Aᵒ 1574', again with Bynneman's monogram (Fig.18.7).[28] When the two engravings, made by Lyne and Hogenberg, are placed side by side, one can see at once that they belong together and indeed complement each other. Impressions were presumably distributed in their own right, as a related pair; the seemingly few that survive do so because in the year after they were first made some were tipped into copies of a composite volume written at Archbishop Parker's behest by his secretary, Alexander Neville (1544–1614), comprising (1) *De furoribus Norfolciensium Ketto duce*, and (2) *Norvicus*, printed as two volumes in one, by Bynneman, in 1575.[29] Parker himself had a close interest in the insurrection known as 'Kett's Rebellion', having preached to the rebels at Mousehold Heath in 1549; but in no sense do these prints illustrate that tract. The prints engraved by Lyne and Hogenberg, as a pair, belong primarily with each other, in 1574; but in 1575 impressions of them, as a pair, were tipped into Neville's second work, on the history of Norwich, on a page which referred to Sigeberht, first

Christian king of the East Angles. Perhaps Bynneman made the association himself, seeing here a link between the design engraved by Lyne and the tract on Norwich;[30] or perhaps both prints had been devised, like the tracts, by Neville himself, at Parker's behest. There might even have been a connection of some kind between the production of these prints, in 1574, and Parker's publication towards the end of that year of a set of historical works beginning with his edition of Asser's *Life of King Alfred*.[31] The archbishop is known to have been eager to present the 'first' copy of the life of Alfred to the Queen herself, sumptuously coloured and bound;[32] and it is apparent that he also intended to present a copy, 'but meanly bound', to Lord Burghley, 'and to certain others of my good lords'.[33] Perhaps the two engravings were distributed in much the same way, as a form of historical instruction offered by the archbishop to those in high office. About 150 years later, in the 1720s, George Vertue was at Ruckholts, in Low Leyton, Essex, which he described as 'the mansion house of the family of the Hickes's Baronets (whose ancestor was Secretary to the Ld. Treasurer Burghley)'; and in this house he noticed impressions

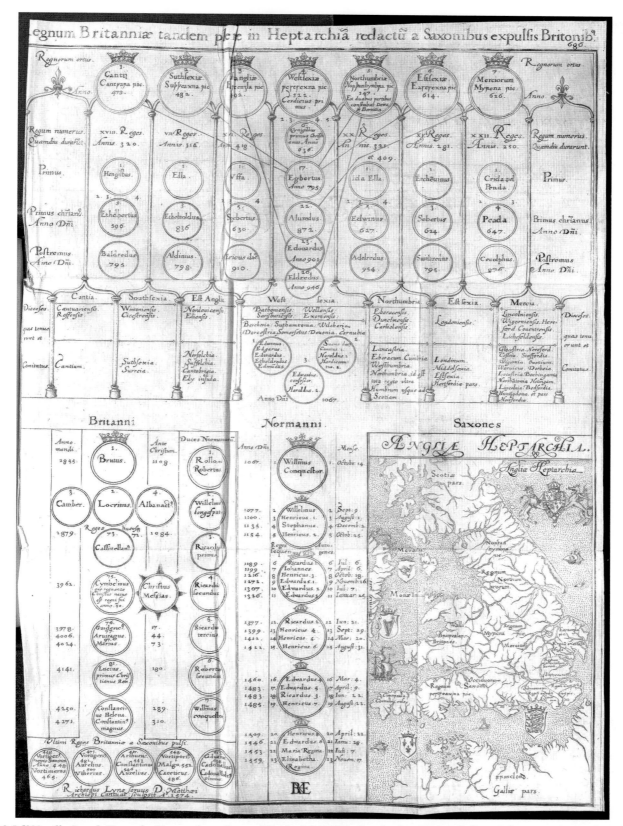

Fig. 18.5 [?Neville-Lyne], From the Heptarchy to Queen Elizabeth I (1574). Cambridge, Trinity College Library, VI.1.117 (folded table) (The Master and Fellows of Trinity College, Cambridge).

Fig. 18.6 [?Neville-Lyne], Angliæ Heptarchia *(1574), detail from Fig. 18.5. Cambridge, Trinity College Library, VI.1.117 (folded table, detail) (The Master and Fellows of Trinity College, Cambridge).*

of both prints (Lyne's and Hogenberg's),[34] perhaps displayed as a pair on a wall, in which case perhaps also gathering dust where they might have hung for many years.

In 1576, two years after Lyne had made his engraving for Archbishop Parker, a number of impressions from Lyne's plate seem to have been trimmed in such a way that the decorated version of Lambarde's map of the Heptarchy, from the lower right corner of the print, could be used for a different purpose. That is to say, the map, evidently trimmed down from impressions of Lyne's original plate (in several cases still showing all or part of the word 'Saxones', from the print, above the map itself), was inserted into copies of the first printed edition of Lambarde's *Perambulation of Kent*, where it

was accompanied by the expanded version of its 'exposition'.[35] Lambarde's map was used also in 1576 for an edition of John Fox's 'Book of Martyrs', printed by John Day, in a form which indicates that Day simply re-used the block originally made for and used by him in Lambarde's *Archaionomia* (1568), now positioned underneath a printed title ('A description of England, as it was diuided in the Saxones tyme into vii kyngdomes'), and accompanied by historical information on each of the kingdoms (Foxe 1576, 110–13. Shirley 1991, 50 (no. 115a); Goffart 1997, 55). For the next (1596) edition of Lambarde's *Perambulation of Kent*, advertised on its title-page as 'increased and altered after the Authors owne last Copie', and printed in London by Edmund Bollifant, a wood-block was newly cut for the map of the Heptarchy, modeled closely on Lyne's engraving of 1574, incorporating the same heading ('Angliæ Heptarchia'); the map was again accompanied, as intended, by the expanded exposition.[36]

The Lambarde-Lyne map of the Heptarchy thus had a complex history from its almost casual appearance in 1568 to the more assertive forms it took in 1574, 1576 and 1596. Yet one could not doubt its impact as the cartographic realization of a deep rooted and compelling perception of the Anglo-Saxon past. The first edition of Holinshed's *Chronicles* (1577) reflected a certain ambivalence about the political arrangements which had obtained among the early English; but the concept of the 'Heptarchy' was deployed to better effect in the revised and augmented edition, published ten years later (1587).[37] The difference lay in part, perhaps, with the publication of the first edition (in Latin) of Camden's *Britannia*, which appeared in 1586.[38] In *Britannia*, Camden promoted the Heptarchy with great conviction, in the fond belief that the Angles and Saxons had formally divided the land into seven kingdoms; taking Bede's famous list of kings who held *imperium* over others (*HE* II. 5) as evidence that there was always 'monarchy' within the Heptarchy; and stating that Egbert of Wessex issued an edict and proclamation that the Heptarchy should be called England or Anglia (Camden 1586, 48, 55–6). The first illustrated edition of *Britannia* (still in Latin) appeared in 1600. The book opens with a very fine engraved title-page, signed by William Rogers; the illustrations also include a pair of engraved maps, both of which are unsigned, but both of which are designed and executed in the same manner as the engraved title-page, and as each other. Rogers is described by the leading authority in the field as 'the greatest of the English engravers in the Tudor period' (Hind 1952, 258–80, at 258); and with very good reason, shown even in maps of this kind. The first of the maps represents Roman Britain (*Britannia Provincia Romanorum*), and is evidently the product of close collaboration between the antiquary and the artist-engraver.[39] The second map, representing Anglo-Saxon England, stands firmly in the Lambarde-Lyne tradition of maps of the Heptarchy, but in this manifestation the design has been raised to an altogether different level (Fig. 18.8).[40] The principal decorative feature is an elaborate cartouche, in the upper right corner. It provides

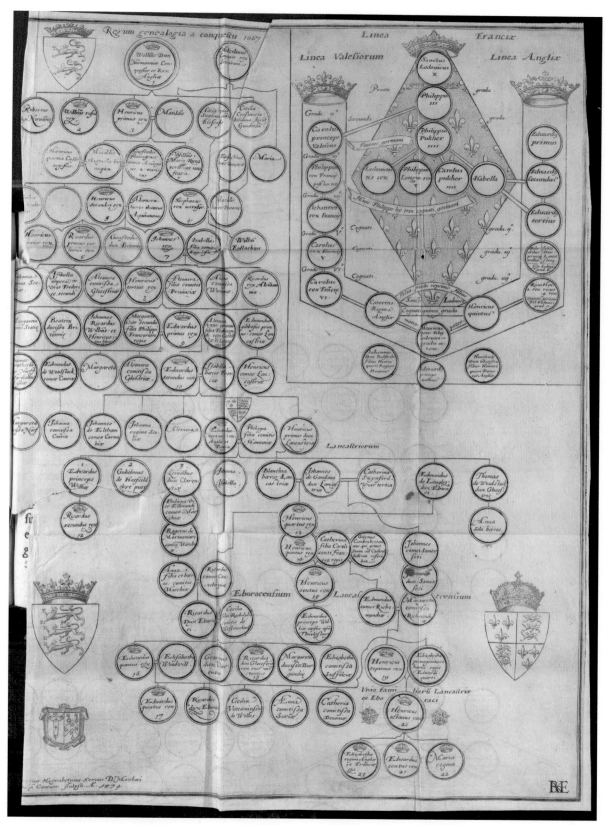

Fig. 18.7 [?Neville-Hogenberg], Genealogical table of English Monarchs (1574). Cambridge, Trinity College Library, VI.1.117 (folded table) (The Master and Fellows of Trinity College, Cambridge).

Fig. 18.8 [Camden-Rogers], The unified kingdom of England, from Britannia *(1600). Cambridge, Trinity College Library, VI.8.22 (The Master and Fellows of Trinity College, Cambridge).*

a new title for the map (*Englalond Anglia Anglosaxonum Heptarchia*), thereby acknowledging Camden's view of King Egbert's role in the rebranding of the Heptarchy, and thus suggesting that the map represents the newly unified kingdom of England, as the combination of its component parts. The fine crown in the centre, enclosing an array of seven sceptres, points in the same way to a period of unification, as indeed does the use of the defiant slogan 'Terra armis animisque potens', adapted from Virgil's *Aeneid*.[41] The sea is now teeming with ships and monsters (surpassing Lyne in this respect), with a particularly fine dragon lying off the coast of Wales; and the land is covered with a profusion of little mountains, to indicate high ground, and little trees, to indicate forest, in the

best tradition of the county maps devised in the late sixteenth century by Saxton and Norden. Most significantly, a selection of places has been added to the map, located by appropriate symbols, and identified using Old English forms written in a convincing attempt at a generically 'Anglo-Saxon' script (with a key to the special characters provided in the top left corner). The selection of names must have been determined by Camden himself, and deserves respect as the product of his own work on place-names, adding at the same time a new dimension to the mapping of Anglo-Saxon England. Another illustrated edition of *Britannia* was published in 1607, in a larger format to suit the addition of a series of county maps; for which purpose the map of the Heptarchy was re-engraved by William Hole (probably a pupil of William Rogers, in this his first year of recorded activity), retaining most of its features but in the process of enlargement losing some of its charm (Fig. 18.9).[42] Hole's engraving was used again for Abraham Whelock's edition of Lambarde's *Archaionomia*, published by the Cambridge University Press in 1644, re-issued in the same year as an additional element in Whelock's edition of the Old English Bede and the 'G' manuscript of the *Anglo-Saxon Chronicle*, with Latin translations (originally published in 1643).[43]

The most elaborate, renowned and decorative of all Anglo-Saxon historical maps (now readily accessible as a jigsaw puzzle) appeared for the first time in John Speed's *Theatre of the Empire of Great Britain*, a magnificent volume complemented by Speed's *History of Great Britain under the Conquests of the Romans, Saxons, Danes and Normans*, published as a pair in 1611 (Speed 1611). The map in question is labeled 'Britain – as it was divided in the time of the English Saxons especially during their Heptarchy', and is followed by Speed's famous series of county maps (Shirley 1991, 122–3 (no. 317); Goffart 1997, 57–9; also Nicholson and Hawkyard 1988, 29–32 (Heptarchy, with illustration), and *passim* (counties)). The work was overtly 'political' in its intention, produced for King James VI and I, and the map thus extends to include the whole of Scotland, as well as England and Wales (Fig. 18.10).[44] Each kingdom is identified not only by its name but

Fig. 18.9 [Rogers-Hole], The unified kingdom of England, from Britannia *(1607). Cambridge, Trinity College Library, VI.3.79 (The Master and Fellows of Trinity College, Cambridge).*

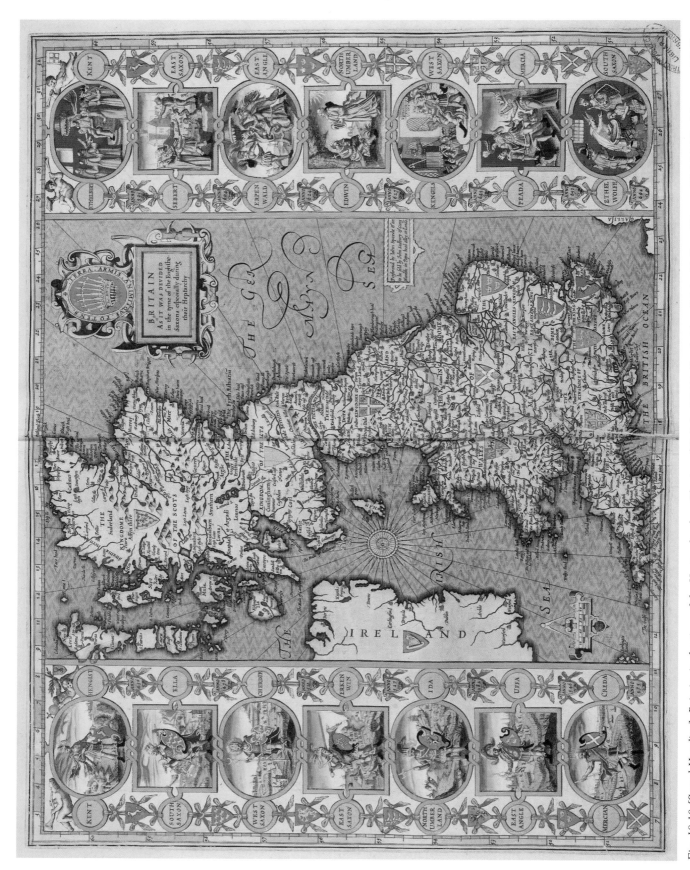

Fig. 18.10 [Speed-Hondius]. Britain, in the time of the Heptarchy, from Theatre of Britain (1611). Cambridge, Trinity College Library, VI.5.34 (The Master and Fellows of Trinity College, Cambridge).

also by the coat of arms which had come to be attributed to it.[45] In the seven frames of the border on the left, images are provided of the founding fathers of each kingdom, with a key date, beginning at the top with Hengist of Kent (456), followed by Ella of Sussex (478), Cherdik of Wessex (519), Erkenwin of Essex (527), Ida of Northumbria (582), Uffa of East Anglia (546), and Creda of Mercia (575). Each king bears a shield with an appropriate heraldic device (differing from the map in the cases of Wessex and Northumbria), posing against an imaginary background. In the seven frames of the border on the right, the chronology continues with images of the first Christian king of each kingdom, depicted in a way intended to capture an aspect of each king's story, beginning at the top with Ethelbert of Kent in 595 (enthroned, receiving a book from St Augustine), followed by Sebert of Essex in 604 (founding a church at Westminster), Erpenwald of East Anglia in 624 (killed by heathens), Edwin of Northumbria in 627 (and his vision of Paulinus), Kengils of Wessex in 635 (listening to Birinus preaching), Peada of Mercia in 650 (killed by his wife's treachery), and Ethelwolfe (*recte Æthelwealh*) of Sussex in 662 (baptized by Wilfrid, in the presence of King Wulfhere). The design thus reaches across 200 years of English history, with names and events linked to each of the kingdoms. The seven-sceptered crown, and the Virgilian motto, were taken over from Camden's map of 1600. Many more places are named than were named by Camden, and are given in modern forms, though now the selection is not obviously historical. The most striking aspect of the map is of course the representation of the founding fathers, on the left, and the first Christian kings, on the right. The idea seems likely to have been suggested by the Lambarde-Lyne design of 1574, but was applied here in the light of some re-consideration of the evidence (for example Earpwald replaces Sigeberht as the first Christian king of East Anglia). One should also note the references to the Irish Sea, the German Sea, and 'The British Ocean' (in the Channel), reflecting the adoption of the doctrine of the 'sovereignty of the seas', which would loom large as the seventeenth century wore on.[46] The map of the Heptarchy, decorated in this form, reappeared in the many editions of Speed's atlas published thereafter in the first half of the seventeenth century (Shirley 1991, 128 (no. 344), 130 (no. 353), 137 (no. 380), 139 (no. 386), 144 (no. 399), 154 (no. 433), 196 (nos. 587, 589, 590), and 211 (no. 668); Goffart 1997, 58–9); it flourished also in the 1640s, in the many atlases produced in Amsterdam by Willem J. Blaeu, Jan Jansson and others, sometimes with 'improved' vignettes (Shirley 1991, 151–2 (no. 423), 188 (no. 549), 192 (no. 572), 193–4 (no. 577), 195 (no. 581), 197 (no. 594), 198 (nos. 597, 601), 199 (nos. 605, 609), 200 (no. 613), 201 (nos. 617, 620), 202 (nos. 623, 626), 204 (no. 639), 205 (no. 643) and 206 (nos. 647, 651). Goffart 1997, 58–9). Speed had been assisted in the engraving and ornamentation of his original maps by Jodocus Hondius (1563–1612), in Amsterdam, giving them their particular Netherlandish flavour; one can but guess what effect this had on the way the opposing sides viewed each other after the start of the Anglo-Dutch wars in the 1650s.

As a historical construct, the 'Heptarchy', like 'Britain' and 'England', served well during the period from 1550 to 1650 as a way of packaging and conveying an understanding of the Anglo-Saxon past. The line from Nowell-Lambarde 1568, via Lambarde-Lyne 1574 and Lyne-Camden 1600, to Camden-Speed 1611, could be traced onwards into the eighteenth and nineteenth centuries. What had begun, however, as a powerfully simple idea would lead in time to levels of complexity which began to undermine its value. For example, the map of *Britannia Saxonica* devised for Rapin de Thoyras's *History of England*, first published in the 1720s, served its purpose well enough; but the large unfolding sheet in the same work, headed 'A Chronological and Synchronical Table of the Seven Kingdoms of the Anglo-Saxons from the Founding to the Dissolution of the Heptarchy', with Egbert of Wessex triumphant along the bottom line, shows what dangers lay not far beneath the surface.[47] In 1833 George William Collen took matters further, creating an Octarchy out of the Heptarchy by counting Northumbria as two, and providing a chronology for all kingdoms in parallel columns, over several pages, intended to show how the kingdoms remained separate or came together, down to the end of the ninth century (Collen 1833). The tabulation of synchronic chronologies would always serve a useful purpose; but it was shown before the end of the seventeenth century that the way forward lay along a different route.

Mapping the Chronicle and Bede

Two maps, one published in 1692 and the other in 1722, both devised to illustrate important historical texts, represent a new and promising development. The earliest map of the *Anglo-Saxon Chronicle* was that published by Edmund Gibson (1692). Gibson (1669–1748) had entered The Queen's College, Oxford, in 1686, and graduated in 1690. It was perhaps the golden age of Anglo-Saxon studies at Oxford. With the advice and encouragement of George Hickes, and others, and while still in his early twenties, Gibson set to work on a new edition of the *Chronicle* (with translation into Latin). It was based on the 'E' manuscript, in the Bodleian Library, but drew also on Whelock for manuscript 'G' (itself a copy of 'A') and on transcripts of some of the other manuscripts to which Gibson had no direct access.[48] The concept of the edition falls short of modern standards and expectations, but for its time it represented a significant step forward in a highly complex editorial task. Gibson's edition also deserves respect for the close attention paid to historical topography. The map, engraved by Michael Burghers (Fig. 18.11), is in the tradition of the earlier maps devised by Camden (1600) and Speed (1611), with the seven-sceptred crown, and the captions and heraldic badges which identify each of the kingdoms. Yet it has many other features which are innovative, commendable, and clearly the product of close study of the particular text. The cartouche in the upper left corner is evidently symbolic of the unified kingdom of England, as indicated by the crown itself and by

Fig. 18.11 [Gibson-Burghers], The unified kingdom of England, from Chronicon Saxonicum *(1692). Private collection.*

the coats of arms on the shields held by the supporting kings (representing Egbert and Edward the Confessor). The two holy men in the upper right corner (seemingly engaged in the act of surveying) draw attention to a key, itself bearing symbols for a religious place, an episcopal see, an estate, a castle, and the site of a battle (crossed swords), as well as *f* (*forsan*), denoting a degree of uncertainty. The selection of names aims to show as many as possible of the places named in the text, given in their vernacular forms and in 'Anglo-Saxon' script. Gibson was following here in the footsteps of Camden, and thus also provides a short essay on the principles of investigating place-names, followed by a long discursive gazetteer. For those who might have wondered, *Clofesho* is at Abingdon, and *Brunanburh* near Lindisfarne. The map also shows the course of Watling Street, mentioned in the annal for 1013; but other major Roman roads are not included. The map was re-engraved by John Sturt for inclusion in Gibson's translation of Camden's *Britannia*, published in 1695.[49] It was not superseded, however, until James Ingram produced a modified and larger version of what is essentially the same map (moving *Clofesho* east into Kent, and *Brunanburh* south into Lincolnshire) for his edition of the Chronicle, with English translation (Ingram 1823).

The second map, illustrating Bede's *Ecclesiastical History*, was included in the edition of that work produced by Dr John Smith (1659–1715), of Durham, and his eldest son George (1693–1756), published at Cambridge in 1722.[50] The father is known to have been still at work on the edition in 1713, but it is clear from the son's preface that the work was unfinished on his father's death two years later (when George was 22). The folded sheet, which unfolds to a large size (53 by 60cms), was pasted into the printed book opposite the second of several appendices, headed 'De provinciarum heptarchiæ limitibus', defining the kingdoms in terms of the counties contained within each. The map itself, however, was patently not conceived as a map of the Heptarchy. It is headed 'Britannia Saxonica juxta Baedam', and shows Ireland and the whole of Britain (Fig. 18.12), extending also to the North Sea littoral so that it would indicate whence came the Angles, the Saxons, and the Jutes. It recognizes that for Bede the appropriate context was the whole of Britain, and seems to have been intended by its creator to show the location of all of the places mentioned which could be identified (including *Mons Badonicus* and *Clofesho*), or accommodated in the available space. In other words, it is a map which breaks free from the long shadow of the Heptarchy, and like Gibson's map of the Chronicle places the emphasis on the elucidation of a text.

The legacy of Lambarde, Speed, Camden, Gibson and Smith

The mapping of the Anglo-Saxon past has come a long way forward since these formative years in the later sixteenth, seventeenth and early eighteenth centuries. The class of essentially 'static' maps, showing boundaries which obtained at particular times, and the location of significant places, has been extended to include dioceses, shires, and earldoms, all bringing problems of their own. A good example was set in the late 1860s by E. A. Freeman, whose six-volume *History of the Norman Conquest* contains a number of effective maps, including one of 'The English Empire in the Tenth and Eleventh Centuries', another showing 'The dioceses of England under Eadward the Confessor', and two showing the earldoms in England as they stood at different points in Edward's reign (1045 and 1065). (Freeman 1867–79, ii. 555–69 ('The Great Earldoms during the Reign of Eadward', with maps), followed by Barlow 1970, 358–9, and by Hill 1981, 105). The all-inclusive map of 'England and Wales before the Norman Conquest', compiled by W. H. Stevenson and published as part of a large historical atlas in 1902, is no less remarkable for the depth of scholarship which lies behind it.[51] The mapping of dioceses remains a challenge, in relation to our imperfect understanding of the ways in which bishoprics were defined, divided, and combined, and in relation to our understanding of the administration of pastoral care, and of the emerging structures of royal government and local administration in different regions (Hunter Blair 2003, 145 and 171; see also Hill 1981, 148). The ealdordoms, or earldoms, seem at first sight to offer an interesting analogy, though it is unclear how far it should be pressed. The arrangements which obtained in ninth-century Wessex are readily understood, at a certain level, though similar arrangements need not have applied elsewhere. Arrangements in the tenth century, and in the earlier part of the eleventh, south as well as north of the Thames, seem to have been more complicated, and to some extent of a different nature. The question arises how they might compare with arrangements in the Confessor's reign, for which Freeman's example has been taken further by Dr Stephen Baxter, in a series of 12 coloured maps, tracking the story through more of its intermediate stages, especially in the 1050s (Baxter 2010, 77–118, with maps I–XII; also Higham and Ryan 2013, 392).

A separate class should be invented for 'dynamic' maps, which attempt to capture a particular sequence of events, and to convey a sense of movement from one to the next. The itineraries which have been constructed for Carolingian, Ottonian and Salian rulers in the ninth, tenth and eleventh centuries, show the potential (see, *e.g.*, McKitterick 2008, 188–97, and Bernhardt 1993, with further references). It has to be admitted, however, that the 'itineraries' of Anglo-Saxon rulers, constructed largely from the evidence of law-codes and royal diplomas, are rarely of the same quality (Hill 1981, 82–91). The kings moved around their kingdom in much the same way; but the problem is that the diplomas are normally dated by year alone (not by the day of the month in that year), and that the place of issue is rarely specified. In fact it is only for a short period in the reign of King Æthelstan that the evidence is representative of the reality.[52] Mapping is rather more effective for tracking the course of the viking

Fig.18.12 [Smith], Britain, from Historia Ecclesiasticae ... Libri Quinque *(1722). Private collection.*

invasions during a particular campaign, drawing in this case largely on the evidence of the *Anglo-Saxon Chronicle*. The best opportunities are provided by accounts of the warfare against the Danes during the reign of King Alfred (Kendrick 1934; Hodgkin 1952, ii, opp. pp. 523, 557, 563, 656–7, 660 and 664; Hill 1981, 38–42), by the co-ordinated campaign of Edward the Elder and Æthelflæd in 914–20 (Hill 1981, 54–9), and (perhaps especially) by the activities of the vikings in England during the reign of King Æthelred the Unready (Kendrick 1934; Hill 1981, 63–71; Falkus and Gillingham 1981, 50–1 (multicoloured map); Haywood 1995, 118–21; Lavelle 2002; Howard 2003; and Hart 2006, xiii (list of maps). For an unpublished series of maps, see n. 63). Further opportunities are provided by the warfare between the English, the Norwegians, the Normans, and the Danes, in 1066–71, from Duke William's arrival at Pevensey Bay to the siege of Ely (Falkus and Gillingham 1981, 54–5). In each case the exercise is worthwhile because the *Chronicle*, supplemented by other source material, provides relatively detailed information, and because the action took place over an extended period and across a wide area. Single battles present more of a problem, even when they can be located. Leaving aside all the decisive battles of the seventh, eighth and earlier ninth centuries, we should like to know more than we do about the battles of Ashdown (871), Edington (878), Tettenhall (910), *Brunanburh* (937), Maldon (991), Ringmere (1010), and *Assandun* (1016); unfortunately, the information only begins to be fit for purpose with the battle of Hastings (1066).

The mapping of information contained in particular texts has itself progressed beyond Bede's *Historia Ecclesiastica*, and the *Anglo-Saxon Chronicle*, into the smaller worlds of documents such as the wills of King Alfred and King Eadred, and the text known as 'Resting-Places of Saints'.[53] The value of mapping, or of the representation of content in graphic form, is especially striking in the case of the texts known as the 'Tribal Hidage' and the 'Burghal Hidage'. The Tribal Hidage is challenging because of the uncertainty which attaches not only to its date, and intended purpose, but also to the identification, on the ground, of several of the peoples listed in the main body of the text; yet any attempt at mapping its content still offers a precious view of the separate (if in some cases unknown) identities of the several peoples who lived in the midst of the larger and perhaps better established peoples whose names had come to define the major Anglo-Saxon kingdoms (Hill 1981, 76–81, with references to earlier work). If the Tribal Hidage thus offers an antidote to the assumptions which flow from a conventional view of the 'Heptarchy', the Burghal Hidage offers an insight into the operation of homeland defence in the late ninth and early tenth centuries. The essential facts are: (a) that the text indicates how many hides were assigned for manning the defences at each place, from which one can work out how many men would be involved and so what total length of wall or rampart could be covered at the required rate; and (b) that one can visit each place, survey and study it closely,

and estimate the length of the defensive line. David Hill's contribution was: (a) to plot 'calculated' length of a defensive work along the x-axis of a graph, and 'actual' length along the y-axis, and then to draw in the line where the two values would happily intersect, with a small margin for error to each side; and (b) to position a dot for each place on the graph, determined by the length of its defences as calculated from the text (on the x-axis), and by the length of its defences as measured on the ground (on the y-axis). (Hill 1978, 184; Hill 1981, 85). Almost all of the dots fall along the line of intersecting values, or within the margins for error, from which it follows: (a) that we may place our confidence in the text; and (b) that the text is most likely to emanate from the 'centre', because no-one other than someone at the centre would have had access to information drawn from across the entire network. To my mind, there could not be a better example of what David Hill was able to bring to our understanding of a text by the process involved in converting its content into graphic form.

The mapping of borders, and of places named in texts, is generally a relatively straightforward exercise. Many new dimensions to our understanding of the period began to take shape as the exercise came to be extended to the mapping of information derived from complementary disciplines. Four groundbreaking examples must suffice to symbolize the advances made in these other fields. In 1903, G. Baldwin Brown published what aimed to be a comprehensive list, with distribution map, of about 180 'Saxon' churches in England; twenty years later, after receiving many letters from clergymen disappointed by the omission of their own church, he published a new edition, in which the number of buildings admitted into the list had increased to nearly 240.[54] In 1913, E. T. Leeds mapped the distribution of early Anglo-Saxon burial places, commenting on their relationship with the river-system, as distinct from the system of Roman roads; many more maps showing the distribution of particular artifacts would follow (Leeds 1913, 18–19). In 1956 A. H. Smith published a map headed 'The Scandinavian Settlement', which has been reproduced probably more times than most other maps of its kind for this period (Smith 1956, pt 1, in back pocket). It would be customary now to express reservations about the arrows coming in from the sea, since they hardly do justice to the protracted campaigns which led to the recorded acts of settlement, and to insist at the same time that the distribution represents the product of the whole period of 200 years between the initial settlements and the Domesday survey; yet Smith's famous map remains none the less a graphic, even iconic, demonstration of the incidence of 'Scandinavian' names in England, largely confined within an area to the north and east of the boundary set down in the treaty between King Alfred and King Guthrum, *c.* 880. Perhaps most striking of all is the map, published at about the same time as Smith's, in which Michael Dolley and Michael Metcalf plotted the distribution of 'stray' or single finds of coins of the early Anglo-Saxon period (7th–9th centuries), showing that the circulation of 'Mercian' coinage 'was limited for all practical purposes to the area south and east of a line from the Solent, through the Northampton uplands, to the Wash' (Dolley and Metcalf 1955–7, 462; also Hill 1981, 120–32. For a more recent discussion, see Naismith 2013, 199–201). There has since been a significant increase in the amount of evidence on which such a map can be based, yet the distribution remains essentially the same; so there could hardly be a more compelling reflection of the essential truth that the use of money was concentrated in south-eastern England, either side of the Thames estuary, providing the obvious explanation for the strong interest shown in the area by successive rulers of the Mercians (and concomitantly for the different kind of interest shown in lands to the west and north).

The mapping in this way of evidence derived from other disciplines was soon combined with the longer established forms of more overtly 'historical' mapping. The way forward was shown by the series of 'period' maps produced and published under the authoritative imprint of the Ordnance Survey, in the second and third quarters of the twentieth century (Seymour 1980, 239, 328). The series was planned in the early 1920s, under the auspices of O. G. S. Crawford, Archaeology Officer at the Ordnance Survey from 1920 to 1946; Crawford was succeeded by C. W. Phillips, who maintained the tradition until his own retirement in 1965, completing his work in the decade which followed. The maps are distinguished not only for their scope, covering Britain as a whole, their superb cartography (as one would expect), and all the expertise which lies behind them, but also for their vision of an understanding of the past based on the *integration* of many different yet complementary forms of evidence. Named places were plotted from a combination of literary and documentary sources, and close attention was paid (on the map itself or in the accompanying text) to the evidence of archaeology, church architecture, stone sculpture, and place-names. An OS map of Roman Britain was first published in 1924 and was revised in 1928; a third edition, showing the whole of Britain on a single sheet, was published in 1956. The south sheet of the OS map of *Britain in the Dark Ages* [O. G. S. Crawford] covering the period 410–871, was first published in 1935, followed by the north sheet in 1938. The list of scholars involved in the provision of data included F. M. Stenton, Kenneth Jackson, J. E. Lloyd, Eilert Ekwall, and others; and the sheer weight of scholarship was complemented by cartographic design and production of the first order. After the war, and following the publication in the early 1950s of the north and south sheets of a map of Monastic Britain (1066–1539), and in 1962 of a map of Southern Britain in the Iron Age, a second edition of *Britain in the Dark Ages* [C. W. Phillips], in one sheet, was published in 1966. It was not quite as stunning to behold as in its first incarnation; but a better impression overall was created by the inclusion of Roman roads (previously omitted), and by clearer marking of the archaeological evidence (significantly increased in quantity). These maps were joined in 1973 by a map of *Britain before the Norman Conquest* [C. W. Phillips], covering the period 871–1066. The data was derived as before from many different kinds of evidence, but now in a period for which it was possible to make more effective use of coinage (mints and hoards); an especially strong (even overpowering) impression is made by the bright red line for the Alfred-Guthrum boundary, and by the red dots indicating the incidence of 'Scandinavian' place-names to the north and east. Unfortunately, the series of these incomparable maps did not extend further to cover Anglo-Norman England, as might have been wished by those eager to see the evidence of the Domesday survey deployed to its full advantage.[55]

The emergence of properly 'integrated' medieval studies, across many disciplines (including archaeology, architecture, sculpture, place-names, and numismatics), was represented in one way by the Ordnance Survey maps of Britain in the early medieval period; and since the maps were as decorative as they were instructive, they served as essential if unwieldy props for lectures on Anglo-Saxon England for many years (and retain their great value precisely because they show so much detail, across the whole country). The development was represented in a rather different but inventive and spirited way by David Hill's *Atlas of Anglo-Saxon England* (1981). The *Atlas* was in certain respects a reaction *against* the way in which the massive authority and matchless cartography of the Ordnance Survey maps might seem (unintentionally) to reduce the complexities of the period to order; and perhaps his book might be read as an exercise in raising awareness of deeper complexities and wider dimensions. One of the most striking pages in the *Atlas* is the one on which a bar-chart representing the distribution of surviving charters, decade by decade, from 600 to 1070, is placed directly above another bar-chart, on the same scale, representing the length of the annals in the *Anglo-Saxon Chronicle*, for each decade, across the same period (Hill 1981, 26). One can see at a glance that the central decades of the tenth century were the golden age for charters, with diplomas trailing off in the early eleventh century as the writs kicked in. One can see also that while chroniclers had much to say about an escapade in the 750s, and about the warfare in the 870s, 890s and 910s, they had rather little to say about the period for which the evidence of charters is so good, though they resumed writing about warfare for the 990s, 1000s and 1010s, followed after another break (in the 1020s and 1030s) by some serious politics in the 1040s and 1050s. Therein, one might say, lies the tale. Some part of the explanation is to be found in an understanding of the *Chronicle* itself, as one can see when the *Chronicle* is 'exploded' into its component parts.[56] More of it is to be found deeper within four of the forms of evidence on which historians of this period depend, and which were largely (though not entirely) beyond the reach of the OS maps: the corpus of Latin saints' *Lives*, and related works in Latin (Lapidge and Winterbottom 1992; Lapidge 2009; Winterbottom and Lapidge 2012); the corpus of Anglo-Saxon charters, comprising royal diplomas, royal writs, and various other forms of documentation, in Latin and in the vernacular;[57] the corpus of Anglo-Saxon law-codes;[58] and the ever expanding corpus of Anglo-Saxon coins (Hill 1981, 120–32; Naismith 2012). The rest of it is another matter.

David Hill seems also to have taken pleasure in introducing into his *Atlas* evidence which one might not have expected to find in a book of its kind. He was renowned for his surveying work on Offa's Dyke, sustained over many years; but his abiding interest in defensive systems also encouraged him to pursue aspects of the subject where the evidence was less tangible. His belief in the existence of a network of signaling beacons as part of a coastal watch and early warning system against the threat of invasion from the sea, represented by his map of 'Hampshire beacons', arose in part from obscure references in contemporary sources, and in part from the compelling evidence of the Armada system in the 1580s (Hill 1981, 92). The point is only strengthened by the map of beacons in Kent, prepared by William Lambarde in 1585.[59] There is good reason to believe that arrangements for a beacon system of such a kind existed already during the reign of King Æthelred the Unready; so that when one looks at Lambarde's map, one begins to understand how news of a hostile fleet landing at Sandwich, as happened in 991, 1006, 1009, 1013, and 1015, might have been transmitted back to Canterbury, Rochester and London.[60]

The legacy of David Hill's *Atlas of Anglo-Saxon England*

The legacy of Hill's *Atlas* lies in the way it demonstrated, in one context after another, the value of the display of information in graphic form, whether in maps or in diagrams, thus enabling the user of the book to appreciate something about a subject which might otherwise be hidden from view. In *The Anglo-Saxons* (1982), edited by James Campbell, an authoritative text was complemented at every turn by a well-chosen selection of illustrations, including landscape, churches, objects, manuscripts and coins, as well as diagrams and maps (including several derived from the *Atlas*). Each of the two books was the first of its kind, and both introduced new dimensions into the perception of the Anglo-Saxon past. One of the most interesting of the maps in *The Anglo-Saxons* was that of 'Early dioceses and minsters', devised in the first instance by Patrick Wormald and developed by him with corrections from another publication.[61] One can see from its key that it was the product of familiarity with a wide variety of evidence, and it combines this evidence with a representation of diocesan boundaries. The effect lies not so much in the distribution, which is in itself the product of a combination of various extraneous factors, as in demonstrating quite simply that there were far more minsters on the ground, throughout the country, than one might imagine from a reading of Bede's *Ecclesiastical History*. Reference

might also be made here to a series of maps drawn over a period of 20 years (1991–2012), on my own behalf (but very much in the spirit of David's *Atlas*), by the late Mr Reginald Piggott, of Potter Heigham, Norfolk. Mr Piggott's work can be recognized in a large number of books published since the 1950s by the Cambridge University Press, Penguin Books, and various other publishers, and his style has been widely imitated. The maps take advantage of the flexibility made possible by hand drawing and labelling, and display a variety of decorative and other devices reaching back to the little mountains and little trees of Saxton and Norden in the late sixteenth century. Most are 'static', and were devised for teaching purposes to illustrate particular periods;[62] others are 'dynamic', including a set illustrating the course of the viking raids during the reign of King Æthelred the Unready;[63] and there are also a few intended to aid the exposition of a particular subject, or a particular text.[64] Needless to say, there remain many aspects of the subject which have yet to be unlocked and opened out in graphic form. One cannot safely judge the significance of one royal diploma, in relation to others, until its boundary-clause has been 'solved', and mapped, and until its role as a title-deed can be set in the context of other title-deeds for the same estate or for other estates in the same vicinity. One can produce maps for places named in a single document (such as a will), or for a group of documents (such as the diplomas in favour of a particular person or family group); but again, much more depends on being able to visualize the totality of the surviving evidence for all holders of land in a particular shire, or larger region. Moreover, all such evidence would take on a new meaning when viewed in relation to roads, rivers, woodland, high ground, villages, churches, towns, bridges, local defensive works, and so on.

We have come a long way from the day in the late 1560s when William Lambarde took Laurence Nowell's map of England and made it the basis for his own map of the Anglo-Saxon Heptarchy. The mapping of data of any kind, for a period in the past, is most rewarding when the sheer quantity of information available creates the need, provides the opportunity, and produces the result. Classic examples from other fields show that the principles had reached a considerable degree of sophistication already in the nineteenth century;[65] and those who have been devising historical maps during the past hundred years have thus taken their place in a long and distinguished tradition. There is no shortage of information about the Anglo-Saxon past which would respond to more detailed mapping. David Hill worked with a rapidograph, and sheets of Letraset. The technology now exists for producing electronic maps with multiple layers or levels of information (from the underlying geology upwards to modern county boundaries), with zooming scales, and with all the other advantages that come with geographic information systems. If only Nowell and Lambarde could have known what they started.

Notes

1 Hill 1981. A second edition had been planned, but did not materialize; he also planned an atlas of early medieval Europe.

2 *Antiquity* 57 (1983), 66–7. Reviews of the *Atlas* are registered in *ASE* 12 (1983), 324, and thereafter.

3 BL Cotton Tiberius B. v, fol. 56v. Images of the map, showing Britain and Ireland in the lower left-hand corner, are available on the website of the British Library.

4 Laws of Wihtred, ch. 28, and laws of Ine, ch. 20. The occurrence of similar clauses in two separate but near-contemporary law-codes suggests agreement between the kingdoms; see also the annal in the 'common stock' of the *Anglo-Saxon Chronicle*, for the year 695.

5 For itineraries, see Barrow 2012. For an itinerary used by Archbishop Sigeric when returning from Rome to England, in 990, see Ortenberg 1990; for a map, see also Keynes 1997, 102.

6 Oxford, Corpus Christi College, MS. 157, pp. 39–45 (bishops) and 47–54 (kings). For the text, see Petrie 1848, 616–44. A new edition and study of this material is in preparation, as part of the edition of the chronicle of John of Worcester (Oxford Medieval Texts); co-edited by David Woodman.

7 Oxford, Corpus Christi College, MS. 157, pp. 43 (bishops) and 50 (kings). High quality images of the manuscript are available on the 'Early Manuscripts at Oxford University' website (image.ox.ac.uk), in the section for 'Corpus Christi College', under 'MS. 157'.

8 For a useful set of royal genealogies in tabular form see Whitelock 1979, 935–48 (Tables 1–12).

9 For a valuable and well illustrated account of this strand in the historiographical tradition, see Holladay 2010.

10 See Holladay 2010, 120–32. A fine example from the fourteenth century (BL Royal 14 B vi) is readily accessible on the internet (British Library, Catalogue of Illuminated Manuscripts); see also Bovey 2005.

11 I obtained a copy of this booklet from the library of the late Patrick Wormald, but suspect that it may not be generally accessible.

12 For Nowell, see entry in Lapidge *et al.* 2014, 342–3, with references; to which should now be added Brackmann 2012.

13 BL Lansdowne MS. 6, fol. 135, cited by Tyacke and Huddy 1980, 10; see also Barber 1983b. For Cecil and Nowell see also Alford 2008, 147, 236–7, and Brackmann 2012, pp. 13–15.

14 BL Add. 62540 [acquired in 1982], fols. 3v–4r, headed 'A general description of England & Ireland with the costes adioyning'. See Shirley 1991, x–xi; Tyacke and Huddy 1980, 10–11; Barber 1983a; and Brackmann 2012, 148–61.

15 Hesiod, *Works and Days*, lines 96–8 (Barber 1983a, 20).

16 It has been noted that the barking dog appears to have an erection, giving rise to a particular line of argument (Brackmann 2012, 159–61). For the more prosaic interpretation, that the barking dog is a product of a convention found on surveyors' maps of this period, see Tyacke and Huddy 1980, 10, and a group of maps made in the 1580s by one John Darby (d. 1609). See, in particular, P. Barber, 'John Darby's Map of the Parish of Smallburgh in Norfolk, 1582', *Imago Mundi* 57.1 (2005), 55–8; R. Frostick, 'A 16th Century East Anglian Surveyor, and Pieter Bruegel', *Journal of the International Map Collector's Society* 101 (2005), 33–9, with reference to a map of Mousehold Heath, Norfolk; and R. Frostick, 'The Map of Blakeney Haven and Port of Cley – 1586', *Glaven Historian* 9 (2006), 29–30, with further references.

17 For Lord Burghley's use of the map, see Barber 1983b, on the annotations (itineraries).

18 For Mercator's map, see Shirley 1991, x and 36–9 (no. 75), with illustration; see also Tyacke and Huddy 1980, 9–11, and Barber 1983a, 20–1.

19 BL Cotton Otho B, xi, on which see Ker 1957, 230–4 (no. 180).

20 BL Add. 43703, on which see Brackmann 2012, 38–9 and 95–100, with references. For this version of the Burghal Hidage, see Hill 1969; Keynes and Lapidge 1983, 193–4 and 339–41; and Hill and Rumble 1996.

21 BL Cotton Domitian [A.] xviii, on which see Brackmann 2012, 161–78, esp. 171–8.

22 J. Norden, *Speculum Britanniae* (1591–8), with Tyacke and Huddy 1980, 43–5; see also Worms and Baynton-Williams 2011, 585 (Saxton) and 494–5 (Norden).

23 Reproduced here from Cambridge, Trinity College Library, VI.1.75 (ex Lord Lumley). Shirley 1991, 41 (no. 83b); Goffart 1997. Images of the sixteenth- and seventeenth-century printed books cited in this article are available on Early English Books Online ('EEBO'), reproduced from microfilm of copies in various collections.

24 Maidstone, Kent History and Library Centre, U47/48. See Warnicke 1973, 29–33, with plate II; see also Brackmann 2012, 136–47.

25 Letter from Parker to Burghley, dated 9 May 1573 (Bruce 1853, 424–6).

26 Reproduced here from Cambridge, Trinity College Library, VI.1.117. For Lyne, see Hind 1952, 81–4, citing his well known bird's-eye plan of Cambridge, and his 'Genealogy of British, Anglo-Saxon, Norman and Later English Monarchs' (no. 4), both published in 1574; see also Worms and Baynton-Williams 2011, 420–1. The entry on Lyne in *ODNB* has become garbled in transmission; see also Knapp 2003, 179–80.

27 That Lambarde had intended to include a heading, and perhaps some further explanation or decoration, is suggested by a space marked for a purpose in the upper right corner of his original map of 1570 (Warnicke 1973, Plate II).

28 Reproduced here from Cambridge, Trinity College Library, VI.1.117. For Hogenberg, see Hind 1952, 72–8 (no. 11).

29 A. Neville, *De furoribus Norfolcensium Ketto duce*, and *Norvicus*, 2 vols in one (London, 1575), pasted down in *Norvicus*, p. 113. Hind 1952, 76, 78, 83; Shirley 1991, 47–8 (no. 106); Goffart 1997, 54–5. For Neville (whose younger brother was Thomas Neville, Dean of Canterbury and later Master of Trinity College, Cambridge), see the entry by E. Leedham-Green in *ODNB*. The copies available on 'Early English Books Online' do not have the plates.

30 Hind 1952, 76, observes that in the three copies of the book which he had examined, containing impressions of both prints (Oxford, Bodleian Library; Trinity College, Cambridge; and the Folger), Lyne's print is placed before Hogenberg's, which (historically) is how it should be; see also his plates 42 (Hogenberg) and 43 (Lyne).

31 The list of Parkerian publications in the early 1570s, before his death in 1575, is impressive. Three of the items published in 1574 – the *Life of Alfred*, Thomas of Walsingham's *Historia breuis*, and Thomas of Walsingham's *Ypodigma Neustriae vel Normanniae* – seem usually to have been bound together as a single volume.

32 For this copy of Parker's book, see Fletcher, *et al.* 2007, 90–2.

33 Letter from Parker to Burghley, dated 23 November 1574 (Bruce 1853, 467–8).

34 Vertue 1932, 71–2, from BL Add. 23070, fol. 62v. In 1597 Michael Hickes had been favoured with a visit by Queen Elizabeth to Ruckholts, and had hoped then for reward.

35 Lambarde1576, map, with pp. 1–5 (exposition). Shirley 1991, 50 (no. 116); Goffart 1997, 55; Brackmann 2012, 136–7. Several seemingly 'perfect' copies of the book lack the map, which suggests that supplies of the map, cut down from impressions of Lyne's engraving, might not have been sufficient to supply; but one would need to examine more copies of the book in order to clarify the matter.

36 The 1596 edition of *Perambulation* also contains a woodblock of a map of the beacon system of Kent, as it existed in the 1580s, showing how news of an invasion in the south-east would have been spread, and passed back to London. The original map by Lambarde, dated August 1585 (BL Add. 62935), and made for Lord Burghley, differs in various respects from the published version; see also Barber 1992, 57–98.

37 For the texts of the 1577 and 1587 editions of Holinshed's *Chronicles*, see 'The Holinshed Project', online at <www.cems.ox.ac.uk/Holinshed/>. For those who worked on the later edition, see Summerson 2013; Herendeen 2013.

38 For Camden's *Britannia*, see Herendeen 2007, 180–242 and 265–89. The Latin text of the 1586 edition is available online, with the English translation by Philemon Holland (1610), at <www.philological.bham.ac.uk/ cambrit>.

39 Shirley 1991, 95 (no. 231). For Camden and Roman Britain, see Hingley 2008, 24–43.

40 W. Camden, *Britannia* (London, 1600), fol. 107. Shirley 1991, 95 (no. 232); Goffart 1997, 57. Reproduced here from a copy in the library of Trinity College, Cambridge.

41 Virgil's Italy was *terra antiqua, potens armis atque ubere glebæ* ('an ancient land, powerful in arms and in the fertility of its soil'); the unified Heptarchy of England was powerful not only in arms, but also in the courage or firm resolve of its people.

42 W. Camden, *Britannia* (London, 1607), between pp. 98 and 99. Shirley 1991, 113–14 (no. 280); Goffart 1997, 57. Reproduced here from a copy in the library of Trinity College, Cambridge.

43 [A. Whelock], *Archaionomia* (Cambridge, 1644), and *Historiæ Ecclesiasticæ Gentis Anglorum Libri V ... Quibus accesserunt Anglo-Saxoniæ Leges* (Cambridge, 1644), printed on the inside of a bifolium which carries Lambarde's exposition of the Heptarchy on the other side.

44 Reproduced here from Cambridge, Trinity College Library, VI.5.34 (the copy presented by Speed to King James's queen, Anne of Denmark).

45 A significant role, immediately before Speed, seems to have been played by Sir William Segar (d. 1633), Garter Principal King of Arms. When he was first presented to King James, in 1604, the king asked him 'some questions touching the Coat Armour of England'; Segar's response, as Garter, is represented by London, College of Arms, MS 14, fols. 362–84, and by BL Harley MS. 6085. For the heraldry of the Heptarchy, see also Keynes 1999, nn. 65, 114, 210.

46 The theme of the sovereignty of the seas can be traced from the so-called *Altitonantis* charter, in the name of King Edgar, to the writings of John Dee, in the sixteenth century, and of John Selden, in the seventeenth; with the surprising result that King Edgar pervades the decorative scheme, and features as figurehead, on King Charles I's flagship, *Sovereign of the Seas*. See Sobecki 2011; a paper on 'John Selden and the *Sovereign of the Seas*', which I gave at a conference marking the 400th anniversary of Selden's first publication, held at the University of Oxford in June 2010, is not yet published.

47 R. de Thoyras, *The History of England*, 2 vols., 2nd ed. (London, 1732). For this work, see Keynes 1999, 272–4 and 276.

48 For further details, see Keynes 2012, 551–2. As a student in Oxford, Gibson would not have been able to consult the manuscripts in the Cottonian library ('B', 'C', 'D', 'F', 'G' and 'H'). He planned to produce a second edition, with the help of Humfrey Wanley, who in 1709 borrowed 'C', 'D' and 'G' from the library for the purpose [slipping, and spraining his left leg, on the way home]; see Heyworth 1989, 11 (Wanley to Tanner) and 255–8 (Wanley to Gibson).

49 E. Gibson, *Camden's Britannia, Newly Translated into English; with Large Additions and Improvements* (London, 1695), pp. cxx–cxxi. Goffart 1997, 60. This edition of Camden has been re-published in facsimile, with contributions by Stuart Piggott and Gwyn Walters (Newton Abbot: David and Charles Reprints,1971).

50 *Historiæ ecclesiasticæ gentis Anglorum libri quinque, auctore sancto & venerabili Bæda, presbytero Anglo-Saxone*, ed. J. Smith (Cambridge, 1722). See Towers 1976; there are entries for both father and son in the *ODNB*.

51 Poole 1902, Map XVI (marked as 'Plate 16'), accompanied by further explanation, including a list of all places marked (given in Old English forms, as on the map, and also identified – including *Brunanburh*). The map was highly commended by Stenton 1971, 729–30.

52 For further details, see Keynes 2013, 33–6, and above, pp. 147–8.

53 For Alfred's will, see Hill 1981, 84; Keynes and Lapidge 1983, 173–8 (with map) and 313–26; and Miller 2001, 3–12. For Eadred's will, see Hill 1981, 89, and Miller 2001, 76–81. For 'Resting-Places of Saints', see Hill 1981, 152, following a study of the text by David Rollason.

54 Baldwin Brown 1903 and Baldwin Brown 1925, with maps. For comparison, the list given in Taylor 1978, 766–72, comprises 267 churches.

55 Hill 1981, 100–5 and 154 (religious houses in DB); see also Campbell 1982, p. 239 (density of population). The mapping of Domesday data is central to the project 'Profile of a Doomed Elite: the Structure of English Landed Society in 1066' (Dr Stephen Baxter, King's College, London).

56 For a diagram attempting to show its development from the 'Common Stock', see Keynes 2012, 542; a more elaborate version of the diagram, in colour, is available on the 'Kemble' website (www.kemble.asnc.cam.ac.uk). For further discussion, see Baxter 2007 and Brooks 2011.

57 Hill 1981, 22–5. The new edition, of which the first volume appeared in 1973, has now reached half-way: Brooks and Kelly 2013. The opportunities presented by vernacular boundary-clauses for recreating the landscape of southern England in the tenth and eleventh centuries require no advertisement; for further information, see the 'LangScape' website (www.langscape.org.ok). The tables in Keynes 2002, available on the 'Kemble' website, represent an attempt to capture and to convey an impression of the evidence of the diplomas, and especially their witness-lists, across the period as a whole.

58 Hill 1981, 97–8. The diagrams in Oliver 2011, comparing rates of compensation for bodily injury (as in the law-codes of Æthelberht and Alfred), serve here as a good example.

59 For Lambarde's map of the Kentish beacons, see above, n. 36.

60 Hill and Sharp 1997, with Baker and Brookes 2013. For Sandwich and the Wantsum Channel, see Hill 1981, 14; see also the entry on Sandwich in Lapidge *et al.* 2014, 418–19.

61 Wormald 1982, 71, with 'The Making of the English Church', in Falkus and Gillingham 1981, 35.

62 The subjects include Bede's Britain; the region of the Middle Angles; southern England in the eighth century; southern England in the ninth century; the 'kingdom of the Anglo-Saxons'; a series of six representing England, or southern England, during the reign of Edward the Elder, Æthelstan, Edmund and Eadred, Eadwig, Edgar, and *c.* 1000; and a four-in-one map representing England in successive stages of its political development (*c.* 700, *c.* 800, *c.* 900 and *c.* 1000). These maps and the others mentioned below are available on the 'Kemble' website.

63 These originated with a map showing the raids in 991–1005, published in 1991. This has since been superseded by a set of three four-in-one maps, representing respectively the early raids (*c.* 980–1005), the devastating raids of 1006–7 and 1009–12, and the major invasions of 1013 and 1015 (both of which led directly or indirectly to Danish conquest), used for teaching purposes.

64 England and Rome in the ninth century; the contexts of the Fonthill Letter; recorded meeting-places of the king and his councillors, 900–1066; Ælfric of Cerne Abbas and of Eynsham; estates of the archbishop of York; estates of the bishop of Wells; churches and estates of Regenbald of Cirencester.

65 Charles Joseph Minard's graphic showing the fate of Napoleon's army on its way to and from Moscow in 1812, first published in 1869, is readily accessible on the internet; see also Tufte 2001, 40–1.

Bibliography

Printed works

Abels, R. P. (1988) *Lordship and Military Obligation in Anglo-Saxon England*. London: British Museum Publications.

Abrams, L. and Parsons, D. N. (2004) Place-names and the history of Scandinavian settlement in England. In J. Hines, A. Lane and M. Redknap (eds) *Land, Sea and Home. Proceedings of a conference on Viking-period settlement in England*, 379–431. Leeds: Maney.

Ager, B. and Williams, G. (2007) No. 310. Penrith Area, Cumbria: Viking silver jewellery and coin hoard (2005 T471). *Treasure Annual Report* 2006, 101–2.

Ager, B. and Williams, G. (2011) The Vale of York Viking hoard: preliminary catalogue. In T. Abramson (ed.), *Studies in Early Medieval Coinage. Volume 2. New Perspectives*, 135–45. Woodbridge: Boydell and Brewer.

Alcock, L. (1995) *Cadbury Castle, Somerset: the Early Medieval Archaeology*. Cardiff: University of Wales Press.

Alford, S. (2008) *Burghley: William Cecil at the Court of Elizabeth I*. New Haven, CT: Yale University Press.

Allan, J. (2002) The Anglo-Saxon mint at Lydford. *Transactions of the Devonshire Association for the Advancement of Science, Literature and Art* 134, 9–32.

Allan, J., Henderson, C. and Higham, R. (1984) Saxon Exeter. In J. Haslam, *Anglo-Saxon Towns in Southern England*, 385–414. Chichester: Phillimore.

Allen, M. (2012) *Mints and Money in Medieval England*. Cambridge: University Press.

Andrews, P. (1997) *Excavations at Hamwic: volume 2: excavations at Six Dials*. Council for British Archaeology Research Report 109. London: Council for British Archaeology.

Anlezark, D. (2006) Reading 'The Story of Joseph' in MS Cambridge, Corpus Christi College 201. In H. Magennis and J. Wilcox (eds), *The Power of Words: Anglo-Saxon Studies Presented to Donald G. Scragg on his Seventieth Birthday*, 61–94. Morgantown, WV: West Virginia University Press.

Anon. (1863) Note. In *Proceedings of the Somerset Archaeological and Natural History Society* 12, 7.

Anon. (1886) *Otago Witness*. Issue 760, 23 June, p. 16.

Anon. (2008) *Royal Engineers Pocket Book*. Chatham: Royal Engineers.

Appleton, H. (forthcoming) A Pattern of Islands: *Durham* and the Cult of Cuthbert.

Archibald, M. M. and Blunt, C. E. (1986) *Sylloge of Coins of the British Isles 34. British Museum, Anglo-Saxon Coins V. Athelstan to the Reform of Edgar. 924–c. 973*. London: British Museum.

Armit, I. (2001) Warfare, Violence and Slavery in Prehistory and Protohistory, *Past: The newsletter of the Prehistoric Society* 37, 10–11.

Ashbee, P. and Jewell, P. (1998) The Experimental Earthworks Revisited, *Antiquity* 72 no. 277, 485–504.

Ashley, S., Penn, K. and Rogerson, A. (2009) Rhineland Lava in Norfolk Churches, *Church Archaeology* 13, 27–33.

Ashworth, T. (2000) *Trench Warfare 1914–1918: The live and let live system*. London: Pan.

Aston, M. (1984) The towns of Somerset. In J. Haslam (ed.) *Anglo-Saxon Towns in Southern England*, 167–201. Chichester: Phillimore.

Aston, M. (1986a) Post-Roman central places in Somerset. In E. Grant (ed.), *Central Places, Archaeology and History*, 49–78. Sheffield: University of Sheffield.

Aston, M. (1986b), The Bath region from late prehistory to the middle ages. *Bath History* 1, 61–98.

Aston, M. and Leech, R. (1977) *Historic Towns in Somerset*. Bristol: Committee for Rescue Archaeology in Avon, Gloucestershire and Somerset.

Atherton, M. (2013) Coins, Merchants and fear of the King: the Old English *Seven Sleepers* story. In G. R. Owen-Crocker and B. W. Schneider (eds) *Royal Authority in Anglo-Saxon England*, British Archaeological Report 584, 63–74. Oxford: Archaeopress.

Attenborough, F. L. (ed. 1922) *The Laws of the Earliest English Kings*. Cambridge: Cambridge University Press.

Bachrach, B. (1993). Logistics in Pre-Crusade Europe. In J. Lynn. (ed.), *Feeding Mars: Logistics in Western Warfare from the Middle Ages to the Present*, 57–78. Oxford: Westview.

Baker, J. and Brookes, S. (2011) From frontier to border: the evolution of northern West Saxon territorial delineation in the ninth and tenth centuries. *Anglo-Saxon Studies in Archaeology and History* 17, 104–119.

Baker, J. and Brookes, S. (2013) *Beyond the Burghal Hidage: Anglo-Saxon civil defence in the Viking age*. Leiden: Brill.

Baker, N. and Holt, R. (2004) *Urban Growth and the Medieval Church: Gloucester and Worcester*. Aldershot: Ashgate.

Baldwin Brown, G. (1903) *The Arts in Early England, II: Ecclesiastical Architecture in England*. London: John Murray.

Baldwin Brown, G. (1925) *The Arts in Early England, II: Anglo-Saxon Architecture*, 2nd ed. London: John Murray.

Baldwin Brown, G. (1937) *The Arts in Early England, VI.ii, Anglo-Saxon Sculpture*, ed. E. H. L. Sexton. London: John Murray.

Barber, P. M. (1983a) A Tudor mystery: Laurence Nowell's map of England and Ireland, *Map Collector* 22.1, 16–21.

Barber, P. M. (1983b) Ld Burleigh carried this map always about him, *Bulletin of the Friends of the British Museum* 43, 18–19.

Barber, P. M. (1992) England II: monarchs, ministers and maps, 1550–1625. In D. Buisseret (ed.), *Monarchs, Ministers and Maps:*

the Emergence of Cartography as a Tool of Government in Early Modern Europe, 57–98. Chicago: University of Chicago Press.

Barker, K. (1986) Pen, Ilchester and Yeovil: a study in the landscape history and archaeology of S E Somerset. *Proceedings of the Somerset Archaeological and Natural History Society* 130, 11–45.

Barker, P. (1994) *A short architectural history of Worcester Cathedral.* Worcester Cathedral Publications 2. Worcester: Dean and Chapter of Worcester.

Barker, P. (2005) Reconstructing Wulfstan's cathedral. In J. Barrow and N. Brooks (eds), *St Wulfstan and his World*, 167–88. Aldershot: Ashgate.

Barlow, F. (1970) *Edward the Confessor.* London: Eyre and Spottiswoode.

Barrow, J. (1996) The community of Worcester, 961–c.1100. In N. Brooks and C. Cubitt (eds), *St Oswald of Worcester: life and influence*, 84–99. London: Leicester University Press.

Barrow, J. (2005) The chronology of forgery production at Worcester from c. 1000 to the early twelfth century. In J. Barrow and N. Brooks (eds), *St Wulfstan and his World*, 105–22. Aldershot: Ashgate.

Barrow, J. (2012) Way-stations on English episcopal itineraries, 700–1300, *EHR* 127, 549–65.

Barrow, J. and Brooks, N. (eds 2005) *St Wulfstan and his World.* Aldershot: Ashgate.

Bassett, S. (1989) Churches in Worcester before and after the conversion of the Anglo-Saxons, *Antiquaries Journal* 69, 225–56.

Bately, J. [M.] (ed. 1980) *The Old English Orosius*, Early English Text Society, supplementary series 6. Oxford: University Press.

Bately, J. M. (ed. 1986) *MS. A.* The Anglo-Saxon Chronicle, a collaborative edition 3, eds D. Dumville and S. Keynes. Cambridge: D. S. Brewer.

Bately, J. [M.] (2006) The place which is called 'at x': a new look at old evidence. In M. Swan (ed.) Essays for Joyce Hill on her Sixtieth Birthday. *Leeds Studies in English* ns 37, 343–63.

Bates, S., Hoggett, R. and Schwenninger, J. (2008). An Archaeological Excavation at Devil's Ditch, Riddlesworth and Garboldisham, Norfolk. Unpublished excavation report. Report 1436, BAU 1307. Norfolk Archaeological Unit, Norwich.

Batt, M. (1975) The Burghal Hidage: Axbridge, *Proceedings of the Somerset Archaeological and Natural History Society* 119, 22–25.

Baxter, S. (2007) MS C of the *Anglo-Saxon Chronicle* and the politics of mid-eleventh-century England, *EHR* 122, 1189–1227.

Baxter, S. (2010) Edward the Confessor and the succession question. In R. Mortimer (ed.), *Edward the Confessor: the Man and the Legend*, 77–118. Woodbridge: Boydell Press.

Beresford, M. R. and H. P. R. Finberg (1973) *English Medieval Boroughs. A Hand-List.* Newton Abbot: David and Charles.

Bernhardt, J. W. (1993) *Itinerant Kingship and Royal Monasteries in Early Medieval Germany, c. 936–1075.* Cambridge: University Press.

Besteman, J. C. (1989) The pre-urban development of Medemblik: from an early medieval trading centre to a medieval town. In H. A. Heidinga and H. H. van Regteren Altena (eds), *Medemblik and Monnickendam. Aspects of medieval urbanisation in northern Holland*, 1–30. Amsterdam: Universiteit van Amsterdam, Albert Egges van Giffen Instituut voor Prae- en Protohistorie.

Besteman, J. C. (1990) North Holland AD 400–1200: turning tide or tide turned? In J. C. Besteman, J. M. Bos and H. A. Heidinga (eds), *Medieval Archaeology in the Netherlands*, 91–120. Assen: Van Gorcum.

Biddle, M. (1962–3) Finds from the Fleam Dyke, Fen Ditton, *Proceedings of the Cambridge Antiquarian Society* 56/57, 125–127.

Biddle, M. (1976) Towns. In D. M Wilson (ed.), *The Archaeology of Anglo-Saxon England*, 99–150. London: Methuen.

Biddle, M. (1984) London on the Strand, *Popular Archaeology* 6.1, 23–7.

Biddle, M. (1990) Object and Economy in Medieval Winchester: *Winchester Studies* 7,2. Oxford: Clarendon.

Biddle, M. (2000) *Felix urbs Winthonia*: Winchester In the age of monastic reform. In D. A. E. Pelteret (ed.) *Anglo-Saxon History: Basic Readings*, 289–316. London and New York: Garland. Originally published in D. Parsons (ed. 1975) *Tenth-Century Studies: Essays in Commemoration of the Millenium of the Council of Winchester and the Regularis Concordia*, 123–140. Chichester and London: Phillimore.

Biddle, M. (ed. 2012) The Winchester Mint and Coins and Related Finds from the Excavations of 1961–71. *Winchester Studies* 8. Oxford: University Press.

Biddle, M. and Hill, D. (1971) Late Saxon Planned Towns, *Antiquaries Journal* 51, 70–85.

Birch, W. de G. (1885–99) *Cartularium Saxonicum.* 3 vols and index. London: Whiting.

Black, J. (1997) *Maps and History: Constructing Images of the Past.* New Haven, CT: Yale University Press.

Blackburn, M. A. S. (1989a) The Ashdon (Essex) hoard and the currency of the Southern Danelaw in the late ninth century. *British Numismatic Journal* 59, 13–38.

Blackburn, M. [A. S.] (1989b) The earliest Anglo-Viking coinage of the southern Danelaw (late 9th century). In I. A. Carradice (ed.), *Proceedings of the 10th International Congress of Numismatics, London 1986*, 341–8. London: International Association of Professional Numismatists.

Blackburn, M. [A. S.] (1996) Mints, burhs and the Grately Code cap. 14.2. In D. Hill and A. R. Rumble (eds), *The Defence of Wessex. The Burghal Hidage and Anglo-Saxon Fortifications*, 160–75. Manchester: University Press.

Blackburn, M. A. S. (1998) The London Mint in the Reign of Alfred. In M. A. S. Blackburn and D. N. Dumville (eds) *Kings, Currency and Alliances: History and Coinage in Southern England in the Ninth Century*, 105–23. Woodbridge: Boydell.

Blackburn, M. [A. S.] (2000) Metheltun not Medeshamstede: an Anglo-Saxon mint at Melton Mowbray rather than Peterborough Abbey. *British Numismatic Journal* 70, 143–5.

Blackburn, M. [A. S.] (2001) Expansion and control: aspects of Anglo-Scandinavian minting south of the Humber. In J. Graham-Campbell (ed.), *Vikings and the Danelaw. Select Papers from the Proceedings of the Thirteenth Viking Congress, Nottingham and York 21–30 August 1997*, 125–42. Oxford: Oxbow Books.

Blackburn, M. [A. S.] (2003a) Alfred's coinage reforms in context. In T. Reuter (ed.), *Alfred the Great*, 199–217. Aldershot: Ashgate.

Blackburn, M. [A. S.] (2003b) 'Productive' Sites and the Pattern of Coin Loss in England, 600–1180. In T. Pestell and K. Ulmschneider (eds), *Markets in Early Medieval Europe: Trading and 'Productive' Sites, 650–850*, 20–36. Macclesfield: Windgather.

Blackburn, M. [A. S.] (2004) The coinage of Scandinavian York. In R. Hall (ed.), *Aspects of Anglo-Scandinavian York, Archaeology of York* 8/4, 325–49. York: York Archaeological Trust.

Blackburn, M. [A. S.] (2005) Currency under the Vikings. Part 1: Guthrum and the earliest Danelaw coinages. *British Numismatic Journal* 75, 18–43.

Blackburn, M. [A. S.] (2006a) Currency under the Vikings. Part 2: The two Scandinavian kingdoms of the Danelaw, *c. 895–954. British Numismatic Journal* 76, 204–26.

Blackburn, M.[A. S.] (2006b) Two new types of Anglo-Saxon gold shillings. In B. Cook and G. Williams (eds), *Coinage and History in the North Sea World, AD 500–1250: Essays in Honour of Marion Archibald,* 129–35. Leiden: Brill.

Blackburn, M.[A. S.] (2011) *Viking Coinage and Currency in the British Isles,* British Numismatic Society Special Publication 7. London: British Numismatic Society.

Blackburn, M. and Leahy, K. (1996) A Lincoln mint-signed coin from the reign of Edgar, *Numismatic Chronicle* 156, 239–41.

Blackburn, M. and Keynes, S. (1998) A corpus of the Cross-and-Lozenge and related coinages of Alfred, Ceolwulf II and Archbishop Æthelred. In M. A. S. Blackburn and D. N. Dumville (eds), *Kings, Currency and Alliances. History and Coinage of Southern England in the Ninth Century,* 125–50. Woodbridge: Boydell and Brewer.

Blackburn, M. and Pagan, H. (2002) The St Edmund coinage in the light of a parcel from a hoard of St Edmund pennies. *British Numismatic Journal* 72, 1–14.

Blackburn, M. A. S., Bonser, M. J. and Conte, W. J. (1993) A new type of Edward the Confessor for the 'Newport' mint. *British Numismatic Journal* 63, 125–6.

Blair, J. (1994) *Anglo-Saxon Oxfordshire.* Thrupp: Alan Sutton Publishing.

Blair, J. (1997) Palaces or minsters? Northampton and Cheddar reconsidered, *ASE* 25, 97–121.

Blair, J. (2005) *The Church in Anglo-Saxon Society.* Oxford: University Press.

Blair, P. (1955) The Northumbrians and their Southern Frontier, *Archaeologia Aeliana* 4.26, 98–126.

Blunt, C. E. (1974) The coinage of Athelstan, king of England 924–939. *British Numismatic Journal* 42, 35–160.

Blunt, C. E. (1985) Northumbrian coins in the name of Alwaldus. *British Numismatic Journal* 55, 192–4.

Blunt, C. E. and Lyon, C. S. S. (1990) Some notes on the mints of Wilton and Salisbury. In K. Jonsson (ed.), *Studies in late Anglo-Saxon coinage in memory of Bror Emil Hildebrand. Svenska Numismatiska Foreningen Numismatiska Meddelanden* 35, 25–34. Stockholm: Swedish Numismatic Society.

Blunt, C. E., Stewart, B. H .I. H. and Lyon, C. S. S. (1989) *Coinage in Tenth-Century England from Edward the Elder to Edgar's Reform.* Oxford: University Press.

Bond, E. A. (1873–8) *Facsimiles of Ancient Charters in the British Museum,* 4 vols. London: Trustees of the British Museum.

Boughton, D., Williams, G. and Ager, B. (2012) Viking hoards: buried wealth of the Norse North-West. *Current Archaeology* 264 (Mar. 2012), 26–31.

Bovey, A. (2005) *The Chaworth Roll.* London: Sam Fogg.

Bowlt, C. (2008) A possible extension to Grim's Dyke. In J. Clark, J. Cotton, J. Hall and H. Swain (eds), *Londinium and Beyond: essays on Roman London and its hinterland for Harvey Sheldon,* 107–111. York: Council for British Archaeology.

Brackmann, R. (2012) The Elizabethan invention of Anglo-Saxon England: Laurence Nowell, William Lambarde and the study of Old English, *Studies in Renaissance Literature* 30. Cambridge: D. S. Brewer.

Bray, W. (1783) *Sketch of a tour into Derbyshire and Yorkshire.* London: B. White.

Breeze, D. and Dobson, B. (2000) *Hadrian's Wall.* London: Penguin.

Brewster, T. C. M. (1957) Excavations at Newham's Pit, Staxton, 1947–8, *Yorkshire Archaeological Journal* 39, 193–223.

Brewster, T. C. M. (1963) T*he Excavation of Staple Howe.* Wintringham: East Riding Archaeological Research Committee.

Brewster, T. C. M. (1981) The Devil's Hill, *Current Archaeology* 76, 140–1.

Bristow, C. R. and Freshney, E. C. (2012) Regional geology. In R. Bryant, *Corpus of Anglo-Saxon Stone Sculpture, X, The Western Midlands,* 28–45. Oxford: University Press.

Brooks, N. P. (1971) The development of military obligations in eighth- and ninth-century England. In P. Clemoes and K. Hughes (eds), *England Before the Conquest,* 69–84. Cambridge: University Press.

Brooks, N. P. (1996) The administrative background of the Burghal Hidage. In D. Hill and A. R. Rumble (eds), *The Defence of Wessex. The Burghal Hidage and Anglo-Saxon Fortifications,* 128–50. Manchester: University Press.

Brooks, N. [P.] (2005) Introduction: how do we know about St Wulfstan? In J. Barrow and N. Brooks (eds), *St Wulfstan and his World,* 1–21. Aldershot: Ashgate.

Brooks, N. P. (2011) Why is the *Anglo-Saxon Chronicle* about kings? *ASE* 39, 43–70.

Brooks, N. [P.] and Cubitt, C. (eds 1996) *St Oswald of Worcester: life and influence.* London: Leicester University Press.

Brooks, N. P. and Kelly, S. E. (eds 2013) *The Charters of Christ Church, Canterbury,* 2 pts. Oxford: University Press.

Brown, D. (1991). *Bury my Heart at Wounded Knee.* London: Vintage.

Bruce, J. (ed. 1853) *Correspondence of Matthew Parker D.D., Archbishop of Canterbury.* Cambridge: University Press.

Bryant, R. (1999) Sculpture and architectural stone. In C. Heighway and R. Bryant, *The Golden Minster: the Anglo-Saxon minster and later medieval priory of St Oswald at Gloucester,* CBA Research Report 117, 146–93. York: Council for British Archaeology.

Bryant, R. (2012) *Corpus of Anglo-Saxon Stone Sculpture, X, The Western Midlands.* Oxford: University Press.

Buchanan, M., Jermy, K. E. and Petch, D. F. (1975) Watling Street in the Grounds of Eaton Hall: excavations north of Garden Lodge, 1970–1. *Chester Archaeological Journal* 58, 1–14.

Burne, A. (1950) Ancient Wiltshire battlefields, *Wiltshire Archaeological Magazine* 53, 397–412.

Burrow, I. C. G. (1981) *Hillfort and Hill-top Settlement in Somerset in the First Millenium AD.* British Archaeological Report 91. Oxford: British Archaeological Reports

Burrow, I. C. G. (1982) Hillforts and hilltops – 1000 BC to 1000 AD. In M. Aston and I. Burrow (eds), *The Archaeology of Somerset – a Review to 1500 AD,* 83–98. Taunton: Somerset County Council.

Bush, J. R. E. (1974) Langport. In R. Dunning (ed.), *A History of the County of Somerset, Volume III [VCH Somerset iii],* 16–38. London and Oxford: Oxford University Press for the Institute of Historical Research.

Caird, Sir J. (1852) *English Agriculture in 1850–51.* London: [s.n.].

Calder, J. (2004) Early ecclesiastical sites in Somerset: three case studies, *Proceedings of the Somerset Archaeological and Natural History Society* 147, 1–28.

Camden, W. *Britannia* … London: R. Newbery, 1586; London, Bishop's Court Press, Georg. Bishop, 1660; London: Georgii Bishop & Ioannis Norton, 1607.

Cameron, K. (1978) The minor names and field-names of the Holland Division of Lincolnshire. In T. Andersson and K. I. Sandred (eds), *The Vikings,* 81–8. Uppsala: Almqvist and Wiksell.

Cameron, K. (1996) *English Place Names*. New edition. London: Batsford.

Campbell, A. (1959) *Old English Grammar*. Oxford: Clarendon.

Campbell, J. (ed. 1982) *The Anglo-Saxons*. Oxford: Phaidon.

Campbell, J. (2001) What is not known about the reign of Edward the Elder? In N. J. Higham and D. H. Hill (eds), *Edward the Elder 899–924*, 12–24. London and New York: Routledge.

Campbell, J. (2010) Secular and political contexts. In S. DeGregorio (ed.), T*he Cambridge Companion to Bede*, 25–39. Cambridge: University Press.

Carelli, P. and Kresten, P. (1997) Give us this day our daily Bread: a study of Late Viking Age and Medieval Quernstones in South Scandinavia, *Acta Archaeologica* 68, 109–137.

Chapman, V. (1953) Open fields in West Cheshire. *Transactions of the Historical Society of Lancashire and Cheshire* 104, 35–60.

Charles-Edwards, T. M. (1972) Kinship, Status and the Origins of the Hide. *Past and Present* 56, 3–33.

Charlton, B. and Mitcheson, M. (1984) The Roman cemetery at Petty Knowes, Rochester, Northumberland [16 burials in small circular barrows, late 2nd–early 3rd century], *Archaeologia Aeliana* 5th series 12, 1–31.

Cheney, M., Smith, D., Brooke, C. and Hoskin, P. M. (eds 2007) *English Episcopal Acta, 33, Worcester 1062–1185*. Oxford: University Press.

Clark, J. (1954) *Excavations at Star Carr: An Early Mesolithic site at Seamer near Scarborough, Yorkshire*. Cambridge: University Press.

Clark, J. (1999) King Alfred's London and London's King Alfred. *London Archaeologist* 9, 35–8.

Clark Hall, J. R. *A Concise Anglo-Saxon Dictionary*. 4th ed. Toronto: University Press.

Clarke, W. N. and Symons, D. (2007) The mint of Aylesbury. *British Numismatic Journal* 77, 173–89.

Clemoes, P. (ed. 1997) *Ælfric's Catholic Homilies: The First Series: Text*, Early English Text Society Supplementary Series 17. Oxford: University Press.

Colgrave, B. and Mynors, R. A. B. (eds 1969) *Bede's Ecclesiastical History of the English People*. Oxford: Clarendon Press.

Collen, G. W. (1833) *Britannia Saxonica: a map of Britain during the Saxon octarchy*. London: William Pickering.

Cooper, A. R. (2006) *Bridges, Law and Power in Medieval England, 700–1400*. Woodbridge: Boydell.

Corder, P. and Kirk, J. L. (1928) Roman Malton: a Yorkshire Fortress and its neighbourhood. *Antiquity* 2.1, 69–82.

Costen, M. (2011) *Anglo-Saxon Somerset*. Oxford: Oxbow Books.

Couppé, J. (1987) *La Calotterie: L'Officine de Potiers Gallo-Romaine et La Nécropole Carolingienne*. Etaples: Société Quentovic.

Cowie, R. (1987) *Lundenwic*: 'Unravelling the Strand'. *Archaeology Today* 8.5, 30–4.

Cowie, R. (2001) Mercian London. In M. Brown and A. Farr (ed.), *Mercia – An Anglo-Saxon Kingdom in Europe*, 194–209. London and New York: Continuum.

Cowie, R. (2004) The evidence for royal sites in Middle Anglo-Saxon London, *Medieval Archaeology* 48, 201–9.

Cowie, R. and Whytehead, R. (1989) *Lundenwic*: The Archaeological Evidence for Middle Saxon London, *Antiquity* 63, 706–18.

Cramp, R. (2005) *Wearmouth and Jarrow Monastic Sites*, vol. 1. Swindon: English Heritage.

Crampton, C. (1966) An interpretation of the pollen and soils in cross-ridge dykes in Glamorgan, *Bulletin of the Board of Celtic Studies* 21.4, 376–90.

Crawford, S. J. (ed. 1969) *The Old English Version of the Heptateuch*, Aelfric's Treatise on the Old and New Testament, and his Preface to Genesis, Early English Text Society original series 160. London: Oxford University Press.

Crick, J. (2011) Script and the sense of the past in Anglo-Saxon England. In J. Roberts and L. Webster (eds), *Anglo-Saxon Traces, Medieval and Renaissance Studies* 405, 1–29. Tempe, AZ: Arizona Center for Medieval and Renaissance Studies.

Croft, R. A. and Adkins, R. (1988) East Lyng, Locketts Cottage, *Proceedings of the Somerset Archaeological and Natural History Society* 132, 222–4.

Crook, J. (2005) The physical setting of the cult of St Wulfstan. In J. Barrow and N. Brooks (eds), *St Wulfstan and his World*, 189–217. Aldershot: Ashgate.

Cubbin, G. P. (ed. 1996) *MS D*. The Anglo-Saxon Chronicle: a collaborative edition 6, eds D. Dumville and S. Keynes. Cambridge: D. S. Brewer.

Cubitt, C. (2009) 'As the lawbook teaches': Reeves, lawbooks and urban life in the anonymous Old English *Legend of the Seven Sleepers. English Historical Review* 124 (510), 1021–149.

Cullen, P., Jones, R. and Parsons, D. N. (2011) *Thorps in a Changing Landscape*. Hatfield: University of Hertfordshire Press.

Cunliffe, B. (1984) Saxon Bath. In J. Haslam (ed.), *Anglo-Saxon Towns in Southern England*, 345–58. Chichester: Phillimore.

Darby, H. C. and Finn, R. W. (eds 1967) *The Domesday Geography of South-West England*. Cambridge: University Press.

Darlington, R. R. (ed. 1968) *The Cartulary of Worcester Cathedral Priory (register I)*, Pipe Roll Society new series 38. London: Pipe Roll Society.

Darlington, R. R. and McGurk, P. (eds 1995) *The Chronicle of John of Worcester, II, The Annals from 450 to 1066*. Oxford: Clarendon.

de Thoyras, R. (1732) *The History of England*, trans. N. Tindal. London: James, John and Paul Knapton.

Deedes, C. (ed. 1913–14/1924) *Registrum Johannis de Pontissara episcopi Wintoniensis 1282–1304*, Canterbury and York Society 19 and 30. London: Canterbury and York Society.

Dekker, K. (2007) Anglo-Saxon encyclopaedic notes: tradition and function. In R. H. Bremmer and K. Dekker (eds), *Foundations of Learning: the Transfer of Encyclopaedic Knowledge in the Early Middle Ages*, 279–315. Leuven: Peeters.

Dixon, P. (1993) The Anglo-Saxon Settlement at Mucking: an interpretation, *Anglo-Saxon Studies in Archaeology and History* 6, 125–147.

Dobbie, E. V. K. (ed. 1942) *The Anglo-Saxon Minor Poems*. The Anglo-Saxon Poetic Records vol. VI. New York: Columbia University Press.

Dobbie, E. V. K. (ed. 1953) *Beowulf and Judith*. The Anglo-Saxon Poetic Records vol. IV. London: Routledge and Kegan Paul.

Dodgson, J. McN. (1970) *The Place-Names of Cheshire Part 2*. English Place-Name Society XLV. Cambridge: University Press.

Dodgson, J. McN. (1972) *The Place-Names of Cheshire Part 4*. English Place-Name Society XLVII. Cambridge: University Press.

Dodgson, J. McN. (1996) A linguistic analysis of the place-names of the Burghal Hidage. In D. Hill and A. R. Rumble (eds), *The Defence of Wessex. The Burghal Hidage and Anglo-Saxon Fortifications*, 98–121. Manchester: University Press.

Dodwell, C. R. (1982) *Anglo-Saxon Art: a new perspective*. Manchester: University Press.

Dodwell, C. R. and Clemoes, P. (eds 1974) *The Old English illustrated Hexateuch. British Museum Cotton Claudius B. IV*. Early English manuscripts in facsimile 18. Copenhagen: Rosenkilde and Bagger.

Dolley, R. H. M. (1952–54) A new Anglo-Saxon mint – Medeshamstede, *British Numismatic Journal* 27, 263–5.

Dolley, R. H. M. (1954) The sack of Wilton in 1003 and the chronology of the Long Cross and Helmet types of Ethelred II, *Saertryck af Nordisk Numismatisk Unions Medlemsblad* 5, 152–6.

Dolley, R. H. M. and Metcalf, D. M. (1955–7) Two stray finds from St. Albans of coins of Offa and of Charlemagne, *British Numismatic Journal* 28, 459–66.

Draper, S. (2008) The significance of Old English *Burh* in Anglo-Saxon England, *Anglo-Saxon Studies in Archaeology and History* 15, 240–253.

Dugdale, W. (1817–30) *Monasticon Anglicanum*, eds J. Caley, H. Ellis and B. Bandinel, 6 vols in 8. London: Longman [and others]

Dumville, D. N. (1976) The Anglian collection of royal genealogies and regnal lists, *ASE* 5, 23–50.

Dunning, G. C. (1956) Trade relations between England and the Continent in the late Anglo-Saxon period. In D. B. Harden (ed.), *Dark-Age Britain: studies presented to E. T. Leeds*, 218–33. London: Methuen.

Dunning, R. W. (1975) Ilchester: a study in continuity, *Proceedings of the Somerset Archaeology and Natural History Society* 119, 44–50.

Dunning, R. W. (1985) St Decumans, including Watchet and Williton, *A History of the County of Somerset, Volume V [VCH Somerset v]*, 143–71. London and Oxford: Oxford University Press for the Institute of Historical Research.

Dyer, C. C. (1968–9) The Saxon Cathedrals of Worcester. In P. Barker (ed.), *The Origins of Worcester. Transactions of the Worcestershire Archaeological Society* 3rd. series 2, 34.

Dyson, T. (1978) Two Saxon land grants for Queenhithe. In J. Bird, H. Chapman and J. Clark (eds), *Collectanea Londiniensia: Studies presented to Ralph Merrifield*, 200–15. London: London and Middlesex Archaeological Society.

Dyson, T. (1990) King Alfred and the restoration of London. *The London Journal* 15.2, 99–110.

Dyson, T. and Schofield, J. (1980) *Archaeology of the City of London*. London: City of London Archaeological Trust.

Dyson, T. and Schofield, J. (1984) Saxon London. In J. Haslam (ed.) *Anglo-Saxon Towns in Southern England*, 285–313. Chichester: Phillimore.

Eaglen, R. J. (1999) The mint of Huntingdon. *British Numismatic Journal* 69, 47–145.

Eaglen, R. J. (2001) The ranking of mints in the reign of Edward the Confessor. *Spink Numismatic Circular* 109, 361–2.

Eaglen, R. J. (2002) Further coins from the mint of Huntingdon. *British Numismatic Journal* 72, 15–19.

Eaglen, R. J. (2006) *The Abbey and Mint of Bury St Edmunds to 1279*. British Numismatic Society Special Publication 4. London, British Numismatic Society.

Earle, J. (1888) *A hand-book to the land-charters and other Saxonic documents*. Oxford: Clarendon.

Ellmers, D. (1972) *Frühmittelalterlichen Handelschiffart in Mittel-und Nordeuropa*. Neumunster: Wachholtz.

Ellmers, D. (1974) Nautical Archaeology in Germany. *International Journal of Nautical Archaeology* 3, 137–45.

Engel, U. (trans. H. Heltay 2007) *Worcester Cathedral: an architectural history*. Chichester, Phillimore.

Erskine, J. (2007) The west Wansdyke: an appraisal of the dating, dimensions and construction techniques in the light of excavated evidence, *The Archaeological Journal* 164, 80–108.

Erskine, R. W. H. (ed. 1986) *Great Domesday: facsimile*. London: Alecto.

Erskine, R. W. H. (gen. ed. 1988) *The Cheshire Domesday, Folios and Maps*, Cheshire: Folios 262–70. London: Editions Alecto (Domesday) Limited.

Evans, J. (1915) *Poems from the Books of Taliesin*. Llanberog: Tremvan.

Everson, P. and Stocker, D. (1999) *Corpus of Anglo-Saxon Stone Sculpture, V, Lincolnshire*. Oxford: University Press.

Falkus, M. and Gillingham, J. (1981) *Historical Atlas of Britain*. London: Granada.

Fellows Jensen, G. (1978) *Scandinavian Settlement Names in the East Midlands*. Copenhagen: Akademisk Forlag.

Fellows-Jensen, G. (1985) Scandinavian Settlement Names in the North-West. Copenhagen: C. A. Reitzels Forlag.

Fellows-Jensen, G. (1988) Danske stednavne på -by i England og det sydlige Skotland fra vikingetiden. In J. K. Hellesen and O. Tuxen (eds), *Historisk Atlas Danmark*. Copenhagen: G. E. C. Gads Forlag.

Fellows-Jensen, G. (1989–90) Scandinavians in southern Scotland? *Nomina* 13, 41–60.

Fellows-Jensen, G. (1991) Scandinavians in Dumfriesshire and Galloway: the place-name evidence. In R. D. Oram and G. P. Stell (eds), *Galloway Land and Lordship*, 77–95. Edinburgh: Scottish Society for Northern Studies.

Fellows-Jensen, G. (1998) Little thwaite, who made thee? *Proceedings of the XIXth International Congress of Onomastic Sciences* 2, 101–6. Aberdeen: Department of English.

Fellows-Jensen, G. (2007) Nordic and English in East Anglia in the Viking period. *Nowele* 50/51, 93–108.

Fellows-Jensen, G. (2009) A few more words on place-names in thorp in England. In P. Dam *et al.* (eds), *Torp som ortnamn och bebyggelse*, 43–53. Lund: Institutet för språk och folkminnen.

Fenwick, V. (1978) *The Graveney Boat*. British Archaeological Report 53. Oxford: British Archaeological Reports.

Feveile, C. (1995) *Tufstenkirkerne i Sydvestjylland – set i handelshistorisk arkaeologisk Belysning. By, marsk og geest* [Ribe Museum (Antikvariske Samlung)] 8, 31–51.

Feveile, C. (2010) Myen lava Quern Stones from the Ribe Excavations 1970–76. In M. Bencard and H. B. Madsen (eds), *Ribe Excavations 1970–76* 6, 133–56. Hojbjerg: Jutland Archaeological Society.

Finberg, H. P. R. (1964) *The Early Charters of Wessex*. Leicester: Leicester University Press.

Finberg, H. P. R. (1972a) *Anglo-Saxon England A.D. 43–1042*. The Agrarian History of Britain, vol. I.ii. Cambridge: University Press.

Finberg, H. P. R. (1972b) *The Early Charters of the West Midlands*. 2nd ed. Leicester: University Press.

Fleming, R. (1993) Rural elites and urban communities in late-Saxon England. *Past and Present* 141, 3–37.

Fletcher, H. G. *et al.* (eds 2007) *The Wormsley Library: a Personal Selection by Sir Paul Getty K. B. E.*, 2nd ed. London: Maggs Bros.

Foot, S. (2000) *Veiled Women*, 2 vols. Aldershot: Ashgate.

Foot, S. (2010) Church and monastery in Bede's Northumbria. In S. DeGregorio (ed.) *The Cambridge Companion to Bede*, 54–68. Cambridge: University Press.

Foot, S. (2013) Wilfrid's monastic empire. In N. J. Higham (ed.), *Wilfrid: Abbot, Bishop, Saint. Papers from the 1300th Anniversary Conferences*, 27–39. Donington: Shaun Tyas.

Foreman, S., Hiller J, and Petts D. (2002) *Gathering the People, Settling the Land: The archaeology of a Middle Thames landscape, Anglo-Saxon to post-medieval.* Thames Valley Archaeological Monograph 14, Oxford: Oxford Archaeology.

Fowler, P. J. (1971) Hillforts AD 400–700. In M. Jesson and D. Hill (eds), *The Iron-Age and its Hillforts; papers presented to Sir Mortimer Wheeler on the occasion of his eightieth year,* 203–13. Southampton: Southampton University Archaeological Society.

Fowler, P. [J.] (2002) *Farming in the First millennium AD: British agriculture between Julius Caesar and William the Conqueror.* Cambridge: University Press.

Fox, C. (1955) *Offa's Dyke: A field survey of the western frontier-works of Mercia in the seventh and eighth centuries AD.* London: Oxford University Press.

Fox, C., Palmer, W. and Duckworth, W. (1924–5). Excavations in the Cambridgeshire Dykes: V: Bran or Heydon Ditch, first report, *Proceedings of the Cambridge Antiquarian Society* 27, 16–42.

Fox, J. (1576) *The first(-second) volume of the Ecclesiasticall History ... [Book of Martyrs].* London: John Daye.

Franks, J. W. (1957) Pollen analysis: a technique for investigating early agrarian history. *The Agricultural History Review* 5.1, 2–10.

Frantzen, A. J. and Moffat, D. (eds 1994) *The Work of Work: servitude, slavery, and labor in medieval England.* Rochester, NY: Boydell and Brewer.

Freeman, A. (1983–85) Reading: its status and standing as a minor Late Anglo-Saxon mint. *Berkshire Archaeological Journal* 72, 53–8.

Freeman, A. (1985) *The Moneyer and the Mint in the Reign of Edward the Confessor.* British Archaeological Report 145, 2 vols. Oxford: British Archaeological Reports.

Freeman, E. A. (1867–79) *A History of the Norman Conquest of England,* 6 vols. Oxford: University Press.

Freshwater, T. (1996), A lava quern workshop in late Saxon London. *London Archaeologist* 8.2, 39–45.

Fryde, E. B., Greenway, D. E., Porter, S. and Roy, I (eds 1986) *Handbook of British Chronology.* 3rd ed. London: Royal Historical Society.

Gammeltoft, P. (2003) 'I sauh a tour on a toft, tryelyche i-maket', part two: on place-names in -toft in England, *Nomina* 26, 43–63.

Gelling, M. (1973–74), *The Place-Names of Berkshire Parts One and Two,* English Place-Name Society Volumes XLIX–L, Cambridge: English Place-Name Society.

Gelling, M. (1976) The evidence of place-names. In P. H. Sawyer (ed.), *Medieval Settlement,* 200–11. London: Edward Arnold.

Gelling, M. (1984) *Place-Names in the Landscape.* London: J. M. Dent.

Gelling, M. (1988), *Signposts to the Past: Place-names and the history of England.* 2nd ed. Chichester: Phillimore.

Gelling, M. (1992) *The West Midlands in the Early Middle Ages.* Leicester: University Press.

Gelling, M., and Cole, A. (2000) *The Landscape of Place-Names.* Stamford: Shaun Tyas.

Gem, R. D. H. (1980) The Romanesque rebuilding of Westminster Abbey, *Anglo-Norman Studies* 3, 33–60, 203–9.

Gibson, E. (1692) *Chronicon Saxonicum.* Oxford: Sheldon.

Gibson, E. (1695) *Camden's Britannia, Newly Translated into English; with Large Additions and Improvements.* London: printed by F. Collins, for A. Swalle and A. & J. Churchil. Facsimile edition, with an introduction by S. Piggott and a bibliographical note by G. Walters. Newton Abbot: David and Charles Reprints, 1971.

Gillmor, C. (1988) The logistics of fortified bridge-building on the Seine under Charles the Bald, *Anglo-Norman Studies 11: Proceedings of the Battle Conference 1988,* 87–105.

Gluhak, T. M. and Hofmeister, W. (2008) Provenance analysis of Roman millstones: mapping of trade in Roman Europe. In R. I. Kostov, B. Gaydarska and M. Gurova (eds), *Geoarchaeology and Archaeomineralogy; Proceedings of the International Conference, Sofia, 29–30 October 2008,* 111–5. Sofia: St Ivan Rilski Publishing House.

Gluhak, T. M. and Hofmeister, W. (2009) Roman lava quarries in the Eifel region (Germany): geochemical data for millstone provenance studies, *Journal of Archaeological Science* 36.8, 1774–82.

Gluhak, T. M. and Hofmeister, W. (2011) Geochemical provenance analysis of Roman lava millstones north of the Alps; a study of their distribution and implications for the beginning of Roman lava quarrying in the Eifel region, *Journal of Archaeological Science* 38.7, 1603–1620.

Gneuss, H. (2001) *Handlist of Anglo-Saxon Manuscripts: A list of manuscripts and manuscript fragments written or owned in England up to 1100.* Medieval and Renaissance Texts and Studies, 241. Tempe, AZ: Arizona Center for Medieval and Renaissance Studies.

Godsal, P. (1913) *Woden's, Grim's and Offa's Dykes.* London: Harrison and Sons.

Goffart, W. (1997) The first venture into 'medieval geography': Lambarde's map of the Saxon heptarchy (1568). In J. Roberts and J. L. Nelson, with M. Godden (eds), *Alfred the Wise: Studies in honour of Janet Bately on the occasion of her sixty-fifth birthday,* 53–60. Cambridge: D. S. Brewer.

Goffin, R. (2003) The quernstones. In G. Malcolm, D. Bowsher and R. Cowie (eds), *Middle Saxon London: Excavations at the Royal Opera House 1989–91.* Museum of London Archaeological Service Monograph 15. London: Museum of London.

Goodrich, M. (1994) The White Ladies of Worcester: their place in contemporary medieval life, *Transactions of the Worcestershire Archaeological Society* 3rd series 14, 129–47.

Goodrich, M. (2008) *Worcester Nunneries: the nuns of the medieval diocese.* Chichester: Phillimore.

Graham, T. (2000) John Joscelyn, pioneer of Old English lexicography. In T. Graham (ed.), *The Recovery of Old English: Anglo-Saxon studies in the sixteenth and seventeenth centuries,* 83–140. Kalamazoo, MI: Medieval Institute, Western Michigan University.

Grant, E. (1985) Langport, Bow Street, *Proceedings of the Somerset Archaeological and Natural History Society* 129, 16–17.

Gray, H. L. (1915) *English Field Systems.* Cambridge MA: Harvard University Press.

Green, S. (1971) Wansdyke, Excavations 1966 to 1970, *The Wiltshire Archaeological and Natural History Magazine* 66, 129–146.

Green, V. (1796) *The History and Antiquities of the City and Suburbs of Worcester,* 2 vols. London: W. Bulmer.

Greenway, D. (ed. and trans. 1996) *Henry, Archdeacon of Huntingdon, Historia Anglorum: The History of the English People.* Oxford: Clarendon Press.

Greenwell, W. (1877) *British Barrows, a Record of the Examination of Sepulchral Mounds in Various Parts of England.* Oxford: Clarendon.

Gretsch, M. (2001) Winchester vocabulary and Standard Old English: the vernacular in late Anglo-Saxon England. The Toller Memorial Lecture 2000, *Bulletin of the John Rylands University Library of Manchester* 83, 41–87.

Grierson, P. and Blackburn, M. (1986) *Medieval European Coinage with a Catalogue of the Coins in the Fitzwilliam Museum.* Cambridge: University Press.

Grimshaw, T. S. (1829) *A memoir of the Rev. Legh Richmond*, New York, J. Leavitt; Boston, Crocker and Brewster.

Grocock, C. W. (2013) Wilfrid, Benedict Biscop and Bede – the Monk who knew too much? In N. J. Higham (ed.), *Wilfrid: Abbot, Bishop, Saint. Papers from the 1300th Anniversary Conferences*, 93–111. Donington: Shaun Tyas.

Grocock, C. W., and Wood, I. (2013) *Abbots of Wearmouth and Jarrow.* Oxford Medieval Texts. Oxford: University Press.

Grundy, G. B. (1927) The Saxon Charters of Somerset. *Proceedings of the Somerset Archaeological and Natural History Society* 73, appendix, 1–32.

Gryson, R. (ed. 2007) *Biblia sacra iuxta vulgatam versionem.* 5th ed. Stuttgart: Deutsche Bibelgesellschaft.

Gunn, V. (2009) *Bede's Historiae: Genre, rhetoric and the construction of Anglo-Saxon church history.* Woodbridge: Boydell.

Guy, C. (1994) Excavations at Worcester Cathedral, 1981–1991, *Transactions of the Worcestershire Archaeological Society* 3rd series 14, 1–73.

Guy, C. (2011) The Refectory Undercroft. In C. Guy (ed.), *Archaeology at Worcester Cathedral: Report of the Twentieth Annual Symposium, March 2010*, 2–11. Worcester: Dean and Chapter of Worcester.

Halpin, P. (1994) Women religious in late Anglo-Saxon England, *Haskins Society Journal* 6, 97–110.

Halsall, G. (1989) Anthropology and the study of pre-Conquest warfare and society: The ritual war in Anglo-Saxon England. In S. C. Hawkes (ed.), *Weapons and Warfare in Anglo-Saxon England*, 155–177. Oxford: Oxford University Committee for Archaeology.

Hamer, R. F. S. (1970) *A Choice of Anglo-Saxon Verse.* London: Faber.

Hamerow, H. (1993) *Excavations at Mucking Volume 2: The Anglo-Saxon Settlement*, English Heritage Research Report 21. London: English Heritage in association with British Museum Press.

Hamerow H. (2002) *Early Medieval Settlements, The Archaeology of Rural Communities in North-West Europe 400–900.* Oxford: University Press.

Hamerow H. (2012) *Rural Settlements and Society in Anglo-Saxon England.* Oxford: University Press.

Hankinson, R. and Caseldine, A. (2006) Short dykes of Powys and their origins, *The Archaeological Journal* 163, 264–269.

Hanson, W. and Maxwell, G. (1983) *Rome's North west Frontier: the Antonine Wall.* Edinburgh: University Press.

Hare, M. (1997) Kings, crowns and festivals: the origins of Gloucester as a royal ceremonial centre, *Transactions of the Bristol and Gloucestershire Archaeological Society* 115, 41–78.

Harmer, F. E. (1952) *Anglo-Saxon Writs.* Manchester: University Press.

Hart, C. (1977). The Kingdom of Mercia. In A. Dornier (ed.), *Mercian Studies*, 43–61. Leicester: University Press.

Hart, C. (2006) *Chronicles of the Reign of Æthelred the Unready: an edition and translation of the Old English and Latin Annals.* Lampeter: Edwin Mellen Press.

Hart, S. (1995) The Aldewerke and Minster at Shelford, Cambridgeshire, *Anglo-Saxon Studies in Archaeology and History* 8, 43–68.

Haslam, J. (1984a) The towns of Devon. In J. Haslam (ed.) *Anglo-Saxon Towns in Southern England*, 249–83. Chichester: Phillimore.

Haslam, J. (1984b) The towns of Wiltshire. In J. Haslam (ed.) *Anglo-Saxon Towns in Southern England*, 87–148. Chichester: Phillimore.

Haslam, J. (2005) King Alfred and the Vikings: strategies and tactics, 876–886 AD, *Anglo-Saxon Studies in Archaeology and History* 13, 121–153.

Haslam, J. (2009) The development of late Saxon Christchurch, Dorset, and the Burghal Hidage, *Medieval Archaeology* 53, 95–108.

Haslam, J. (2010) The development of London by King Alfred: a reassessment, *Transactions of the London and Middlesex Archaeological Society* 61, 109–43.

Haslam, J. (2011a) Daws Castle, Somerset, and civil defence measures in southern and midland England in the ninth to eleventh centuries, *Archaeological Journal* 168, 196–227.

Haslam, J. (2011b) King Alfred, Mercia and London, 874–886: a reassessment, *Anglo-Saxon Studies in Archaeology and History* 17, 120–46.

Haslam, J. (2012) *Urban-rural Connections in Domesday Book and late Anglo-Saxon Royal Administration.* British Archaeological Report 571. Oxford: Archaeopress.

Haslam, J. (2013a) A probable late Saxon *burh* at Ilchester, *Somerset, Landscape History* 34.1, 5–22.

Haslam, J. (2013b) The *burh* of Wallingford and its context in Wessex. In J. Christie, K. S. B. Keats-Rohan, and D. R. Roffe (eds), *Wallingford: the Castle and Town in Context.* 400–407. British Archaeological Reports, British Series. Oxford: Archaeopress.

Haughton, C. A. and Powlesland, D. J. (1999) *West Heslerton – The Anglian Cemetery, Landscape Research Centre Archaeological Monographs 2 vols.* Yedingham: Landscape Research Centre.

Hayes, L. and Malim, T. (2008) The Date and Nature of Wat's Dyke: a Reassessment in the Light of Recent Investigations at Gobowen, Shropshire, *Anglo-Saxon Studies in Archaeology and History* 15, 147–179.

Hayward, P. A. (ed. 2010) *The Winchcombe and Coventry Chronicles: hitherto unnoticed witnesses to the work of John of Worcester.* Medieval and Renaissance Texts and Studies 373, 2 vols. Tempe AZ: Arizona Center for Medieval and Renaissance Studies.

Haywood, J. (1995) *The Penguin Historical Atlas of the Vikings.* London: Penguin Books.

Healey, A. diP. (ed. 2007). *Old English Dictionary: A–G.* Database. Toronto: University of Toronto.

Hearne, T. (ed. 1723) *Hemingi Chartularium Ecclesiæ Wigorniensis*, 2 vols. Oxford: E Theatro Sheldoniano.

Henderson, C. G. and Bidwell, P. T. (1982) The Saxon Minster at Exeter. In S. M. Pearce (ed.), *The Early Church in Western Britain and Ireland: studies presented to C.A. Ralegh Radford arising from a conference organised in his honour by the Devon Archaeological Society and Exeter City Museum*, BAR British Series 102, 145–176. Oxford: British Archaeological Reports.

Herendeen, W. H. (2007) *William Camden: a Life in Context.* Woodbridge: Boydell Press.

Herendeen, W. H. (2013) Later historians and Holinshed. In P. Kewes, I. W. Archer and F. Heal (eds), *The Oxford Handbook of Holinshed's 'Chronicles'*, 235–50. Oxford: University Press.

Heyworth, P. L. (1989). *Letters of Humfrey Wanley: Palaeographer, Anglo-Saxonist, Librarian 1672–1726.* Oxford: University Press.

Higham, N. J. (1988) The Cheshire Land-holdings of Earl Morcar, *Historical Society of Lancashire and Cheshire* 137, 139–47.

Higham, N. [J.] (1993a) *The Kingdom of Northumbria.* Stroud: Alan Sutton.

Higham, N. J. (1993b) *The Origins of Cheshire.* Manchester: University Press.

Higham, N. [J.] (1997) The Context of *Brunanburh*. In A. Rumble and A. Mills (eds), *Names, People and Places: An onomastic miscellany in memory of John McNeal Dodgson*, 144–56. Stamford: Paul Watkins.

Higham, N. J. (2000) The Tatton Park Project, Part 2: the medieval estates, settlements and halls. *Journal of the Chester Archaeological Society* 75, 61–133.

Higham, N. J. (2002) The Tatton Park Project, Part 3. *Journal of the Chester Archaeological Society* 76, 81-125.

Higham, N. J. (2004a) *A Frontier Landscape: The North West in the Middle Ages*. Macclesfield, Windgather Press.

Higham, N. [J.] (2004b). Northumbria's southern frontier: a review, *Early Medieval Europe* 14.4, 391–418.

Higham, N. J. and Cane, T. (1999) The Tatton Park Project, Part 1: Prehistoric to Sub-Roman Settlement and Land Use. *Journal of the Chester Archaeological Society* 74, 1–61.

Higham, N. J. and Hill, D. H. (eds 2001) *Edward the Elder*. London: Routledge.

Higham, N. J. and Ryan, M. J. (2013) *The Anglo-Saxon World*. New Haven, CT: Yale University Press.

Higson, P. J. W. (1993) Pointers towards the structure of agriculture in Handbridge and Claverton prior to Parliamentary Enclosure. *Transactions of the Historic Society of Lancashire and Cheshire* 142, 55–86.

Hilberg, V. (2009) Hedeby in Wulfstan's days: a Danish emporium of the Viking Age between East and West. In A. Englert and A. Trakadas (eds),Wulfstan's Voyage: the Baltic Sea region in the early Viking age as seen from shipboard. *Maritime Culture of the North* 2, 79–113. Roskilde: Viking Ship Museum in Roskilde.

Hill, D. [H.] (1967) The Burghal Hidage – Lyng, *Proceedings of the Somerset Archaeological and Natural History Society* 111, 64–6.

Hill, D. [H.] (1969) The Burghal Hidage: the establishment of a text, *Medieval Archaeology* 13, 84–92.

Hill, D. [H.] (1975–6) Bran Ditch – The Burials Reconsidered, *Proceedings of the Cambridge Antiquarian Society* 66, 126–9.

Hill, D. [H.] (1978) The Origins of the Saxon Towns. In P. Brandon (ed.), *The South Saxons*, 174–89. Chichester: Phillimore.

Hill, D. [H.] (1978) Trends in the development of towns during the reign of Ethelred the Unready. In D. Hill (ed.), *Ethelred the Unready: Papers from the Millenary Conference*, British Archaeological Report 59, 213–26. Oxford: British Archaeological Reports.

Hill, D. [H.] (1981) *An Atlas of Anglo-Saxon England 700–1066*. Oxford: Basil Blackwell.

Hill, D. [H.] (1982) The Anglo-Saxons 700–1000 AD. In M. Aston and I. Burrow (eds), *The Archaeology of Somerset – a Review to 1500 AD*, 109–18. Taunton: Somerset County Council.

Hill, D. [H.] (1985) The construction of Offa's Dyke, *Antiquaries Journal* 65.1, 140–2.

Hill, D. [H.] (1988) Unity and diversity – a framework for the study of European towns. In R. Hodges and B. Hobley (eds), *The Rebirth of Towns in the West AD 700–1050*, Council for British Archaeology Research Paper 68, 8–15. London: Council for British Archaeology.

Hill, D. [H.] (1996a) Gazetteer of Burghal Hidage sites. In D. Hill and A. R. Rumble (eds), *The Defence of Wessex. The Burghal Hidage and Anglo-Saxon Fortifications*, Appendix IV, 189–231. Manchester: University Press.

Hill, D. [H.] (1996b) The nature of the figures. In D. Hill and A. R. Rumble (eds), *The Defence of Wessex. The Burghal Hidage and Anglo-Saxon Fortifications*, 74–87. Manchester: University Press.

Hill, D. [H.] (2000) Athelstan's urban reforms, *Anglo-Saxon Studies in Archaeology and History* 11, 173–85.

Hill, D. [H.] (2000). Offa's Dyke: Pattern and purpose, *Antiquaries Journal* 80, 195–206.

Hill, D. H. (2001) End piece: definitions and superficial analysis. In D. H. Hill and R. Cowie (eds), *Wics: The early medieval trading centres of northern Europe*, 75–84. Sheffield: Academic Press.

Hill, D. H. (2010a) The Anglo-Saxon plough: A detail of the wheels. In N. J. Higham and M. J. Ryan (eds), *Landscape Archaeology of Anglo-Saxon England*, 169–74. Woodbridge: Boydell.

Hill, D. [H.] (2010b) *The Quality of Life Deerhurst Lecture 2005*. Deerhurst, The Friends of Deerhurst Church.

Hill, D. [H.] and Rumble, A. R. (eds 1996) *The Defence of Wessex. The Burghal Hidage and Anglo-Saxon Fortifications*. Manchester: University Press.

Hill, D. H. and Seddon, D. (1998) An unrecorded Anglo-Saxon cross shaft, now at Blackden, Holmes Chapel, Cheshire SJ 789 707. *Transactions of the Lancashire and Cheshire Antiquarian Society* 94, 145–9.

Hill, D. [H.] and Sharp, S. (1997) An Anglo-Saxon beacon system. In A. R. Rumble and A. D. Mills (eds), *Names, Places and People: an onomastic miscellany in memory of John McNeal Dodgson*, 157–65. Stamford: Paul Watkins.

Hill, D. [H.] and Worthington, M. (2003) *Offa's Dyke: History and guide*. Stroud: Tempus.

Hill, D. H., Barrett, D., Maude K., Warburton, J. and Worthington, M. (1990) *Quentovic* defined. *Antiquity* 64.242, 51–8.

Hill, D., Worthington, M., Warburton, J. and Barrett, D. (1992) The definition of the early medieval site of *Quentovic*, *Antiquity* 66 253, 965–9.

Hinchcliffe, J. (1975) Excavations at Grim's Ditch, Mongewell, 1974, *Oxoniensia* 40, 122–35.

Hind, A. M. (1952) *Engraving in England in the Sixteenth & Seventeenth Centuries: a descriptive catalogue with introductions, I: The Tudor period*. Cambridge: University Press.

Hingley, R. (2008) *The Recovery of Roman Britain 1586–1906: a Colony so Fertile*. Oxford: University Press.

Hirst, S. M. (1985) *An Anglo-Saxon Inhumation Cemetery at Sewerby, East Yorkshire*, York University Archaeological Publications 4. York, Department of Archaeology, University of York.

Hodges, R. (1982) *Dark Age Economics: The origins of towns and trade AD 600–1000*. London: Duckworth.

Hodges, R. (1989) *The Anglo-Saxon Achievement: archaeology and the beginnings of English society*. London: Duckworth.

Hodgkin, R. H. (1952) *A History of the Anglo-Saxons*, 2 vols (Oxford, 1935), 3rd ed. Oxford: University Press.

Holladay, J. A. (2010) Charting the past: visual configurations of myth and history and the English claim to Scotland. In R. A. Maxwell (ed.), *Representing History, 900–1300: Art, music, history*, 115–32, 232–5. University Park, PA: Pennsylvania State University Press.

Holmberg, B. (1946) *Tomt och toft som appellativ och ortnamnselement*. Uppsala: Lundequistska Bokhandeln.

Hooke, D. (1990) *Worcestershire Anglo-Saxon Charter-Bounds*. Studies in Anglo-Saxon History 2. Woodbridge: Boydell.

Hope-Taylor, B. (1975–6) The Devil's Dyke Investigations, 1973, *Proceedings of the Cambridge Antiquarian Society* 61, 123–6.

Hörter F., Michels, F. X. and Röder, J. (1951) Die Geschichte der Basaltlavaindustrie von Mayen und Niedermendig 1, *Jahrbuch für Geschichte und Kultur des Mittelrheins und seiner Nachbargebeite* 2, 1–32.

Hörter, F., Michels, F. X. and Röder, J. (1955) Die Geschichte der Basaltlavaindustrie von Mayen und Niedermendig 2, *Jahrbuch für Geschichte und Kultur des Mittelrheins und seiner Nachbargebeite* 6, 7–32.

Howard, I. (2003) *Swein Forkbeard's Invasions and the Danish Conquest of England*, 991–1017. Woodbridge: Boydell Press.

Howe, N. (2008) *Writing the Map of Anglo-Saxon England*. New Haven, CT: Yale University Press.

Hunter Blair, P. (2003) *An Introduction to Anglo-Saxon England*, 3rd ed. Cambridge: University Press.

Hutcheson, A. R. L. (2006) The origin of King's Lynn? – control of the wealth of the Wash prior to the Norman Conquest, *Medieval Archaeology* 50, 71–104.

Ingram, J. (trans.; 1823). *The Saxon Chronicle*. London: Longman.

Irvine, S. (ed. 2004) *MS. E*. The Anglo-Saxon Chronicle, a collaborative edition 7, eds D. Dumville. and S. Keynes. Cambridge: D. S. Brewer.

Jacob, K. A. (1984) The mint of Cambridge. *Seaby Coin and Medal Bulletin* 786, 34–43; 787, 72–6.

Jankuhn, H. (1963) *Haithabu, ein Handelsplatz der Wikingerzeit*. 4th ed. Neumunster: K. Wachholtz.

Jarman, A. (1988) *Aneirin: Y Gododdin*. Llandysul: Gomer Press.

Jarvis, K. S. (ed. 1983) *Excavations in Christchurch 1969–80*. Dorset Natural History and Archaeological Society, Monograph Series 5. Dorchester: Dorset Natural History and Archaeological Society.

Jellema, D. (1955) Frisian trade in the Dark Ages, *Speculum* 30, 15–36.

Jones, M. U. J. (1973) An ancient landscape palimpsest at Mucking, *Essex Archaeology and History* 5, 6–12.

Jones, M. U. J. (1974) The Mucking excavations 1974, *Journal of the Thurrock Local History Society* 18, 32–41.

Jones, M. U. J. (1979) Saxon sunken huts: problems of interpretation, *Archaeological Journal* 136, 53–9.

Jones, M. U. J. (1980) Mucking and the Early Saxon rural settlements in Essex. In D. Buckley (ed), *Archaeology in Essex to AD 1500*, Council for British Archaeology Research Report 34, 82–9. London: Council for British Archaeology.

Jonsson, K. (1987a) Grantham – a new Anglo-Saxon mint in Lincolnshire, *British Numismatic Journal* 57, 104–5.

Jonsson, K. (1987b) *The New Era: The Reformation of the Late Anglo-Saxon Coinage*, Commentationes de Nummis Saeculorum IX–XI in Suecia Repertis, new series 1. Stockholm: The Royal Coin Cabinet.

Jonsson, K. and van der Meer, G. (1990) Mints and moneyers *c*. 973–1066. In K. Jonsson (ed.), *Studies in Late Anglo-Saxon Coinage in Memory of Bror Emil Hildebrand*, Svenska Numismatiska Meddelanden 35, 47–136. Stockholm: Svenska Numismatiska Föreningen.

Kars, H. (1980) *Early Medieval Dorestad, an Archaeo-Petrological Study*, Part 1: General Introduction. The Tephrite Querns. Berichten van der Rijksdienst voor het Oudheidkundig Bodemonderzoek 30, 393–422.

Kelly, S. (1992) Trading privileges from eighth-century England. *Early Medieval Europe* 1, 3–28.

Kelly, S. E. (ed. 1998) *Charters of Selsey*. Anglo-Saxon Charters 6. Oxford: University Press.

Kelly, S. E. (ed. 2000–1) *Charters of Abingdon Abbey*. 2 vols. Anglo-Saxon Charters 8–9. Oxford: University Press.

Kelly, S. E. (ed. 2007) *Charters of Bath and Wells*. Anglo-Saxon Charters 13. Oxford: University Press.

Kelly, S. E. (ed. 2009) *Charters of Peterborough Abbey*. Anglo-Saxon Charters 14. Oxford: University Press.

Kemble, J. M. (1839–48) *Codex diplomaticus aevi Saxonici*. 6 vols. London: English Historical Society.

Kendall, C. (1988) Let us now praise a famous city: wordplay in the OE *Durham* and the cult of St Cuthbert. *Journal of English and Germanic Philology* 87, 507–521.

Kendrick, T. D. (1934) Maps illustrating the Viking invasions of England, *Saga-Book of the Viking Society* 11, 61–70.

Ker, N. R. (1948) Heming's Cartulary: a description of the two Worcester cartularies in Cotton Tiberius A. xiii. In R. W. Hunt, W. A. Pantin and R. W. Southern (eds), *Studies in Medieval History Presented to Frederick Maurice Powicke*, 49–75. Oxford: Clarendon.

Ker, N. R. (1957) *Catalogue of Manuscripts Containing Anglo-Saxon*. Oxford: Clarendon.

Ker, N. R. (1962) The Bodmer fragment of Ælfric's Homily for Septuagesima Sunday. In N. Davis and C. L. Wrenn (eds), *English and Medieval Studies Presented to J. R. R. Tolkien on the Occasion of his Seventieth Birthday*, 77–83. London: Allen and Unwin.

Ker, N. R. (1964). *Medieval Libraries of Great Britain: A list of surviving books*. London: Royal Historical Society.

Keynes, S. (1980) T*he Diplomas of King Æthelred 'the Unready': A Study in their Use as Historical Evidence*. Cambridge: University Press.

Keynes, S. (1992) George Harbin's Transcript of the lost Cartulary of Athelney Abbey, *Proceedings of the Somerset Archaeological and Natural History Society* 136, 149–59.

Keynes, S. (1994) Cnut's earls. In A. R. Rumble (ed.) *The Reign of Cnut: King of England, Denmark and Norway*, 43–88. London: Leicester University Press.

Keynes, S. (1997) Anglo-Saxon entries in the 'Liber Vitae' of Brescia. In J. Roberts and J. L. Nelson, with M. Godden (eds), A*lfred the Wise: Studies in honour of Janet Bately on the occasion of her sixty-fifth birthday*, 99–119. Cambridge: D. S. Brewer.

Keynes, S. (1998) King Alfred and the Mercians. In M. A. S. Blackburn and D. N. Dumville (eds), *Kings, Currency and Alliances. History and Coinage of Southern England in the Ninth Century*, 1–45. Woodbridge: Boydell and Brewer.

Keynes, S. (1999) The cult of King Alfred the Great, *ASE* 28, 225–356.

Keynes, S. (2002) *An Atlas of Attestations in Anglo-Saxon Charters, c. 670–1066*. Cambridge: Department of Anglo-Saxon, Norse, and Celtic.

Keynes, S. (2005) Between Bede and the *Chronicle*: London, BL, Cotton Vespasian B. vi, fols. 104–9. In K. O'Brien O'Keeffe and A. Orchard (eds), *Latin Learning and English Lore. Studies in Anglo-Saxon Literature for Michael Lapidge*, 2 vols., i. 47–67. Toronto: University Press.

Keynes, S. (2012) Manuscripts of the *Anglo-Saxon Chronicle*. In R. Gameson (ed.), *The Cambridge History of the Book in Britain, I: c. 400–1100*, 537–52. Cambridge: University Press.

Keynes, S. (2013) Church councils, royal assemblies, and Anglo-Saxon royal diplomas. In G. R. Owen-Crocker and B. W. Schneider (eds), K*ingship, Legislation and Power in Anglo-Saxon England*, 17–182. Woodbridge: Boydell Press.

Keynes, S. and Lapidge, M. (trans. 1983) *Alfred the Great: Asser's Life of King Alfred and Other Contemporary Sources*. Harmondsworth, Penguin.

King, D. (1986) Petrology, dating and distribution of querns and millstones. The results of research in Bedfordshire,

Buckinghamshire, Hertfordshire and Middlesex. *University of London Institute of Archaeology Bulletin* 23, 65–126.

Kirby, D. (1977) Welsh bards and the border. In A. Dornier (ed.), *Mercian Studies*, 31–42. Leicester: University Press.

Kirby, D. P. (1991) *The Earliest English Kings*. London: Unwin Hyman.

Kitson, P. (2008) Fog on the barrow-downs? In O. J. Padel and D. N. Parsons (eds), *A Community of Good Names: Essays in honour of Margaret Gelling*, 382–94. Donington: Shaun Tyas.

Knowles, D. (1963) *The Monastic Order in England*. 2nd ed. Cambridge: University Press.

Knapp, J. A. (2003) *Illustrating the Past in Early Modern England: the representation of history in printed books*. Aldershot: Ashgate.

Krapp, G. P. and Dobbie, E. V. K. (eds 1936) *The Exeter Book*. Anglo-Saxon Poetic Records vol. IV. London: Routledge and Kegan Paul.

Kreis, S. (2003) *Skandinavische-Schottische Sprachbeziehungen im Mittelalter: Der altnordische Lehneinfluss*. Odense: University Press of Southern Denmark.

L'Anson, W. M. (1913) The castles of the North Riding, *Yorkshire Archaeological Journal* 22, 362.

Lambarde, W. (1568) *Archaionomia ...* London: ex officina Ioannis Daij.

Lambarde, W. (1576) *Perambulation of Kent*. London: Ralphe Newberie.

Lang, J. T. (1977) The St Helena Cross, Church Kelloe, Co. Durham, *Archaeologia Aeliana* 5th series 5, 105–19.

Lang, J. T. (1991) *Corpus of Anglo-Saxon Stone Sculpture, III, York and Eastern Yorkshire*. Oxford: University Press.

Lapidge, M. (trans. 1979) The prose *De virginitate*. In M. Lapidge and M. Herren, *Aldhelm: The Prose Works*, 49–132. Cambridge, D. S. Brewer.

Lapidge, M. (1983) Ealdred of York and MS Cotton Vitellius E. xii, *Yorkshire Archaeological Journal* 55, 11–25.

Lapidge, M. (ed. 2003) *The Cult of St Swithun*. Winchester Studies, 4, ii. Oxford: Clarendon.

Lapidge, M. (ed. 2009) *Byrhtferth of Ramsey: the Lives of St Oswald and St Ecgwine*. Oxford: University Press.

Lapidge, M. and Winterbottom, M. (eds 1992) *Wulfstan of Winchester: the Life of St Æthelwold*. Oxford: University Press.

Lapidge, M., Blair, J., Keynes, S. and Scragg, D. (eds 2014) *The Wiley-Blackwell Encyclopedia of Anglo-Saxon England*, 2nd ed. Chichester: Wiley Blackwell.

Latham, R. E. and Howlett, D. R. (eds 1975–97) *Dictionary of Medieval Latin from British Sources*. Vol. 1. Oxford: University Press.

Lavelle, R. (2002) *Æthelred II, King of the English 978–1016*. Stroud: Tempus.

Leach, P. J. (1976) Excavations at East Lyng, Somerset, 1975, *Proceedings of the Somerset Archaeological and Natural History Society* 120, 29–38.

Leach, P. [J.] (ed. 1994) *Ilchester. Vol. 2: Archaeology, excavations and fieldwork to 1984*. Sheffield Excavation Report 2. Sheffield: Collis.

Lebecq, S. (1990) On the use of the word 'Frisian' in the 6th–10th centuries written sources: some interpretations. In S. McGrail (ed.), *Maritime Celts, Frisians and Saxons*. Council for British Archaeology Research Report 71, 85–90. London: Council for British Archaeology.

Leech, R. H. (1986) Excavations at Whatley Lane/The Hill, Langport 1976, *Proceedings of the Somerset Archaeological and Natural History Society* 130, 165–7.

Leeds, E. T. (1913) *The Archaeology of the Anglo-Saxon Settlements*. Oxford: University Press.

Lehmann-Brockhaus, O. (1955–60) *Lateinische Schriftquellen zur Kunst in England, Wales und Schottland vom Jahre 901 bis zum Jahre 1307*, 5 vols. Munich: Prestel.

Lerer, S. (1999) Old English and its Afterlife. In D. Wallace (ed.) *The Cambridge History of Medieval English Literature*, 7–34. Cambridge: University Press.

Leman, P. (1981) Contribution à la localisation de Quentovic ou la relance d'un vieux débat, *Revue du Nord* 63 (251), 935–45.

Lethbridge, T. (1938) Anglo-Saxon remains. In L. Salzman (ed.), *The Victoria History of the County of Cambridgeshire and the Isle of Ely: Volume 1*, 305–33. London: Oxford University Press.

Lethbridge, T. (1957) The Riddle of the Dykes, *Proceedings of the Cambridge Antiquarian Society* 51, 1–5.

Lethbridge, T. and Palmer, W. (1927–8) Excavations in the Cambridgeshire Dykes: VI: Bran Ditch second report, *Proceedings of the Cambridge Antiquarian Society* 30, 78–96.

Lewis, S. (1987) *The Art of Matthew Paris in the Chronica Majora*. Aldershot: Scolar Press.

Lilley, K. (2000) Mapping the medieval city: plan analysis and urban history, *Urban History* 27.1, 5–30.

Lindkvist, H. (1912) *Middle-English Place-Names of Scandinavian Origin*. Uppsala: University Press.

Locke, A. A. (1912) *In Praise of Winchester*. London: Constable.

Loveluck, C. (2009) A note on the lava querns from Flixborough. In D. H. Evans and C. Loveluck (eds), Life and economy at early medieval Flixborough *c*. AD 600–1000: The artefact evidence. *Excavations at Flixborough* 2, 248–9. Oxford: Oxbow Books.

Luard, H. R. (ed. 1864–9) *Annales monastici*. Rolls Series 36, 5 vols. London: Longman.

Luard, H. R. (ed. 1865) *Annales monasterii de Wintonia (A.D. 519–1277)*, Annales monastici ii. Rolls Series 2. London: H.M.S.O.

Lund, N. (1976). Thorp-names. In P. H. Sawyer (ed.) *Medieval Settlement: Continuity and change*, 223–5. London: Edward Arnold.

Luscombe, P. (2005) Charters, place-names and Anglo-Saxon settlement in south Devon, *Report of the Transactions of the Devon Association for the Advancement of Science* 137, 89–138.

Lyon, S. (2000) Review of M. A. S. Blackburn and D. N. Dumville (eds), Kings, Currency and Alliances. History and Coinage of Southern England in the Ninth Century, *British Numismatic Journal* 60, 169–71.

Lyon, S. (2001). The coinage of Edward the Elder. In N. J. Higham and D. H. Hill (eds), *Edward the Elder 899–924*, 67–78. London: Routledge.

MacArthur, E. M. (1995) *Columba's Island: Iona from past to present*. Edinburgh: University Press.

Maddicot, J. R. (1989) Trade, industry and the wealth of King Alfred, *Past and Present* 123, 3–51.

Magennis, H. (1985) Style and method in the Old English version of the *Legend of the Seven Sleepers*. English Studies 66, 285–295.

Magennis, H. (1991) The anonymous Old English *Legend of the Seven Sleepers* and its Latin source. *Leeds Studies in English*, New Series 22, 43–56.

Magennis, H. (ed. 1994) *The Anonymous Old English Legend of the Seven Sleepers*. Durham: Durham Medieval Texts.

Mainman, A. J. (1993) *Pottery from 46–54 Fishergate, The Archaeology of York* 16.6. York: Council for British Archaeology

Malim, T., Penn, K., Robinson, B., Wait, G. and Welsh, K. (1996) New evidence on the Cambridgeshire dykes and Worsted Roman road, *Proceedings of the Cambridge Antiquarian Society* 85, 27–122.

Manby, T. G. (1975) Neolithic occupation sites on the Yorkshire Wolds. *Yorkshire Archaeological Journal* 47, 23–59.

Manco, J. (1998) Saxon Bath: the legacy of Rome and the Saxon rebirth, *Bath History* 7, 27–54.

Mangartz, F. (2008) *Römischer Basaltlava-Abbau zwischen Eifel und Rhein*. Monographien des Römische-Germanisches Zentralmuseum 75, gleichzeitig Vulkanpark-Forschungen 7. Mainz: Römisch-Germanisches Zentralmuseum.

Mawer, A. and Stenton, F. M. (1927) *The Place-Names of Worcestershire*. English Place-Name Society 4. Cambridge: University Press.

McAvoy, F. (1986) Excavations at Daw's Castle, Watchet, 1982, *Proceedings of the Somerset Archaeological and Natural History Society* 130, 47–60.

McGowan, J. P. (2012) Introduction to Bodmer 2. In *Manuscripts in Switzerland. Anglo-Saxon Manuscripts in Microfiche* Facsimile 20. Tempe, AZ: Arizona Center for Medieval and Renaissance Studies.

McKitterick, R. (2008) *Charlemagne: the formation of a European identity*. Cambridge: University Press.

Metcalf, D. M. (1978) The ranking of the boroughs: numismatic evidence from the reign of Æthelred II. In D. Hill (ed.), *Ethelred the Unready: Papers from the Millenary Conference*, British Archaeological Report 59, 159–212. Oxford: British Archaeological Reports.

Metcalf, D. M. (1980) Continuity and change in English monetary history *c.* 973–1086. Part 1. *British Numismatic Journal* 50, 20–49.

Metcalf, D. M. (1981) Continuity and change in English monetary history *c.* 973–1086. Part 2. *British Numismatic Journal* 51, 52–90.

Metcalf, D. M. (1987) 'A penny life will give you all the facts', *Numismatic Chronicle* 147, 184–8.

Metcalf, D. M. (1998) *An Atlas of Anglo-Saxon and Norman Coin Finds, c. 973–1086*. Royal Numismatic Society Special Publication 32. London and Oxford: Royal Numismatic Society and Ashmolean Museum.

Miller, S. (ed. 2001) *Charters of the New Minster Winchester*. Anglo-Saxon Charters 9. Oxford: University Press.

Milne, G. (1990) King Alfred's plan for London. *London Archaeologist* 6.8, 206 7.

Milne, G. and Dyson, T. (2002) The tradition of a Saxon palace at Cripplegate. In G. Milne with N. Cohen, *Excavations at Medieval Cripplegate: archaeology after the Blitz*, 127–9. London: English Heritage.

Mitchell, B. and Robinson, F. C. (2007) *A Guide to Old English*. 7th ed. Oxford: Blackwell.

Moore, J.W. (1966) An Anglo-Saxon settlement at Wykeham, North Yorkshire, *Yorkshire Archaeological Journal* 41, 403–44.

Mortimer, J. R. (1905) *Forty years' Researches in British and Saxon burial mounds of East Yorkshire*. London: A. Brown and sons.

Muir, R. (1981) *Riddles in the British Landscape*. London: Thames and Hudson.

Naismith, R. (2012) *Money and Power in Anglo-Saxon England: the Southern English Kingdoms, 757–865*. Cambridge: University Press.

Naismith, R. (2013) The English monetary economy, *c.* 973–1100: the contribution of single-finds. *Economic History Review* 66, 198–225.

Naylor, J. (2004) *An Archaeology of Trade in Middle Saxon England*. British Archaeological Report 376. Oxford: Archaeopress.

Nelson, J. L. (trans. and annotated 1991) *The Annals of St-Bertin*, Manchester Medieval Source Series, Manchester: University Press.

Nenk, B., Margeson, S. and Hurley, M. (1992) Swaffham Prior, Devil's Dyke, *Medieval Archaeology* 36, 203.

Neville, A. (1575) *De furoribus Norfolcensium Ketto duce and Norvicus*, 2 vols. in one. London: ex off. H. Binnemani.

Nicholson, N. and Hawkyard, A. (1988) *The Counties of Britain: a Tudor atlas by John Speed*. London: Pavilion Books.

Nicolaisen, W. F. H. (1967) Notes on Scottish place-names: 29. Scandinavian personal names in the place-names of south-east Scotland. *Scottish Studies* 11, 223–44.

Nielsen, L. C. (1986) Omgård. The Viking Age Water-mill Complex, *Acta Archaeologica* 57, 177–204.

Nunneley, J. (1998) *Tales from the East African Rifles*. London: Cassell and Co.

O.A.N. (2008) A66 (Package A) Road Improvement Scheme Greta Bridge to Scotch Corner: Archaeological Post-excavation Assessment, unpublished report, Oxford Archaeology North.

O'Brien O'Keeffe, K. (ed. 2001) *MS C. The Anglo-Saxon Chronicle, a collaborative edition* 5, eds D. Dumville and S. Keynes. Cambridge: D. S. Brewer.

O'Connell, M. O. and Poulton, R. (1984) The towns of Surrey. In J Haslam (ed.) *Anglo-Saxon Towns in Southern England*, 53–86. Chichester: Phillimore.

Oliver, L. (2011) *The Body Legal in Barbarian Law*. Toronto: University Press.

Oliver, P. (2007) Geology and building stones. In A. Brooks and N. Pevsner, *The Buildings of England: Worcestershire*. 2nd ed., 3–10. New Haven CT and London: Yale University Press.

Orchard, A. (2008) Reconstructing *The Ruin*. In V. Blanton and H. Scheck (eds), *Intertexts: Studies in Anglo-Saxon Culture Presented to Paul E. Szarmach*, 45–68. Turnhout: Brepols.

Ortenberg, V. (1990) Archbishop Sigeric's journey to Rome, *ASE* 19, 197–246.

Orwin C. S. and Orwin C. S. (1938) *The Open Fields*. Oxford: University Press.

O'Sullivan, D. (2011) Normanising the North: the evidence of Anglo-Saxon and Anglo-Scandinavian sculpture, *Medieval Archaeology* 55, 163–91.

Pagan, H. (1990) The coinage of Harold II. In K. Jonsson (ed.), *Studies in Late Anglo-Saxon Coinage in Memory of Bror Emil Hildebrand*, Svenska Numismatiska Meddelanden 35, 177–205. Stockholm: Svenska Numismatiska Föreningen.

Pagan, H. (1995). Mints and moneyers in the West Midlands and at Derby in the reign of Eadmund (939–46). *Numismatic Chronicle* 155, 139–61.

Pagan, H. (2008) The pre-reform coinage of Edgar. In D. Scragg (ed.), *Edgar, King of the English, 959–975: New Interpretations*, 192–207. Woodbridge: Boydell and Brewer.

Pagan, H. (2011) The Pacx type of Edward the Confessor. *British Numismatic Journal* 81, 9–106.

Page, W. and Willis-Bund, J. W. (eds 1913) *The Victoria History of the County of Worcestershire*, III. London: Archibald Constable.

Palmer, W., Leaf, C. and Lethbridge, T. (1930–1) Further excavations at the Bran Ditch, *Proceedings of the Cambridge Antiquarian Society* 32, 54–56.

Parkhouse, J. (1976) The Dorestad Quernstones, *Berichten van der Rijksdienst voor het Oudheidkundig Bodemonderzoek* 26, 181–8.

Parkhouse, J. (1977) Early medieval basalt lava quernstones and their use as an indicator of trade. Unpublished MA thesis, University of Manchester.

Parkhouse, J. (1991) An assemblage of lava querns from the Thames Exchange site, City of London. Unpublished archive report for Museum of London.

Parkhouse, J. (1997) The distribution and exchange of Mayen lava quernstones in early medieval northwestern Europe. In G. de Boe and F. Verhaeghe (eds), *Exchange and Trade in Medieval Europe: Papers of the medieval Europe Brugge 1997 conference* 3, 97–106. Zellik: Instituut voor het Archeologisch Patrimonium.

Parsons, D. N. (2011) On the origin of 'Hiberno-Norse inversion compounds'. *The Journal of Scottish Name Studies* 5, 115–52.

Parsons, D. N. and Styles, T. (2000) *The Vocabulary of English Place-Names*. Vol. 2 Brace-Caester. Nottingham: Nottingham Centre for English Name Studies, English Place-Name Society.

Peacock, D. P. S. (1980) The Roman millstone trade: a petrological sketch, *World Archaeology* 12.1, 43–53.

Pelteret, D. A. E. (1990) *Catalogue of English Post-Conquest Vernacular Documents*. Woodbridge: The Boydell Press.

Pelteret, D. A. E. (1995) *Slavery in Early Mediaeval England: From the reign of Alfred until the twelfth century*. Studies in Anglo-Saxon History. Rochester, NY: Boydell and Brewer.

Pennar, M. (1988) *Taliesin poems*. Lampeter: Llanerch Enterprises.

Pestell, T. (2003) The afterlife of 'productive' sites in East Anglia. In T. Pestell and K. Ulmschneider (eds), *Markets in Early Medieval Europe: Trading and 'productive' sites, 650–850*, 122–137. Macclesfield: Windgather.

Petrie, H. (1848) *Monumenta Historica Britannica*. London: Record Commission.

Phillips, A. D. M. (1989) *The Underdrainage of Farmland in England during the Nineteenth Century*. Cambridge: University Press.

Phillips, C. (1948) Ancient earthworks. In L. Salzman (ed.), *The Victoria County History of Cambridgeshire and the Isle of Ely: Volume 2*, 1–47. London: Oxford University Press.

Phillips, C. (2000) *The Greatest Raid of All*. London: Pan Books.

Picavet, P. (2011) Les meules romaines de sept chefs-lieux de cité de Gaule Belgique occidentale, étude du matériel et synthèse bibliographique, *Revue du Nord* 93, 167–226.

Pirie, E. J. E. with Archibald, M. M. and Hall, R. A. (1986) *Post-Roman Coins from York Excavations 1971–81, The Archaeology of York* 18/1. York: York Archaeological Trust.

Plummer, C. (ed. 1892–99) *Two of the Anglo-Saxon Chronicles Parallel with Supplementary Extracts from the Others*, 2 vols. Oxford: Clarendon Press.

Plummer, C. (ed.; 1895) Bede, Historia Abbotum. In C. Plummer (ed.), *Venerabilis Bædae Opera Historica*, 364–87. Oxford: Clarendon.

Plummer, C. and Earle, J. (eds 1972) *Two of the Saxon Chronicles Parallel*, Oxford: Clarendon.

Pohl, M. (2010) Quern-stones and tuff as indicators of medieval European trade patterns, *Papers from the Institute of Archaeology* 20, 148–53.

Pohl, M. (2011) Querns as markers for the determination of medieval northern European trade spheres. In D. Williams and D. Peacock (eds), *Bread for the People: The Archaeology of Mills and Milling. Proceedings of a colloquium held in the British School at Rome 4th–7th November 2009*. Southampton University Archaeological Monograph 3. British Archaeological Report S2274, 169–77. Oxford, Archaeopress.

Poole, R. L. (ed. 1902) *Historical Atlas of Modern Europe from the Decline of the Roman Empire*. Oxford: University Press.

Pope, J. C. (ed. 1967–68) *Homilies of Ælfric: A supplementary collection*. Early English Text Society, 2 vols. London: Oxford University Press for the Early English Text Society

Pounds, N. G. (1994) *An Economic History of Medieval Europe*. 2nd ed., London: Longman.

Powlesland, D. J. (1998b) Early Anglo-Saxon settlements, structures form and layout. In J. Hines (ed.), *The Anglo-Saxons from the Migration Period to the 8th Century: An ethnographic perspective*. Woodbridge: Boydell.

Powlesland, D. J. (1999) The Anglo-Saxon Settlement at West Heslerton, North Yorkshire. In J. Hawkes and S. Mills (eds), *Northumbria's Golden Age*, 55–65. Stroud: Alan Sutton.

Powlesland, D. J. (2000) West Heslerton settlement mobility: a case of static development. In H. Geake and J. Kenny (eds), *Early Deira*. Oxford: Oxbow Books.

Powlesland, D. J. (2009) Why Bother? Large scale geomagnetic survey and the quest for Real Archaeology. In S. Campana and S. Piro (eds), *Seeing the Unseen, Geophysics and Landscape Archaeology*, 167–82. Boca Raton and Leiden: CRC Press/Balkema.

Powlesland, D. J. (2011) Identifying the unimaginable – managing the unmanageable. In D. Cowley (ed.), *Remote Sensing for Archaeological Heritage Management in the 21st century*, EAC Occasional Paper 5, 17–32. Brussels: EAC.

Powlesland, D. J., Haughton, C. A. and Hanson, J. H. (1986) Excavations at Heslerton, North Yorkshire 1978–82, *Archaeological Journal* 143, 53–173.

Pryor, F. (2007) *Britain in the Middle Ages. An Archaeological History*. London: Harper.

Pye, G. R. (1976) Excavations at Crossgates near Scarborough 1957–65, *Transactions of the Scarborough Archaeological and Historical Society* 3.19, 1–22.

Pye, G. R. (1983) Further Excavations at Crossgates near Scarborough 1966–1981, *Transactions of the Scarborough Archaeological and Historical Society* 25, 3–12.

Rahtz, P. and Fowler P. J. (1972), Somerset AD 400–700. In P. J. Fowler (ed.), *Archaeology and the Landscape*, 187–221. London: John Baker.

Rahtz, P. and Meeson, R. (1992) *An Anglo-Saxon Watermill at Tamworth*. Council for British Archaeology Research Report 83. York: Council for British Archaeology.

Raine, J. (ed. 1879–94) *The Historians of the Church of York and its Archbishops*. Rolls Series 71, 3 vols. London: Longman.

Redin, M. (1919) *Studies on Uncompounded Personal Names in Old English*. Uppsala: A.-B. Akademiska Bokhandeln.

Reed, M. (1984) Anglo-Saxon charter boundaries. In M. Reed (ed.) *Discovering Past Landscapes*, 261–306. London and Canberra: Croom Helm.

Reynolds, A. (2009) *Anglo-Saxon Deviant Burial Customs*. Oxford: University Press.

Reynolds, A. and Langlands, A. (2006) Social Identities on the macro scale: a maximum view of Wansdyke. In W. Davies, G. Halsall and A. Reynolds (eds), *People and Space in the Middle Ages, 300–1300*, 13–44. Turnhout: Brepols.

Richards, M. P. (2000) Fragmentary versions of Genesis in Old English prose: Context and function. In R. Barnhouse and B. C. Withers (eds), *The Old English Hexateuch: Aspects and Approaches*, 145–163. Kalamazoo, MI: Medieval Institute Publications.

Riley, H. T. (ed. 1867–9) *Chronica Monasterii S. Albani: Gesta Abbatum Monasterii Sancti Albani a Thoma Walsingham*. 3 vols. London: Longmans, Green, Reader, and Dyer.

Rippon, S. (2004) Making the most of a bad situation? Glastonbury Abbey, Meare, and the medieval exploitation of wetland resources in the Somerset Levels, *Medieval Archaeology* 48, 91–130.

Rippon, S. (2008) *Beyond the Medieval Village: The diversification of landscape character in southern Britain.* Oxford: University Press.

Ritchie, A., and Fisher, I. (2001) *Iona Abbey and Nunnery.* Edinburgh: Historic Scotland.

Roberts, J. and Nelson, J. L. with Godden, M. (eds 1997) *Alfred the Wise: Studies in honour of Janet Bately on the occasion of her sixty-fifth birthday.* Cambridge: D. S. Brewer.

Robertson, A. J. (ed. 1925) *The Laws of the Kings of England from Edmund to Henry I.* Cambridge: University Press.

Robertson, A. J. (ed. and trans. 1939) *Anglo-Saxon Charters.* Cambridge: University Press.

Rodwell, W. (2001) *Wells Cathedral: Excavations and Structural Studies, 1978–93,* 2 vols. London: English Heritage.

Roe, F. (2002) Worked stone. In S. Foreman, J. Hiller and D. Petts (eds), *Gathering the people, settling the land: The archaeology of a Middle Thames landscape; Anglo-Saxon to post-medieval.* Thames Valley Landscapes Monograph 14 (appendix on CD-ROM). Oxford: Oxford Archaeology.

Rogers, N. (1988) Quern Queries. *Interim* [Bulletin of the York Archaeological Trust] 13.4, 35–8.

Rogers, N. (1993) *Anglian and Other Finds from 45–56 Fishergate, York. Archaeology of York* 17.9, 1321–29. York: Council for British Archaeology.

Rogerson, A. (2003) Six middle Anglo-Saxon sites in west Norfolk. In T. Pestell and K. Ulmschneider (eds), *Markets in Early Medieval Europe: Trading and 'productive' sites,* 650–850, 110–121. Macclesfield: Windgather.

Rollason, D. (2003) *Northumbria, 500–1100.* Cambridge: University Press.

Rollason, D. (2004) Anglo-Scandinavian York: the evidence of historical sources. In R. Hall (ed.), *Aspects of Anglo-Scandinavian York, Archaeology of York* 8/4, 305–24. York: Council for British Archaeology.

Rønneseth, O. (1968) Das Zentrum der ältesten Mühlsteinindustrie in Norwegen. In M. Claus, W. Haarnagel and K. Raddatz (eds), *Studien zur europäischen Vor- und Frühgeschichte.* Neumünster: Karl Wachholtz Verlag.

Royal Commission on Historical Monuments (RCHM) (1959) Wareham west walls, *Medieval Archaeology* 3, 120–38.

Royal Commission on Historical Monuments (RCHM) (1980) *Ancient and Historical Monuments in the City of Salisbury.* London: HMSO.

Royal Commission for Historic Monuments (RCHM) (1994) *Medieval Village Research Group Index.* London: HMSO.

Royal Commission for Historical Monuments of England (RCHME) (1970). *An Inventory of historical monuments in the County of Dorset, Volume 3 Central Part 2.* London: Royal Commission on Historical Monuments.

Royal Commission for Historical Monuments of England (RCHME) (1972). *An Inventory of the historical monuments in the County of Cambridge, Volume 2 North-East Cambridgeshire.* Worcester and London: Trinity Press.

Rumble, A. R. (1980) Descriptive list of the contents of the *Codex Wintoniensis,* with an index. In The Structure and Reliability of the *Codex Wintoniensis,* Appendix 1. Unpublished Ph.D thesis, University of London.

Rumble, A. R. (1981) The Purposes of the *Codex Wintoniensis. Anglo-Norman Studies* 4, 153–66, 224–32.

Rumble, A. R. (1996) The known manuscripts of the Burghal Hidage. In D. Hill and A. R. Rumble (eds), *The Defence of Wessex. The Burghal Hidage and Anglo-Saxon Fortifications,* 36–58. Manchester: University Press.

Rumble, A. R. (2001) Edward the Elder and the churches of Winchester and Wessex. In N. J. Higham and D. H. Hill (eds), *Edward the Elder 899–924,* 230–47. London and New York: Routledge.

Rumble, A. R. (2002) *Property and Piety in Early Medieval Winchester: Documents relating to the topography of the Anglo-Saxon and Norman City and its Minsters.* Winchester Studies 4, iii. Oxford: University Press.

Rumble, A. R. (ed. forthcoming) *Charters of the Old Minster, Winchester.* British Academy Anglo-Saxon Charters Series. Oxford.

Russo, D. G.(1998) *Town Origins and Development in Early England, c. 400–950 A.D.* Westport, CT and London: Greenwood.

Ryan, M. J. (2011), That 'Dreary old question': The hide in Early Anglo-Saxon England. In N. J. Higham and M. J. Ryan (eds), *Place-Names, Language and the Anglo-Saxon Landscape,* 207–23. Woodbridge: The Boydell Press.

Ryder, P. F. (1982) *Saxon Churches in South Yorkshire.* Barnsley: South Yorkshire County Council.

Sadler, J. C. (2010) *The Ipswich Mint c. 973–c.1210. Volume I: Eadgar to the End of Aethelred II c. 973–c. 1016.* Ipswich: J. C. Sadler.

Sadler, J. C. (2012) *The Ipswich Mint c. 973–c. 1210. Volume II. Cnut the Great to the end of Edward the Confessor 1016–1066.* Ipswich: J. C. Sadler

Salvador-Bello, M. (2008) The Edgar panegyrics in *The Anglo-Saxon Chronicle.* In D. G. Scragg (ed.) *Edgar, King of the English: New Interpretations,* 252–272. Woodbridge: Boydell.

Sandred, K. I. (1990) Language contact in East Anglia, Some observations on the Scandinavian place-names in -thwaite in Norfolk. *Proceedings of the XVIIth International Congress of Onomastic Sciences,* 310–7. Helsinki: The University of Helsinki.

Sandred, K. I. (1994) Nordisk i Norfolk. Kungl. *Humanistiska Vetenskaps-Samfundet i Uppsala Årsbok,* 129–54.

Sauvage, E. P. (ed. 1888) Vita Sancti Swithuni, Wintoniensis Episcopi. *Analecta Bollandiana* 7, 373–380.

Sawyer, P. (1995) The last Scandinavian kings of York, *Northern History* 31, 41–4.

Sawyer, P. H. (1968) *Anglo-Saxon Charters: An annotated list and bibliography.* London: Royal Historical Society.

Sawyer, P. H. (1979) *Charters of Burton Abbey.* Anglo-Saxon Charters 2. Oxford: British Academy.

Scharer, A. (1982) *Die angelsächsische Königsurkunde im 7. und 8. Jahrhundert.* Veröffentlichungen des Instituts für österreichische Geschichtsforschung 26. Vienna: Böhlau.

Schlauch, M. (1941) An Old English *Encomium Urbis. Journal of English and Germanic Philology* 40, 14-28.

Schön, V. (1989) *Betrachtungen zum Handel des Mittelalters am Beispiel von Mühlsteinfunden aus Schleswig-Holstein,* Hammaburg 9, 185–190.

Schön, V. (1995) *Die Mühlsteine von Haithabu und Schleswig.* Berichte über die Ausgrabungen in Haithabu, 31. Neumünster: Wachholtz Verlag.

Scragg, D. (1973) The compilation of the Vercelli Book, *ASE* 2, 189–207.

Scragg, D. (2005) A late Old English Harrowing of Hell Homily from Worcester and Blickling Homily VII. In K. O'Brien O'Keeffe and A. Orchard (eds), *Latin Learning and English Lore: Studies in Anglo-Saxon literature for Michael Lapidge*, 2 vols, II, 197–211. Toronto: University Press.

Scragg, D. (2012a) *A Conspectus of Scribal Hands Writing English, 960–1100*. Cambridge: D. S. Brewer.

Scragg, D. (2012b) Sin and laughter in late Anglo-Saxon England: The case of Old English (h)leahtor. In S. McWilliams (ed.), *Saints and Scholars: New perspectives on Anglo-Saxon literature and culture in honour of Hugh Magennis*, 213–23. Cambridge: D. S. Brewer.

Scull, C. (1997) Urban centres in pre-Viking England? In J. Hines (ed.), *The Anglo-Saxons from the Migration period to the eighth century – an ethnographic perspective*, 269–310. Woodbridge: Boydell.

Seymour, W. A. (1980) *A History of the Ordnance Survey*. Folkestone: Ordnance Survey.

Shirley, R. W. (1991) *Early Printed Maps of the British Isles 1477–1650* [1973], rev. ed. East Grinsted: Antique Atlas Publications.

Shortt, H. de S. (1950) Bibliography of Wiltshire coins in early medieval hoards, *Wiltshire Archaeological Magazine* 52, 413–8.

Sisam, K. (1953) *Studies in the History of Old English Literature*. Oxford: Clarendon.

Slater, T. R. (1991) Controlling the South Hams: the Anglo-Saxon *burh* at Halwell, *Report of the Transactions of the Devon Association for the Advancement of Science* 123, 57–78.

Smith, A. H. (1956) *English Place-Name Elements*. 2 vols. English Place-Name Society 25–6. Cambridge: University Press.

Smith, A. H. (1961) *The Place-Names of the West Riding of Yorkshire Part 3*. Cambridge: University Press.

Smith, J. (ed. 1722) *Historiæ ecclesiasticæ gentis Anglorum libri quinque, auctore sancto & venerabili Bæda, presbytero Anglo-Saxone*. Cambridge: typis academicis.

Smith, P. and Cox, P. (1986) *The Past in the Pipeline: Archaeology of the Esso Midline*. Salisbury: Trust for Wessex Archaeology.

Smyth, A. (1995) *King Alfred the Great*. Oxford: University Press.

Sobecki, S. I. (2011) Introduction: Edgar's archipelago. In S. I. Sobecki (ed.), *The Sea and Englishness in the Middle Ages: Maritime narratives, identity, and culture*, 1–30. Cambridge: D. S. Brewer.

Spain, B. (2001) *Spon's Estimating Costs Guide to Minor Works, Alterations and Repairs to Fire, Flood, Gale and Theft Damage*. London: Spon.

Speed, J. (1611) *The Theatre of the Empire of Great Britaine and The History of Great Britaine under the Conquests of the Romans, Saxons, Danes and Normans*. London: s.n.

Squatriti, P. (2002) Digging ditches in early medieval Europe, *Past and Present* 176, 11–65.

Squatriti, P. (2004) Offa's Dyke between nature and culture, *Environmental History* 9.1, 37–56.

Stenton, F. M. (1911) *The Place-Names of Berkshire. An Essay*. Reading: University College.

Stenton, F. M. (1971) *Anglo-Saxon England* (Oxford, 1943), 3rd ed. Oxford: University Press.

Steuer, H. (1987) Der Handel der Wikingerzeit zwischen Nord- und Westeuropa aufgrund archäologischer Zeugnisse. In K. Düwel *et al.* (eds), *Untersuchungen zu Handel und Verkehr der vor- und frühgeschichtlichen zeit in Mittel- und Nordeuropa* 4, 113–97. Göttingen: Vandenhoeck and Ruprecht.

Stevenson, W. H. (ed. 1904) *Asser's Life of King Alfred together with the Annals of Saint Neots Erroneously Ascribed to Asser*. Oxford: Clarendon Press.

Stewart, I. (1982) The anonymous Anglo-Viking issue with sword and hammer types and the coinage of Sitric I. *British Numismatic Journal* 52, 108–16.

Stewart, I. (1988) English coinage from Athelstan to Edgar. *Numismatic Chronicle* 148, 192–214.

Stewart, I. and Lyon, S. (1992) Chronology of the St. Peter coinage. *Yorkshire Numismatist* 2, 45–73.

Stocker, D. with Everson, P. (1990) Rubbish recycled: a study of the re-use of stone in Lincolnshire. In D. Parsons (ed.), *Stone: Quarrying and building in England, AD 43–1525*, 83–101. Chichester: Phillimore.

Summerson, H. (2013) Sources: 1587. In P. Kewes, I. W. Archer and F. Heal (eds), T*he Oxford Handbook of Holinshed's 'Chronicles'*, 77–92. Oxford: University Press.

Sumner, H. (1931) Combs Ditch and Bokerly Dyke, reviewed, *Proceedings of the Dorset Natural History and Archaeological Society* 52, 59–74.

Swanton, M. J. (ed. and trans. 1996) *The Anglo-Saxon Chronicle*, London: Dent.

Sweet, H. (1922) *An Anglo-Saxon Reader in Prose and Verse*. 9th edition, revised C. T. Onions. Oxford: Clarendon.

Sylvester, D. (1956) The open fields of Cheshire. *Transactions of the Historical Society of Lancashire and Cheshire* 108, 1–33.

Sylvester, D. (1969) *The Rural Landscape of the Welsh Borderland: A study in historical geography*. New York: Humanities Press.

Symons, D. J. (2003) Aspects of the Anglo-Saxon and Norman Mint of Worcester, 975–1158. Unpublished PhD thesis, University of Birmingham.

Symons, D. J. (2006) The moneyers of the Worcester mint, 1066–1158: Some thoughts and comments. In B. Cook and G. Williams (eds), *Coinage and History in the North Sea World, c. AD 500–1200. Essays in Honour of Marion Archibald*, 545–88. Leiden and Boston: Brill.

Tait, J. (1936) *The Medieval English Borough*. Manchester: University Press.

Tatton-Brown, T. (1986) The topography of Anglo-Saxon London, *Antiquity* 60, 21–8.

Tatton-Brown, T. (1988) The Anglo-Saxon towns of Kent. In D. Hooke (ed.) *Anglo-Saxon Settlements*, 213–32. Oxford: Blackwell.

Taylor, C. (1904) The date of Wansdyke, *Transactions of the Bristol and Gloucestershire Archaeological Magazine* 27, 131–155.

Taylor, H. M. (1978) *Anglo-Saxon Architecture* III. Cambridge: University Press.

Taylor, H. M. and Taylor, J. (1965) *Anglo-Saxon Architecture*, 2 vols. Cambridge: University Press.

Thacker, A. (1996) Saint-making and relic collecting by Oswald and his communities. In N. Brooks and C. Cubitt (eds), *St Oswald of Worcester: life and influence*, 244–68. London: Leicester University Press.

Thompson, P., McKenna, L. and Mackillop, J. (1982) *Ploughlands and Pastures: The imprint of agrarian history in four Cheshire townships*. Chester: Cheshire County Council.

Thorn, C., and Thorn, F. (ed. 1980) *Domesday Book 8: Somerset*. Chichester: Phillimore.

Thorn, F. R. (1991) Hundreds and Wapentakes. In A. Williams (ed.-in-chief) and R. W. H. Erskine (gen. ed.), T*he Cheshire Domesday*, 26–46. London: Alecto Historical Editions.

Thorn, F. and Thorn, C. (ed. 1982) *Domesday Book 16: Worcestershire.* Chichester: Phillimore.

Thorn, F. and Thorn, C. (ed. 1983) *Domesday Book 17: Herefordshire.* Chichester: Phillimore.

Tinti, F. (2002) From episcopal conception to monastic compilation: Hemming's Cartulary in context, *Early Medieval Europe* 11, 233–61.

Tinti, F. (2010) *Sustaining Belief: the Church of Worcester from* c. *870 to* c. *1100.* Farnham: Ashgate.

Tipper J. (2004) *The Grubenhaus in Anglo-Saxon England: an analysis and interpretation of the evidence from a most distinctive building type.* Landscape Research Centre Monograph Series 2, Vol. 1.Yedingham: Landscape Research Centre.

Toulmin Smith, L. (ed. 1906–10) *The Itinerary of John Leland in or About the Years 1535–43,* 5 vols. London: G. Bell.

Towers, T. (1976) Smith and Son, editors of Bede. In G. Bonner (ed.), *Famulus Christi: Essays in commemoration of the thirteenth centenary of the birth of the Venerable Bede,* 357–65. London: SPCK.

Treharne, E. (ed. and trans. 2010) *Old and Middle English c. 890–c. 1450. An Anthology.* 3rd ed. Oxford: Wiley-Blackwell.

Treveil, P. and Rowsome, P. (1998), Number 1 Poultry – the main excavation: late Saxon and medieval sequence, *London Archaeologist II,* 283–91.

Tufte, E. R. (2001) *The Visual Display of Quantitative Information.* Cheshire, CT: Graphics Press.

Tummuscheit, A. (2003) Groß Strömkendorf: A market site of the eighth century on the Baltic Sea coast. In T. Pestell and K. Ulmschneider (eds), *Markets in Early Medieval Europe: Trading and 'productive' sites, 650–850,* 208–220. Macclesfield: Windgather.

Turner, A. G. C. (1953) Some Old English passages relating to the episcopal manor of Taunton. *Proceedings of the Somerset Archaeological and Natural History Society* 98, 118–26.

Tweddle, D., Biddle, M. and Kjølbye-Biddle, B. (1995) *Corpus of Anglo-Saxon Stone Sculpture, IV, South-East England.* Oxford: University Press.

Tyacke, S. (ed. 1983) *English Map-Making 1500–1650: Historical essays.* London: British Library.

Tyacke, S. and Huddy, J. (1980). *Christopher Saxton and Tudor Map-making.* London: British Library.

Tyler, D. (2011) Offa's Dyke: a historiographical appraisal, *Journal of Medieval History* 37, 145–61.

Tyler, D. J. (2002) Kingship and Conversion – Constructing Pre-Viking Mercia. Unpublished PhD thesis, University of Manchester.

Ulmschneider K. and Pestell T (2003) Introduction: Early Medieval markets and 'productive' sites. In T. Pestell and K. Ulmschneider (eds), *Markets in Early Medieval Europe: Trading and 'productive' sites, 650–850,* 1–11. Macclesfield: Windgather.

Ulmschneider, K. (2000) Settlement, economy and the 'productive' site in Anglo-Saxon Lincolnshire, AD 650–780. *Medieval Archaeology* 44, 53–79.

Vertue, G. (1932) Note Books, pt 2, *Walpole Society* 20, 1–93.

Vince, A. (1983) In search of Saxon London: The view from the pot shed. *Popular Archaeology* 5.4, 33–7.

Vince, A. (1984) The Aldwych: Mid-Saxon London discovered, *Current Archaeology* 93.8, No. 10, 310–12.

Vince, A. (1988) The economic basis of Anglo-Saxon London. In R. Hodges and B. Hobley (eds), *The Rebirth of Towns in the West, AD 700–1050,* 83–92. London: Council for British Archaeology.

Vince, A. (1990) *Saxon London: An archaeological investigation.* London: Seaby.

Wallace-Hadrill, J. M. (1988), *Bede's Ecclesiastical History of the English People: a historical commentary.* Oxford Medieval Texts. Oxford: Clarendon Press.

Warnicke, R. M. (1973) *William Lambarde: Elizabethan antiquary 1536–1601.* Chichester: Phillimore.

Warre, F. (1863) Earthworks at Langport, *Proceedings of the Somerset Archaeological and Natural History Society* 40, 194–8.

Webber, T. (1992) *Scribes and Scholars at Salisbury Cathedral c. 1075–c. 1125.* Oxford: University Press.

Webster, L. (1973) Cambridgeshire: Newmarket, *Medieval Archaeology* 17, 138.

West, S. E. (1985) *The Anglo-Saxon Village at West Stow. 2 vols.* East Anglian Archaeology 24. Ipswich: Suffolk County Planning Department.

Wheelhouse, P. and Burgess, A. (2001) The linear earthworks. In I. Roberts, A. Burgess and D. Berg (eds), *A New Link to the past: The archaeological landscape of the M1-A1 Link Road,* 123–48. Leeds: West Yorkshire Archaeology Service on behalf of West Yorkshire Joint Services.

[Whelock, A.] (1644) *Archaionomia.* Cambridge: s.n.

White, G. J. (1995) Open fields and rural settlement in medieval west Cheshire. In T. Scott and P. Starkey (eds), *The Middle Ages in the North West,* 15–35. Liverpool: Leopard's Head Press.

White, G. J. (2012) *The Medieval English Landscape: 1000–1540.* London: Bloomsbury.

Whitelock, D. (ed. and trans. 1930) *Anglo-Saxon Wills.* Cambridge; University Press.

Whitelock, D. (ed. 1955) *English Historical Documents* c. *500–1041.* London, Eyre and Spottiswoode.

Whitelock, D. (1961) The numismatic interest of the Old English version of the Legend of the Seven Sleepers. In R. H. M. Dolley (ed.) *Anglo-Saxon Coins: Studies Presented to F. M. Stenton,* 188–194. London: Methuen.

Whitelock, D. (ed. 1979) *English Historical Documents* c. *500–1042,* 2nd ed. London: Eyre Methuen.

Whitelock, D. with Douglas, D. C. and Tucker, S. I. (1961) *The Anglo-Saxon Chronicle: a revised translation.* London: Eyre and Spottiswoode.

Wickham, C. (2005) *Framing the Early Middle Ages: Europe and the Mediterranean, 400–800.* Oxford: University Press.

Wileman, J. (2003) The purpose of the Dykes: Understanding the linear earthworks of early medieval Britain, *Landscapes* 4.2, 59–66.

Williams, A. (1996) The Spoliation of Worcester, *Anglo-Norman Studies* 19, 383–408.

Williams, G. (2008a) *Early Anglo-Saxon Coins.* Oxford and New York: Shire.

Williams, G. (2008b) 'RORIVA CASTR: a new Danelaw mint of the 920s'. In O. Järvinen (ed.), *Scripta varia numismatico Tuukka Talvio sexagenario dedicata, Suomen Numismaattisen Yhdistyksen julaisuja* 6, 41–7. Helsinki: Suomen Numismaattisen Yhdistysken.

Williams, G. (2008c) The coins from the Vale of York Viking hoard: preliminary report. *British Numismatic Journal* 78, 228–34.

Williams, G. (2011) Coinage and monetary circulation in the northern Danelaw in the 920s in the light of the Vale of York hoard. In T. Abramson (ed.), *Studies in Early Medieval Coinage. Volume 2. New Perspectives,* 146–55. Woodbridge: Boydell and Brewer.

Williams, G. (2012) A new coin type (and a new king?) from Viking Northumbria. *Yorkshire Numismatist* 4, 261–75.

Williams, G. and Archibald, M. (2011) The Cuerdale coins. In J. Graham-Campbell (ed.), *The Cuerdale Hoard and Related Viking-Age Silver and Gold from Britain and Ireland in the British Museum*, British Museum Research Publication 185, 39–71. London: British Museum Press.

Williams, I. (1935) *Canu Llywarch Hen.* Cardiff: University of Wales Press.

Williams, M. (1970) *The Draining of the Somerset Levels.* Cambridge: University Press.

Williams, S. R. (1984) Aerial Archaeology and the Evidence for Medieval Farming in West Cheshire. *Transactions of the Historical Society for Lancashire and Cheshire* 133, 1–24.

Williams, T. (1993) *The Origins of Norfolk.* Manchester: University Press.

Williams, T. J. T. (2012) The mint at Wallingford: and introduction to the corpus. *Yorkshire Numismatist* 4, 141–57.

Willis-Bund, J. W. and Page, W. (eds 1906) *The Victoria History of the County of Worcestershire, II.* London: Archibald Constable.

Wilson, D. (1987) The medieval moated sites of Cheshire. *Transactions of the Antiquarian Society of Lancashire and Cheshire* 84, 143–54.

Winterbottom, M. and Lapidge, M. (eds 2012) *The Early Lives of St Dunstan.* Oxford: University Press.

Winterbottom, M. and Thomson, R. M. (ed. and trans. 2002) *William of Malmesbury, Saints' Lives: Lives of SS. Wulfstan, Dunstan, Patrick, Benignus and Indract.* Oxford: Clarendon.

Withers, B. C. (2007) *The Illustrated Old English Hexateuch, Cotton Claudius B.iv. The Frontier of Seeing and Reading in Anglo-Saxon England.* London: British Library.

Wood, I. N. (2008) *The Origins of Jarrow: the monastery, the slake and Ecgfrith's minster.* Bede's World Studies 1. Jarrow: Bede's World.

Wood, I. N. (2010) The foundation of Bede's Wearmouth-Jarrow. In S. DeGregorio (ed.), *The Cambridge Companion to Bede*, 84–96. Cambridge: University Press.

Wormald, P. (1982a) The Age of Bede and Æthelbald. In J. Campbell (ed.), *The Anglo-Saxons*, 70–100. Oxford: Phaidon.

Wormald, P. (1982b) The Age of Offa and Alcuin. In J. Campbell (ed.), *The Anglo-Saxons*, 101–31. Oxford: Phaedon.

Worms, L. and Baynton-Williams, A. (2011) *British Map Engravers: a Dictionary of Engravers, Lithographers and their Principal Employers to 1850.* London: Rare Book Society.

Worthington, M. (1993) *Quentovic*: Local and imported wares. In D. Piton (ed.), *La Céramique du Vième au Xième siècle, dans l'Europe du Nord-Ouest: Actes du Colloque d'Outreau (avril 1992)*, 377–383. [s.l.], Groupe de Recherches et d' Études sur la Céramique dans le nord-pas-de-Calais.

Wroe-Brown, R. (1999) The Saxon Origins of Queenhithe, *Transactions of the London and Middlesex Archaeological Society* 50, 12–16.

Yorke, B. A. E. (1990) *Kings and Kingdoms of Early Anglo-Saxon England.* London: Routledge.

Youngs, S. (1981) Medieval Britain in 1980: Pre-conquest, *Medieval Archaeology* 25, 166–86.

Zarnecki, G., Holt, J. and Holland, T. (eds 1984), *English Romanesque Art 1066–1200.* London, Arts Council of Great Britain.

Electronic Resources

Boswell, J. (1785) The Journey of a Tour of the Hebrides, 11. Iona to Mull, at http://www.undiscoveredscotland.co.uk/usebooks/boswell-hebrides/11-iona-mull.html.

Crittal E. (ed.), (1962), Victoria County History: Wiltshire, vi. http://www.british-history.ac.uk/source.aspx?pubid=273explore-isle-of-iona (2012), at www.explore-isle-of-iona.co.uk.

Gathercole, C. (2003). Watchet. English Heritage Extensive Urban Survey – Somerset Somerset County Council. Online at <http://www1.somerset.gov.uk/archives/hes/eus/index.htm >.

Grimshawe, T. S. (1829), *A Memoir of the Revd. Legh Richmond*, New York: J. Leavitt; Boston, Crocker & Brewster. On openlibrary.org., at http://archive.org/stream/memoirofrevleghr01grim#page/104/mode/2up, accessed 28.08.2013.

Haslam, J. (2003) Excavations at Cricklade in 1975, *Internet Archaeology* 13. <http://intarch.ac.uk/journal/issue14/haslam_index.html>image.ox.ac.uk.

Kemble Website on the study of Anglo-Saxon charters http://www.kemble.asnc.cam.ac.uk.

LAARC [London Archaeological Archive and Research Centre Online Catalogue] BIG82 London Archaeological Archive for Billingsgate Market Lorry Park, Lower Thames Street, EC3.

LAARC [London Archaeological Archive and Research Centre Online Catalogue] NFW74 London Archaeological Archive for New Fresh Wharf, 2–6 Lower Thames Street, EC3.

LAARC [London Archaeological Archive and Research Centre Online Catalogue] PEN79 London Archaeological Archive for Peninsular House 112–116 Lower Thames Street, EC3.

LAARC [London Archaeological Archive and Research Centre Online Catalogue] WAT78 London Archaeological Archive for Watling Court 11–14A Bow Lane, 39–53 Cannon Street, 19–28 Watling Street, EC4.

Mitchell, I. (2006) Scott in Mull and Iona (Sir Walter Scott), at http://www.scotlandmag.com/magazine/issue30/12007614.html.

Montgomery, J. (2006) Lead and Strontium Isotope Compositions of Human Dental Tissues as an Indicator of Ancient Exposure and Population Dynamics: PhD thesis, University of Bradford (2002), http://archaeologydataservice.ac.uk/archives/view/montgomery_2005/.

Nurse, K. (2001) Wat's in a name?, http://www.wansdyke21.org.uk/wansdyke/wanart/matthews2.htm.

Powlesland, D. J. (1980) The Heslerton Parish Project, Landscape Research Centre, distributed manuscript (http://www.landscaperesearchcentre.org/AATier1 Primary Headings/heslerton_parish_project.htm).

Powlesland, D. J. (1998a) West Heslerton – The Anglian Settlement: Assessment of Potential for Analysis and Updated Project Design, Internet Archaeology 5 (http://intarch.ac.uk/journal/issue5/pld/index.html).

Powlesland, D. J. (2012a), Landscape Research Centre Digital Atlas of the Archaeology of Heslerton in the Vale of Pickering http://www.landscaperesearchcentre.org/atlas/LRC_VOP.html.

Powlesland, D. J. (2012b) Death and Taxes in Anglo-Saxon Sherburn http://thelrc.wordpress.com/death-and-taxes-in-anglo-saxon-sherburn.

Powlesland, D., Lyall, J. and Donoghue, D. (1997) Enhancing the record through remote sensing: the application and integration of multi-sensor, non-invasive remote sensing techniques for the enhancement of the Sites and Monuments Record, Heslerton Parish Project, N. Yorkshire, England, Internet Archaeology 2 (http://intarch.ac.uk/journal/issue2/pld/index.html).

Prosopography of Anglo-Saxon England (PASE) database http://www.pase.ac.uk.

Richardson, M. (2002) Ilchester, English Heritage Extensive Urban Survey – Somerset. Somerset County Council. Online at <http://www1.somerset.gov.uk/archives/hes/eus/index.htm >.

Richardson, M. (2003a) Axbridge, English Heritage Extensive Urban Survey – Somerset. Somerset County Council. Online at: <http://www1.somerset.gov.uk/archives/hes/eus/index.htm >.

Richardson, M. (2003b) Langport and Frog lane, *English Heritage Extensive Urban Survey* – Somerset. Somerset County Council. Online at: <http://www1.somerset.gov.uk/archives/hes/eus/index.htm >.

Richardson, M. (2003c) Lyng and Athelney, English Heritage Extensive Urban Survey – Somerset. Somerset County Council. Online at:<http://www1.somerset.gov.uk/archives/hes/eus/index.htm >.

sacred-destinations.com (2012), at www.sacred-destinations.com/scotland/iona-abbey.

Somerset Historic Environment Record – online at http://webapp1.somerset.gov.uk/her/text.asp.

Wessex Archaeology (2010), Balinscale, Isle of Mull. Archaeological Evaluation and Assessment of Results. At http://www.scribd.com/doc/53531551/Time-Team-Baliscate-Isle-of-Mull.

www.cems.ox.ac.uk/Holinshed
www.kemble.asnc.cam.ac.uk
www.langscape.org.uk
www.philological.bham.ac.uk/cambrit

Index

Place-names are located to current English and Scottish counties and current countries

Numerals in italics relate to illustrations

Index of Manuscripts